BAD BOY DRIVE

ALSO BY ROBERT SELLERS

Hellraisers: The Life and Inebriated Times of Richard Burton, Richard Harris, Peter O'Toole and Oliver Reed

Sting: A Biography

The Films of Sean Connery

Sigourney Weaver

Tom Cruise: A Biography

Harrison Ford: A Biography

Sean Connery: A Celebration

Always Look on the Bright Side of Life: The Inside Story of HandMade Films

Cult TV: The Golden Age of ITC

The Battle of Bond: The Genesis of Cinema's Greatest Hero

BAD BOY DRIVE

The Wild Lives and Fast Times of Marlon Brando,
Dennis Hopper, Warren Beatty
and Jack Nicholson

ROBERT SELLERS

preface
publishing

Published by Preface 2009

10 9 8 7 6 5 4 3 2 1

Copyright © Robert Sellers 2009

Robert Sellers has asserted his right to be identified as the author of this work under the
Copyright, Designs and Patents Act 1988

First published in Great Britain in 2009 by Preface Publishing
1 Queen Anne's Gate
London SW1H 9BT

An imprint of The Random House Group Limited

www.rbooks.co.uk
www.prefacepublishing.co.uk

Addresses for companies within The Random House Group Limited
can be found at www.randomhouse.co.uk

The Random House Group Limited Reg. No. 954009

A CIP catalogue record for this book is available from the British Library

ISBN 978 1 84809 122 1 (Hardback edition)
ISBN 978 1 84809 123 8 (Trade paperback edition)

The Random House Group Limited supports The Forest Stewardship
Council (FSC), the leading international forest certification organisation. All our titles that are
printed on Greenpeace-approved FSC certified paper carry the FSC logo.
Our paper procurement policy can be found at
www.rbooks.co.uk/environment

Typeset in Dante MT by Palimpsest Book Production Limited,
Grangemouth, Stirlingshire
Printed and bound in Great Britain by Clays Ltd, St Ives plc

To

Bradley, Doug, Keith, Marc, Martin

Contents

I would like to thank the following who contributed to and agreed to be interviewed for this book:

Don Aly
Vic Armstrong
Alexandra Bastedo
Tony Bill
Richard Bradford
Kit Carson
Doug Claybourne
Roger Corman
Alex Cox
Clive Donner
Freddie Fields
David Foster
Gary Foster
William Fraker
James Frawley
Gray Frederickson
John Gilmore
John Glen
Trevor Griffiths
George Hickenlooper
Dwayne Hickman
Marty Ingels
Henry Jaglom
Shirley Jones
Michael Lake
Jon Landau
Charles Langston
Tom Mankiewicz
George Miller
Matthew Modine

Dan Paulson
Karyn Rachtman
Kevin Reynolds
Marion Rosenberg
Albert S Ruddy
Richard Rush
Robert H Solo
Richard Stanley
Leon Vitali
Michael Winner
Susannah York

Picture Credits

Select Bibliography

The following previous books on our bad boys proved most useful:
Songs My Mother Taught Me by Marlon Brando (Century, 1994)
Brando by Richard Schickel (Pavilion Books, 1999)
Marlon Brando by Patricia Bosworth (Weidenfeld & Nicolson, 2001)
Brando Unzipped by Darwin Porter (Blood Moon, 2005)
Dennis Hopper by Elena Rodriguez (St. Martin's Press, 1988)
Warren Beatty and Desert Eyes, by David Thomson (Doubleday, 1987)
Warren Beatty by John Parker (Hodder Headline, 1993)
Warren Beatty: The Sexiest Man Alive by Ellis Amburn (Virgin Books, 2003)
The Joker's Wild by John Parker (Macmillan, 1991)
Jack's Life by Patrick McGilligan (Hutchinson, 1994)
Jack Nicholson: The Life and Times of an Actor on the Edge by Peter Thompson
(Mainstream, 1998)

Other books proved helpful with miscellaneous stories:
Julie Christie by Michael Feeney Callan (W.H. Allen, 1984)
The Kid Stays in the Picture, By Robert Evans (Hyperion, 1994)
Easy Riders and Raging Bulls by Peter Biskind (Simon & Schuster Ltd, 1998)
*The Keys to the Kingdom: The Rise of Michael Eisner and the Fall of Everybody
Else* by Kim Masters (Collins, 2001)
Natasha: The Biography of Natalie Wood, by Suzanne Finstad (Century, 2001)
Undressing Emmanuelle by Sylvia Kristel (Fourth Estate, 2007)
Madonna: An Intimate Biography by J. Randy Taraborrelli (Simon &
Schuster, 2007)
Joan Collins: Biography of an Icon, by Graham Lord (Orion, 2007)

I'd also like to thank the staff of the British Film Institute library for
allowing me access to their vast collection of magazine and newspaper
cuttings regarding our bad boys.

Freddie Fields quote from unpublished interviews with Freddie Fields by
David Rensin, 2004.

Introduction

Mulholland Drive is a long, winding road that snakes through one of the prettiest and most desolate hillsides in Hollywood, high above the smog and pestilence below. For three decades two of the movie industry's most powerful stars, Marlon Brando and Jack Nicholson, shared the same driveway and lived in homes just a few minutes' walk apart through dense wood; their pal Warren Beatty lived just several houses away. Dennis Hopper, by contrast, lived in Mexico, then Venice Beach, always the outsider, Hollywood's interloper, though he did make Jack a star. Together they formed a kind of unholy union that led local cops to nickname Mulholland Drive 'Bad Boy Hill'. Jack always preferred Bad Boy Drive.

A beauty spot, full of hiking trails and millionaires' residences, miles from the sound of LA gunfire and crack dens, Mulholland Drive was by no means immune to the seedier side of Hollywood life. In the late seventies the hillside strangler caused panic in the community, torturing, raping and murdering ten women. One of the victims was found behind Brando's house. A little later one of his near neighbours was murdered, strangled in the bathroom. 'Mulholland Drive is full of crazy people,' he said. 'We have nuts coming up and down all the time.' Is it any wonder David Lynch made a film about the place?

Jack, suiting his personality, was pretty lackadaisical about security, believing no one would wish to cause him harm – didn't the whole planet just adore him? – though the odd nutty fan did get in from time to time. As for Marlon, he bought a gun just days after the Manson murders, admitted pointing the thing in the face of at least three intruders, and progressively turned his home into a fortress. Jack said Brando was

1

paranoid about anyone getting near his front door. One time a couple of visitors, arriving for a barbecue at Jack's, turned left instead of right and ended up in Marlon's compound and face to face with two mean-looking guys brandishing shotguns. Tom Mankiewicz, creative consultant on *Superman*, recalls arriving there with director Richard Donner to ask Brando if he fancied playing Superman's pop. 'We drove into the courtyard and as we were about to get out suddenly four dogs came running at the car, they were Rottweilers and Dobermanns, and we stayed inside and were honking and honking and the dogs were snarling and jumping on the bonnet. All of a sudden Brando appeared in the doorway wearing a caftan, clapped his hands three times and the dogs came running towards him. I said, "Dick, I think we're in trouble here."'

Inside Brando's domain, you'd never have known a movie star lived there. All his showbiz souvenirs, annotated scripts of *The Godfather* and suchlike, worth an absolute fortune, he stored like junk in an outhouse in the grounds.

In stark contrast, Jack proudly displays his Oscar statuettes and Golden Globe trophies. It's entirely his place. It's where, in the late sixties, as part, no doubt, of some mystical find-yourself bollockry, he spent three months walking round completely naked from dawn till sunset, not giving a damn about visitors or the 'For God's sake, Dad' pleadings of his daughter. It's where Marlon used to come calling when Jack wasn't home and raid his fridge, because the silly bugger had padlocked his own as part of his latest starvation diet, which obviously wasn't working. Curiously the Great One would often leave behind his underpants.

Warren bought his pad in the mid-seventies just to be near his pal Jack; before then he lived mostly out of hotel rooms. 'The house was one of the most spectacular that I've been to in Los Angeles,' says *Dick Tracy* producer Jon Landau. 'But it felt like a home. Often you go into a star's house and it doesn't. This one felt lived in, very comfortable.' But it took Warren years to settle in and furnish the place. In 1978 a British reporter paid a visit, surprised that it was still half-finished. Security guards patrolled the grounds, obviously not very well since they'd let her straight in, no questions asked. 'I suppose Warren's reputation as a woman chaser had got me in.' When there was another murder nearby

Warren stepped up his personal security, installing a kidnapper-proof vault, replete with thick, half-inch steel-plated walls and closed-circuit TV. Get into that, you fuckers!

Warren's terminal indecisiveness, taking years to choose wallpaper, is one of many curious personality quirks. This is a man who travelled with the fast crowd yet rarely drank, snorted or smoked, a multimillionaire who wore dirty jeans for three days in a row and made coast-to-coast plane reservations for six consecutive flights, then missed all of them.

And there are the women, of course – lots of them. When Woody Allen was asked what he would like to come back as in another life he gave the classic response: 'Warren Beatty's fingertips.' The women Warren has supposedly bedded is a roll call of some of the most beautiful and legendary of the twentieth century – Julie Christie, Brigitte Bardot, Madonna, Princess Margaret, Cher, Vivien Leigh, Jane Fonda, Catherine Deneuve, Barbra Streisand, Jackie Kennedy Onassis, Goldie Hawn, Diane Keaton, Maria Callas, Natalie Wood, Britt Ekland, even Emmanuelle herself: Sylvia Kristel. It's a miracle his cock didn't drop off.

There were tales that if you were an aspiring actress just arrived in Hollywood, maybe waitressing while awaiting your big break, it was really only a matter of time before you got a call from good ol' Warren. Ask Nicole Kidman. Literally within weeks of arriving in Tinsel Town from her native Australia Nicole found herself chased by Warren. He wasn't her type, so she bagged Tom Cruise instead. According to friend and production designer Richard Sylbert: 'Warren told me once he had made a decision, "I'm either going to fuck a lot of women or be a politician. I've made a choice, I'm gonna fuck a lot of women."'

Jack is Jack and will never change – thank God. He gets away with the kind of bad-boy behaviour that other celebs or mere mortals would be publicly crucified for. Attack a guy's car with a golf club? 'No problem, Jack,' say the LAPD, 'we'll let you off.' He's also bald and paunchy yet chases nubile actresses around and has talked openly about drug taking with barely a tabloid titter. I mean, this is a guy who wears shades indoors, for Christ's sake, and doesn't get the piss taken out of him. Such is his mythic status now that the *LA Times* said he had the gravitational pull of Jupiter.

And what of Dennis, a man who everyone, including himself, thought would be dead by the time he reached thirty, a man who used to take three grams of cocaine so he could sober up enough to drink more, who on *Easy Rider* didn't change his clothes for six months and punched a hole in a coffee table with a local drug dealer's head? A man whose seduction techniques included walking up to women in the street and saying, 'Hi, I'm Dennis Hopper. Do you wanna fuck?'

Between the four of them, God knows how many women have been hammered – more than the Allied landing force in Normandy, probably. And how many joints smoked, lines snorted, faces punched, reputations soiled and tantrums thrown. It's a wonder Hollywood survived. It did, but after our bad boys were finished with it, it was never to be the same again.

1

Legends Are Born

My old man used to hit harder than that.

Near the end of his life Marlon Brando was asked: 'If you could live your life over again, what would you do differently?' Scarcely skipping a beat he replied, 'I wouldn't get married and I'd kill my father.' Life is never that simple, but the great Brando might have avoided a lot of grief if he'd done just that.

Marlon grew up terrified of his own father, Marlon Brando Sr, a man of unpredictable mood swings and often fierce rages. He was a travelling salesman and threw his money around in whorehouses and speakeasys, fucking or drinking anything he could lay his hands on. Rumours of his wayward lifestyle filtered back to the simple house in Omaha, Nebraska, that Marlon shared with his two elder sisters and his mother Dorothy, known by all as Dodie, a fragile, creative spirit who acted in local theatre and dared to dream of Broadway success. Ashamed of her husband's infidelity, Dodie could hit the bottle hard too, and on nights they both got loaded the lounge became a battleground where the children feared to trespass.

Born on 3 April 1924, the young Marlon, nicknamed Bud, had a hectic wildness in him that needed controlling, being taken to kindergarten on a leash, in case he ran away. He once even dropped the neighbour's dog down a well. At night he crawled into bed with his eighteen-year-old half-Danish, half-Indonesian nanny Ermi and they'd sleep naked together. The five-year-old sometimes playfully touched Ermi's ample creamy brown breasts and writhed around on top of her as if she were a bouncy castle. 'She belonged to me and me alone.' Not for long, though, and when Ermi left after two years to get married Marlon was devastated. 'My mother had long ago deserted me for her bottle, now Ermi was gone too. From that day forward I became estranged from this world.' Marlon was a very serious and let's say strange little chap.

If he turned to his parents for comfort, they were incapable of giving it to him. His father, when he wasn't being a bully, giving orders and issuing ultimatums, fostering in his son a lifelong aversion to authority, was an emotional cripple. There were no father-and-son bondings, no shared tender moments, no hugs or 'Well done, son,' just constant lashing out. Dodie instilled in the young Marlon a love of nature and the arts, but too often was legless or borderline conscious, her son reduced to play-acting for her in an attempt to grab some attention and love. When he was older Marlon often brought Dodie home after she'd spent the night drunk in jail, events that traumatised the young boy. 'I admire Marlon's talent,' Anthony Quinn once said. 'But I don't envy the pain that created it.'

On many a Sunday afternoon Marlon and his sister Frances would run away from home. For kicks he enjoyed setting off fire alarms then hiding to watch the emergency services roar down the street. When his pet chicken died and Dodie buried it in the garden, Marlon repeatedly dug the poor thing up until it resembled some monstrosity from the nightmare cupboard of Tim Burton.

When the family uprooted and moved to rural Illinois, Dodie was forced to leave her theatrical and bohemian friends behind, her artistic dreams crushed. But Marlon loved the new place; it was a veritable zoo with a horse, a cow, a Great Dane, several rabbits and twenty-eight cats. To this menagerie Marlon would occasionally add a wounded snake or broken bird he'd found somewhere. He was a champion of the defence-less, once even turning up at home with an elderly bag lady who had fainted outside in the street, fussing over her while the doctor was called. He became naturally drawn to troubled children, perhaps because they reflected something in himself. One such boy, frail with glasses and bullied at school, was Wally Cox, and the two boys became inseparable, even after Marlon tied poor Wally to a tree in a wood and left him there all night. Their friendship lasted until Cox's premature death in the early seventies and, rather spookily, beyond. Brando kept Cox's ashes in his house and confessed to talking to them most nights.

Aware that her marriage was more compost heap than bed of roses, Dodie was hitting the bottle even harder. Hubby still enjoyed his wayward trouser dropping, and when Dodie spotted lipstick stains on his underpants the rows got worse. Marlon had heard his parents argue and fight before but, now a strapping twelve-year-old, was at last confident physically to confront the man he'd grown to despise, a taskmaster who'd raised his family by the strict rules of the Bible but who was nothing but a fraud and hypocrite. The gloves were off, and their frequent clashes were so volcanic that the neighbours could hear them warring. One night Marlon burst into the bedroom while his father was beating Dodie and threatened to kill him if he didn't stop.

It's no surprise that Marlon scarcely discussed his childhood when pressed by friends or reporters. The memories were just too painful. His mother had been the only brightness that shone out from the muck and gloom, and he had had to watch her spiral into drunken promiscuity and darkness, fighting her horrendous private demons. Often she'd disappear on wild binges and Marlon spent tortured nights in bed waiting for her to come home, or he'd search out the streets, the saloons and seedy hotels, often finding her passed out in her own vomit. One time he brought her home naked in a cab from some miserable hell-hole and fought off his father as he rained his fists down on his wretched wife's head.

Is it any wonder, with such a home life, that school seemed a total inconsequence to Marlon, who gladly treated it as such, flunking lessons and misbehaving, like the time he burned the word SHIT on the blackboard with corrosive chemicals. Only for sports and drama did he show any kind of aptitude. When it was discovered he'd failed all his subjects and was being held back a year, his father exploded. Marlon didn't care and got himself expelled when he orchestrated one prank too many, placing cheese into the air-conditioning unit and stinking out his classroom.

Marlon Sr was at a loss about what could be done with his son. The boy needed discipline, that was for sure, and as a product of military school himself, he decided that the army could beat it into him more productively than he ever could. So in 1942 Marlon found himself at Shattuck Military Academy in Minnesota, up before dawn, inspections, drills, hikes, marching about, and lights out at 21.30. If anything his rebellious nature found a greater outlet to express itself, and there were pranks galore: stealing every piece of cutlery from the canteen so his fellow cadets couldn't eat, emptying a chamber pot out of the dormitory window as someone was passing and shimmying up a tower to disable and then bury the school bell, which chimed every quarter hour and drove him to distraction.

As for women, he fucked conveyor-belt fashion local lasses from waitresses to farm girls. According to one fellow cadet, Marlon was an equal-opportunity fucker; he happily screwed ugly, pretty, fat or thin girls. They just had to be fuckable.

He enjoyed facing down bullies, too, acting tough and winning friends with his outrageous disobedience. But the outside world could still scar him. His parents never wrote or visited their son at the academy and during the holidays Marlon, rather than going straight home, sometimes lived like a hobo, riding the trains with fellow drifters, sharing their food and stories by the campfire.

As time went on his behaviour at Shattuck got worse. He dyed his hair red and got out of classes by feigning illness. 'I did my best to tear the school apart and not get caught at it,' Brando confessed. 'I hated authority and did everything I could to defeat it. I would do anything to avoid being treated like a cipher.'

His grades were, unsurprisingly, appalling; only in drama did he seem to make any effort. One day during manoeuvres Marlon's insolence went too far when he talked back to his commanding officer. Confined to barracks, Marlon grew bored so broke out and headed into town for a bit of fun. His absence was reported and he was expelled for grand insubordination. Such was Marlon's popularity that the students threatened to go on strike until he was reinstated. In an unprecedented move the principal wrote inviting him back in order that he could graduate; Brando told him to shove it.

You know, this used to be a helluva good country. I can't understand what's gone wrong with it.

Dennis Hopper's upbringing sounds like a corny western. He was born on 17 May 1936 on a wheat farm in Kansas, just a few miles outside Dodge City, half a century after Wyatt Earp tamed the town before moving on to Tombstone; corrupt folk heroes have fascinated Hopper ever since. The place was a dustbowl, so bad little Dennis had to wear a gas mask to school. It was a time of depression, the middle of America was wiped out, people queued for bread and soup.

The farm was twelve acres of wide-open land and Dennis pretty much had the run of the place. His was a solitary existence with no neighbours and no kids to play with, just a train that came though once a day. Dennis used to spend hours wondering where it came from and where it went to. The farm belonged to his grandparents, who pretty much raised him as their own. For years Dennis struggled to come to terms with the feeling that his parents had let him down, that they didn't show the same kind of love and commitment his grandparents did. They were distant figures mostly. His mother Marjorie was a Bible-thumping fundamentalist who worked over in Dodge City at a swimming pool, and Dennis cherished the times, all too rare, when she'd take him to work and he could have her to himself all day. His father Jay was absent from the homestead most of the time, working on the railroad as a postal clerk.

Dennis was barely five when he was given the news that his father was dead. America had just entered the war and Jay had been called up, but there'd been a terrible accident during his basic training and he'd been killed. Too young to fully appreciate the gravitas of what his mother was telling him, Dennis understood her promise that he'd be meeting his daddy again one day in heaven.

It was easy back then to just skip out of reality sometimes, Saturdays especially, during trips to the local movie house. Dennis was five when he was taken to the cinema for the first time and, bang, it hit him in an instant: the places he saw on screen were the places the train went to and came from, that flickering image on white canvas was the real world, and he wanted so much to be a part of it.

But no Hollywood scriptwriter could possibly have dreamed up the following scenario.

When the war ended Jay Hopper returned from the dead, quite literally. His death had been faked – a James Bond-type ruse so that he could undertake top-secret intelligence work. So while little Dennis believed his dad was decaying in the earth, in reality he was in China, Burma and India, fighting Maoists and taking the surrender of the Japanese in Peking.

The young Dennis welcomed his father back disbelievingly and for a time hero-worshipped him like a character ripped from the pages of a *Boy's Own* adventure. His feelings towards his mother were altogether different. She'd known the truth all along, the only one in the family who had. How could she have lied to him? It was the worst kind of betrayal. She tried explaining that the government had sworn her to secrecy and forced her to live as a grieving widow, but Dennis had trouble swallowing it.

After this incredible emotional rollercoaster, Dennis's family life returned to some kind of normalcy, and therein lay the problem. Again his parents grew distant, Jay going back to work on the railroad, carrying a gun to guard the mail, Marjorie working over in Dodge City. Again Dennis was left on the farm in his grandparents' care, feeling deserted.

It was now that his trend for experimentation began. By his own future standards it started innocently enough, snorting gasoline fumes from his grandfather's truck and gently tripping, seeing clowns and goblins in the clouds. That was until he overdosed one day and went wild, attacking the truck with a baseball bat, thinking it was a monster, smashing out the lights. 'That was the end of my gasoline-sniffing.' Grandpa was put out, to say the least, and Dennis was banned from going to the cinema until he'd learned his lesson. Trouble was, he never did, but instead graduated to drinking beer, stealing cans from the fridge and running into the wheat fields to pour the sweet nectar down his throat. The fantasy worlds of his boyhood, Dennis discovered, could just as easily be summoned up by alcohol as by his imagination. It was an interesting short cut.

As Dennis got older he lent a hand on the farm, daydreams supplanted by the cold, smelly reality of cleaning up pig shit. And if he didn't do his chores properly he'd be punished, and not just with a spanking. 'I'd say more like a whipping. That's just the way it was in those days.'

Then, like a bolt out of the blue, his parents told him they were leaving the farm and moving to Kansas City. It was a huge adjustment and, once there, Dennis rebelled. Not quite a teenager, he started hanging out with the wrong crowd, returning home at odd hours reeking of beer, reducing his mother to tears and causing his father to yell at him that he was a no-good son.

In 1950 the family were on the move again, this time to San Diego, just a few hours' drive up the freeway from fabled Hollywood. Dennis started to knuckle down at school, which he'd always seen as a chore, impressing teachers with his art work and winning prizes for drama. Consumed with a desire to be an actor, this interest in the arts created a gulf between him and his parents. Why couldn't he be a doctor or a lawyer, they asked, anything but a career in the theatre, which they saw as populated with the same kind of bohemian rebels and bums who'd led him astray in Kansas City. Dennis was beyond redemption in any case, already a committed boozer and close to discovering the wonders of weed. He also liked to party hard. Discussions on the subject always ended up in rows with Marjorie screaming and throwing things. Speaking of his parents years later Dennis admitted, 'I didn't love either one of them. They weren't bad, I just felt out of place.'

Home was becoming something of a nightmare. Jay drank too much and tended to get maudlin about the glory days of his war. He'd often row and fight with Marjorie, creating a hostile atmosphere that deeply affected the young Dennis. It took years, as he himself failed as a family man prone to rages, for him to forgive his parents for the malignancy he believed their soul-destroying scraps planted in his psyche.

So one night during the summer holidays sixteen-year-old Dennis packed a small suitcase and fled the hundred or so miles to Pasadena, calling his parents in the morning to tell them he was still alive. Managing to talk himself into a job shifting scenery in a professional theatre, Dennis soaked up the vibes – 'It was fabulous, man' – and didn't even resent the fact that he wasn't paid. To survive he flipped burgers at a roadside café.

It had been an adventure for sure, and he returned home to finish his schooling more determined than ever to be an actor.

It was Dorothy McGuire, a successful film actress, who saw something in Dennis worth nurturing and cast him in a small role in a production of *The Postman Always Rings Twice* at San Diego's La Jolla playhouse, which she helped run. For the first time since he'd left the farm Dennis felt wrapped up in a warm and inspiring environment. After successful stints performing in Shakespeare he was advised by Dorothy to set his sights on Hollywood. She had some contacts in the movie world who might help. Dennis was on his way to the town of his childhood fantasies. As for the theatre, he never really had any desire to go back: 'Where's the fucking close-up, man!?'

I never know what I'm going to do next. I just live for kicks.

Warren Beatty arrived in the world on 30 March 1937, three years after his sister, who was to become one of America's greatest all-round entertainers – Shirley MacLaine. It must have been an amazing household with those two embryonic egos in it. He was hardly out of nappies before Shirley started to resent her little brother's bid to hold centre stage, sparking off a lifelong sibling rivalry. 'Warren spent most of his time as a baby yelling,' she later said. 'And with growing finesse and sometimes astounding precision, has been doing so ever since.'

Proper little darlings at home, around the neighbourhood they raised hell, setting off fire alarms, dumping rubbish on their next-door neighbour's lawn and halting traffic on busy crossings by pretending to be handicapped and limping across theatrically. They even took to lying in the middle of the road waiting for a good Samaritan to arrive, only then to jump up and run away. 'Warren and I breathed the breath of rebellion into each other,' said Shirley.

Play-acting came naturally, I guess, since both their parents were frustrated performers. Father Ira wanted to be a musician but opted for the more secure profession of teaching, wondering for the rest of his life if he'd ever made the right decision. Mother Kathlyn wanted to be an actress but instead taught drama. After they married both receded into a comfortable middle-class existence in Richmond, Virginia, to raise a family. Perhaps the pangs of thwarted creativity in the Beatty household coloured their children's choice of career.

Growing up, Warren was the moody type, introverted and withdrawn, someone who, in the words of his sister, 'always had a private world no one could penetrate where he could hide away and be alone'. His love for books and writing cruelly marked him out as bully fodder. Incapable of fighting back, it was Shirley's fists that got him out of jams, until she discovered such butch behaviour didn't get her many dates. So the tomboy became a beautiful young woman and poor Warren had to fend for himself.

He didn't get much help from his father, with whom he never developed a truly close relationship. Ira could be distant and unapproachable, a bit too schoolmasterly in the household. A drinker, Ira often passed out in front of the television and on one occasion, in a drunken stupor, accidentally set the house on fire. Warren's main influences came from women, from his mother, his sister and aunts, all of whom had a strong and positive effect on his development. 'And I was fortunately not smothered by them.' By his own admission Warren came to trust women far more than men.

By the time Warren reached high school things were radically different. No longer bullied, the blistering looks that would make him a sex symbol were emerging and girls were starting to take note. He had his pick of them, and became something of a flirt. 'Warren always loved the opposite gender,' former classmate Art Eberdt told *People* magazine in 1990. 'What he does in Hollywood, he was just like that in high school. He dated everybody he could date,' even the senior girls. Whether he lost his virginity at this point is debatable, but Warren told friends that he believed he'd marry the first girl he fucked and that they'd always stay together. He also thought that the only reason for marriage was to have children, and that fatherhood would satisfy his ego. He'd have to wait some forty years to find out.

He ditched his precious books, too, replacing them with football boots. The abandonment of creative aspirations was because 'I was too occupied in proving myself a male.' 'Mad Dog Beatty', as they called him, excelled on the sports field to such a degree that in his senior year Warren was elected class president.

This desire to achieve merely hid the fact that Warren was still a resolute loner, fearing commitment of any kind. It may also have had something to do with a drive to compete with his big sister's recent successes. After graduating Shirley had gone off to New York to be a dancer, hoofing it like mad in Broadway chorus lines. She was spotted by a talent scout and cast in Alfred Hitchcock's *The Trouble with Harry* (1955), quickly establishing herself as the new darling of Hollywood, winning the ultimate accolade of membership into Frank Sinatra's Rat Pack, as their sort of sexually off-limits mascot.

Warren was still at school when Shirley hit the big time. He ditched sports and took up the arts again. This was a big gamble, since spurning his fellow jocks could have backfired nastily, but Warren was no longer a wimp who needed his sister to bail him out of fights: his masculinity went unquestioned. But eyebrows were raised when, following graduation, he turned down ten college sports scholarships. Athletes, he said, 'get their nose splashed all over their faces and their teeth knocked down their throats'. Ignoring his father's advice to study law, Warren wanted to follow in Shirley's footsteps and go into show business, even taking a holiday job at a theatre in Washington as a rat catcher. 'I was supposed to stand in the alley to keep the rats from going in the stage door. I never saw any rats, except on stage.'

Then it was off to Chicago and drama school, but after just a year he dropped out, convinced they'd nothing left to teach him and that he was ready to strike out on his own.

I'm a goddamn marvel of modern science.

When he reached the age of seventy Jack Nicholson announced he'd been thinking about writing his memoirs. All he'd got so far, he confessed, was the first line. He flashed his devilish trademark grin as he recited: 'It seems to me that my life has been one long sexual fantasy,' he paused, leering for effect. 'But more of that later . . .'

Jack was born in Neptune, New Jersey, on 22 April 1937 in extraordinary circumstances. For the first thirty-eight years of his life he never realised that his sister was in fact his mother and the woman he'd grown up calling Mom was actually his grandmother. How the hell did that happen?

Back in the thirties you'd be less of a social pariah as a child molester than as a teenage single mum, but that's exactly what faced seventeen-year-old June Nicholson. Desperate to avoid a local scandal, her family secretly bundled June off to a hospital in New York to have the child and did the cinema-going public a big favour by deciding against an abortion. When she returned with the baby boy a charade began that was to last almost four decades as June's mother, Ethel May, took over the raising of her grandson, passing him off as her own. As for June, she slipped quietly into the role of Jack's older sister until he was two, then she left home to try her luck in show business, ending up marrying a dashing test pilot, starting a new family and settling down on Long Island, where Jack visited on school holidays.

The cover-up was discovered in 1974 by a reporter for *Time* magazine, who confronted Jack with the facts. After shaking off his disbelief he called his other sister Lorraine to see if it was true, June and Ethel May by this time both having passed away. Lorraine confirmed it: yes, June was his real mother. 'Such is the price of fame,' he later said. 'People start poking around in your private life, and the next thing you know your sister is actually your mother!'

On the surface Jack seemed to take the news on the chin, remaining controlled, getting on with his life. 'By that time I was pretty well psychologically formed.' But those closest to him were only too aware that the revelation had deeply wounded him. According to his friend Peter Fonda it gave him a, 'real deep hurt inside; there's no way of resolving it, ever'. And Michelle Phillips, Jack's girlfriend at the time, told *Vanity Fair* in 2007 that the news 'was horrible for him. Over the weeks, the poor guy had a very tough time adjusting to it. He'd been raised in this loving relationship, surrounded by women. Now I think he felt women were liars.'

Of course, the great Nicholson family secret spewed up one further question: who the hell was the father? Accusing fingers pointed at Don Furcillo-Rose, a handsome vaudevillian who performed with bands at holiday resorts on the New Jersey shore. He and June shared a brief romance, despite the fact he was ten years her senior and already married with a young child. When Ethel May learned of the affair she told Furcillo-Rose to stay away from her daughter or she'd have him thrown in jail for corruption of a minor.

For years Furcillo-Rose kept tabs on little Jack, attending his school plays and watching him run back home after classes, sighing, 'That's my son.' Despite the circumstantial evidence, Jack has always declined to accept Rose as his father, or to submit to a blood test, preferring to let the matter rest. For good or for bad Ethel May's ne'er-do-well husband, John J. Nicholson, was Jack's dad, in his memories at least, however sour they were. The guy was practically out of the door by the time he arrived. A devout Catholic and upstanding local citizen, John Nicholson descended into alcoholism and became something of a bum, reappearing for holidays or special family gatherings, then taking off again. Maybe sometimes he'd take little Jack to a baseball game or a movie, and there were trips to bars where the kid drank eighteen sarsaparillas to his dad's thirty-five shots of neat brandy. 'He was an incredible drinker.' Strangely, there was no hostility towards John from other family members; they just accepted the way he was – 'a quiet, melancholy, tragic figure', in the words of Jack. 'I felt sorry for him because he couldn't help it.' So peripheral was his father in his life that when he died in 1955 Jack, then a poverty-stricken young actor in California, declined to fly back home for the funeral.

It was Ethel May, a formidable and resourceful matriarch, whose resolve and great self-sacrifice kept the family's head above water in those lean post-Depression years. Her thriving beauty business, conducted from the living room of her home, allowed them to live in one of Neptune's more favoured neighbourhoods. There Jack grew up surrounded and suffocated by the adoration of women, his mother, his sisters, aunts and female customers, hearing them all gossip beneath hair dryers; 'It's a miracle that I didn't turn out to be a fag.'

It's hardly surprising that in adult life Jack constantly sought the company of women, why he fixated on them, desperate to please them, 'because my survival depended on it'. He knew also how to exploit his status as the only male in the household, turning on the charm like a car stereo, but there was a temper, too, 'that rocked the house like an earthquake' when he didn't get his way, said sister Lorraine. One Christmas, as punishment for sawing a leg off the dining-room table, his present was a piece of coal. He hollered the place down until a proper gift was forthcoming.

At school Jack was a mischief maker par excellence, suspended three times: for smoking, swearing and vandalism. He later bragged that during his sophomore year he had to stay after class every day. 'I was the toughest kid in my area.' There was also an anger in him that's never truly gone away. Jack has confessed to having 'a tremendous violence in me', and said that all through his life he's had to learn to subdue it. Even playing golf it's there, waiting to burst out. 'I'm not a very Zen guy. I've laid in sand traps and cried, and hurled clubs in lakes.'

Some teachers saw behind this rebellious façade to a deeply unhappy boy, disappointed by his father's absence, though Jack claimed he was only doing what most adolescents did at school, 'making a big show that they don't give a fuck'. When he needed to knuckle down he was capable of producing skilled work; he merely chose to hide his not inconsiderable intelligence since it wasn't cool to be seen as a geek.

If Jack wasn't a geek, by no stretch of the imagination was he ever going to be a jock, though he loved sport and hung around the periphery of the school basketball team. After one away game, incensed at the opponents' dirty tactics, he snuck back into their gym and trashed the electrical scoreboard equipment. That was Jack's first moment of notoriety – and boy did it feel good.

Such clowning around was perhaps his first realisation of a desire to perform. Whatever, he joined a drama group, not initially out of any theatrical bent but because it was a chance to hang around with 'chicks'. Although he never got the chance to do much with them. The school prom was the only time Jack was seen arm in arm with a girl. And she wasn't terribly amused when he spent the bulk of the evening in a bathtub while his friends poured cold water over his head in an effort to sober him up.

There was little direction in the life of Jack. He sported a DA hairstyle, wore blue jeans and a motorcycle jacket, sort of bummed around, counting the days till the end of school. 'It's crazy,' said classmate Gil Kenney, later a local chief of police. 'We never thought Jack would go anywhere. He was a clown, wasn't serious about anything.'

2

The Methody Fifties

I coulda been a contender. I coulda been somebody.

Having burned his bridges at Shattuck Military Academy, the question for Marlon Brando was what to do now. There was some vague notion about maybe trying something in the theatre. 'That's for faggots!' his father scoffed. 'Who'd want to pay to see a shit-kicking Nebraska boy on stage?' It was an attitude that seemed to sum up their relationship. Nothing Marlon did ever pleased or interested his father, who took malicious pleasure in telling his son he'd never amount to anything. Marlon was determined to get the hell out and prove him wrong.

Both his sisters had already fled to New York and Marlon soon joined them in that cultural maelstrom of the war years, clay ready to be moulded, but moulded into what? He'd no clear idea when he landed on the doorstep of Frances in Greenwich Village in 1943. He enjoyed the bohemian lifestyle all right: parties, late nights – women. A South American señora who lived across the hall, ten years his senior, had a young son and a husband away fighting in the war. Marlon pounced, but saw other women quite flagrantly, immune to the hurt he caused. A few years later when the flat was taken over, the new occupier was kept up all hours of the day and night by girls beating on the door after Marlon. To preserve her sanity she attached a sign outside: 'Marlon Brando doesn't live here any more.'

Work was plentiful in the bustling city and for short stretches Marlon was a cook, a nightwatchman, a truck driver till he crashed it and an elevator operator at a department store, quitting after four days because it embarrassed him to call out such words as 'lingerie'. His other sister Jocelyn was studying drama under the brilliant Stella Adler, a proponent of a new naturalistic form of acting called the method, which emphasised that authenticity in acting is achieved by drawing on inner reality to expose deep emotional experience. At her suggestion, Marlon joined the class. Why the hell not – he'd nothing else to do – though there was an ulterior motive involved: fellow graduate Walter Matthau said Marlon only wanted to be an actor 'so that he could get fucked from here to Timbuktu'.

It didn't take Stella long to home in on Brando's raw talent; she was mesmerised by his sheer energy and sex appeal. 'In those days Marlon looked as if he might hump you at any moment like a beast in the field.' Also by his creative originality. One day she told her class to act like chickens alerted to an atomic bomb strike. Everyone started flapping and clucking maniacally, except Marlon, who just squatted on the ground, miming laying an egg. 'What the hell does a chicken know about nuclear fission?' he said. Soon Stella was telling anyone who'd listen that this nineteen-year-old student would be 'the best young actor in the American theatre'.

Suddenly Marlon's mother Dodie arrived in New York. Marlon Sr had tried to get them both to join Alcoholics Anonymous; she'd chosen the booze over her marriage and fled. Brando often visited her apartment and delighted in shocking her, camping it up in her frilly bathrobe or pissing in the kitchen sink while she watched. 'Oh Buddy,' she cried out. 'Why don't you stop this shit?' The close bond they shared was plain for all to see, but Dodie's drinking remained out of control and Marlon would once again be forced to search the streets and alleyways for her. Some nights when he couldn't find her he'd crash into a state of depression. She even missed her son's triumphant Broadway debut in October 1944 because she was nursing a hangover.

It was a nothing role, anyway, ironically in a play called *I Remember Mama*, a rather anodyne affair about an immigrant family. To alleviate the boredom Marlon played practical jokes on the cast, like pouring salt in the coffee veteran actress Mady Christians had to drink on stage, making her violently sick. He also aroused himself in the wings so as to arrive on stage with a full-blown erection that couldn't be missed by ladies in the front stalls.

As for his dressing room, it was a den of iniquity. Marlon boasted that his 'noble tool', as he was wont to call his cock, had never been so busy. Broads were queuing up outside his door. One night after the show Marlene Dietrich waltzed in and without saying a word dropped to her knees and gave him an expert blow job.

Just as Marlon was tasting stage success Dodie returned to his father. Marlon knew deep down that she 'was mad about the bastard', but couldn't help but see her leaving him as desertion, as choosing her husband over her son. 'My love wasn't enough. She went back.' Over the next few weeks Marlon lost his appetite, shed twenty-five pounds and began to stammer. After the curtain fell at the theatre he'd wander the streets for hours on end, lost in thought. It was, 'a kind of nervous breakdown' that lasted for months.

Stella Adler came to his rescue, taking Marlon into the bosom of her family. 'She may have saved my sanity.' Along with her husband, theatre director Harold Clurman, Stella listened for hours as Brando talked and explored his angst. Clurman later wrote. 'Marlon suffers untold misery because of his mother's condition. The soul-searing pain of his child-hood has lodged itself in some deep recess of his being.' Clurman also revealed that Brando said he smoked pot and admitted, with a measure of guilt, his rabid sexual promiscuity.

Living in close proximity for weeks on end inevitably drew Marlon and Stella closer together and a great deal of flirtatiousness entered the relationship. Often Marlon deliberately went into Stella's bedroom while she was changing and stared at her in her bra and knickers. 'Oh, Marlon, please,' she'd complain while coyly covering herself up. 'I'm getting dressed.' He'd say, 'That's why I'm here, to see that you're dressed prop-erly.' He'd even sit next to her at moments like this, a few times cupping her breasts in his sweaty palms. 'Marlon, don't do that or I'll slap you.' Brando would playfully look at Stella and reply, 'You know you don't want to do that to me.'

As luck would have it, Clurman was preparing to direct a new play on Broadway, *Truckline Café*, and Stella recommended Marlon for the important role of a psychopathic war veteran who murders his cheating wife. His audition was a disaster. 'He mumbles,' complained producer Elia Kazan. 'They won't be able to hear him past the fifth row.' Clurman remained insistent: 'Look, this boy's got real talent.'

Kazan would soon become a major force in Brando's life, but at that first meeting the two men circled each other like competing predators, each sizing the other out and then moving off, not a single word exchanged.

When *Truckline Café* opened in early 1946 Broadway had never seen such raw, naturalistic acting. For the dramatic scene in which his character confesses his crime, Marlon ran up and down the basement stairs of the theatre each night while stagehands doused him with a bucket of cold water so he appeared on stage in an effectively frenzied demeanour, out of breath, wet and trembling. Movie critic Pauline Kael was in the audience one night and thought the young actor was in the middle of a genuine convulsion. 'Then I realised he was acting.'

Kazan was dazzled by it, too. 'It's like he's carrying his own spotlight.' Brando literally stopped the show. The audience shouted, they screamed, they stamped their feet. 'In fifty years in the business, I've never seen it happen before,' said co-star Karl Malden. 'And it's never happened since.' The play itself, however, didn't find public favour and closed within a week. But Brando had announced himself.

Marlon found other jobs, starring in a touring production of *Candida* in Washington, DC, where he spent most of his spare time wandering the nation's capital covering the heads of famous statues with paper bags. If he encountered one with an outstretched hand he'd place a coffee cup in it. The local police thought a nutter was on the loose. He also seemed to take a perverse pleasure in turning down work. When a top Broadway producer offered him a major role in Noël Coward's comedy *Present Laughter*, Marlon said he couldn't possibly appear in such fluffy nonsense when millions of people were starving in Europe and Asia. Besides, he detested it, telling Coward to his face that his play was like 'having a diarrhoea attack with no toilet in sight'.

He said yes, though, to working opposite former screen legend Tallulah Bankhead, by then so faded as to be virtually invisible. She'd casting approval for her new play, a wretched thing called *The Eagle Has Two Heads* by Jean Cocteau, and wanted to interview Marlon at her mansion. An enthusiastic boozer, she was well tanked up by the time he arrived. 'Are you an alcoholic?' said Brando, not giving a damn for protocol. 'No, darling, just a heavy drinker.' She was also a nymphomaniac who seduced her young leading men and was very quickly trying to grope at the bulge in Brando's jeans. 'I would rather be dragged over broken crockery than make love to Tallulah,' he wrote to his sister afterwards. But it's generally accepted he did.

When the play opened on tour Brando proceeded to upstage the diva at every opportunity: he picked his nose, scratched his balls and leered at the audience, even mooned them. Then he ate garlic before his big love scene with Tallulah, 'Avoiding her tongue as best I could'. He drove the poor woman nuts and was fired when one night he stood at the back of the stage and pissed against the scenery. 'The next time Miss Bankhead goes swimming,' Marlon declared. 'I hope that whales shit on her!'

Unemployed again, things were about to change radically for Marlon. Tennessee Williams had written a new play about a repressed Southern belle raped and driven mad by her brutal brother-in-law. Elia Kazan was set to direct it on Broadway. Convinced Brando was perfect for the lead role, Kazan thrust twenty dollars into his palm and told him to go and see Williams out at his holiday home on Cape Cod, where he was vacationing with his gay lover. The cash went straight on food and booze because Marlon was broke so he hitchhiked all the way and arrived three days late. The house was in chaos when he got there; the power was out and the toilets blocked and overflowing. Williams was in a dreadful panic. Brando astonished him, first by mending the fuses and sorting out the plumbing, then with his audition. 'I had never seen a man of such extraordinary beauty,' Williams gushed. He'd found his Stanley Kowalski. The play was *A Streetcar Named Desire*.

When *Streetcar* went into rehearsals Brando was erratic. Unable to get a fix on the character, he fell back on his familiar mumbling. 'Speak up!' one actor yelled at him. 'I can't hear a bloody word you're saying.' Another smashed his fist against a wall in sheer frustration. Few in the production quite knew what to make of him, this wild man who sometimes slept at the theatre and once disappeared for days on end, returning unshaven and looking like shit.

By opening night, 3 December 1947, bang, Brando was there, totally in the zone, to such an extent that, smashing a dinner plate during one scene, he continued his dialogue while picking shards of china from his bloodied fingers. 'Once on stage, he became a character so much he wasn't Marlon any more,' said co-star Karl Malden.

Streetcar quickly became the hottest ticket in town. When Marlon made his first appearance in tight-fitting blue jeans and ripped T-shirt people simply gasped, nothing quite so threateningly sexual had been unleashed before on an American stage; some women in the audience began hyperventilating. It was a performance that redefined acting, practically revolutionised it overnight. This wasn't an actor merely acting, this was an actor *being*.

Brando's dressing room was undoubtedly the social centre of the theatre; young actors were drawn to him like moths to a flame. Starlets too fell at his feet, and he took ruthless advantage. Kazan said he was like 'a fuck machine'. Parades of women of all races, creeds and colours passed through; some he serviced during the twenty-minute interval in which he was off stage. It was not unusual either for some girl to crash through the stage door ranting and raving that Marlon should pay for her abortion. He also, ahem, 'entertained' the rich and famous, including Ingrid Bergman, Joan Crawford, Wendy Barrie (a raging nympho and former girlfriend of gangster Bugsy Siegel), Veronica Lake and Hedy Lamarr, whose previous shagmates included Hitler and Mussolini, so he was in good company.

His apartment door was open most of the time, too, for the odd bit of skirt or devotee to come calling. Sometimes upwards of fifteen actors or down and outs he'd picked up would cram inside. He was their leader, no question, helping them out with food and money; he liked to feel needed. It was a pretty squalid flat, no hot running water and just a few tables and chairs, plus a mattress thrown on the floor amongst piles of books. A Broadway star he may have been, but he didn't live like one, preferring to eat peanut butter straight from the jar and wear slovenly clothes until they started to stink, and then throw them away and buy new ones.

His only concession to fame was the Harley-Davidson motorcycle that he was seen roaring around the back alleyways of the theatre district or giving colleagues lifts home on. One night he was arrested for dangerously overloading the machine. Another time he was hauled over by a traffic cop in Times Square and asked for his licence. He didn't have one. As he vainly searched his pockets some unanswered parking tickets fell out. It was off to jail and the play's producer had to bail him out. 'Why'd you do that?' Marlon complained. 'I was having a fine time in there. Met a lot of interesting people. Great experience.'

As *Streetcar* settled down into a long run Brando grew restless and started playing up, putting dog shit in the food on stage, stuff like that. The main target of his childish japes was leading lady Jessica Tandy; God knows what she'd done wrong. He once told a bunch of sex-crazed sailors he met in the street that if they visited Jessica's dressing room after the show she'd satisfy the lot of them. They actually turned up, but were prevented from getting inside by security. Another time a mysterious voice on a phone informed theatre management that if Jessica appeared on stage that night she'd be shot. Police mingled amidst theatregoers as Jessica bravely gave her performance. No one ever found out who made the call, but fingers pointed in Marlon's direction. Asked to sum up Marlon, Jessica did so in four words: 'A selfish, psychopathic bastard.'

To keep fit Marlon organised boxing matches down in the theatre's boiler room. One night – crack – he took a surprise punch that busted his nose real good. Doctors pumped him full of anaesthetic and reset it, and the thing healed pretty quickly, much to Marlon's dismay. *Streetcar* had been running for about a year now and he was pretty sick of it and fancied a longer convalescence. When he heard the play's producer Irene Selznick was coming to visit he went to work on himself with bandages, iodine, the lot. 'When she walked in the door, I looked like my head had been cut off and sounded as though I were dying.' Irene was aghast. 'Oh, Marlon, you poor boy!' Struggling to sit up, he replied, 'Don't you worry, I'll be back in the show tonight!' 'Don't you dare!' she said. 'You're in no condition, you poor darling. I forbid you to come to the theatre.' So Marlon got to stay in hospital, 'and had myself a ball'.

Playing Stanley Kowalski night after night was now sheer tedium to Marlon, nor could he deal with what was happening to him in terms of celebrity. Fame when it arrived caused massive problems; he began suffering from insomnia, got searing headaches, even anxiety attacks, which forced him to lie down in the street on a couple of occasions until they passed. He hated the attention his acting success had brought, running away from people in the street when they recognised him. He confided to Kazan that he succumbed to dark and powerful rages and was terrified he might seriously injure someone while under their influence. The director suggested he see an analyst; psychoanalysis was all the rage at the time, Kazan even told his actors to turn their trauma into drama. For the next eleven years Brando was to see a psychiatrist five days a week whenever he was in New York.

The bizarre behaviour continued, though. He collected manure from police horses and dropped bags of the stuff from his roof onto unsuspecting passers-by. He enjoyed hanging out of his apartment window until friends screamed in terror for him to get back inside, and took delight in creeping unannounced into the homes of his friends, either just to borrow a book or to camp down for the night. Sometimes an unknowing house guest would watch terrified as a window slid open and the figure of Marlon appeared. He'd also be deliberately rude. The morning after an elegant dinner party the hostess phoned to ask if he'd enjoyed himself. 'I had a terrible time,' said Brando. 'Why?' said the hostess. 'Because you're dull and your guests are repulsive.'

When he wasn't insulting his swanky friends he was thieving from them. After one high-society party he'd attended the hostess noticed her collection of miniature antique clocks was missing. Convinced the culprit was Marlon, word was put around and that very evening the items miraculously showed up outside her apartment door with a note: 'Oops! (signed) a thief.'

Marlon was glad when he finally left the cast of *Streetcar*; he'd given everything to the production and now turned his back on the theatre for good. Years later, when asked why he never pursued a theatrical career and if he missed the spontaneous applause from a live audience,

Marlon snapped, 'Who cares about applause? God, do I have to turn into an applause junkie in order to feel good about myself?'

For a bit of rest and recuperation Marlon holidayed in Europe, getting up to his usual tricks, seducing a local gangster's convent-reared daughter in Italy, taking her virginity. The guy erupted like Vesuvius. Since he had vowed that 'even if her own husband attempts to fuck my daughter, I'll have his dick cut off', Marlon knew he was in trouble and legged it.

Hollywood was the obvious next destination, although Marlon was to treat the place with utter contempt for the rest of his life, calling it a 'cultural boneyard', a place that stood for 'greed, avarice, phoniness and crassness'. He agreed to star in *The Men* (1950), as an embittered paraplegic war veteran, only 'because I don't yet have the moral strength to turn down the money'. Arriving wearing his only suit, with holes in the knees and a rip up the arse, no one quite knew what to make of him, or his unusual working methods. In order to feel what it was like to be completely immobilised in a wheelchair Brando asked to be admitted to a veterans' hospital. There he was able to blend in and make friends with real amputees and lend his characterisation unprecedented authority.

Most nights Marlon joined the guys when they went out in their wheelchairs to a nearby bar. A woman, obviously pissed, approached them one time babbling on about the healing powers of Jesus Christ. Brando couldn't resist it and urged the woman to try an on-the-spot conversion on him. Gradually he struggled to his feet. 'I'm cured!' he shouted. 'It's a miracle!' before tap dancing round the bar, much to the amusement of his crippled buddies.

When Marlon returned to New York he moved into classier digs, but his slovenly habits soon turned the place into a dump. A guy arriving to deliver a vacuum cleaner declared, 'That boy doesn't need a vacuum cleaner, he needs a plough.' Setting about decorating the place, Marlon gave up after painting just one wall and for the next year buckets of paint and brushes lay on the living-room floor. Guests just stepped round them.

His old school friend Wally Cox shared the place with him, along with a third flatmate, a pet raccoon called Russell, a gift from Dodie. Marlon had a way with animals, though not this furry little bastard. So vicious was it that poor Wally was eventually forced out. Brando couldn't help but love the critter though, and they were practically inseparable for the next two years. It accompanied him onto the sets of movies and at parties would perch on his shoulder. Marlon once asked a press agent, 'Do you know where my raccoon can get laid?' Another time he held up a flight because he wanted to bring Russell aboard the plane as a passenger.

But even the Great One's patience wore thin as the animal became more uncontrollable. Arriving home from vacation to discover it had pissed over his entire record collection – 'the apartment looked as though it had been through a drug raid' – he booted out the moth-eaten shit ball.

Though reluctant to return to Hollywood, Marlon had little choice when Kazan wanted him for the screen version of *Streetcar*, although he wasn't sure if he wanted to revisit Stanley and all the incumbent psychological baggage. At least he had a new and exotic leading lady, Scarlett O'Hara herself, Vivien Leigh, whose personal life at the time horribly mirrored that of Williams's character Blanche. Haunted by depression, Vivien was a notorious nymphomaniac and on the fast track to a full mental collapse.

People were nervous how the pair would get on. One afternoon Brando asked why she always wore perfume. 'I like to smell nice, don't you?' Evidently not; Brando said he didn't even take regular baths, instead 'I just throw a gob of spit in the air and run under it.' As filming got under way there was raw tension between them, but an undeniable chemistry. Marlon prowled around Vivien like a caged animal and in letters to Wally Cox admitted he wanted to fuck her so much his teeth ached.

It was, however, rumoured that around this time Marlon began an affair with Marilyn Monroe that lasted on and off for several years. After one date back at Marlon's place he said, 'For God's sake, Marilyn, get out of that dress. Those tits of yours look like they need to be liberated.' The two of them remained close friends and Marlon was one of the last people to talk to Marilyn before her untimely death in 1962.

Another blonde bombshell, Shelley Winters, was a regular visitor to the *Streetcar* set. One day Brando locked her in his trailer and began to simulate lovemaking by violently shaking the room, pounding the walls and screaming with delight. Shelley was perplexed, to say the least, and when she refused to yell loud enough for him he whispered, 'You're not helping my image enough. For God's sake, you studied voice projection. Use it!'

Brando's playfulness had certainly not subsided in the spotlit environs of Hollywood. He once drove down Sunset Strip with a fake arrow through his head, enjoyed painting moustaches on statues in parks, shook hands vigorously with a powerful producer while holding an egg and laughed as the executive instinctively rubbed his messy hand down his expensive Italian silk suit, and kept his neighbours up all night pounding on African drums.

He was no respecter of Hollywood tradition either. When the legendary showbiz reporter Hedda Hopper arrived to interview Marlon, he couldn't give less of a fuck, paying her no attention at all. 'Do you care to answer my questions?' she finally said, exasperated. 'I don't believe so.' She stormed off, never to interview Brando again. Along with Louella Parsons, who wrote that Marlon had 'the manners of a chimpanzee and a swelled head the size of a navy blimp', Hedda was Hollywood's premier gossipmonger; both could ruin careers with one stroke of a pen, such had been their influence over decades. But Brando was a tornado that couldn't be stopped, and besides, they represented the past, Brando the future.

Marlon never would be a conventional interview subject. He might suddenly ask the reporter, 'What kind of underwear do you wear?' Or, 'Who would you have been in the eighteenth century?' He hated the whole idea of self-promotion: 'I don't want to spread the peanut butter of my personality on the mouldy bread of the commercial press.' In publicity handouts he'd tell whopping fibs about having been born in Outer Mongolia and that he ate gazelle's eyes for breakfast. Or claim he'd been born in Rangoon during a zoological expedition and that his father was a leader in the Chinese revolution, sometimes a big-game hunter, an English diplomat or a cattle rustler.

The film of *Streetcar* opened in September 1951 and was a smash hit. Watching in the stalls was a whole generation of actors who'd be influenced by Brando's breathtaking performance. 'It was shocking to see an actor with that vitality and that reality; no one had ever done it before,' says *Godfather* producer Albert Ruddy. *Streetcar* ended up with twelve Oscar nominations, including Brando for best actor. Ever the joker, Brando informed the press that he wouldn't be attending the ceremony but sending a cab driver in his place to pick up the award, should he win. He didn't, losing out to Humphrey Bogart's infectious turn in *The African Queen*, though one columnist did actually see a cabby sitting in his place.

Eager to work with Brando again, Kazan searched for a suitable vehicle for them both, finding it with *Viva Zapata* (1952), a historical drama based on the life of the great Mexican revolutionary Emiliano Zapata. Darryl F. Zanuck, who owned 20th Century Fox and was paying the bills, wanted anyone but Brando in the lead; he would probably have preferred Russell the raccoon to the great mumbler. Zanuck swore he couldn't understand a word that came out of Brando's mouth and his fee of $100,000 was a joke. Marlon hit back, saying the tycoon with his buck teeth resembled Bugs Bunny. 'When he entered a room his front teeth preceded him by about three seconds.' Kazan wouldn't budge and began the picture with Brando but Zanuck continued to butt in; the film was falling behind schedule, said the tycoon, Brando's moustache was stupid, and he still couldn't understand a bloody thing the actor said.

Zanuck wouldn't be the only one. During rehearsals for *The Fugitive Kind* (1960), the actors all sat round a table to read the script, speaking their lines in a low mumble, taking the lead from Marlon. Finally, cast member Maureen Stapleton couldn't take it any longer. 'What the fuck are you doing, Marlon? I can't hear a word anyone is saying. Have I gone deaf or what? For all that money you're getting you ought at least to let everyone hear what you're saying.' Marlon burst into laughter and everyone felt a huge release. Sitting at the back was the author Tennessee Williams, 'Thank God, darling,' he said. 'I haven't heard a bloody thing all week.'

While filming *Viva Zapata* Marlon got up to his usual tricks, setting off firecrackers in a hotel lobby, dropping tarantulas into the dressing room of the actresses and serenading leading lady Jean Peters from a treetop at three in the morning. Kazan also recalled the amazing number of women who hung around the set, making themselves very available to him, though he rarely responded. His warmest relations seemed to be with the men. Well, not all of them, certainly not Anthony Quinn, cast as his brother. The two hardly spoke at all. Quinn was pissed off that Kazan asslicked Brando constantly, attending always to his needs to the detriment of everyone else's. One day the two actors took a walk, during which Marlon got his dick out and started pissing. He suggested Quinn do the same. 'At least we can relieve ourselves together.' After that the pair had contests to see who could piss the furthest.

Then all hell broke loose. In the climactic fight between the two brothers Kazan wanted authenticity, he wanted his actors at each other's throats for real, so spread malicious lies to Quinn that Marlon had bad-mouthed him and vice versa. When the cameras rolled both men went wild. Marlon especially lost it, yanking out tufts of hair. 'I wanted to stick my sword in him,' Quinn said later. Kazan kept his deception secret and as a result the two actors didn't speak to one another for fifteen years until the misunderstanding was resolved. 'He inspired a lot of actors,' Brando said of Kazan. 'But you paid a price.'

Over the past few years Kazan had become a mentor for Brando, an integral part of his creative life, which made what the director was about to do all the more shocking. This was the age of the McCarthy witch-hunts, of Reds-under-the-bed paranoia, and after going through private torture for months Kazan agreed to testify before the House Un-American Activities Committee (HUAC), naming former colleagues who, like himself, had once been communist sympathisers. Many in Hollywood would never forgive Kazan such treachery. Could Brando? He was working on a new film, *Julius Caesar* (1953), when someone told him what Kazan had done and he was poleaxed by the revelation. The director, Joe Mankiewicz, later recalled Brando coming to him on the set virtually in tears, saying, 'What'll I do when I see him, bust him in the nose?'

For now Marlon had to put Kazan's betrayal to one side and concentrate on his biggest challenge yet, Shakespeare's Mark Antony, quite a stretch after playing a Mexican and the masturbatory fantasies of Tennessee Williams. Critics, naturally, scoffed but the British Film Academy voted him best foreign actor of the year. 'Dad always liked to point out,' says Tom Mankiewicz, 'that the Brits, especially in those days, would rather have committed mass suicide than give an American actor an award for Shakespeare. But he was wonderful in it.'

Riding a huge wave of popularity, Brando had still to come to terms with fame, still detested the intrusion into his personal space by both fans and those darker elements like stalkers and general nutters. There were three girls who camped on his doorstep and refused to leave, and a woman who festooned her bedroom walls with pictures of her idol as she plotted his kidnap and cannibalisation. One time a gaggle of girls, including a young Mary Tyler Moore, waited outside his house for him to appear. An old man with a limp exited and got in a car. It was Brando in disguise. They tailed him for about a quarter of a mile until he stopped, got out and walked over. The limp was gone, so too the grey wig. 'He walked to us in the slowest, sexiest walk I'd ever seen,' Moore later recalled. He bent down and briefly scanned the passengers before saying, 'Don't you girls have anything better to do on a Saturday night?'

Brando solidified his place as the archetypal bad boy when he was cast as Johnny, the swaggering leather-clad leader of a motorcycle gang that terrorises a small town. *The Wild One* (1954) was amongst the first films to address a new and pressing problem in fifties America, juvenile delinquency. Terribly tame by today's standards, even blissfully nostalgic, the film provoked huge controversy at the time with moralists claiming it glamorised anti-social behaviour. In one scene a girl asks Johnny what he's rebelling against. His defiant response. 'Whaddya got?'

Brando was now moving with alacrity from one classic to another, but turned down *On the Waterfront* (1954) when it was first offered, not because he didn't want to do it, but because Elia Kazan was attached as director. The true story of mob rule on the New York docks and one young worker's determination to testify against the crime bosses had obvious resonance for Kazan, but Brando was still in turmoil over what he'd done by selling out his friends to McCarthy paranoia. So Frank Sinatra was installed as star. All the time, though, Marlon, by far the greater box-office draw, was being secretly wooed by producer Sam Spiegel. After much persuasion Brando gave in; the role of Terry Malloy was just too good to turn down. More than most, Marlon could relate to a character 'driven crazy by his inner conflicts'. As for Sinatra, he was incensed at being dumped and no doubt planned to put a horse's head in both Spiegel's and Brando's beds.

Although he still respected Kazan professionally, calling him 'the best director I ever worked with', all intimacy had gone and there was an uneasy atmosphere on set. They never worked together again. In order to achieve greater realism, Kazan spurned studio sets to shoot amidst the slum dwellings of the dock area where weeks earlier Marlon had hung out with workers loading crates. It was dangerous, though, with the local Mob keeping tabs on the production. One afternoon Kazan and Brando lunched with gangsters to get permission to shoot in a particular area they controlled.

Cast as Terry's girl was Eva Marie Saint, who marvelled at how Brando never once stepped out of character. 'He *was* Terry.' Their relationship on screen is beautifully tender. He may also have saved her life. In a scene where both are chased down an alleyway by a truck, they had to run through a door to escape. On 'action', when they got to the door the thing was locked, a crew hand had goofed. With seconds to spare Marlon broke a window pane, slashing his hand, flung open the door and threw himself and Eva inside just as the truck hurtled past.

As filming continued Kazan could only stop and admire what Brando was giving him. 'If there is a better performance by a man in the history of film in America, I don't know what it is.' Every word Brando spoke seemed not something memorised but the spontaneous expression of an inner experience. And there's no better example than the archetypal scene, staged with Rod Steiger in the back of a taxi, where Marlon famously emotes, 'I could have been a contender.' Having trouble with the dialogue, so pissing off further a screenwriter already maddened by his endless ad-libbing, Marlon got Kazan to allow him to virtually take over. 'I never could have told him how to do that scene as well as he did it,' Kazan later admitted.

When a rough cut of the movie was screened for the first time the mood was ebullient as the lights came back on, but of Brando there was no sign; he'd gone, walked out without even speaking to Kazan. 'I thought it was terrible,' he later said, criticising his own performance. Such misgivings were utterly unfounded. *On the Waterfront* was a major commercial and critical success, winning eight Oscars, including best picture and best actor for Brando. Everyone expected him to cause chaos at the event, swing on the chandeliers, try to mate with Bette Davis, but he was civil and gracious in his acceptance speech, though for years he contemptuously used the statuette as a doorstop before someone stole it.

Never greater in demand, Brando found himself turning down scripts left, right and centre, spurning the chance to play in *East of Eden* (1955), so leaving the door open for a certain James Dean to make his film debut. When it opened, reviewers remarked on the plagiaristic resemblance between Dean's acting mannerisms and Brando's. Both Midwestern farm boys recast as rebels, Brando saw this attempt to copy him, including his lifestyle, as Dean's way of dealing with his own insecurities. Dean took to wearing the same brand of jeans as Brando, started riding motorcycles and for a while dated the same women, including future Bond girl Ursula Andress. When Marlon sat down to write his autobiography in the nineties he called Ursula at her house in Rome, first complimenting the actress upon her eternal beauty and then making the ultimate faux pas by asking her if they'd ever had an affair. When her former husband John Derek got to hear about this he fumed, 'Who wouldn't remember fucking Ursula Andress? Marlon must be coming down with Alzheimer's disease.'

Often Marlon would listen to Dean's sensitive voice talking to the answering service, asking for him, but never spoke up and never called back. They finally met at a party, where Dean was 'throwing himself around, acting the madman'. Brando took him aside and, recognising the personal demons eating into his skull, gave him the number of his analyst, suggesting he pay a swift visit. 'You need help.' Whether Dean ever sought it is unrecorded.

You're tearing me apart!

Dennis Hopper arrived in LA at the close of 1954 with virtually the clothes he stood up in and hardly any cash, but most importantly with the name of a casting agent scribbled on a piece of paper by his acting sponsor Dorothy McGuire that was worth its weight in gold.

Thanks to her he won an audition for a substantial guest role in the TV hospital-drama series *Medic*. It was to play an epileptic patient and Dennis was up against a dozen other actors with much more experience than he had. The director looked at this young buck, heard him read and didn't think very much. 'Can you portray an epileptic fit?' he asked. Dennis remained silent, but his eyes began to roll in their sockets and his body started to jerk from side to side. The director was starting to wonder if he'd been sent a real epileptic by mistake. Dennis stopped as abruptly as he'd begun and stared back at his inquisitor. 'We'll let you know.' He got the part.

While he waited for his episode to air, and with money desperately tight, Dennis took any menial job he could find, even stealing milk and orange juice from his neighbour's front porch to sustain himself. Eventually lack of funds and near starvation drove him back to his folks and he took a soul-destroying job delivering phone books around the local area, where he'd be met on doorsteps with taunting looks from friends who'd seen him head off to Hollywood with high ideas of stardom. 'I thought you were an actor now!'

Dennis rammed those words down their throats when his *Medic* episode was broadcast a few weeks later. The family all sat in silence watching it, mesmerised by his performance, especially his convincing epileptic fit. 'It's similar to what Grandma described when you were sniffing gasoline back on the farm,' said his mother. Joking aside, everyone was duly impressed, including Hollywood. Seven studios wanted to put the eighteen-year-old under contract. Coolly he chose Columbia and went along to check the place over. Head of the studio was the fearsome Harry Cohn, a man who ruled the place with an iron will, ranting and raving at his stable of stars. Hedda Hopper said, 'You had to stand in line to hate him.' Dennis knew of his reputation, that his workers visibly cowered in his presence, but didn't give a shit as he walked into his office flanked by his agent, looking around at shelves groaning under the weight of awards.

'I seen your TV show, kid; you got it, you're a natural, like Monty Clift. What else you done?' Dennis was elated: Clift was a hero. 'I've done Shakespeare at the –' Cohn butted in, Shakespeare, or culture in general, was anathema to the mogul. 'Oh my God,' he said, as if Dennis had taken a dump on his prize mohair carpet. He turned to face a minion. 'Give this kid some cash and put him under contract. Then get him started with a coach to wipe out that Shakespeare crap.'

Dennis stood up. He wasn't taking this from Harry Cohn or anyone. 'Go fuck yourself!' he hollered and stormed out. Cohn went purple with rage. 'Don't ever let that bastard set foot in my studio again, or his fucking agent.' Then, screaming at the rapidly disappearing Dennis: 'You'll never work at Columbia, not even a crowd scene.' The mogul was true to his word, Dennis never worked for them until 1969, by which time Cohn was long gone and Dennis had a little film called *Easy Rider* to sell.

A much better impression was made over at Warner Brothers and Dennis was given their standard seven-year contract. Director Nicholas Ray was the first to seize on Hopper's talent and cast him as a gang member in the studio's latest teenage angst movie, *Rebel Without a Cause* (1955), starring James Dean. Ray also asked Dennis to stand in for Dean at a series of screen tests with prospective leading ladies, one of them former child star Natalie Wood. The next day Dennis got a call from Natalie confessing she fancied him like mad and wanted to have sex with him. 'A helluva line,' Hopper recalled. 'In the fifties, to be aggressive like that as a woman was really amazing. It was an amazing turn on to me.'

Dennis jumped into his car and raced over to pick Natalie up outside her hotel. As they drove up into the Hollywood Hills she confessed to having just come from the bed of Nicolas Ray. Aged sixteen, Natalie was still a minor, illegal goods for either man to tamper with, but at least Dennis was only a couple of years her senior – Ray was in his mid-forties. Dennis eased the car down an uninhabited stretch of Mulholland Drive and the two youngsters made out together for the first time.

After that Dennis saw Natalie a lot, reassuring her that she was bound to get the role opposite Dean: she was fucking the director, after all. Returning home from a drive one day their car was involved in an accident with another vehicle and the couple were thrown into the road. Dennis escaped with minor bruising but Natalie suffered concussion and was taken to hospital. Later the police arrived to question them both, and afterwards Natalie called Ray. 'The cops called me a goddamn juvenile delinquent; now do I get the part?'

As filming commenced on *Rebel*, Dean cut a posturing figure on the set, treating Hopper and other cast members with unconcealed disdain. Dennis didn't give a shit, he was the best actor around, he was gonna take Hollywood by storm, wasn't he? All that changed when he saw Dean act. It blew him away. When cameras finished rolling on the scene Dennis grabbed Dean, or so the story goes, and threw him inside a car. 'What the hell are you doing?' he yelled in his face. 'I thought I was the best young actor in the world until I saw you. I gotta know how you do it!' It was the beginning of Dennis's idolisation of Dean, as the star sometimes took time out during filming to watch his takes and offer advice, for example, 'Smoke the cigarette, don't act smoking the cigarette.' In other words, just do it, don't show it. Both also learned they had a mutual hatred for their parents and used that anger as an outlet in their acting. 'I'm gonna show you, I'm going to be somebody,' that was the drive, as it was for Brando, too.

Dennis hung out with a lot of the *Rebel* cast, smoking dope at a time when regular offenders were thrown in jail. Worse, he also tried peyote, dried cactus top, shit the Indians smoked; this when it wasn't cool to mention the fact even to your closest buddies. Dennis ended up hooked on the stuff for years, until he quit after a bad trip. According to friends, when they popped over to see him at home there was always a pot of the stuff simmering on the hob ready for use. Dennis later claimed peyote 'helps you communicate with God or the universe. Once when I took peyote I saw the world as a cancerous growth.' It's official, Dennis was the first hippie.

Actor, writer and friend of James Dean, John Gilmore also befriended Dennis on the *Rebel* set and hung out with him. One particularly memorable night was spent at the Hollywood home of Maila Nurmi, aka Vampira, the original glamour ghoul girl who hosted late-night horror movies on TV. A few of the *Rebel* cast, including Dennis, were relaxing on the living-room floor, chatting with Maila. Suddenly she jolted up and cried, 'Kiss my ass, stupid.' This Dennis viewed not as an insult but as an invitation to pull down Maila's jeans and proceed as instructed.

She fought him off, but Dennis's gander was up and he'd yanked her pants partway down before noticing she wasn't wearing knickers. Embarrassed and vexed, Vampira, according to Gilmore, punched Dennis hard in the face. He tried to laugh it off but the next day arrived on set with a glorious shiner.

It didn't take Gilmore long to realise that Dennis was into sex in a big way. He accompanied him one afternoon to a burlesque show downtown, 'and Dennis started jacking off in the middle of it. Someone called the manager and he asked us to leave and Dennis shouted, "I'm Dennis Hopper, man. I'm with Warner Brothers and I'll have your fucking job!" The guy said if we didn't leave he'd call the cops. "We don't allow no jacking off in here!"'

Dennis and Natalie remained an item all through the shooting of *Rebel*, creating such a bad atmosphere on set between himself and the director that Dennis challenged him to a fist fight. 'Kid,' Ray said, 'someday you're going to learn to put your fists away.' Dennis consoled himself with the fact that, even though Natalie was shagging the old guy, 'she was *with me*.'

One day Dennis and Natalie decided to have a good old-fashioned Hollywood orgy and invited another couple round to Dennis's apartment. No one really knew what the rules were, so Natalie got things rolling by crying out, 'Let's have a champagne bath.' Good idea, thought Dennis, who popped out quickly and returned with a couple of cases of cheap bubbly and proceeded to fill the bath with it. Natalie stripped and slowly lowered herself in. Within seconds she was in absolute agony, her vagina inflamed by the alcohol. A half-dressed Dennis had to rush her to the ER.

Within weeks of finishing work on *Rebel* Dennis was cast in James Dean's next movie, the epic *Giant* (1956) with Elizabeth Taylor. When that was over both returned to LA, Dean ecstatic that he could drive his Porsche Spyder again after studio executives had banned him from car racing during filming. He even took Dennis for a spin in it. On 30 September 1955, on his way to a race meeting, Dean was involved in a head-on collision with another car at a lonely intersection. Rushed to hospital, he was pronounced dead on arrival. He was twenty-four.

Minutes after the news came over the radio a mutual friend was banging on the door to Dennis's apartment. It was a bad idea. Recovering from a hectic night, Dennis couldn't comprehend what he was being told and reacted with violence, shoving the guy against a wall and thwacking him one. He thought it was a sick joke. 'Don't you ever put me on like that again, man.' Then the reality sank in. 'It was horror. It was unbelievable.'

Dennis had placed Dean on a pedestal, above anyone else he'd ever met. Now his idol was gone and he was left devastated, wondering how a person of destiny could die just like that. The aftershock of the tragedy would echo inside him for years.

When the time comes when nobody desires me . . . for myself . . . I'd rather not be . . . desired . . . at all.

Determined to be an actor, Warren Beatty hit New York with all the explosive energy of a damp squib, working as a dishwasher, as a sandhog during the construction of a new section of the Lincoln Tunnel and also picking up the odd gig as, would you believe, cocktail-lounge piano man, all the while living in filthy conditions that even Marlon might have turned his nose up at: an unheated apartment in a run-down tenement. The previous occupant had been a junkie and the place still reeked of his habit. With very little income, Warren seemed to be just about surviving on peanut butter sandwiches, until he collapsed and ended up in hospital with hepatitis.

With little experience behind him it was Brando's old drama coach Stella Adler who gave Warren the, 'arrogant, self-confidence', in his words, that would spur him on to success and equip him with the balls to say no to roles he didn't like. Quite a courageous thing for an out-of-work actor to do. At one audition, when a director criticised his low voice, saying that he was mumbling like Brando, Warren simply gave the script back and walked out. Stella loved Warren the minute he joined her acting class, but her praise alone didn't pay the bills and the young actor continued to live on the breadline, literally starving, before he won a few roles in daytime soaps, one-off television dramas and off-Broadway plays.

And there were women, of course. Warren was spending a lot of time with a young actress called Diane Ladd, the future wife of Bruce Dern and mother of *Blue Velvet* and *Jurassic Park* star Laura Dern. They met through acting class; Diane was barely sixteen years old. She loved Warren's company, thought he was fun to be around. 'He'd take me home and kiss me goodnight – then say hello to my roommates and kiss them too.' Others found him overbearing and too cocky by half. Neither did they appreciate his sometimes wild sense of humour.

One of Diane's flatmates was seventeen-year-old Rona Barrett, later to become a popular TV showbiz reporter in the seventies, to whom Ryan O'Neal famously mailed a live tarantula. Early one morning Rona was awoken by loud rapping at the door and a voice demanding, 'Open up.' She was hardly going to do that at 2 a.m., not until the mystery voice identified itself, which it refused to do. 'Open the door,' it went on, then menacingly: 'I'm gonna rape you.' Startled, Rona replied, 'No you're not. Who is it?' It was Warren, of course, coming to visit his girl-friend. Finally, Diane came running down the hall. 'Oh my God, it's only Warren,' she said, as if this were a daily occurrence. Invited in, he took one look at Rona and blurted out, 'This is it, baby! You're finally gonna lose that fucking cherry.'

Not surprisingly, Rona was never attracted to Warren, even though 'he had relationships with a number of my girlfriends'. But, rape threats aside, she found him charm personified. Already the Beatty seduction technique was taking shape: an ability to captivate a woman entirely, to be attentive only to her, to make her feel she was the one person in the room, nay the world, who mattered at that moment. As one woman who enjoyed a brief affair with Warren explained to *Time* magazine in 1978. 'He doesn't just want to seduce you but to quite literally charm the pants off you. He tells you you're fabulous and laughs at all your jokes. He's so in love with himself that it's contagious.'

Like before, Superman, two or three goons holding me while you do the punching.

Jack Nicholson did a lot of thinking about his future during the summer of 1954. He'd enough grades to go to college, but that meant work and lots of it. 'And I was too lazy for that. I wasn't filled with a burning desire to make something of myself in those days.' So he bummed around for a while, worked as a lifeguard, even making the local papers when in a choppy storm he muscled a boat out, surviving huge waves, to rescue a party of five swimmers who'd got into trouble. 'What the paper didn't mention is that as soon as I beached the boat, I puked my guts out in front of about 40,000 people.'

Another summer job was working as the assistant manager of a local movie theatre. *On the Waterfront* was showing and the young Jack must have seen every performance, unable to take his eyes off Brando. 'He was spellbinding, a genius. There was no way to follow in his footsteps. He was just too large and just too far out of sight.'

By coincidence, or was it providence, June had settled in a suburb of LA with her children after her marriage to the test pilot broke up. Jack, still unaware that his sister was his mother, packed his bags and headed west to stay with her for a while, keen on catching some Californian rays before deciding what to do next with his life. Immediately he connected with the place, its atmosphere, the buzz, it just felt like home. For money he played the horses at the local race track and hustled pool at night, and there was also a part-time job in a toy store. But that wasn't enough for June; she thought Jack ought to be looking for more secure employment. Both hot-headed, the pair often clashed and after one particularly fierce argument June threw him out into the street. Angry, he walked for hours before stumbling, exhausted, onto Sunset Boulevard. At last, Jack had arrived in the heart of Hollywood.

On the verge of returning home, feeling he really ought to get serious about his life and go to college, Jack landed a job as a mail boy in the animation department of MGM, for Tom and Jerry creators William Hanna and Joseph Barbera. Although the studios were far from the giants they once had been, they were still imposing places and Jack was intoxicated by the sheer vibe of working there. He'd visit sound stages and watch them shoot pictures, see stars like Bogart and Liz Taylor; 'It was hog heaven for me.' He once confessed to lying down flat on a studio lawn to get a good look at Lana Turner's knickers as she boarded a coach. He even had the temerity to ask Joan Collins for a date; she turned him down.

To this day Jack still recalls the day Marlon arrived on the MGM lot. The staff there were blasé about seeing movie stars, but every venetian blind flew up and all the secretaries stuck their heads out the window to take a peek at him. Jack even snuck onto the sound stage to watch up front and personal his hero in action.

Moving out of June's place, Jack rented a small apartment above a garage with an old school pal. They'd go out at night with like-minded souls, wasting hours over a cappuccino in the coffee bars of Sunset Strip talking about movies and worshipping their acting idols, Brando, Dean and Clift. They'd try to hit on girls, without success. At one nightclub Jack plucked up the courage to ask for a dance but rushed back minutes later. 'I've got to find the men's room.' His friends were perplexed. 'What happened?' Jack explained. 'I was dancing with this girl and she danced so damn close to me that I exploded in my pants!'

Walking down a corridor one day at MGM Jack passed producer Joe Pasternak. 'Hiya, Joe,' he grinned. Pasternak paused, then said, 'Hey, kid – how'd ya like to be in pictures?' Yes, that really used to happen, you just had to be in the right place at the right time. For days Jack sweated over his audition, daring to dream of stardom. Reality hurt when it hit him: he wasn't good enough, the test was a disaster and Nicholson was back on the mail run. His gawky, unconventional looks just didn't fit in with the current emphasis on brooding Roman gods like Marlon and Rock Hudson. 'Hiya, Joe,' Jack greeted Pasternak in the corridor a few days after. The producer stopped for a moment, mulling over the earnest youth's face. Then he spoke: 'Hey – how'd ya like to be in pictures?' Jack shrugged his shoulders over the fickle business he'd chosen to be a part of and walked away.

Get up! Get up, you scum-suckin' pig!

Despite all the success Marlon Brando had enjoyed he remained a psychological mess. Sometimes he'd walk the streets till dawn or chat for hours on the phone with friends until succumbing to sleep. Financially things were looking precarious, too. In an effort to mend the relationship with his father he'd taken on Marlon Sr as a business manager, which was a recipe for disaster. When a cattle ranch the old man invested in went belly up the son needed money fast, so signed a contract to appear in a piece of historical nonsense called *The Egyptian* for 20th Century Fox, the first time he'd agreed to make 'crap for money'. Then he read the script – 'It was shit' – and walked. The studio was incensed. Acting fast, Brando got his shrink to write a letter saying he couldn't make the film because he was 'mentally confused'. It was the ultimate sick note, but Fox weren't buying it and sued Brando for breach of contract. A compromise was reached: Marlon would make another film for Fox, *Desirée* (1954), starring as Napoleon.

Either he wasn't interested in the role or it was the biggest sulk in movie history, but Marlon's performance as the diminutive dictator was one big fat void. Critics and the public wholeheartedly agreed. At one screening Marlon's Napoleon emoted on screen, 'When did you stop loving me?' To which one member of the audience heckled, 'When you made this shit-kicker.' Marlon's spirits fell and he told a reporter he felt like giving up movies for a while and finding a hideaway somewhere in the South Pacific, where he could 'fuck brown-skinned teenage gals until I've doubled the island population'.

Amidst all this wrangling Dodie was taken seriously ill. Marlon and his sisters rushed to her bedside and for the next three weeks held vigil as she slipped in and out of a coma, waking up sometimes to talk with her children, telling Brando to promise her, 'to try and get along with people. Don't fight with them, Bud.'

Then one night she held Marlon's hand softly and whispered, 'I'm not scared, and you don't have to be.' Then the woman Stella Adler called 'this heavenly, girlish, lost creature' was gone. Brando broke down, emotionally spent. Dodie had borne her illness with incredible courage and dignity; Brando later told friends she taught him how to die. Marlon did not fall completely to pieces after Dodie's death, as friends feared he might, but there were occasions he came mighty close. Like when he drove playwright Clifford Odets home late one night and suddenly started dredging up memories of pulling his mother's drunken body out of bars as a kid. Tears welled up in his eyes, impairing his vision, and his driving grew erratic, the car swerving from side to side on the perilously steep bends along the Hollywood Hills. Odets was convinced his number was up, but Marlon managed to regain composure and all was well.

After their fruitful collaboration on *Julius Ceasar* Joe Mankiewicz wanted Marlon to star in the screen version of the Broadway smash musical *Guys and Dolls* (1955). As Joe's son Tom recalls, 'Marlon was in Europe and Dad sent him a telegram saying, "How would you like to play Sky Masterson?" And Marlon sent a telegram back saying, "Actually more terrified than playing Shakespeare for the first time, never have done a musical before." And Dad sent him back a telegram saying, "Don't worry about it, neither have I." And that's how they started. And they became artistically very close. Marlon once said to me, "Your old man was the only person who would have cast me in Shakespeare and a musical."'

His co-star was Frank Sinatra, still pissed at Brando for stealing *On the Waterfront* from under his nose and now even more narked because he was giving his old lady Ava Gardner a good seeing-to on a regular basis. One morning Marlon got a call from Frank. 'Listen, creep, and listen good. Stay away from Ava. You got that? First offence, broken legs. Second offence, cracked skull. If you live through all that, cement shoes.'

Inevitably tensions surfaced between the two men on set. Sinatra's nickname for Brando was 'Mumbles'. Marlon said of Sinatra's voice, 'I'd prefer a castrated rooster at dawn.' On set one day Marlon asked Frank to run through lines with him. 'Don't pull that Actors Studio shit on me,' blasted the singer. Their working methods certainly differed. Sinatra liked things done swiftly, if it was a good take, that's it, let's move on. 'That was not Marlon's way of working,' says Tom Mankiewicz. 'And it wasn't my father's way of working either.'

Brando's rivalry with Sinatra never boiled over into open hostility in public, his best put-down about the crooner being, 'He's the kind of guy that, when he dies, he's going up to heaven and give God a bad time for making him bald.' The nearest it came to blows was during the filming of a scene in a restaurant booth with Sinatra eating a slice of cheesecake. 'Just for fun, Marlon kept blowing his line,' says Mankiewicz. 'And of course every time he blew his line they'd start again and they'd put a new piece of cheesecake in front of Sinatra. And Frank didn't want to eat a lot of cheesecake, and during a break Brando said to Dad, "I'm

gonna make this son of a bitch eat till he starts shitting in the booth."
Frank knew Marlon was fluffing his lines intentionally just to irritate him
because he had a show to do that night in Vegas.'

A substantial box-office hit, *Guys and Dolls* remained the one and only
musical Marlon ever made, believing as he did that his voice sounded
'like the wail of a bagpipe through wet tissues'.

In an interview Marlon once declared his intention of marrying within
the year and was predictably inundated with offers from women in
various states of desperation. One postcard arrived from a sixteen-year-
old Eskimo girl who ended: 'Me make best wife, know how to keep
husband warm in very cold.' Brando replied. 'No good in California.'

When he did finally marry, Marlon chose a suitably exotic creature,
Anna Kashfi, who claimed to have been born in Calcutta of pure Indian
parentage. She was just another of his numerous girlfriends until struck
down with tuberculosis, whereupon Marlon, a sucker for the helpless,
nursed her back to health and then claimed he was smitten, presenting
Kashfi with the ring he'd taken from his dead mother's finger and
declaring, 'I'm glad she's dead! If she was alive, I never could have loved
you. She wouldn't have let me go.'

Then it was off to Europe to film the war drama *The Young Lions*
(1958), in which Brando played a Nazi. To help him get into the part
director Edward Dmytryk hired an ex-Wehrmacht officer and every day
he and Brando hurled German abuse at each other. During one meeting
with Dmytryk Marlon announced he needed to take a leak. Instead of
going to the bathroom Marlon removed some flowers from a vase,
opened his flies and, 'In front of me,' Dmytryk later recalled, 'he took
a horse piss into the vase.'

While filming in Paris Marlon was mobbed; fans tore off his coat and
ripped his shirt. Fame was still very much a Kafkaesque nightmare and
he grew increasingly paranoid that people used him just for money or
status. He described himself as 'a bomb waiting to go off'. Much of his
anger was directed at the paparazzi. In Hollywood he knocked a camera
out of a photo journalist's hand, while in Rome half throttled a paparazzo
who dared take a picture of him with a girlfriend. (By the seventies
his antipathy for them hadn't dimmed, as evidenced when he broke a

photographer's jaw. Undaunted, the paparazzo wore a football helmet next time he went snapping photos of Brando.)

With *The Young Lions* in the can Brando's marriage to Kashfi could go ahead. Marlon Sr was not amongst the invited. 'I'll bury him first,' he told friends. If it were possible, relations between father and son were worse than ever. At a party given by Marlon for his father, Sr complained about the noise some of his son's friends were making and told him to ask them to leave. When Marlon refused he was treated to a vicious slap across the face. Though seized with anger, Marlon did not retaliate. Many people have speculated that it was Marlon's hatred for his father that fuelled his acting, and that it was Stella Adler who showed him how to focus that anger and channel it creatively. Marlon claimed that one of the few positive aspects of playing the motorcycle thug in *The Wild One* was that it released some of his inner violence. 'Before *The Wild One* I thought about killing my father. After *The Wild One*, I decided that I shouldn't actually kill him, but pull out his corneas.'

Marlon and Anna Kashfi were married in October 1957. After a brief honeymoon the happy couple returned to Hollywood. Bizarrely, on that first night back Marlon clambered through the window of his sister Jocelyn's house, crashing on the sofa and telling her, 'Well, I did it. I got married. Now what do I do?'

In May 1958 Kashfi gave Marlon a much-longed-for son, despite the trauma of being forced to change delivery rooms to avoid press photographers dressed as doctors who were roaming the ward. Tears welled up in Marlon's eyes as he held the child, whom they named Christian. But parenthood couldn't save the marriage, and the couple argued and fought constantly. Kashfi claimed that Marlon insisted on behaving like a 'bachelor' at weekends, and at other times took off at all hours, returning early in the morning without explanation – 'None of your business where I've been,' he'd growl.

Brando found solace from marital woes in his pet project, a revenge western called *One-Eyed Jacks* (released in early 1961 after a lengthy delay), which he wanted Stanley Kubrick to direct. For months they sweated over a script that never quite worked. 'Marlon, I still can't figure out what this movie is about,' Kubrick said one day. 'It's about the $350,000

I've spent so far,' replied Brando. Kubrick walked and made *Spartacus* instead. 'So there wasn't anything for me to do except direct it myself,' said Marlon. 'Or go to the poorhouse.' This news was met with consternation by Paramount's terrified executives, weary of Brando's erratic behaviour. But he was a star, one the studio's top brass believed could be controlled; big mistake.

Out on location Brando out-Leaned David Lean, waiting hours for the right kind of light or cloud formation before shooting. A two-month schedule dragged on to nearer six, and the budget ballooned from $2m to $6m. Brando was out of control and the studio got nervous, very nervous. In the end the head of Paramount himself, Y. Frank Freeman, arrived on the set to personally read the riot act to Brando, since no one else could summon up the courage. 'You're going to see how to deal with Marlon Brando.' Freeman told his fellow executives.

Marlon was sitting on a fence as Freeman approached, the crew looking on and waiting for the fireworks to begin. 'Marlon,' said Freeman. 'I saw the dailies.' There was a pause, the tension was unbearable. 'They're brilliant. I want to tell you what a great job you're doing.' The crew nearly died laughing. Freeman was so intimidated by coming face to face with Marlon, who hadn't even opened his mouth, he couldn't say anything bad. 'Everyone forgets Marlon was a big powerful man,' says *Godfather* producer Albert Ruddy. 'Believe me, you wouldn't try to push him around; this guy was a boxer, he had fucking arms on him bigger than most people's legs. No one ever tried to intimidate him. And they didn't, because his presence overwhelmed them.'

When Brando got back to Hollywood his first cut of the movie ran five hours. Agonising for months trying to trim it down, in the end Marlon gave up and let Paramount make the final edit. The film never found an audience. 'Marlon admitted to me that he found directing tough, an ass-breaker,' says Tom Mankiewicz. 'Very few actors have become really good directors because it's a completely different deal. You see, when you're acting, everybody takes care of you; when you're directing, you have to take care of everybody else. It's just a totally different job. And Marlon said, "I did the one picture and never again."'

According to Karl Malden, during the shooting of *One-Eyed Jacks*

Brando would have, 'two steaks, potatoes, two apple pies and a quart of milk' for dinner, necessitating constant altering of his costumes. Even before he let himself get obese and ballooned up to Hindenburg proportions, over 350 pounds, Marlon's eating habits were legendary. Close friend Carlo Fiore told how as early as the late fifties and early sixties Brando went on crash diets before shooting movies, but when he lost his willpower would gorge himself on huge breakfasts consisting of corn flakes, sausages, eggs, bananas and cream, and a huge stack of pancakes drenched in syrup. During a birthday party for Brando on *One-Eyed Jacks* a sign was placed below the cake saying, 'Don't feed the director.' It was an amusing aside, but Marlon's battle with his weight had only just begun.

Had to shoot me a Mexican.

When *Rebel Without a Cause* hit cinemas James Dean had been dead for only a month, but the legend was already growing out of control. Elvis Presley saw the film forty-four times; he was obsessed with it and when he came to Hollywood sought Dennis Hopper's friendship because he'd been close to Dean. After two weeks of hanging out Elvis asked Hopper for some acting advice. He'd just read the script for his debut movie *Love Me Tender* and saw major problems over a fight scene involving his leading lady. 'I've never hit a woman and I never will,' Elvis fretted. 'I don't know how I'm gonna do that scene.' Gently Dennis tried to explain. 'Well, Elvis, we don't really hit people in the movies. We fake all that.' Elvis was convinced Dennis was pulling his leg. 'Yeah, next thing you're gonna tell me is those ain't real bullets I see hitting the ground.' 'No, Elvis,' said Dennis, dumbfounded at the pelvis thruster's utter naivety. 'I'm gonna let that one slide.'

Not long after *Rebel* came the premiere of *Giant*. The studio demanded Dennis take Natalie Wood as his date, but he refused, escorting instead the then unknown and future Mrs Paul Newman, Joanne Woodward, who he had the hots for. Afterwards Dennis insisted on taking Joanne home, and then tried to sweet-talk himself through the door of her apartment. Joanne barred the entrance with her arm but Hopper wouldn't budge. Finally she'd no choice but to physically throw him down the stairs. For years Dennis never figured out why, until Newman told him that he was waiting for Joanne inside that night. 'I was behind the door. We both had a good laugh.'

Bewildering as it may have been to him that Joanne preferred Paul Newman, female company was hardly a problem for Dennis; there were rumours of romantic trysts with Joan Collins and Ursula Andress. 'None of these affairs were too serious,' he said. 'But I don't think there was a starlet around who could have been had in those days that I didn't have.'

With Dean dead, Dennis saw himself as the natural inheritor of his rebellious mantle. He made this very obvious to Dean's old friend John Gilmore when they bumped into each other again. 'Dennis was peeing in the long trough in a men's room on the Warners lot one afternoon. He was coming on very strange, like, fuck Warner Brothers, they're not gonna tell me what to do, blah, blah. He was doing a Jimmy Dean kind of thing, but it didn't work at all.' Dennis was determined to be the new rebel in town and give the executives hell. 'Only they don't know it yet,' he said to Gilmore, wagging his cock in the direction of the front office. 'But they're going to find out, man.'

Dennis had plenty to rebel against, like the old-timers who'd been running the movie business for decades and grown fat and complacent on past successes. He was going to give it to 'em, but good. 'I was temperamental,' he later confessed. 'I figured I knew a hell of a lot more about acting than they did. Which was probably true.' Not just Dean, Hopper also looked to the likes of John Barrymore and Errol Flynn, the rebels of Hollywood's golden age, and saw that it was a great actor's responsibility to raise hell. Maybe the studio would take you more seriously the more outrageously you behaved.

Quickly Dennis acquired a reputation as a perfectionist and screwball. When he was late on set one time, according to Gilmore, Warners sent a letter detailing the expense this had cost the studio in the cast and crew having to hang around, a not inconsiderable sum. Dennis framed it. He revelled in his nickname of 'Dennis the Menace', bragging that Warners now knew they had another volatile talent on their hands who needed special handling the same as Jimmy Dean.

Not everyone thought this rebellious attitude was a good idea.

Jack Nicholson was at a party at Dennis's house once, listening to the man rant and rave, condemning his paymasters, the fat, useless moguls, and clearly saw that this wasn't an ideal course of action. When Dennis left the room to find more dope, Jack turned to Gilmore and said, 'Man, this is suicide! What the fuck's he doing?' Other friends felt the same way. Gilmore recalls noticing a silver tray at the home of *Rebel* screen-writer Stewart Stern that had a peculiar dent in it. 'Joanne Woodward told me that at a dinner party there one evening she'd become so impatient with Dennis's "moaning drivel" about cutting Hollywood down to size that she grabbed the tray and smacked him on top of the head as hard as she could, "Hoping in some way," she said. "To knock sense into him."'

A head-on collision was inevitable and it arrived when Dennis was loaned out to 20th Century Fox to work for Henry Hathaway on a movie called *From Hell to Texas* (1958). Hathaway was just the sort of old-school director Dennis abhorred, the kind who didn't understand, or want to understand, new approaches in acting. 'I walked off the picture three times,' said Dennis. 'I wouldn't take direction.' What cheesed off Dennis the most was Hathaway's habit of telling his actors where to move, how to walk, how to talk. Inspired by Dean, Dennis was now trying to, 'live in the moment', do things with his acting without preconceived ideas. 'Look,' said Dennis, 'I'm a method actor. I work with my ears, my sight, my head, and my sense of smell.' Hathaway must have thought he had a real nutcase on his hands.

On the last day of shooting Dennis decided to make a stand and refused to perform a scene Hathaway's way. 'Listen,' said the director, 'I own forty per cent of this studio and you're going to do the scene how I want it.' It was a battle of wills. Whose would crack first? They started at seven in the morning. By lunch Dennis was still defiant; by dinner he was still giving Hathaway the finger, doing the lines his way; by 11 o'clock, after eighty takes and fifteen hours, it was Dennis who caved in, physically and mentally drained. In tears, he asked Hathaway how the director wanted him to play the scene. He did it and then walked off the set. Not before he heard, ringing in his ears, Hathaway's curse: 'You'll never work in this town again, kid! I guarantee it!'

Few in Hollywood had ever known a young actor behave like this. In the past the industry forgave unspeakable things in the name of genuine, saleable talent, but the consensus was that Dennis Hopper didn't have any such talent, so Warners dropped him as quickly as they would a dog-shit sandwich. In the words of studio executives, he was dead meat. 'I was blackballed, which means the executives call each other and say, don't hire this kid – he's a nightmare.' Dennis didn't make another Hollywood movie for seven years.

Disillusioned, he headed east to New York, where he stayed with John Gilmore. 'When he flew in Dennis had this BOAC bag that was half full of marijuana. And he was totally stoned all the time, and drinking, just incredibly stoned.' His sex drive was enormous, out of control. According to Gilmore, 'Dennis would stop girls on the street and say. "Hi, I'm Dennis Hopper. Do you wanna fuck?" They'd laugh or just glare with indignation – "Who the hell is Dennis Hopper?"'

A friend of Gilmore thought it might be a good idea to get a couple of nuns from a nearby convent to come by and try and save the soul of Dennis. They arrived decked out in traditional black habits and clutching their rosaries. Out of it on dope and booze, Dennis wasted little time in propositioning the younger of the two sisters to a romp with a 'live pulse'. Gilmore's friend stepped in. 'Excuse me, Sister,' he said, and picked Dennis up and threw him onto a bed, warning, 'Don't move a muscle. I'm escorting the sisters out of here.' Before leaving the nuns turned to the bedraggled form of Dennis. 'I can see he's in pain. We will pray for him.' Considering what was to befall Dennis over the next couple of decades, she obviously didn't pray hard enough.

Gilmore continued to see Dennis on and off for the next few years but the two men fell out over a film script and never spoke to one another again. 'Dennis liked to probably sell the idea that he was this wild Hollywood rebel,' says Gilmore. 'He was wild. At parties he'd get weird and piss on the wall, but he really wasn't a rebel, he was just this self-destructive asshole.'

In New York Dennis studied with Lee Strasberg at the Actors Studio and guest starred in the odd TV series, 'strictly for the bread, man'. More often than not he appeared in the pilot episode, 'usually as the bad guy who'd get knocked off by the hero before he got his own series'. Most of these shows were westerns, such as *Wagon Train*, *Bonanza* and *Gunsmoke*, and Dennis enjoyed standing in front of mirrors to practise his quick draw. 'I almost shot my toe off once.'

Mostly he soaked himself in the underground culture of the Big Apple, floating in and out of jazz clubs where the atmosphere of drugs, broads and booze appealed. He met fellow purveyors of decadence, hard drinkers and druggies who, like Dennis, could stay up all night drinking and still be standing upright, just, by dawn. He went beatnik basically, grew his hair long and started a Marlon Brando for President campaign.

Most importantly for his sanity, Dennis discovered a real passion for art and became a self-confessed 'gallery bum'. Hardly a day went by that he wasn't wandering around the city's many art galleries. Frustrated by the deliberate stifling of his film career, Dennis turned to art and photography for creative stimulus, beginning with abstract subjects like walls and landscapes. Dennis was reluctant to photograph people – from his own experience in Hollywood he knew how intrusive a photojournalist's lens could be – but gradually he began to document with his camera the burgeoning sixties vibe, especially the new bohemians he hung out with, an arty crowd of abstract expressionists and pop-art artists that included Andy Warhol, Roy Lichtenstein and Jasper Johns. Dennis was at the cutting edge, if you wanted to know something about what the scene was, Dennis could tell you.

So how about making up your mind: are you my girl or aren't you?

Aside from early forays into television, Warren Beatty managed some theatre, too, and in the summer of 1958 a production took him out to Connecticut, where he met a remarkable young woman destined, like himself, to become an icon – Barbra Streisand. Her plain looks and foghorn nose didn't put Warren off; far from it, he was quite definitely turned on by the sixteen-year-old high-school student. Finding out where she was babysitting that evening, Warren turned up and they chatted for hours, but his intentions weren't exactly honourable: he wanted her there and then, nappies or no nappies. Barbra was no pushover and Warren's pants stayed firmly on. 'She seemed to be a person of strong moral convictions,' Warren said later. 'One of her convictions seemed to be that with the recent loss of my virginity, I might be experiencing too much of a good thing.' Indeed, it was hands off when it came to Barbra, at least for now.

Ultimately it was theatre that brought about Warren's big break-through, appearing in a touring play in New Jersey at which the first five rows were full of agents. 'I really thought I was hot shit.' It was *South Pacific* director Joshua Logan who first spotted Warren's talent, along with gay playwright William Inge. Much salivating must have gone on in the stalls when the beauteous Warren entered stage left. Inge, amongst America's most celebrated playwrights, was, according to Logan, in love with Warren at first sight, gushing, 'I absolutely must have him,' a statement that can be given two quite different though probably equally accurate interpretations. It was Logan who had Warren first (professionally, that is), flying him out to Hollywood for a screen test opposite another celluloid virgin, Jane Fonda. The audition was a love scene, 'We were thrown together like lions in a cage,' recalled Warren, and it went so well that the young couple were still swapping tonsils long after the director yelled, 'Cut! Stop! That's enough!' As Jane later recalled, 'We kissed until we had practically eaten each other's heads off.'

Hollywood was Warren's kind of town and he was quickly snapped up by MGM, who put him under contract at $400 a week. Flush with money, he checked into the Chateau Marmont off Sunset Boulevard and exploited his sister's fame by gatecrashing industry parties where he could network and hunt pussy at the same time. His lifetime pursuit of Hollywood's most glamorous women had begun.

First on the Beatty conveyor belt was British sexpot Joan Collins, who found him, 'appealing and vulnerable'. Their eyes first met across a crowded restaurant one night in 1959. Dining with Jane Fonda, who, according to Joan, 'hung on to Warren's every word', the Lothario couldn't help sneaking the odd appreciative peep over at Joan. At one point she returned his gaze and Warren, playing it cool, smiled and raised his glass. They quickly hooked up, and on that first night hit the sack and were still rutting in the early hours of the morning. We know this thanks to Joan's gleeful confession to a friend that she was amazed at the man's stamina and that, if Warren kept up such bedroom activity, 'in a few years, I'll be worn out'.

It was love, addictive love, for Joan, who was twice suspended by 20th Century Fox, with whom she was under contract, for refusing film roles in order to be with Warren. Considering his sex addiction, which meant they got down to it four or sometimes five times a day, every day, it's no surprise that Joan never wanted to be out of his sight, presumably fearing that he might end up rutting the sideboard or an innocent maid who had only popped in to turn down the beds. Joan had good cause to worry about Warren's roving eye: he'd tried to bed starlet Mamie Van Doren, without success. 'Warren drools a lot,' Mamie would say of him. 'He has such active glands.' Joan observed another habit, that Warren talked on the phone during copulation.

Dating a sex bomb like Joan Collins gave Warren his first taste of celebrity, but his career had stalled. Over at MGM he was picking up his weekly cheque but sitting on his arse doing nothing. 'I felt I was turning into a very large piece of citrus fruit.' With borrowed money Warren bought his way out of his MGM contract and sought out a mentor. William Inge was only too happy to oblige, casting him in his latest Broadway play *A Loss of Roses*. Rumours quickly spread backstage that the eager young star did very little to discourage Inge's obvious infatuation and jealous friends labelled the ageing playwright 'Warren's fairy godmother.' Safe in this position, Warren started throwing his weight around, debating the meaning of the dialogue, showing up late for rehearsals. It got so bad that his co-star, veteran Broadway actress Shirley Booth, quit in protest. The play opened in the winter of 1959 to poor reviews and closed after just three weeks, ending Warren's first and, as it turned out, only Broadway appearance.

Recovering fast, Warren got a semi-regular role in a new popular TV comedy, *The Many Loves of Dobie Gillis*, starring Dwayne Hickman as a girl-chasing teen. Warren played the neighbourhood 'rich kid' Milton Armitage, and although he appeared in only six episodes made a lasting impression on Hickman. 'Warren Beatty has always acted like a movie star, even when no one knew who he was. He had great confidence in himself and seemed assured of his success, and the fact that he wasn't well known didn't matter.'

Hickman thought him pleasant and very good in the role, 'It was perfect for him.' But Warren 'didn't have much to say to anyone', and when he left to become a genuine star, didn't admit for years that he'd been in *Dobie*. 'Which I thought was strange,' says Hickman. 'Clint Eastwood, Steve McQueen, Jim Garner all had big film careers and had started in television, not to mention the fact the show is on video for anyone to see. Dustin Hoffman used to kid him about it in interviews.'

All these years later one incident remains in Hickman's memory. 'Everybody was on the studio floor and about to shoot. We had these little canvas knock-down dressing rooms just behind the set and one of the crew, as a joke, turned the latch and locked Warren in.' Instead of yelling to get out or trying to kick the thing over, Warren just waited till the cameras rolled and started singing opera. "Cut," the director yelled. "What is that? Who's doing that?" An assistant piped up, "Warren Beatty is locked in his dressing room." "Well, let him out!" implored the director. "We can't shoot with that kind of noise. Good God!"'

No novocaine. It dulls the senses.

Jack Nicholson was advised that if he wanted to get anywhere in show business he ought to gain experience and training first. The best acting classes in town were run by Jeff Corey, an advocate of the method. Though not hamstrung by it, he encouraged playfulness in his class and improvisation, at which Jack excelled. Corey was all for his students making the bizarre choice; 'Be unpredictable,' he'd urge. 'But most importantly, don't copy other actors, be yourself, be original.'

Corey's lessons were important in other ways, too. Valuable friendships were forged with people who were to play significant roles in Jack's life: Robert Towne, the future screenwriter of *Chinatown*, and Carole Eastman, who'd write *Five Easy Pieces*. Jack thought Carole was, 'a knockout', a feeling not exactly reciprocated: she thought the young actor 'defied description', was a bit of an oddball, 'as if he'd been dropped out of outer space'. She had to admit, though, there was something special about him. 'It was like seeing Marlon Brando on stage for the first time – he was *it*.' Nothing sexual developed, however, much to Jack's dismay.

This was fairly indicative of his carnal grabbings at the time. Although Jack liked to call himself the great seducer, Robert Towne remembered things a little differently. Yes, there were plenty of groupies hanging about Hollywood, and great women in acting classes, but few of them wanted to fuck a nobody, a category Jack and his little group of buddies certainly qualified for. As producer Julia Phillips once famously claimed, in Hollywood you fuck up, not down.

In the spring of 1957 the Hanna–Barbera cartoon unit at MGM closed down and Jack was out of work. It was a disruptive period; without a place of his own he'd crash at friends' houses or stay sometimes with June. Inevitably the arguments would begin again. 'She thought that I was lazy, wasn't trying,' Jack confessed to *Vanity Fair* in 1992. 'She thought all I was interested in was running around, getting high, and pussy.' Imagine how tempting it must have been for June to yell out, 'Do as I say because I'm your mother, you prick!' But she daren't, so the rows continued. One time they didn't speak to each other for a whole year. It got that bad.

Meanwhile over at Jeff Corey's class there was a new student, Roger Corman, a maverick director/producer who made films like other people made IKEA wardrobes: quick, cheap and with as little fuss as possible. Stories about him are legion, like the time someone asked for a helicopter to shoot a high angle. 'I'll get you a ladder,' Corman said. He'd enrolled to learn more about how actors prepared and trained, and for him Jack stood out from day one. 'I thought he was an outstanding actor and what I've always liked about Jack is that he's a totally dedicated and sincere actor who can take a dramatic performance and do it very well but bring a little bit of humour to it, which I think makes the perform-ance far more complex.'

Convinced that Jack would emerge as some sort of a name, 'but with no idea that he would become the great star that he did', Corman cast him in *Cry Baby Killer* (1958), playing the sort of mixed-up teenager that proliferated in the wake of James Dean. 'Corman had discovered some-thing that no one else apparently had,' says director Richard Rush.

'That if your cast is the same age as your target audience, they'll come to see it; that was the secret of his exploitation.'

Jack later recalled just turning up for the audition and doing a bit of crazy stuff, screaming louder than anyone else, and getting the role. 'That's it. Movie star.' He thought, 'What's so tough?' The film managed quite the reverse, being so down-market few theatres screened it. At the not so grand opening Ethel May was invited and Jack recalled her whacking with her purse somebody who was heckling him on the screen; 'It was so humiliating.'

So, instead of instant stardom Jack was out of work for a year. Far from glum, he revelled in a hectic social life, staying up all night on Venice Beach, going to parties, catching Lenny Bruce's stand-up act over at some beatnik hangout or watching the latest European art-house movie. As for his career, it was so far down the crapper he couldn't see it. Deciding to take matters into his own hands, Jack teamed up with Robert Towne and out-of-work director Monte Hellman to literally build their own theatre in an abandoned warehouse, stealing timber from building sites at night, yanking a toilet off the wall of a local gas station and nicking electronic and lighting equipment, too. It was like the Sex Pistols stealing the instruments they played on; it was punk theatre.

Doomed to failure, of course, lasting just the one production, and just as well, for Jack had decided to leave theatre well alone and concentrate on cracking film. But would anyone give him a job? Richard Rush had just left his advertising business to set up in the movies, later becoming a cult director with films like *Freebie and the Bean* (1974) and *The Stunt Man* (1980). Back in 1959, setting up his directorial debut *Too Soon to Love*, he advertised in the local papers for young actors to attend a casting session. Rush still vividly recalls the moment Jack walked in. 'He was terrific, stood out like a jewel among stones.'

Annoyingly, the lead role had already been assigned, so Rush could cast Jack in only a minor role, that of a teen hoodlum. 'Even then he was a very accomplished actor, and gave a good performance; he was physically tough and threatening in the role. What I learned about Jack from later working with him much more consistently, first off he's a very smart guy and you can almost call out the number of the IQ you want him to play and he can lower his on-screen intelligence very convincingly, it's a very clever trick. He can play sophisticated people on film and he can play a bum, and play a bum successfully with great imagination, strength and charisma like he did in *Cuckoo's Nest*; it's a strange ability.'

The only other person prepared to hire Jack in any meaningful way was Roger Corman, and over the next few years the actor appeared almost exclusively in a conveyor belt of schlockmeister howlers. 'I either played the clean-cut boy next door, or the murderer of a family of at least five.'

One Corman role stands out from all the others, a sadomasochist patient who gets his kicks in the dentist's chair. *Little Shop of Horrors* (1960) is tatty beyond belief and looks as if it was made in two days (wait a minute – it was!), but it's Nicholson's performance almost as much as the main attraction, a flesh-eating plant, that audiences remember. A cult classic today, *Little Shop* also gave moviegoers their first glimpse of Jack's superb gift for comedy. 'He was great in it,' says Corman. 'He brought all kinds of individual bits of humour to the role. I think the high point of the scene was the way Jack yelled, "Don't stop now!" when the dentist was trying to stop his drilling; it was almost a parody of the sex act, which was the subtext. Jack was great in that part.'

3

The Drugged-Up Sixties

You remarkable pig. You can thank whatever pig God you pray to that you haven't turned me into a murderer.

Midway through shooting *One-Eyed Jacks*, Anna Kashfi walked out on Marlon Brando, fed up with his flagrant infidelity. Both ended up in court fighting over custody of their son. What was revealed did not paint a pretty picture. Marlon accused Anna of coming at him once with a butcher's knife. 'Go ahead if it makes you happy,' he screamed at her. Anna claimed that Marlon bombarded her with phone calls during the night and ransacked her house, and when she protested he 'brutally beat and struck me'. Once, while Marlon was visiting his son, Anna left the house but on her return discovered Marlon having sex with a woman. 'Would you mind leaving the bedroom while I speak to my husband?' The woman refused, so Anna threw a lamp at her. Brando countered by saying that on another occasion his wife had attacked and bitten him in his own bedroom. After giving her a good spanking he'd thrown her out, but Anna had forced her way back in. Pinning her to the ground, Marlon tied her up with dressing-gown cord and called the police. It was, it's safe to say, a messy divorce.

Far from being put off the opposite sex for life, Marlon wasted little time marrying wife number two, in June 1960. Mexican actress Movita Castaneda was nine years his senior. Curiously, after the ceremony she was installed in a separate house and the couple never actually lived together. Obviously Marlon visited from time to time, since she gave birth to a son and daughter.

According to Movita, Marlon was still battling with weight problems due to binge eating. She had to put a lock on their refrigerator to stop him pilfering on the nights he stayed over. She'd usually wake in the morning to find the lock broken. She also related how he often drove down to his favourite all-night hot-dog stand in Hollywood in the early hours of the morning and polish off half a dozen of them.

It was soon back to work for Marlon, turning down *Lawrence of Arabia* in favour of playing Fletcher Christian in a remake of the classic *Mutiny on the Bounty* (1962). It very nearly proved his undoing. The production was a madhouse almost from day one, at least six writers had a go at the script, tropical storms ravaged the Tahitian locations and director Carol Reed and Marlon argued constantly. Stories began to emerge that when Marlon didn't get his way he'd throw a hissy fit or walk off set, slowing the rate of production to a crawl. His weight fluctuated wildly, too, and he regularly split the seat of his pants. The costume department solved the problem by sewing stretch fabric into his trousers.

With shooting running desperately behind schedule, MGM ordered the company back to Hollywood. Carol Reed confessed he couldn't go on and quit. His replacement, Lewis Milestone, a no-nonsense industry veteran, collided with Brando head-on, causing even more friction and collective trauma. Milestone complained that Brando was sulky and argumentative and undermined his authority by taking over the direction of his scenes. 'I've been working in the business for forty-six years and I've never seen anything like it.' He considered quitting but was persuaded to stay on.

Brando's behaviour got worse. Trevor Howard, playing the indomitable Captain Bligh, found the star 'unprofessional and absolutely ridiculous. He could drive a saint to hell in a dogsled.' In the end Milestone could take it no longer and walked, leaving an assistant to shoot Brando's death scene, for which the actor insisted lying on ice to get the death tremors he'd witnessed at his mother's bedside exactly right. Who knew that off screen at this affecting moment an actress was kneeling beside him, just out of camera range, with his lines written out across her forehead?

When the film finished it had cost a whopping $20m, tipping MGM close to bankruptcy. The fingers of blame pointed at Marlon, as stories of his wacko behaviour, including having aeroplanes filled with cases of champagne flown to Tahiti for parties, were leaked to the press. It was clear to Brando that he was being made the scapegoat for the film's spiralling costs, and that Hollywood had begun turning its back on him. 'They start out by seducing you,' he said, 'and then they end up pissing on you.'

That was the least of his problems, though. He had woman trouble again. Out in Tahiti Marlon was steadily getting through most of the island's female population when he fell in love with local beauty Tarita Teriipaia, who played Fletcher Christian's love interest, a role that, ironically, Movita had played in the 1935 Clark Gable version of *Mutiny on the Bounty*! Eighteen years younger than Marlon, Tarita become wife number three in August 1962 after Marlon's quickie divorce from Movita came through. She would give him two children.

Back in Hollywood, Marlon again caused controversy with an appearance on a live TV chat show. Fellow guest Zsa Zsa Gabor was decked out in a low-cut pink evening gown and they got chatting. All of a sudden Marlon leaned forward and leered, 'I don't know why Zsa Zsa has to talk so much. With those boobs she really doesn't have to say anything.' The audience tittered but weren't quite prepared for Marlon's next comment. 'Zsa Zsa,' he went on, 'a man can only do one thing with you: throw you down and fuck you!'

I don't know why I get into gunfights. I guess sometimes I just get lonely.

Still at the Actors Studio, Dennis Hopper met and fell hopelessly in love with former *Vogue* cover model and wannabe actress Brooke Hayward. One of many girlfriends (Dennis was drowning in sex), Brooke was different and there was talk of marriage, provided he cleaned up his lifestyle. Brooke had two children from a previous marriage and didn't want a wild man influencing them.

Devastatingly beautiful, Brooke came from rich and socially prominent Hollywood stock, the daughter of film actress Margaret Sullivan, who'd been Henry Fonda's first wife, and Leland Hayward, who co-produced *South Pacific* and *The Sound of Music* on Broadway. It was odd company for someone like Dennis to be involved with, and Brooke's father immediately railed against his daughter's choice of husband. Tom Mankiewicz, a close friend of the Hayward family, got to know Dennis around this time. 'I adored Dennis, I thought he was great. It was a different story with Leland. I remember he called me up and said, "You have to stop this marriage to Dennis Hopper." I said, "We do?" And Leland said, "The guy is nuts." I said, "Leland, Brooke really loves this guy." He said, "This is going to be a disaster, it's going to be terrible." He carried on, and I said, "So you and Dennis, did you have fights and stuff?" He said, "I've never met him. But I know it's wrong."'

In August 1961 they married in a little chapel in New York. Mankiewicz was amongst the thirty guests. 'I'll never forget, just before Brooke was going to go down the aisle, Leland appeared. And I thought, that's great, at least he's here for his daughter. And he whispered something in her ear and left. I assumed it was, I love you very much honey. Afterwards I asked Brooke, "What did your father say? I'd love to know." And she said, "He told me, there's still time to back out." He said this to her at the top of the aisle!'

It was at the wedding reception that Dennis first made the acquaintance of Peter Fonda, a friend of Brooke's since childhood. Years later Fonda recalled this historic first encounter. 'I thought, this guy's a looney tune. But he sure is interesting.'

Soon after his marriage to Brooke, Hopper decided to return to Hollywood, hoping to resurrect his movie career. The couple moved into a Bel Air mansion furnished with valuable art pieces that had belonged to Brooke's mother before she took her own life with an overdose of barbiturates in 1960. Dennis had a room set aside for his painting and photography. He'd go on to paint hundreds of canvases, even managing to sell some to fellow actors. These included Joanne Woodward, whose husband, Paul Newman, once told Dennis, 'You should really concentrate on your painting.' A put-down if ever there was one.

Just months after moving in Brooke awoke one morning and smelt the unmistakable odour of smoke. There was a fire in the next canyon. Having grown up in the neighbourhood she knew only too well the speed with which such fires could spread amongst the dry California hills, so tried to stay calm, not panicking her family. Out of the window she saw her neighbour watching the fire's progress through binoculars, then race outside and start packing valuables into his car. That was it; Brooke felt they should be doing the same, just to be on the safe side. She ran into the bedroom where Dennis was sound asleep and woke him, explaining the situation, but he seemed not unduly worried and went back to whatever dream he'd been having. Not long after that he was being violently shaken by a hysterical Brooke: the fire was closing in, there was no time left to save anything except themselves – they had to get out now. 'We lost everything,' Brooke later recalled. 'A huge, lovely house, all my clothes, furniture, well, just everything.'

Dennis lost something even more personal: all his paintings and innumerable poems he'd written. Luckily his photographic negatives were in storage ready for his first gallery showing and so were saved. But the loss of his paintings so devastated him that he didn't put brush to canvas again for another two decades.

They resettled in West Hollywood in a more modest home near Sunset Boulevard. This time it was furnished more to Dennis's taste; a feature of the living room was a fourteen-foot papier-mâché clown from Mexico suspended from the ceiling. He also began assembling an impressive collection of modern and pop art, at a time when this kind of stuff was considered radical and unacceptable. Dennis's agent thought he was barmy and threatened not to represent him any more if he didn't get rid of it all, since he was obviously throwing his money away. 'That was the end of my agent,' said Dennis. Most of the paintings were bought direct from the artist's studio. For example Dennis paid just $75 for one of Warhol's first Campbell's soup-can paintings, now worth a few million. He knew everybody in the underground and wasn't frightened by the new and the experimental. 'That was one of the most amazing things about Dennis,' says friend Tom Mankiewicz. 'He had the greatest eye for modern art, it was remarkable. He would load his house up with painters that no one had heard of, like Jasper Johns and Warhol, who at the time was barely on the map. I remember looking at this whole house full of these paintings and saying, "Dennis I wouldn't give you twenty bucks for everything." But he was certainly right and years later there were exhibitions of his art collection. He's always added and subtracted from it.'

With Dennis's film career still in the shitter, Brooke turned to her numerous friends for help. Ironically it was Brooke's social position that ensured Dennis entry to the very Hollywood circles that wouldn't hire him as an actor. Most were alienated by his rebellious persona. They'd be invited to some swish party with important industry figures in attendance, Dennis would start the evening quiet, even reserved, but after a few drinks – well, quite a few, actually – he'd rant and rage at everyone, say how the revolution was coming and they'd be the first lot to get it, that one day he'd make a movie and the old dinosaurs would be slain; hardly the best tactic when you're looking for work. Poor Brooke would have to spend the following day calling everyone to apologise for her husband's behaviour. Many of them had known Brooke since childhood and expressed sympathy with her for being married to 'that madman'.

One person who was prepared to give Dennis a job was first-time director Curtis Harrington. He was putting together a low-budget horror movie, really low-budget, just $50,000, called *Night Tide* (1961), and wanted Dennis to play a sailor hopelessly in love with a mysterious woman who just might be a rampaging sea monster. It sounded kooky but it would be Dennis's first lead role and he worked hard the whole shoot. That was until the last day, when he sunk into a deep depression because filming was coming to an end and got miserably drunk, so drunk that he got into a motorcycle accident, necessitating the whole cast and crew reconvening two weeks later to complete the movie.

Drink and Dennis were now happy comrades. As a teen he'd been very much a beer man, but in Hollywood beer was seen as uncouth; people were drinking Martini instead. 'At first, I thought the stuff tasted awful,' said Dennis. 'It's an acquired taste, I acquired it.'

When Brooke gave birth in 1962 to a daughter, christened Marin, she must have hoped fatherhood would calm Dennis down. Far from it. There was a revolution going on outside, in the streets, and Dennis wanted desperately to be part of it. This was the burgeoning era of free love and abundant drugs and Dennis began experimenting with hallu-cinogenics, barbiturates and speed. 'The sixties was just one big drug party,' he said, a party that lasted twenty years and almost claimed his life.

I'm not even supposed to know girls like that exist.

After his Broadway flop Warren Beatty was to find another mentor in Elia Kazan, who fastened on to the young hopeful straight away. 'He was awkward in a way that was attractive,' said Kazan. 'He was very, very ambitious. He had a lot of hunger.' Immediately the director launched Warren's film debut *Splendour in the Grass* (1961), yet another in a long line of movies exploring how shitty it was to be a teenager with a hard on and square parents.

As he prepared for the role Joan Collins dropped a bombshell – she was pregnant. Warren let the news sink in before enquiring how it had happened. 'The butler did it,' Joan quipped. Both knew the timing was lousy, that as a couple they were simply too immature and career-orientated to start a family. But on the drive over to the abortionist Joan suddenly had second thoughts. At odds with his own raw emotions, Warren tried reassuring her and the abortion went ahead; Joan described the experience as 'horrifying'.

The incident didn't bode very well for their relationship, though Warren stunned Joan one day by proposing marriage, only to later accuse her of having an affair. He'd got marriage jitters and Joan knew it; he just wasn't ready to settle down. An astrologer had told her as much, that as an Aries Warren was, 'ruled by his cock' and wouldn't get married, 'for a long time. Probably not until he's forty-five or older. After many, many women.' The astrologer added, 'He will need a constant inflation of his ego – one woman will not satisfy him sexually.' Prophetic, or what!

Cast alongside Warren in *Splendour* was Natalie Wood and at first the two disliked each other intensely. Well established as an actress by now, her affair with Hopper a distant memory, there was no way Natalie was going to put up with a temperamental and egotistical newcomer who proved so difficult to work with that she christened him 'Mental Anguish'. 'Here comes MA,' she'd joke as Warren sauntered onto the set. Having to share a make-up room increased the friction, which got so bad the producer told a crew hand, 'Natalie can't stand him, she wants him out of there.'

For one thing Natalie couldn't get a handle on Warren's vanity.

Joan Collins once quipped that Warren was 'the only man to get to the mirror faster than me'. One morning assistant director Don Kranze caught the actor grooming himself by separating, with surgical precision, each individual eyelash with a pin. 'This is six feet of pure ego,' said Kranze. Warren ended up wasting so much time gazing at his own image that Kazan had every mirror in his dressing room covered up. The fact that he was an Adonis was undisputed, but such preening got the crew's backs up and they nicknamed him 'Donkey Dick'. After filming Kranze summed up Warren as, 'a pain in the ass. His emotional maturity was about thirteen.'

Suddenly things changed, or they did for Natalie. During a love scene Kazan sensed a spark, some chemistry between them that hadn't been there before. Maybe it had dawned on Natalie that Warren was headed for the top and, unabashed star fucker that she was, she had to have him. Their very public love affair meant curtains for Natalie's husband, poor old Robert Wagner, who watched as his wife of four years fell ravenously addicted to another man. It was, in Kazan's words, nothing short of, 'sexual humiliation'. In his autobiography Wagner claimed he sat with a gun outside Beatty's home many a night, intent on killing him. 'I was pretty young, and I don't think I could have ever gone through with that act, but I was pretty frustrated and upset.'

It was also goodbye to Joan Collins, who in time would reappraise her gushing admiration of Warren's sexual prowess. Responding to Shirley MacLaine's enquiry, 'How was my brother?' Joan replied, 'Overrated.' Decades later in 2006 when Joan was asked whether she and Warren really made love seven times in one day, she replied. 'Maybe he did, but I just lay there.' Meow.

When *Splendour* opened it won Warren instant fame. *Life* magazine called him 'The latest in the line of hostile, moody, sensitive, self-conscious, bright, defensive, stuttering, self-seeking and extremely talented actors who have become myths before they are thirty.' Always uncomfortable as an idol, Warren admitted that he'd become successful far too young, that it went to his head and mixed him up emotionally. Sure he had fun, but he needed a period of adjustment to avoid becoming 'another young actor compulsively working himself towards top billing in an early obituary column'. As his fame grew, so he withdrew more and more, leaning towards complete independence. It's no surprise that one of his pet projects in the sixties and seventies was a biopic of Howard Hughes. His view of fame didn't change much over the years either, but in this modern era of twenty-four-hour mass media and YouTube, it has become both costly and cheap, and Beatty is bewildered by the fact that 'people can become famous in a day for getting out of a cab in the wrong way'.

Everybody wanted a piece of Warren after *Splendour*, even, as it turned out, the president of the United States. A film was to be made about John F. Kennedy's heroic exploits in the navy during the Second World War and Warren was singled out to play him. It was a great honour, but he didn't rate the script and refused. Kennedy shrugged his shoulders and went back to his Camelot whoring. After the film, titled *PT 109* and starring Cliff Robertson, flopped in 1963 the two men ran into each other. 'Boy! Were you right about that movie!' said Kennedy.

It was largely the magic and glamour surrounding the Kennedy presidency that influenced Warren to become active in politics, and he became something of a bridge between Hollywood and Washington. When Kubrick feared his film *Dr Strangelove*, a stinging satire of Cold War sabre rattling, might be blocked, it was to Warren he turned to smooth things over with the administration.

Finishing with Kazan, Warren turned next for guidance to wheeler-dealer agent turned producer Charles Feldman, whose bon vivant approach to life – eat at the best restaurants, stay in the best hotels and fuck the most beautiful women – he adored. Feldman would teach Warren much about the movie business, contracts and negotiating deals, and he'd soak it up like a sponge. Unlike Marlon, Dennis and the other bad boy rebels, Warren wasn't out to shake up the movie establishment but to beat it at its own game. He learned the rules and played it better than any other actor ever did. He talked the moguls' language – money. And he learned that if you have to argue, you must do so from a position of power.

Someone's advice he didn't seek out was his sister's, despite the fact that she was now one of Hollywood's top actresses. To avoid any hint of nepotism Warren tended not to bring up the subject of Shirley in interviews. 'I am *not* Shirley's brother,' he once said. 'She is *my* sister.' It was a stance that led inevitably to rumours of sibling rivalry that have persisted ever since. In 1970 when Shirley was attempting a comeback in a one-woman stage show an audience member yelled, 'Where's Warren?' 'You want Warren?' she shouted back. 'You can have him! Practically every other woman has.'

Warren and Natalie Wood meanwhile had become Hollywood's glamour couple, photographed everywhere they went. They set up home together and Natalie filed for divorce from Wagner, telling the judge that he preferred playing a round of golf to playing around with her. Warren also took a deep interest in Natalie's career, helping research her new film role as a stripper by taking her to burlesque clubs; what a chore that must have been.

But things soon started to turn sour. There were rows and long silences and, according to Natalie's kid sister Lana, then sixteen and just beginning an acting career, a curious lack of intimacy in their relationship outside the bedroom. 'I have since come to think of it as two lives coming together briefly, but always at cross-purposes,' she says. 'There was always a distance between them.'

While holidaying in Europe they went to a nightclub one evening and Wagner showed up. He and Natalie danced for hours and seemed to rejoice in each other's company. Back at the hotel Warren made business calls until dawn, thwarting, deliberately or not, any chance Wagner might have had to put a call through to Natalie. If he'd succeeded, Natalie later confided to a friend, she'd have gone back to him like a shot, having discovered too late that sex not love was the foundation of her relationship with Warren. And it was love that she needed, not a man who she felt was using her as a shag pillow and a photo opportunity.

Warren's blatant philandering hardly endeared him to Natalie either. One incident, jaw-dropping in its brazen insensitivity, occurred when they dinned at top Hollywood restaurant Chasens. Halfway through the meal Warren excused himself to go to the lavatory. After ten minutes and no sign of Warren a search party was dispatched. It was the head waiter's job to inform Natalie that her boyfriend had scored with the well-stacked cloakroom attendant and they'd buggered off to enjoy what turned out to be a marathon three-day sex session. It was public humiliation of the highest order and Natalie took revenge by burning all his clothes and, when he turned up at the house a week later, slamming the door shut in his face. When she'd calmed down Natalie described her Warren romance as, 'changes of heart, flying jars of cold cream, protestations of renewed love and clashing of egos'. She then proceeded to gobble up Hollywood men with such reckless abandon that future co-star Tony Curtis remarked, 'Natalie would have been much happier as a nun or a hooker.'

As for Warren, he got over Natalie by dating a bunny girl at the Playboy Club on Sunset Strip. When he called one night and she wasn't there he chatted up the girl who answered the phone instead and they became lovers too. She later revealed that Warren was always suggesting they do a threesome, despite her aversion to the notion. Invited one evening to his hotel suite, the girl felt compelled to ask on the phone if there wasn't a floozy already up there with him. Warren said he was quite alone. 'If I get there and you've got a chick with you, I'm leaving,' she threatened. Warren greeted her in his bathrobe and carried her into the bedroom, where very obviously there was another woman; you couldn't miss her, she was lying naked on the bed. Feeling duped, the bunny girl was also feeling rather randy; fuck it, who cares, though she drew the line at girl-on-girl action.

Warren followed his startling movie debut by playing an Italian gigolo in the film version of Tennessee Williams's play *The Roman Spring of Mrs Stone* (1961). Warren heard that the gay playwright had casting approval and wanted an authentic Italian for the role. Undeterred, Warren bought a bottle of something called Man Tan, which turned his face orange-yellow, got a plane to Puerto Rico where Williams was holidaying, tracked him down to a casino and personally read for him. It won him the part. Warren then immediately caught a flight back to New York. Williams had to admit that Warren possessed all the right qualities to play a gigolo. 'He is so beautiful,' sighed the playwright. 'Just looking at him brings a tear to my eyes – what a waste!'

His leading lady was Vivien Leigh, twice his age at forty-eight, who, according to Noël Coward, 'was on her way round the bend again' as her marriage to Laurence Olivier headed for the divorce court. She was fascinated by Warren – no surprise there; Joan Collins had noted that he could charm any woman within moments of meeting her. Inevitably rumours began of an affair. Richard Burton spilled the beans to one showbiz reporter. 'They were at it in broom closets, across billiard tables, in telephone kiosks; you have to hand it to the pair of them.'

In Rome Warren also found time to date actresses Inger Stevens and Susan Strasberg, daughter of the famous method-acting teacher Lee, who was so impressed by his tight, revealing pants that she marvelled that he could even sit down in them. 'I found him charming and intelligent,' said Susan. 'With a tremendous need to please women as well as conquer them.' Susan and Warren attended a party at Luchino Visconti's opulent mansion and the director was so fascinated by Hollywood's newest star he even ignored his fawning stable of lap-boys. 'I'm going to the bathroom,' Warren suddenly whispered into Susan's ear. 'Follow me in a few minutes.' Once she arrived he pulled her inside and started to get frisky. She complained the place was too cramped. 'No it's not. You'll see.' When the couple returned to the living room twenty minutes later they were greeted by six pairs of hostile eyes. 'To my embarrassment I realised my blouse was still unbuttoned,' Susan later recalled. 'I wasn't quite sure how to act, but Warren beamed at one and all, an enchanting, ingenuous smile.'

Very quickly Warren was acquiring a certain kind of reputation and recalled those early sixties years as 'a series of very good times, good food, a lot of good-looking girls, and a lot of aimless fun'. Who else would fall for Russia's prima ballerina Maya Plisetskaya and fly to London, Toronto and Moscow just to attend her performances? 'They're madly in love,' said Warren's old acting teacher Stella Adler. 'But of course neither can understand a word the other is saying.'

There was also the briefest of flings with the young Cher, who'd only just dropped out of high school and come to Hollywood seeking a show-business career. She found Warren instead and was easily seduced by him. 'I was only sixteen,' she later excused. 'Maybe I can get out of it with that.'

Don't speak of the dead any more. You're with me now.

While Beatty was establishing himself as Hollywood's new star, getting something like $300,000 per film, Jack Nicholson was on considerably less for his Corman cheapos. Unlike Beatty, though, Jack could date women without fear of them phoning up the night editor on one of the various sleaze magazines. As he put it, he had 'complete anonymity in social exchange', or, more straightforwardly, 'I was able to go around picking up stray pussy without a care in the world.'

Jack lived at the time in a house not far from Sunset Boulevard, sharing with friends. It was, in his own words, the wildest house in Hollywood. Jack's comments that he'd never been in an orgy of more than three people gives you an idea of the kind of parties he threw. Orgies weren't his style, anyway, 'with everybody naked and fucking one another all over the place. I've never been in that scene.'

All this monkey business changed, temporarily, when Jack met actress Sandra Knight. It was a whirlwind affair and they quickly got hitched in June 1962. Clearly in love, Jack did later admit that the ceremony 'was a no big deal act for me'. He was right, since he was never to do it again. As vows were being exchanged he even had the temerity to look heavenward to plea, 'Now, remember, I'm very young, and this doesn't mean I'm not ever going to touch another woman.'

Still suffering in exploitation-movie hell, Jack was only too well aware of the danger of becoming stigmatised in the industry as a B-movie actor. Watching those films today, all he can see is his own 'fearful, desperate ambition. People who haven't seen my early movies are better off than I am.' But, like all actors, he needed the work and has acknowledged that without Corman he might not have survived those tough early years, so is forever thankful. 'Roger also underpaid us and for that he will be eternally grateful.'

But Corman's cheapos were about to get a hell of a lot more interesting. The schlock merchant had left the world of radioactive vegetables on the loose to tread a more cultured path, finding success adapting Edgar Allan Poe horror stories starring Vincent Price. For *The Raven* (1963) Corman added Boris Karloff and Peter Lorre to the mix, plus Jack. It was another camp classic. 'They all got along very well together,' says Corman. 'Because Jack had great respect for Vincent, Boris and Peter, and let them know it, and at the same time they realised from the very beginning that he was a very talented young actor, so accepted him into their group.' No respect, however, was offered by the titular bird, which shat endlessly over everybody. 'My shoulder was constantly covered with raven shit,' complained Jack.

In the film he played Lorre's son and both actors improvised most of their scenes, having been taught techniques originating with Stanislavsky, Jack in Corey's class, Lorre with Brecht in Germany. All this was beyond the understanding of poor old Karloff, who approached the film knowing his lines and ready to give the exact performance that he had prepared. 'With Peter and Jack improvising,' says Corman, 'I would almost use the word outrageously, Boris got a little bit nervous between the two techniques. The mediator in all this was Vincent Price, who understood how both sets of actors worked and was wonderful in bringing Peter and Jack together with Boris, who was more of a classically trained actor.'

On finishing *The Raven*, Corman realised the costumes and sets he'd rented were still his for another forty-eight hours. Karloff, too, remained on the payroll. A light bulb lit above his head like in a cartoon: Why not make another movie? If anyone could make a movie over a weekend, it was Corman. Jack happily accepted the lead, without knowing what the hell it was going to be about. Corman rushed home and bashed out a script entitled *The Terror* (1963), which everyone set to work on the next morning. It was chaos. Karloff later recalled how removal men arrived to take away the sets as they were acting, but Corman carried on filming guerrilla-style.

Unable to complete the film personally Corman handed it over to a couple of friends; Francis Ford Coppola shot some stuff, as did Monte Hellman. 'Finally, for the last sequence,' says Corman, 'there was nobody left to direct and Jack came to me and said, "Rog, every idiot in town has shot part of this picture; lemme direct the last bit." I said, "OK, Jack, you're the director." So Jack got his first taste of directing and the work he did was good.'

Unsurprisingly, *The Terror* is a complete farrago: it has witches, a curse, a creepy castle, but no plot – honestly, no plot whatsoever. Jack looks distinctly uncomfortable in the role of a French soldier, wearing Brando's oversized Napoleon costume from *Desirée*. 'I was absurd,' he says of his performance. 'It was amazingly bad.'

It takes six men to carry a guy to his grave; it takes one woman to put him there.

Because of a series of poor investments made by his father and heavy alimony payments, Marlon Brando's finances were looking decidedly shaky. It was now that he started making movies purely for the money, which partly explains why he made such godawful crap in the sixties. *The Ugly American* (1963), a risible political drama, was followed by *Bedtime Story* (1964), a weak comedy about two con men, that at least Marlon had fun on. 'The one thing Marlon regretted, and he told me this, was that no one came to him to do more comedy, because he loved comedy,' says producer Albert Ruddy. 'He loved to laugh.'

Having less fun on the film was co-star Shirley Jones. Hailing from a largely film musical background (*Oklahoma!*, *Carousel*) she hadn't worked with such an intense actor before. 'People say Marlon's the greatest American actor, I say one of the reasons why is because he wore everybody else down after doing sixty takes on one scene. That's exactly what he did. Marlon had this theory that the next one was going to be better, or let's try it another way, while I always thought my first or second take was the best and from then on it was all repetition.' One wonders how much of this was Marlon seeking perfection and how much a deliberate ploy to hamstring his fellow actors, to render them invisible so it was he who dominated the scene. As Bernardo Bertolucci was later to say of Brando, 'He's an angel as a man and a monster as an actor.'

Something else Shirley found unusual was Marlon's habit of not learning his lines. 'Instead he'd have his dialogue written on his hand or on a table. It fascinated me that he was able to do that and still come across as brilliant as he was.' This was a habit of Marlon's that grew to preposterous levels.

The cast was rounded off by the debonair David Niven, an actor poles apart from Marlon and who confessed to being a shade nervous about working with him, though the two ultimately got on very well. 'Marlon had great respect for David,' recalls Shirley. 'He'd just sit around on the set and listen to him tell stories and laugh and have a wonderful time.'

A misfire, *Bedtime Story* quietly crawled away and was forgotten until it was remade in 1988 as a vehicle for Steve Martin and Michael Caine, *Dirty Rotten Scoundrels*. But Shirley appreciated her Brando experience, one that could have been an even closer encounter. 'He came into my dressing room one time and asked me about my personal life, and if I was happily married, so he came on to me a bit. But I wasn't attracted to him that way at all, and it didn't bother me because I'm sure he did it with everybody.'

Morituri (1965, aka *The Saboteur*), a wartime spy drama, was another flop, and it was not a happy ship. Brando confessed that making it was like, 'pushing a prune pit with my nose from here to Cucamonga'. William A. Fraker, later an award-winning cinematographer on pictures like *Rosemary's Baby* and *Bullitt*, was an assistant cameraman on the film and came away knocked out by Marlon. 'He was sensational. Marlon always had his problems with directors and producers, but he loved the crews, he'd co-operate with them no problem.' No, Marlon's problems on the set weren't with the grips or the sound guys, it was with authority figures.

Aaron Rosenberg was the producer on *Morituri* and the movie was shot off the coast of northern California. Everyone stayed in local motels and one night Fraker was awoken by a big rumpus going on outside. 'There was screaming and hollering. I looked out the window and there was Marlon and Aaron Rosenberg fighting each other. Now Rosenberg was an all-American football player in college, he was no baby, and Marlon was from the streets, and they were just pounding each other and pretty soon Marlon knocked Aaron over the side of this hill and he rolled all the way down. Marlon went after him, picked him up and they both shook hands, put their arms around each other and walked off down the street. Those were great days.'

Maybe to get rid of the stench of making money from shit, Marlon sought to do something worthwhile with his fame, like an attempt to make a documentary for UNICEF on the Bihar famine in India. He visited filthy hospitals and watched a child die right in front of him. He derided how his government in one year spent less helping stop the starvation than was spent in a few hours on the Vietnam War. No one listened. Bitter, he turned down a film role, saying, 'How can I act when people are starving in India?'

Then suddenly news reached him that his father had died. Marlon took the old bugger back to the farm in Illinois and spread his ashes around the fields. But his passing did little to alleviate Marlon's fantasies of revenge. He used to think, just let me have him back for eight seconds that would be enough to break his jaw. 'I wanted to smash his face and watch him spit out his teeth. I wanted to kick his balls into his throat. I wanted to rip his ears off and eat them in front of him. I wanted to separate his larynx from his body and shove it in his stomach.' This kid had issues, obviously. But Marlon knew that he would have to forgive the sins of the father if he was ever to find peace for himself.

What are you hiring a gunman for, Pa?

Like Brando, Dennis Hopper was deeply concerned that the world was taking a big dump on its poorest and most defenceless people, and nobody much was doing anything about it. Impressed and influenced by the speeches of Martin Luther King, he followed much of liberal Hollywood and became interested in the civil rights movement. Actually it was the personal intervention of Marlon that got Dennis actively involved. He was walking down the street when a car pulled up alongside him. It was Brando. 'What are you doing?' Dennis did a double take before replying. 'Nothing.' Marlon said there was a big march planned from Selma to Montgomery, Alabama, so armed with his trusty camera Dennis headed south to participate in what many commentators see as the political and emotional peak of the civil rights struggle, where King eulogized: 'I've been to the mountain; I've seen the Promised Land.'

It was a gruelling five-day trek, during which time Dennis took many now historically important photographs of King and the other marchers, ignoring redneck locals who spat at him and called him a long-haired nigger-loving commie. There was a lot of violence going on all around them, helicopters flying everywhere, people screaming and yelling and waving Confederate flags. It was something to be remembered. Certainly the reaction from these bigoted inbreds really got to Dennis, changed him from an individual who believed the world's problems could be solved peacefully, Gandhi-style, to a man who began to store guns and study martial arts.

The drugs didn't help, of course. Mists of paranoia floated around in his head unchecked; he believed both the CIA and FBI were tracking his movements. Friends revealed he sometimes stalked the neighbourhood late at night, gun in hand, in search of government agents he was convinced were spying on him. He even began to think that Brooke was part of the conspiracy, that he could no longer trust her. She in turn grew increasingly wary of what he might do; hardly surprising, since Dennis was now a black belt in karate. He also made a habit of falling drunkenly asleep in bed with a lit cigarette between his fingers, causing a fire or two. Once Brooke woke up and the room was filled with smoke and flames and she booted Dennis out of bed to safety. More than once Brooke was to look back on that incident and wonder what might have been had she just left the guy to roast.

Back in the closeted fantasy world of Hollywood, Dennis wanted a movie real bad, something mainstream; he hadn't had a role in a studio film for eight years. It was one of Hollywood's biggest ironies that the man who gave it to him was his old adversary Henry Hathaway. The veteran had heard about his marriage to Brooke and hoped it might have calmed him down, so cast Dennis in *The Sons of Katie Elder* (1965), a John Wayne western. Over the years Dennis had thought of every possible way to kill his nemesis on *From Hell to Texas*, 'From poisoning, to a truck running him over.' Instead he kept his counsel and took the job. 'You're not going to make any trouble like you did before, right?' said Hathaway on his first day. 'This is a big Duke picture and you know Wayne doesn't dig any of that method shit. So if you're going to use any of that method shit, get out of here, kid.' Actually Hopper got on swimmingly with Wayne and co-star Dean Martin, boozing royally together; many mornings Hathaway would greet the bleary-eyed trio warily. And there were no problems on set, either. 'That was great, kid,' Hathaway praised Dennis for doing a scene in take one. 'But Henry, I'm a better actor now than I was eight years ago.' Hathaway shook his head. 'No Dennis, you ain't a better actor. You're just smarter.'

That rhinoceros hasn't been innocent since the day he was born.

Since Warren Beatty's social life was more exciting than any script, he decided to bring his exploits to the silver screen himself, portraying 'the plight of the compulsive Don Juan'. The film was called *What's New Pussycat?*, an expression Warren often used when calling up his girls on the phone. He brought in Charlie Feldman as producer and sought the talents of a new young comic, Woody Allen, to write the script. 'Warren and Woody thought they were going to make a low-key, Woody Allen kind of picture,' recalls Clive Donner, who'd been hired to direct. 'Now there was no way Charlie was ever going to do that, that wasn't his style, low-key pictures, he was into big fucking powerful productions.'

Dashing over to Woody's New York apartment for a meeting on 22 November 1963 Warren overheard on the radio the shocking news about Kennedy's assassination. He arrived at Allen's place still numb with shock. 'We sat there, stunned,' Warren later recalled.

Worse than Kennedy's head exploding like a melon was the prospect of starring opposite Feldman's mistress, Capucine. 'Warren and Charlie were very good friends,' says Donner. 'But Warren just didn't want to act with Capucine. He's a lovely guy, Warren, but deadly serious. So we had a big meeting, it went on and on and on, with Warren trying to get his own way.' In the end he confronted Feldman; it was either him or Capucine, and as she was fucking Feldman it was no contest. Warren was out, replaced by Peter O'Toole, and *What's New Pussycat?* turned into one of the biggest comedy hits of the decade.

By 1964 Warren was strapped for cash and hurried into a terrible film called *Lilith*, directed by Robert Rossen. Rossen had made *The Hustler* with Paul Newman, but could do little with this melodramatic tripe about love in a mental hospital. Warren had severe reservations about the script, but his questioning of practically every move and line of dialogue incensed the director. 'If I die,' he moaned, 'it'll be Warren Beatty who killed me.'

Years later Tom Mankiewicz was told a story by his father about Rossen. 'I'm directing this kid Beatty,' Rossen had said. 'And you know what, we had an argument about a scene and he turned around and said, "OK, direct it your way." No actor's ever said that to me in my life. I said, "Of course I'm going to direct it my way, I'm the fucking director!" It was like, he allowed me to direct it my way.' Warren did have something of a reputation for being hard on directors in his early days. 'If the director was indecisive, Warren would absolutely destroy him,' recalled Robert Towne. 'He'd ask so many questions – and he can ask more questions than any three-year-old – that the director didn't know whether he was coming or going.' Some people saw this as nothing short of infuriatingly arrogant and spoiled behaviour. 'Obviously every human being has got their doubters,' says Mankiewicz. 'One of the reasons that people liked him and one of the reasons why some people disliked him, was that he was very cocky, Warren was a cocky guy.'

His unpopularity also extended to the crew on *Lilith*, who trashed his dressing room. Rumour had it that Peter Fonda and a few of the other actors were seriously contemplating doing him in. At a party to celebrate the end of shooting shit-scared studio executives persuaded Warren to leave early in order to stave off any mayhem.

Rossen never made another film and died in 1966. It's debatable what actually killed him: heart disease, diabetes, alcoholism – or annoying actors.

Another director who found Warren, 'difficult . . . impossible', was Arthur Penn when they worked together on *Mickey One* (1965), which had Beatty play a nightclub entertainer on the run from gangsters. Neither did Warren make friends with his stand-in, John Gibson. After working ten weeks with the star Gibson recalled they'd exchanged barely twenty words, the rest of the time it was a volley of orders – 'Get my water!' 'Get my yoghurt!' 'Get my orange juice!' After a few days Gibson told ol' buddy Warren to 'Get lost!'

Warren, bless him, also tried his luck with a nubile extra. 'You can look, but don't touch,' he was told. Yes, that's right, Warren didn't necessarily score with every woman with a pulse; occasionally his pick-up lines fell on deaf ears. 'It's untrue to think I am irresistible to all women,' he once said. 'That's very flattering but I've been turned down by armies of them.' Including *On the Waterfront*'s Eva Marie Saint. Leaving the studio in her station wagon with her two little kids, Warren knocked on the window. She rolled it down and he said, 'Are you really happily married?' She drove off.

Mickey One was poorly received. It seemed that tales of Warren's womanising resonated more with the public than his acting talents. He desperately wanted to be taken as seriously by critics as Brando. Instead, he was considered just a playboy. He was in despair about it. Weary anyway of press interviews, Warren now pretty much banned them altogether, hoping that journalists would forget his Casanova image and focus on his career. More than most actors Warren resents personal publicity. 'I'd rather ride down the street on a camel nude. In a snow-storm. Backwards. Than give what is called an in-depth interview.' When he does agree to speak to the press it's always on his terms; he's mostly evasive and he talks methodically, as if cautiously editing every syllable. His pauses are elephantine. As one reporter said, 'Broadway musicals could be mounted during his pauses.' Critic Rex Reed once said interviewing Beatty was 'like getting a pint of blood out of a haemophiliac'.

Shirley hardly helped her brother's attempt to drop his playboy image with statements like, 'I keep my daughter as far away from him as possible.' Never one to miss an easy opportunity to goad Warren in public, Shirley genuinely disapproved of his reckless shagging habits. 'Warren seems to be quite enthusiastic about sex, to put it mildly,' she told one reporter. What Warren needed was a stable relationship with a strong woman, not all this gallivanting around. And that's exactly what happened when he met the elfin star of *Gigi* Leslie Caron. There was only one snag: she was already married to English theatre director Peter Hall. At thirty-two, she was also six years older than Warren and the mother of two young children, but that didn't stop our man. He was fascinated by her passion and vitality. Hall was incensed when he found out about the affair and allegedly hired a private detective to follow them around London. (Hall, on the other hand, said it was his wife who hired detectives to follow him.)

When news arrived that Leslie intended moving her children out to LA to be closer to Warren Hall filed for divorce and petitioned the British government to make his children wards of court and keep them in England. Leslie had no choice but to stay in London. 'I cannot give up my children.' It was Warren who made the sacrifice and came to live in England, happy to support Leslie during the custody battles ahead. They settled into a large house in Knightsbridge and Warren bought a suitably ostentatious piece of England, a Rolls-Royce that once belonged to the Queen. Their near neighbour was Roman Polanski. Warren already knew the notorious director, having met him at a Hollywood party and discovered their minds were pretty much in the same place when it came to women. Together they'd toured the streets and topless bars along Sunset Strip. 'All I was interested in was to fuck a girl and then move on,' Polanski once confessed. He was Warren's kind of man and a welcome dinner guest in London, along with his soon-to-be-wife, the beautiful actress Sharon Tate.

Warren had arrived in the capital at a propitious moment. It was the mid-sixties and London was beginning to swing. He made a typically dotty sixties spy romp, *Kaleidoscope* (1966), with Susannah York. 'I think we worked well together,' says Susannah. 'Of course, Warren was a bit of a lad, and I was fairly newly married, so I wasn't up for any hi-jinks. He had an annoying habit of pinching my bum and I used to slap his hand. But it was all done in good humour. Besides, Leslie would come onto the set, so there really wasn't any question of taking things any further than just light-hearted banter. I suppose I'm one of the few women who didn't necessarily respond to him; I didn't really fancy him.'

Warren perhaps sensed this and his relationship with Susannah never extended beyond the film. Warren felt more comfortable being friends with women that he'd been in an intimate relationship with. 'But I liked Warren enormously,' says Susannah. 'I thought he was personable, funny, very intelligent, enthusiastic, all qualities I like. Also very quick-thinking, very ambitious. I liked his style. A little bit thinking he was the bee's knees as far as women were concerned. I think sometimes a certain self-regard or vanity might occasionally have got in the way at that time. Probably that was because he was just beginning and it was something that Hollywood fosters in people that could sometimes make him seem a little immature perhaps.'

Just how immature can perhaps be summed up by this story. In London Warren called up his old buddy Charlie Feldman, then producing the spoof Peter Sellers Bond movie *Casino Royale*, asking if he could visit the set. The day Warren arrived just happened to be when 20 nubile and scantily clad young ladies hovered about the place. Inevitably Warren asked to be introduced to them all. Twenty-one-year-old model Alexandra Bastedo (later a TV star in cult show *The Champions*) was amongst them. 'At the time I was sharing a flat with a girlfriend,' Alexandra remembers. 'Her name was Nicole Shelby. That evening we got to bed around midnight and the phone rang. I was nearest so I answered it and this voice said, "Hi Alexandra, this is Warren here. Would you like to come over for a drink?" And I said, "I'm awfully sorry Warren but I've just gone to bed." I put the phone down and went back to sleep. At 3 o'clock in the morning the phone rang again. I staggered back over and this voice said, "Hi Nicole, Warren here. I wonder if you'd like to come over for a drink." He'd obviously worked his way through the film producer's address book. Looking back, I don't regret saying no to Warren, I wasn't a great one for Lotharios. Someone like that terrified me; I kept well away.'

Sensing his career was in jeopardy if he remained in England, Warren returned to Los Angeles. Frightened of losing him, Leslie vacillated between continents, juggling the needs of her lover and those of her children. Leslie was now more in love with Warren than ever and it showed, at least to those in the know. At one Hollywood party she positively glowed, causing a guest to remark, 'Leslie is looking so beautiful.' Overhearing, Natalie Wood said one word: 'Warren.'

Marriage was looking like a real possibility. 'I believe that a fulfilled monogamous relationship can be great,' Warren told reporters. 'But it takes genius to do it.' That's why he retained his bachelor pad over at the Beverly Wilshire Hotel, hardly an indicator of marital intent. Warren was also lining up a possible replacement. In London he'd been introduced to Britain's new star, and the face of the sixties, Julie Christie, an

Oscar winner with *Darling* and also the immortal Lara in *Dr Zhivago*. 'When I met her,' he said. 'I thought she had the most wonderful face.' Yet those glamorously refined looks belied a beatnik sensibility, in her attitude towards both life and sex. She once said, 'For men, I don't think it's sexiness in me that appeals to them, but an air of abandonment. Men don't want responsibilities and neither do I.' She sounded like the perfect match for Warren, if not for the fact that she despised the sort of hollow film-star glamour that he largely personified. Anyway, both were currently in relationships, and Warren had more pressing problems such as rescuing his career from going down the toilet.

Are bras that heavy, Mister Pulver?

In the summer of 1963 Jack Nicholson heard the news that June had been diagnosed with cancer and it was terminal. For years now their relationship had never been less than shaky. 'We used to have incredible fights,' Jack recalled. 'She had a fiery, amazing temper.' Maybe she was bitter that she'd never made it in show business and feared Jack was heading the same way. Neither did she much approve of his bohemian lifestyle, going around with his hair generally a mess, wearing jeans and smoking dope. 'She saw me as a bum.'

Ironically, Jack had just landed a small role in his first major studio picture, *Ensign Pulver* (1964), a sequel to the 1955 hit *Mister Roberts*. The night before he was due to fly out for location shooting in Mexico he visited June in hospital. He settled down in a chair next to June's bed and they started chatting. Strange, June must have known that this was the last time they'd ever speak; surely now was the moment to reveal the truth about his parentage, to unburden herself of this guilty secret. She remained silent. When Jack got ready to leave she looked him in the eye. 'Shall I wait?' Jack looked at her, in these last few months he'd seen her suffer and lose so much weight. The pain was so bad that surely the most humane thing was to wish for her to be taken now. 'No,' Jack replied, looking away. Inside the elevator when the doors closed he collapsed to his knees and sobbed uncontrollably. Almost immediately after arriving on location Jack got the wire. June had passed away at the age of forty-four.

Besides schlockmeister Roger Corman, Jack worked for another bargain-basement producer, Robert Libbert, selling him a script called *Thunder Island* (1963), a potboiler about political assassinations in South America. Director Jack Leewood never forgot the fraught and passionate story conferences during which Jack took it as a personal insult whenever a line or story idea was changed or criticised, actually to the point of violence. 'He'd go for me physically,' said Leewood.

When *Thunder Island* opened to moderate success Libbert requested Jack's services again, this time to co-star in a couple of action B-movies Monte Hellman was shooting back to back in the Philippines: *Flight to Fury* (1964), about hidden treasure and *Back Door to Hell* (1964), about US marines let loose on the Japs in the Second World War. Cast and crew journeyed to the most desolate of locations, hot and humid when it wasn't raining torrents. Giant cockroaches invaded their rooms, poisonous snakes and spiders bigger than saucers were all over the place and there was no hot water or plumbing; little wonder everyone got the shits or worse and that between pictures Hellman collapsed from exhaustion and had to be hospitalised.

Jack was desperately disappointed when both films met with a lukewarm reception; he'd slogged his guts out in a miserable hell hole for months – and for what? He still wasn't getting the breaks and he was still driving the same goddamn car, a battered yellow Volkswagen bug, a car he kept for years once he made it big, just to remind himself of where he'd come from.

When star of *Back Door to Hell* Jimmie Rodgers invited Jack to a party at his huge mansion he noticed that for much of the evening he stood by a wall surveying the scene, the upmarket guests, the lush interior. As Rodgers recalled, 'The look on his face was, so this is what it's like.'

Have you ever been collared, dragged out into the streets and thrashed by a naked woman?

Marlon Brando continued to make films to pay the bills rather than for any idealistic or creative reason. And his resentment too often showed. On the western *The Appaloosa* (1966), it was open hostility between director

Sidney J. Furie and his star; the crew were taking bets who'd lay the other one out first. According to co-star John Saxon Brando would come onto the set to do his close-ups reading a book. 'He would only lower the book when it was action. When it was cut, he'd raise the book again.'

Furie sought the unlikely assistance of Michael Caine, who was in Hollywood filming at the time. Caine, who'd been directed by Furie in *The Ipcress File*, recalled him coming into his dressing room one day almost in tears because of Brando's behaviour. They wandered back onto the set together and Caine got talking to Marlon. 'What do you think of Sidney as a director?' Brando asked. 'I think he's an excellent director,' said Caine, faithfully. Marlon, in front of Furie and the crew, replied, 'I don't think he can direct traffic.'

It's hardly surprising that Marlon fostered a reputation for being diffi-cult with directors. He habitually turned against whatever he was working on, it seemed to comfort him to be dissatisfied and difficult. However, when people dealt with him honestly, there was no one better. Gray Frederickson, who worked twice with Marlon, says, 'He was a professional, never caused a problem. If you were a professional with Marlon he respected you. God forbid the people that didn't know what they were doing around him, he unleashed unholy hell on them.' Before Tom Mankiewicz started working with Marlon on *Superman* he sought advice from the star's former agent Jay Kanter. His opinion was stark: 'Marlon is either at your feet or at your balls.'

It didn't really matter, anyway, Marlon was convinced we were all fucked, nuclear oblivion was just round the corner, and so began a search for a place where he and his family could be self-sufficient and survive. He remembered how much he'd fallen in love with Tahiti during the making of *Mutiny on the Bounty*, and with the Tahitian people, 'because they don't give a damn who you are', so bought his own little piece of paradise there. At first he lived on his island in a modest house, just one large room, a double bed covered by a mosquito net, scant furnishings and a photograph of his mother. But he had grand plans for the place and over the years would pump millions into turning his own small corner of heaven into an arts and science commune, with disastrous results.

But for now it was back to more mundane matters like earning a living, Brando playing a sheriff in a southern backwater town seething with racism, wife-swapping and murder. *The Chase* (1966) boasted an astonishing supporting cast – Angie Dickinson, Jane Fonda, Robert Duvall and a young Robert Redford – but little else. Marlon's beating at the hands of a group of rednecks, however, remains one of the most savage in cinema history. Centre stage in the punch-up was a young Brando-inspired actor called Richard Bradford, who recalls that during rehearsals Marlon told him to slap him around and punch him in the body for real. As cameras rolled Bradford lost himself in the moment. 'There's a bit where I jump up on a desk on top of Marlon and I'm whacking him, kind of going crazy,' he says. 'One of the actors pulled me off, "You're gonna kill him," but they couldn't hold me, I got away and I ran and jumped back up on top and started whacking Marlon again. I think that's the part they used in the film. That fight was so brutal they didn't show the whole of it, the censor wouldn't let them. But I learned something great from Marlon: whenever he was going to fall he just relaxed completely and went down, he didn't try to break his fall, he just went. Once he literally rolled off that desk and bang, hit the floor, he didn't try to support himself or anything. I thought that was fantastic.'

Next Marlon played a repressed homosexual married to Elizabeth Taylor in *Reflections in a Golden Eye* (1967), a role in which co-star Julie Harris believed he was 'exploring his own sexuality'. Rumours have persisted about Marlon's gay leanings or bisexual nature, that he enjoyed numerous affairs with not only women but men as well, from street riff-raff to Hollywood stars such as Laurence Olivier, James Dean, Rock Hudson, Burt Lancaster and Montgomery Clift, about whom Brando apparently told director Fred Zinnemann, 'I made him my bitch.'

Brando himself was quoted in the mid-seventies: 'Like a large number of men I, too, have had homosexual experiences, and I am not ashamed.' His *Last Tango in Paris* co-star Maria Schneider said she got on well with him, 'because we're both bisexual'.

During the filming of *Reflections* Brando socialised with Liz and husband Richard Burton, the trio often getting thoroughly pissed together. 'Brando is very engaging and silly after a couple of small drinks,' Burton wrote in his diary. Brando presented the couple with two memorial antique silver goblets. The first was engraved: 'Richard: Christ, I've pissed in my pants.' And the second: 'Elizabeth: That's not piss, that's come.'

Burton truly admired Brando, often arriving on the set to pick up Liz early so he could watch him at work. It was a combustible friendship that as the years dragged on decayed and died. Burton felt that his fondness for Marlon was not reciprocated. In the early seventies he wrote disparagingly about Brando in his diary after learning from Liz that he'd expressed concern about him during a gossipy telephone chat. 'He really is a smugly pompous little bastard and is cavalier about everybody except Black Panthers and Indians. That sober self-indulgent obese fart being solicitous about me. Sinatra is the same. Gods in their own mirrors. Distorted mirrors.'

She's gorged herself with fresh blood. She's a monster.

After his supporting role in Wayne's *The Sons of Katie Elder*, the only roles on offer for Dennis Hopper were in exploitation gems like *Queen of Blood* (1966), which has Basil Rathbone sending a rocket ship into an unknown galaxy to bring back a blood-sucking alien witch-bitch thing. Dennis plays one of the pilots and is clearly improvising much of his dialogue; I mean, who the hell calls their shipmates 'baby'?

Like many young people at this time, Dennis was being swept up in the counterculture movement; taking part in anti-war demos, political protests for free speech and civil rights. All very high-minded and noble, but the fringe benefits were good, too, namely sex, drugs and rock and roll. And more drugs. A lot more drugs. 'Back in those days, we were all like guinea pigs,' Dennis recalled. 'We were always waiting for the next new drug. It was like, Hey, gimme some of that!'

But the impact it was having at home was considerable. Booze had always been an issue with Dennis, but now he'd embraced the drug scene things got darker and weirder and more dangerous. Brooke believed it was the combination of drink and drugs that warped his personality, changed him and made him more violent, more of a loose cannon. He even made her take mescaline on one occasion, which she later described as, 'one of the most horrific experiences'. She was frightened; saw his eyes 'zipping around like the fourth of July'. At those moments she feared he'd do something that he might not remember the next morning. One time, when Dennis was rehearsing a play and nervous about his performance, Brooke said she had to get home for the kids and couldn't stay to support him. Driving off, Dennis suddenly jumped on the hood of Brooke's car and kicked out the windshield. Brooke started worrying about the safety of her children.

Dennis saw nothing wrong in exposing himself to every new dangerous stimulus going: hadn't the great artists that he aspired to be like done precisely the same thing? John Barrymore, Edmund Kean . . . they'd all got bladdered. Van Gogh, said Dennis, drank for a whole summer to find the perfect yellow to paint his damn sunflowers. Their collective geniuses almost excused Dennis to go hell for leather. 'I was an artist; I was supposed to drink, supposed to take drugs.' It also fitted in well with his plan. From as far back as he could remember he saw himself as destined to achieve the extraordinary. 'I ruled out even the vaguest notions of normal work.' He saw art as the perfect vehicle; guys like Van Gogh gave him faith because, although their lives were tragic ruins, the fruits of their suffering had achieved immortality. 'Dennis did look back at his wild period and compare it to what Van Gogh said about needing to drink to get that perfect yellow,' says film-maker George Hickenlooper. 'Which in retrospect I think Dennis thought was horseshit because in the end drugs and alcohol only limit you as an artist. But at the time drugs and alcohol served as a vehicle for him to act outrageously. It also magnified what was already there, that is a personality and a temperament that is truly an artist trying to function in an industry that proclaims to be about art but is really more about money.' Hopper's difficulty with the Hollywood power structure was almost always over artistic vision, not trailer size or corporate jets.

So, sadly for Dennis, all drinks and drugs did was turn him into something of a stumbling wreck. 'Dennis's mind was all over the map,' says Tom Mankiewicz. 'Everybody started to use drugs then. I recall one time we were driving to Tijuana for the bullfights and stopped off at Disneyland. And there's a ride called the Mad Hatter's Tea Cup which has a circular bar in the centre where the harder you pull on it the faster the cup spins. Dennis had had a lot of joints, and I'd had booze, but Dennis was really wasted, and he started to pull the thing so fast that the announcer on the public address system said, "Would the gentlemen on teacup eight please slow down." And after the ride was over we were ejected, and Dennis said to me, "What a bummer, getting thrown out of Fantasy Land."'

This here's Miss Bonnie Parker. I'm Clyde Barrow. We rob banks.

Warren Beatty's last four films had tanked at the box office and he needed a hit. Actually, he needed a miracle. Salvation came from a pair of outlaw lovers that maybe could speak directly to the anti-war generation – being anti-establishment was a pretty cool thing to be in the late sixties. They were called Bonnie and Clyde.

Warren snapped up a screenplay based on their lives and installed himself as producer and star. But there was one aspect of the story that he refused to countenance: the Clyde character was revealed as having bisexual relationships within his gang. 'Let me tell you one thing right now,' he told the writers. 'I ain't gonna play no fag. The audience won't accept it, they're going to piss all over my leg.' A colourful expression that was one of his favourites. Thinking that Clyde should have at least some kind of sexual dysfunction, Warren instead played him as impotent, a neat subversion of his own Casanova persona.

Not yet ready to take on the responsibility of helming a movie himself, Warren hired Arthur Penn instead, after a host of other directors rejected the offer. At first Penn felt like doing the same, not sure if he wanted to work with Beatty again. 'I'm going to lock myself in a room with Arthur and not let him out until he says yes,' threatened Beatty. Penn caved in.

Warren needed all his powers of persuasion to get the fearsome Jack Warner to agree to finance the movie, especially after a number of studios had already turned him down, worried about his recent lousy track record. When he sensed the pitch wasn't going well – 'Those pictures went out with Jimmy Cagney,' blasted the tycoon – Beatty suddenly dropped to the floor and grabbed Warner round the knees. 'I'll kiss your shoes here,' he said. 'I'll lick them.' Warner must have thought Warren was having a nervous collapse. 'Get off the fucking floor, you crazy bastard.' 'Not until you agree to make this movie,' implored Warren. Probably just to get this nutcase of an actor out of his office Warner agreed to a bargain-basement budget of $2m.

Warren always insisted this never happened, that the story, spread around Hollywood by people who swore they were in the room and witnessed it, is apocryphal. And yet when directly asked by film critic Roger Ebert in 1971 whether he really got down on his knees in Jack Warner's office Beatty replied, 'Probably. Possibly. I used to do all sorts of crazy things with Jack. He thought I was a little crazy. Well, I am a little crazy.' So who knows?

Leslie Caron always assumed she would be first choice to play Bonnie; after all, she was sleeping with the producer. When Warren said her French accent and pixie features weren't quite right for a machine-gun toting bitch from hell, Leslie saw it as an act of betrayal, and it wasn't long before she was gone altogether from Warren's life, perhaps realising that he was never going to commit fully to her personally either. Warren was starting to come out with some real peachy quotes concerning marriage, like this absolute gem: 'The best time to get married is noon. That way, if things don't work out, you haven't blown the whole day.'

Poor Leslie was left devastated; she'd lost Warren and what could have been the role of a lifetime. 'Anyone who has come close to Warren has shed quite a few feathers,' she would say years later. 'He tends to maul you.' As for Warren himself, he confessed to looking back at the messy end of his affair with Leslie 'with a deep and profound sadness'.

Speculation began about who would play Bonnie, with one wag suggesting sister Shirley. 'That would be adding incest to injury,' she quipped. Could they handle the love scenes, reporters asked. 'I guess he couldn't do it with his sister,' said Shirley. 'But come to think of it – maybe he could.' Warren actually wanted Jane Fonda, Ann-Margret, Sharon Tate, or even ex-lover Natalie Wood. Warren visited Natalie at home and talked to her personally about it. Anxious to play Bonnie, Natalie was also anxious to avoid any more emotional distress. 'Working with Warren had been difficult before.' She passed.

In the end a virtual unknown landed the role: Faye Dunaway. Beatty marvelled at Faye's abilities as an actress and desperately wanted to give her one too, but the artist in him said no, this time he wouldn't bang his leading lady. Faye later revealed that she and Beatty had a 'tacit understanding' during filming to keep things on a professional footing. Indeed, Warren was prepared to shun nookie altogether for the duration of the shoot. 'You should be totally abstinent from the start of pre-production,' he announced. 'The film will be better if you never come.' What crap! Filmmaker Kit Carson was a college student at the time and invited to hang out on the set. 'Warren had his own trailer and every afternoon there would be a couple of girls who'd go inside and it would rock backwards and forwards, and then the girls would leave and Warren would come out beaming, "Heh, ready to go, let's shoot."'

The crew took their collective hat off to Warren's stamina as a lover, but were appalled that this snot-nosed pretty boy dared hold such a position of power; back then actors just didn't produce their own movies. But Warren had learned very early in his career that real power was never with the actor, it was with the money men and the producers. No one really believed he could pull it off but in Penn's estimation he was the perfect producer, staying with the picture through editing, mixing and scoring. 'He plain works harder than anyone else I have ever seen.'

They had their problems, though. Working on location in Texas, Warren and Penn clashed over practically every detail. They'd argued before on *Mickey One*, 'deep disagreements' as Penn put it, but this was far worse. 'We had an argument for an hour every day on *Bonnie and Clyde*,' Warren later admitted. 'I like knowledgeable people to argue with me.'

When Gene Wilder arrived on set for his short appearance, he was horrified when Warren and Penn began yelling at each other. 'What's happening?' He asked actress Estelle Parsons. 'Is this movie going to get made?' Estelle gave him a knowing look, 'Oh, don't worry. This happens every day.'

One thing they agreed on from the start was that the violence should shock people. 'It has to be in-your-face,' said Penn. The film's controversial climax, where the outlaw couple die in an orgy of bullets, was the single most shocking piece of cinema up to that time.

Bonnie and Clyde was brought in under budget and Warren oversaw the final cut until it met his exacting standards. He knew he'd made a remarkable film; now he had to convince Jack Warner, the toughest of critics and a man who measured a film's success on how many times he went for a piss. Five minutes into a private screening Warner got up for a leak. Reluctantly, it seemed, he came back, only to excuse himself twice more. His damning pronouncement on *Bonnie and Clyde* was, 'It's a three-piss picture.' Warren tried to smooth things over. 'You know, Jack, this is really kind of an hommage to the Warner Brothers gangster movies of the thirties.' Warner stared back at him and said, 'What's a fucking hommage?' Warren knew he was in serious shit.

Convinced the movie wouldn't make a dime, over August 1967 Warners dumped it with scarcely any publicity in second-rate theatres, where it met with some lousy reviews and public apathy. Warren fell into a deep depression. By year's end he was re-energised by the positive response to the film in Britain and critical reappraisal back home. He walked into Warner Brothers and demanded *Bonnie and Clyde* be re-released, a practically unheard of move, or he was going to sue one of the studio's top executives, Eliot Hyman. 'What the hell would you sue me for?' Hyman hit back. It was a Beatty bluff. He'd heard rumours of some dodgy individuals Hyman had associated with in the past, that's all, so shot him a knowing look and said, 'I think you know.'

It worked. *Bonnie and Clyde* was back in theatres and its turnaround from flop to box office smash was unparalleled, and everything to do with Warren. He'd proved himself not just an artist but a street fighter. He made himself a real pain in the arse to an industry who mocked: Why do we have to deal with this good-looking actor? 'People didn't recognise him as the superior businessman he is,' said Penn. 'They do now. The results of his efforts were absolutely electrifying.'

Warren was now the most important leading male in Hollywood and one of the richest, but, more significantly, also the most powerful. The *Village Voice* sent their star reporter Blair Sobol to interview him, along with a young freelance photographer called Linda Eastman, the future Mrs Paul McCartney. As she squatted at the feet of Warren to reel off a load of film Sobol noticed she wasn't wearing any knickers. 'Warren must have noticed too,' said Sobol. 'Because I didn't see Linda again for two weeks.'

Warren wasn't averse to picking up dates during interviews. *Los Angeles* magazine journalist Thomas Thompson remembered talking with Warren in London when they were joined by a very attractive German reporter decked out in the latest Carnaby Street fashions. It was too much for poor Warren; he took her up to his hotel room with really quite shocking haste.

He also had an unusual hiring method for his personal staff according to Susanna Moore, now an acclaimed novelist, then a nineteen-year-old being interviewed by Warren for a job as his assistant. After the interview she turned to leave when Warren said, 'There's one last thing I haven't checked yet – I need to see your legs. Can you lift up your skirt?' Susanna obliged. 'OK, you got the job.'

Bonnie and Clyde also made Faye Dunaway a star, and she was cast next opposite Steve McQueen in *The Thomas Crown Affair* (1968). It was now, like a heat-seeking missile, that Warren struck. 'Everybody wants you,' he said to her hotly down the phone one night. 'And so do I.' There was no denying Faye found Warren, 'pretty alluring', but she'd made a private vow never to fuck a superstar; most of them were womanisers and that kind of relationship was doomed from the start. When probed years later about Warren's seduction technique, Faye called it 'direct', telling a girl right out front what he wants, and what he wants is to go to bed with her. 'He's one of the most charming men I've ever met. I wouldn't have anything to do with him if my life depended on it. I consider him dangerous.'

Well, the crew on *Bonnie* considered Faye aloof. During filming she seemed never to be truly part of the team. At the wrap party, held at a New York hotel, Kit Carson recalls a bunch of guys showing up with a string of women who were sent round the room to dance with the guests. 'They were hookers, and these guys were really low-rent pimps. At the end of the evening Warren paid for them all and took them to Faye's hotel room. So Faye Dunaway ended up that night with about ten hookers showing up at her hotel. It was Warren's way of getting back at her because she was too much of a stiff.'

Reality is a deadly place. I hope this trip is a good one.

Now thirty, Jack Nicholson had been busting his arse for years. He'd made some fifteen films, written, edited and produced some of them, and for what? He was hardly known outside the midnight-movie crowds, and his big break seemed as elusive as ever. Maybe he was considered too old for stardom by Hollywood standards. There was an air of desperation now, a fear he'd missed his chance. He lost out on *The Graduate*. Despite the fact that 'they were auditioning everyone I was having lunch with', Jack wasn't even seen and the role went to a complete newcomer – Dustin Hoffman. It seemed to sum up Jack's predicament and when he heard the news he got miserably drunk.

While Jack wondered if he was ever going to rid himself of his B-movie millstone, rifts began to appear in his marriage to Sandra. He'd made a fine go of it the first few years and been blessed with a daughter, Jennifer, but his old ways slowly crept back. He seemed to want to carry on his bachelor existence as if he hadn't signed a wedding certificate, so that meant wild parties, drugs and the odd fling. Filming the Monte Hellman movies in the Philippines had been 'prostitute heaven', according to producer Jack Leewood, who revealed that during production he and Jack, 'were screwing the same dames'.

At this rate Jack and Sandra were headed for divorce. But Jack, to his credit, did try his best to work things out, in his own inimitable way, by asking Sandra to drop acid with him. Jack was never one to bother with dreary marriage counsellors; he'd found an analyst whose course of treatment included the administration of LSD. Unfortunately Sandra was given the maximum dosage. 'At one point, she looked at me and saw a demon,' Jack told *Ladies' Home Journal* in 1976. 'A totally demonic figure. For whatever reason, either because it's true about me or because of her own grasping at something, it was pretty bad.' No shit, Sherlock.

So bad was it that Sandra turned to religion for solace. Jack couldn't get with that programme. 'I didn't want to get caught in a situation where I was in competition with God.' He also continued using LSD, much to Sandra's horror. When he refused to give it up, she booted him out of the house and the marriage was dead. The divorce was finalised in 1967 with no residue of hatred. 'Our marriage was lived out rather than failed,' Jack admitted. 'We just grew apart.' The two remained friends and when Sandra moved to Hawaii with Jennifer he was able to see his daughter at regular intervals. As she grew up Jennifer often spent her summer vacation with Jack, visiting him on film sets, and a charming and strong bond developed between them, with Jack deciding not to duck the odd embarrassing question about his affairs; nor did he necessarily hide other aspects of his lifestyle.

Meanwhile the ever dependable Roger Corman had become the first filmmaker to tap into the growing California motorcycle-gang culture with its drugs, sex and sadistic violence. 'I wanted to move away from the studio system and do something reflecting the changing social environment,' he says. 'It was an exciting time because film was changing. I had been shooting primarily studio films such as the Poe pictures, and now everything was shot on location, so it was a whole different feel to the making of films. Also it was the time of the hippie movement and the anti-Vietnam War movement, there was a general rebelliousness amongst the young.'

The Wild Angels (1966), starring Peter Fonda and Nancy Sinatra, was a massive hit, so Corman threw Jack into his own derivative biker movie, *Hells Angels on Wheels* (1967). Prepping the movie, Jack got to meet Sonny Barger, the infamous head of the Hells Angels, who'd agreed to add a little background authenticity to the movie. There stood Barger in cliché black leather and swastika, smoking a joint, his bike parked in his hotel room. He looked over at what he thought was this soft actor and asked, 'A toke for a poke?' Jack had no idea what that meant but was pretty much game for anything. He took a drag from a lethal-looking joint and then Barger punched him full in the stomach – a toke for a poke, Hells Angels humour, I guess. Jack did his best to blend in with them during filming.

Hells Angels on Wheels was directed by Richard Rush, who remembered Jack's impressive audition for him years before and was happy to cast him again. This time he detected an actor 'more aware of his capabilities and desirability' and the flowering of a persona that would eventually explode in *Easy Rider* and *Five Easy Pieces*. 'My films called for those qualities,' says Rush. 'For example, Jack had one thing that was extremely appealing to me, he had a kind of shit-eating grin that said, I don't really mean what I'm saying, I don't mean it to offend you, but it sort of pardoned anything he said or did. It was something he did habitually as a person, a natural quirk, but I liked it very much and called it up for the character.'

And so was born the famous Jack smile, soon to become his trademark. 'An icon of our times,' says *Witches of Eastwick* director George Miller. 'Like those newspaper competitions where they just show you the smile and you have to guess whose it is.'

Drugs were now a major issue in a society perhaps changing too rapidly. The posturing rebellion of Brando and James Dean looked positively anachronistic up against the new drug-fuelled hippie movement; everywhere people were dropping out of society and hitting the road as the reality of Vietnam started to spill out into the streets and campuses of America. 'There was a marijuana scene very strongly going on, both on and off screen,' says Rush. 'But I don't think it hurt anyone's performance or functionality.' Certainly the drug scene was informing the kind of films being made at the time, and the atmosphere of the late sixties. 'I think it was a great time,' continues Rush. 'The sexual revolution had just taken place. The hippies in northern California had created a new culture, make love not war. It was very strongly influencing the rest of the world, kids in particular. Marijuana had become part of the culture, which was a daring part of the rebellion, a rebellion against the restraining holds of society, and we could reflect that in films and in our daily lives as well.'

Ahead of the game once again, Corman seized on the cinematic potential of putting a drug trip up on the screen. He rang Jack: 'Write me a screenplay about this psychedelic craze and LSD.' Jack thought it was a great idea and went to work, drawing heavily upon his own experiences of LSD, which, he told *Playboy* in 1972, he first dropped as early as 1963 'because I was a totally adventurous actor looking for experience to put in his mental filing cabinet for later contributions to art'. Nothing at all to do with getting plain stoned, then. Jack had heard some people were taking the drug, then not seen as harmful but almost of therapeutic value, at a medical practice in LA and so went along. His private session lasted five hours in total, with the therapist administering the drug on hand throughout to supervise the trip, a trip enhanced by the fact he was blindfolded, to aid further introspection. So strong was the overall effect that Jack was still tripping hours after getting home.

Jack readily admitted to being unprepared for the experience. Maybe he thought it was going to be like getting zonked out on grass. If so, he was wrong. Some of the images and feelings were frighteningly vivid, such as the moment he thought that 'my prick was going to be cut off'. He also experienced the sensation of floating inside his mother's womb and being born screaming and kicking into a cold world, overwhelmed by feelings of being unwanted. These were complicated issues to make sense of at the time, and long before he became aware of his family's dark secret.

Jack also confessed to *Playboy* that he'd dropped acid since, but not as much as most of the people in his social circle, and continued to take it occasionally 'because once you've related to acid, there are certain things you perceive that would be impossible otherwise – things that help you understand yourself. If properly used, acid can also mean a lot of kicks.'

Finishing off his screenplay for *The Trip* (1967), Jack gave it to Corman. 'I thought it was terrific,' says Corman. 'The only problem was Jack had written stuff that we couldn't shoot, it was impossible to do. If you've taken LSD the images are so phenomenal that there's no way you can put them on the screen, even if you had all the money in the world. I thought we came pretty close with *The Trip*, but then the studio took out most of the psychedelic trips that took place and I was really disappointed because they were the core of the film.'

Jack's script was also enthusiastically received by stars Peter Fonda and Dennis, pot heads and acid takers themselves. Fonda, who'd dropped acid with the Beatles, drove over to Jack's house to congratulate him personally on producing a script that was, 'right on the nose'.

Everyone, however, was less sure about Corman's counterculture credentials. By the director's own admission he was, 'the straightest man in a fairly wild group'. So, figuring he couldn't make a film about LSD without trying it himself, Corman dropped a tab. 'A whole bunch of other people who were wavering took it with me. We went up to Big Sur, because you're supposed to take it in a beautiful place. It's on the coast in northern California. And we had so many people in cars driving up that it became a caravan. We had to schedule the trips, almost like scheduling a motion picture because you always had to have somebody as the designated straight person in case somebody did something that might get out of control.'

Even forty years later Corman can recall the images and emotions he experienced. 'I remember one of them very vividly, and I was reminded later of the Beatles song "Lucy in the Sky with Diamonds", because I remember seeing a great sailing ship coming towards me in a red sky and as it came closer the sails turned into jewels, all glittering in the setting sun, and then the sails turned into the curves of a woman's body. I thought that was kind of a pleasant experience. But that was only one of a continual stream of images, but they weren't images, you felt that you were in them, that it was reality.'

Jack had written a role in *The Trip* expressly with himself in mind, that of a hippie guru, but Corman refused to cast him, hiring instead Bruce Dern, who remembers Jack being mightily 'pissed off' over the decision. Still, he hung around for the shooting and got pally with Fonda and Hopper, who were given a camera by Corman and sent out to the California desert to capture some weird imagery for the LSD montages, an experience that perhaps whetted their appetites to one day move into direction themselves.

The Trip caused a mild flash of controversy when it opened; amazingly it wasn't passed by the British censor until 2003, due to the belief that it was an advertisement for drug taking. Jack's script worked, then.

Listen, man . . . if you want to try anything freaky, you don't do it with her.

Way back in the early sixties Marlon Brando had become one of the first actor-activists to march for civil rights. Criticised by some as an outsider, another knee-jerk white liberal, others applauded his participation and personal appearances at demonstrations in the Deep South. When Martin Luther King was assassinated in 1968 Brando was amongst those who walked through Harlem in a successful bid to calm riotous unrest and even announced that he was temporarily leaving movies to devote himself to the civil rights movement.

His screen abstinence didn't last long. Maybe it would have been for the best if it had because by the end of the sixties Marlon's choice of movie roles was making even his staunchest fans scratch their heads in befuddlement. What on earth induced him, for example, to appear as a mystical guru in *Candy* (1968), a comedy about the sexual misadventures of a naive girl played by Ewa Aulin? In one scene Marlon, dressed in ceremonial robes and with Indian make-up, attempts to seduce Candy and, according to production manager Gray Frederickson, the actress got the shock of her life. 'The story is that Marlon actually tried to have sex with Ewa for real on camera. I remember she had a bad reaction to it. Well, she freaked out.'

Candy was based on the novel by comic writer Terry Southern, who, towards the end of his life, taught screenwriting classes at Columbia University. One student recalled Southern electrifying a class with a story about a party at Marlon's house in the sixties. None of the students ever found out if it was true or not – hopefully not – but Southern relayed the story as if it really had happened. 'Brando's housekeeper', he said, 'miscarried his baby, right there at the party, this right rave-up. So, dig, Marlon scoops the stillborn infant into a coffee cup, and he proffers this mug to all of the guests, instructing them to "taste the zygote".'

Marlon continued to scrape the barrel with *The Night of the Following Day* (1968), a suspense thriller that he later claimed 'made about as much sense as a rat fucking a grapefruit'. Again he clashed with his director, Hubert Cornfield, who accused Brando of trying to seduce his wife and then having the gall to tell him all about his failed effort. By the end Marlon insisted the final scenes were directed by his co-star Richard Boone, as he could no longer stand the incompetence of Cornfield.

Burn! (aka *Queimada!*, 1969) was another misfire, however appealing the subject matter: colonialism and the exploitation of blacks by whites. As part of his research Marlon met Bobby Seale, a co-founder of the Black Panthers, a group that revolutionised the civil rights campaign in the USA and turned Seale into public enemy number one on the FBI's computer. Fascinated with the group, Marlon began speaking out in their defence. When Panther members were busted he posted their bail, and even attended the funeral of a fallen comrade. It was to be a brief dalliance; Marlon distanced himself when the group succumbed to radicalisation.

For *Burn!* it was off to the jungles of Colombia, and pretty quickly things turned nasty. For a start Brando was convinced the indigenous cast and extras were being exploited and mistreated by the filmmakers, which was pretty ironic, given that the film was about exploitation of the Third World. He also suspected that most of the crew were perpetually stoned on the local grass. Next, director Gillo Pontecorvo made Marlon stand in the searing heat in front of a blazing cornfield and perform forty takes of a scene. It was the last straw. Brando made for the airport and only the personal intervention of the crew got him to change his mind and come back. The truce didn't last long. Feigning illness, Marlon legged it and this time he'd no intention of returning. For months the film was in limbo, until Marlon agreed finally to finish it. He needn't have bothered, *Burn!* was a complete flop, his tenth in a row. Hollywood producers were now better disposed to catching a dose of the clap than to hiring Marlon Brando for a movie.

The only way out for me and my people is to either snuff you out or to sell you.

Back to *The Trip*, which was an important film for Dennis Hopper as well as Jack. In it Hopper played a drug pusher with an eye-catching necklace made from human teeth. Since he was playing a dealer who sells Peter Fonda's character some acid Dennis thought, quite naturally, that he really ought to try the stuff first. 'I'd taken peyote pretty early on in life and had a really bad trip. I saw the whole world charred and burned, and people hanging off trees. It was awful, a terrible nightmare kind of thing. So I wasn't ready to jump into LSD. But I thought I'd better try this before I play the acid dealer. I got some acid from director Bob Rafelson and I took it. And it was an incredible trip. I went back to being a cave man. It was amazing.' He was recommended to Corman by Peter Fonda, but the director was reluctant to hire him, aware of his reputation. 'I know Dennis is a good actor,' he told Fonda, 'but we're shooting this picture over three weeks; we just don't have time for any problems. He's gotta come in and do the performance.' All three went to dinner to see if anything could be worked out. 'And I alluded as tactfully as I could to his reputation,' says Corman. 'Dennis understood immediately what I was hinting at. "Roger," he said, "there will be no problem, I assure you." And he was as co-operative as any actor I've ever seen. He may have caused problems on other pictures, but he understood this was a group of young guys making an inexpensive picture on a subject he himself was involved with and that it was important that he do it right and not do anything to upset the shooting, and he was perfect.'

One scene had Dennis give a two-minute monologue to a group of hippies sitting round him in a circle. Corman didn't want to hold on Dennis the whole time so gradually moved his camera away from him and around the people in the circle and then back on Dennis at the end. 'I was concentrating so much on the movement of the camera,' says Corman, 'that afterwards I just said print it and we went to the next set up. Dennis sounded fine to me. Then the sound man came to me just before we shot the next scene and said, "I played back that tape and I think Dennis has broken the all-time record for saying the word 'man' in one monologue."'

Dennis was now appearing in big mainstream Hollywood movies, albeit in very minor roles. He got shot pretty early on in the Clint Eastwood western *Hang 'Em High* (1968) and hardly says a word in the Paul Newman prison classic *Cool Hand Luke* (1967). Dennis enjoyed recalling that on that picture everyone wore their chains and prison clothes all the time, in restaurants, nightclubs, even slept in them too.

There was also a return match with John Wayne in arguably Duke's most famous film, *True Grit* (1969), leading to a legendary story that Wayne chased Hopper around Paramount studios with a loaded gun. It wasn't quite like that. Wayne used to arrive every morning on set via helicopter, a .45 strapped to his hip, wearing army fatigues. This particular day he wanted to know where 'that Pinko Hopper' was hiding. Dennis was indeed hiding, in Glen Campbell's trailer. The Duke was screaming,

'My daughter was out at UCLA last night and heard this Black Panther leader cussing, and I know he must be a friend of that Pinko Hopper! Where is he? I want that Red motherfucker!' So, though not literally 'running around with a gun', Wayne was certainly on the lookout for Hopper with a loaded .45 at his side. 'But I think he wanted to have a political discussion,' Dennis said, 'as opposed to committing actual manslaughter! That was just Duke.'

Whenever Dennis landed a leading role, it was in some exploitation or drive-in type movie like *The Glory Stompers* (1968), where he's the leader of a motorcycle gang waging war with a rival group. It's one of Quentin Tarantino's favourite films and, according to Dennis, he drove the director to a nervous breakdown and ended up taking over the movie. 'That was my first directorial job.'

Drugs, however, were still an important part of Dennis's day-to-day existence, but he did draw the line somewhere, refusing to do acid trips with Doors frontman Jim Morrison because 'he was always blowing every acid trip I was on. Suddenly the police were there because Jim Morrison was bouncing up and down naked on a Volkswagen.' Ahh, the sixties.

I ain't good. I'm the best!

After proving that he could be a class actor and producer with *Bonnie and Clyde*, Warren Beatty became a social gadfly again as the sixties drew to a close, often bumping into old flames at social gatherings. In a Paris restaurant one night he was little more than sandwich filling wedged between wholesome bloomers Natalie Wood and Julie Christie, each desperate to claim his attention all for herself. Reporter Thomas Thompson recalled the evening: 'The two women threw verbal poison darts at one another from the crudités to the crème caramel. Warren sat uneasily in the middle.'

Warren had the knack of seduction, a talent that made him almost irresistible; he made the woman he was about to go to bed with feel like the most beautiful and desirable woman in the world. And when he flirted with her he did it in such a tender way that she'd melt and do anything he asked for. He tells her she's fantastic and beautiful, the girl he's been looking for all his life. You name it, he says it. And he got so good at it, women believed him. It was hard for a woman not to sleep with Warren when he wanted her to. Just ask Tom Mankiewicz. 'Warren was devastatingly charming with women, especially when he wanted to be; he could turn it on and off like a stereo set. I remember one woman, who has to remain nameless, that I was living with and she was talking about Warren one night and it was so clear that she'd slept with him, and I said, "Jesus Christ, you slept with Warren." And she said, "I don't think you understand, everybody has to sleep with Warren. It's like the mumps or chickenpox, either you do it and you wind up in love with him or you do it and then you're immune." It was like that in those days.'

By far Warren's most noteworthy conquest of the period was Brigitte Bardot, at the time Europe's number one sex symbol. They met in Paris and quickly became lovers, Brigitte being, if anything, even more sexually brazen than Warren. She probably scared him half to death. This was a woman who told reporters she was looking for a man who could 'make me vibrate fully as a woman'.

Brigitte was perfect for Warren. Neither was looking for any sort of commitment from the other and so they became occasional fuck buddies, a situation that lasted on and off for the next few years. 'Warren had a ferocious charm that was impossible to resist,' she claimed. One memorable evening the couple were invited for dinner with Brigitte's former husband Roger Vadim and his current wife Jane Fonda. Warren complimented Jane on the excellent gourmet meal she'd served up then, looking over at Brigitte knowingly, announced that he knew of something that tasted even better. 'In that area,' said Vadim, 'Jane is not quite in Brigitte's class.' Bardot smiled in satisfaction; Jane was more ready to serve divorce papers than dessert.

It wasn't just women who were occupying Warren's time; politics was beginning to take a firm hold on him, growing eventually into a consuming passion that preoccupied him for months and sometimes years at a time, severely curtailing his film output. When in 1968 Robert Kennedy denounced America's involvement in Vietnam and declared his candidacy for the Democratic presidential nomination Warren was amongst the first of Hollywood's liberals to offer his support. After his brutal slaying an outraged Warren became a vocal gun-control advocate. He spoke to a large crowd before a football game, but they didn't take kindly to an actor who'd just made a film about gangsters lecturing them on the perils of owning a rifle. As someone rather succinctly put it: 'Here was Clyde Barrow himself, blathering on about gun control, when only recently we'd watched Faye Dunaway caressing his rod.'

For a time, Julie Christie accompanied Warren on some of his gun-control lectures. They'd met again in San Francisco, where Julie was filming *Petulia*. Being fully aware that she was still in a serious relationship with the artist Don Bessant didn't stop Warren begging her to go out with him, describing how he wanted to do something less selfish with his life besides the soulless and single-minded pursuit of women and fame. Don't knock it, it worked. Eventually she caved in and, you never know, Warren might even have meant it! After *Petulia* was in the can they ran off to Mexico and Bessant was history. Back in LA Warren rented a house that he and Julie could share, but refused to give up his suite at the Beverly Wilshire, in whose corridors Julie was sometimes spotted wearing a see-through white cotton sari.

Warren's suite at the Beverly Wilshire has passed into Hollywood folklore. It comprised three penthouse rooms and was aptly named El Escondido ('The Hideaway'). For such a meticulous person in habits and outlook, the place was a tip: half-eaten room-service sandwiches adorned most surfaces, books, scripts and unopened mail lay in heaps. British playwright Trevor Griffiths, when he worked with Warren on *Reds*, dubbed the suite 'The Pit'. People scratched their heads in bewilderment as to why Warren, a millionaire many times over, preferred to live in these slovenly kept rooms, slipping in and out of the hotel garage to avoid the paparazzi. It was freedom and independence, I guess; the fact he could at a moment's notice just pack up and leave. 'Any need for possessions or roots is unnecessary.'

Maybe Julie was the one to change all that. She was a blast of fresh air for Warren, just the woman he needed, and he loved her inability to bullshit. 'She saves me from my vanity.' As for Julie, Warren's unconventional, rebellious spirit and proud rootless nature had been hard to resist.

Less so his womanising. Even while in relationships Warren sought out the company of other women. Playing around on his current girlfriends became almost a way of life for him, and a thrill. Twenty-one-year-old Jaid Mako, Drew Barrymore's future mum, remembers arriving in Hollywood in the late sixties and finding a job as a waitress at the famous Troubadour, the town's 'in' music venue. The first guy to hit on her was Warren. (Actually, when you think about it, the odds of that happening to young, buxom new arrivals in Hollywood aren't really all that long.) Accompanied that night by Julie Christie, when Warren saw Jaid's dark smouldering Hungarian looks he walked over to her and immediately began flirting. 'I couldn't believe it,' she later recalled. 'Here he was, so handsome and with this beautiful girl, and he's coming on to me.'

Jaid went on to enjoy numerous whirlwind Hollywood romances but Warren never lost interest in her, nor, once she was old enough, in her star teenage daughter Drew. Both were at a restaurant on Sunset Boulevard when Warren invited them over to his table. 'He got very flirtatious,' said Jaid. 'He started kissing and caressing me and eyeing Drew. Finally, he said he was very much into sleeping with one of us, or even both of us.' His offer received a polite but firm refusal.

Jennifer Lee was another new arrival in Hollywood and soon began a tempestuous affair with Warren, claiming that during sex he took calls from Julie Christie. She was also disturbed by his habit of constantly monitoring his partner's responses in bed, analysing what turned them on and giving directions, not only about positions, but about how to feel and react. 'The pressure to have the biggest, most earth-shattering orgasms can get a little relentless,' said Jennifer

It was precisely this kind of reputation that inspired the British director John Schlesinger, who'd launched Julie Christie's film career with *Billy Liar* and *Darling*, to write to his protégée and warn her off the Hollywood Lothario, whom he described as a serial womaniser who 'gets through women like a businessman through a dozen oysters'. Good advice, though she ignored it.

Still coming to terms with Bobby Kennedy's assassination, Warren threw his weight behind the campaign to elect Vice-President Hubert Humphrey to high office. The current incumbent, Lyndon Johnson, was a dead duck because of his Vietnam War policies and Warren, along with many others, saw Humphrey's liberal allegiance as the nation's only hope in the face of Richard Nixon's rabid republicanism. The war was stoking up unrest on the streets of America. At the Democratic convention in Chicago anti-war protestors lined the streets outside the Hilton Hotel, where Humphrey and his team were staying. Warren was tear gassed during one demonstration as he attempted to enter the building.

Humphrey asked Warren to appear in a campaign documentary. Warren's price was simple, and something many of Humphrey's friends were urging him to do anyway: that he should publicly criticise and break with his own administration's stance on Vietnam. 'Don't worry,' said Humphrey, 'that'll be happening within the next week or so.' Warren was satisfied, but Humphrey failed to honour his promise and his defence of the war cost him the support of the large anti-war lobby. That November Nixon claimed the White House.

Upon Warren's return from Chicago, *Los Angeles* magazine gleefully reported a phalanx of girls 'larger than a Broadway chorus call' outside El Escondido. A very nice welcome home present, but the guest directly below his suite had some difficulty getting to sleep, what with the bumping and grinding noises emanating from above his head. 'What goes on up in that penthouse apartment?' he asked the manager. 'I hear the strangest noises at all hours of the night.' Had the guest known who the occupant above was, he might not have asked such a stupid question.

To say that a conveyor belt of crumpet perpetually wound its way through Beatty's hotel suite is not much of an exaggeration. 'When he was in town he'd have various people over there,' says Tom Mankiewicz. 'And a couple of times he said to me, you wanna come up, I've got this and that going on. I don't think Warren wanted me to go up as much as he wanted me to know what he was up to. He had a real reputation, and I think he loved every minute of that reputation. I think he's very clear that he did it and I think he didn't mind that people knew that he did it. I've always thought Warren, in the best sense of the word, was one of the most shameless people I've ever seen.'

Hey hey we are the Monkees, you know we aim to please. A manufactured image with no philosophies.

After the positive reaction to his script for *The Trip*, Jack Nicholson was giving serious consideration to dumping acting altogether and concentrating on writing, and maybe directing. His next screenplay, *Psych-Out* (1968) was a paean to flower children and all that hippy-dippy shit; the problem was, by the time the cast and crew arrived at Haight Ashbury in San Francisco, home of the hippie movement, the summer of love had turned to winter, hard drugs were being taken, the counterculture was for sale. 'The kids on the street,' says Richard Rush, brought in by Jack to direct, 'took one look at us in our studio trucks and decided that we were the enemy, we were the establishment come to exploit them.' Knives were pulled on some of the actors, and the film-makers couldn't call the cops lest they alienate the very group they wanted to film. 'So I called the Hells Angels,' says Rush. 'I called Sonny Barger and said, "Listen, can you send a couple of guys to police this for us?" and he did, and it worked beautifully because both the Angels and the kids on the street had dope in common and the tide turned to friendliness at once. So it worked out fine except that I felt like I had just called the Nazis to police the French underground.'

Jack had taken a role in the film and once again Rush found him easy going, 'although very demanding in terms of what he was doing. Inevitably he'd bring you a performance with a lot of invention in it.' It was the last time they'd work together. When they met up again years later Rush was surprised how unchanged he was by superstardom. 'He was very much the same old Jack, but he'd become an international icon. I wasn't surprised he became a star, he was such a naturally magnetic leading man, with terrific range and the ability to handle anything on screen. There's a common-man appeal in him that's reached everybody, they all root for Jack whether it's on the screen or at a Lakers game.'

There was also a new woman in Jack's life, Mimi Machu, a former model he'd met on a movie set. The pair were immediately attracted to each other and began a passionate and occasionally stormy affair. Occasionally they'd hang out at the home of director Bob Rafelson.

Dennis and Brooke would also be there, the atmosphere was warm and friendly, and the dope was good. Rafelson was riding high as one of the creators of the hit TV show *The Monkees* and planned to use the group for a surreal assault on the big screen, turning to Jack to help with the script – the result was *Head* (1968). Both worked on the screenplay, 'stoned out of our minds' on acid, says Rafelson. But audiences didn't get the joke and the proposed sequel never happened. Shame. The ads would have read: 'From the people who gave you *Head*.'

Rafelson would become a key Nicholson collaborator; he was starting to collect them thick and fast. Another powerful new friendship was with Robert Evans, a former movie actor who had been appointed head of Paramount. Evans was backing a Roman Polanski film called *Rosemary's Baby* and suggested Jack play the father of the devil child. Polanski wasn't convinced; Jack was a too unknown and off-the-wall choice. 'For all his talent, his faintly sinister appearance ruled him out,' said the director, who preferred Warren, though he said he'd rather play the part of Rosemary. As with *The Graduate*, Jack had missed out on another break-through role. It only added credence to his own argument that he should quit acting altogether.

Cutting off her nipples with garden shears! You call that normal?

Marlon Brando's career was in free fall and his personal life wasn't faring any better. It was around this time that his *Bedtime Story* co-star Shirley Jones met up with him again – sort of. Shirley was the star of a new TV series called *The Partridge Family*, playing the mother of a teen pop group. She also often appeared as a guest on the TV game show *Hollywood Squares* and became friends with Marlon's best pal Wally Cox, who also appeared on it from time to time. One evening Wally invited Shirley and her husband to dinner at his home. When they arrived Wally opened the door and rushed out. 'Now Shirley, don't say anything, Marlon's here and he doesn't want to see anybody or talk to anybody, so just make like he's not here.' A little taken aback, Shirley replied, 'Oh, really.' Wally said, 'Yeah, he's in a very bad mood, he's having problems with his kids.' So Shirley went inside. 'They had a whole table set out with food,' she recalls. 'It was a buffet, we could go and get our dinner whenever we wanted. As I approached the table to get some food, underneath was Marlon Brando, sitting in a crouched position. And he stayed there all evening until the people started to leave and then gradually he got up and just left.'

Marlon's friendship with his old roommate was really rather odd indeed. Marlon often stayed at his house or sometimes broke in when Wally and his wife were away, and they'd return to see him slouched on a coach eating peanut butter out of a jar. The two men shared the same mischievous sense of humour and intellectual pursuit of life. Rumours that they were lovers have always been dismissed by family and friends, although Marlon could be incredibly possessive of Wally and never wanted him to marry. He did, though, three times. His third wife, Patricia, never saw any evidence of bisexuality or any other shenanigans. 'I knew Wally pretty well. Even though Marlon had orgies, Wally never participated in them.' But eyebrows were raised when Marlon told one journalist, 'If Wally had been a woman, I would have married him and we would have lived happily ever after.'

Marlon was in Tahiti in February 1973 when he learned of Wally's death from a heart attack, aged just forty-eight. He was devastated, and just like the wrestling from his life of his mother, he'd never get over it. He flew in for the funeral but refused to join his fellow mourners, staying the entire time in Wally's room, sleeping that night in his old pal's pyjamas. Later he wrenched Wally's ashes away from his widow, promising to scatter them himself in the place where they used to go hiking together. Instead, for years Marlon kept them at home or under the front seat of his car. When he revealed to the press that he talked to them nightly, Wally's widow was furious at being lied to and threatened to sue in order to have them returned, but in the end decided, 'Marlon needed the ashes more than I did.'

Hey, man. All we represent to them, man, is somebody who needs a haircut.

One night during a publicity junket for *The Trip* Peter Fonda lay whacked out on vodka and weed in his hotel room when an idea suddenly hit his brain that was so enlightening he had to tell someone about it there and then. He called Dennis Hopper. 'Listen to this, man.' Fonda outlined his idea of a modern western, two buddies on motorbikes instead of horses travelling across America on one final dope deal. 'Whaddaya think?' We'll take the two leading roles.'

'Wow, man, that's great,' said Dennis. 'Jesus, that's great, man.'

'I'm going to produce this movie and I want you to direct it,' said Fonda. 'Will you do it?'

'Gee whiz, man, are you kidding me? Wow, babe. Jesus, that's great. Of course I'll fucking do it. What's the title?'

'*Easy Rider*.'

'Wow, man.'

Dennis seized on the project, realising no sane film executive would ever give him the chance to direct his own picture. As Jack said, 'You know Dennis, you don't exactly just turn over some money to him and say, no problem, you know what I mean.'

After hiring Terry Southern, a hot writer with *Dr Strangelove* to his credit, to turn their story outline and ramblings into a coherent script, Hopper and Fonda pitched the idea around the studios, but there were no takers. Maybe Dennis's manic way of describing the story, all shouting and arm waving, scared producers.

So they tried the private sector, in the shape of the reclusive American supermarket tycoon Huntington Hartford. Dennis's heartfelt pitch to the businessman went down so well that Hartford declared, 'I will give you the money.' Denis couldn't believe it. 'You will?' Hartford smiled. 'Yes, I can see you're impassioned and this will be a great movie. So I will give you the money. You only have to do one thing for me.' He looked Dennis straight in the eye. 'A man with your kind of passion should be able to levitate.' Dennis was dumbfounded as Hartford carried on. 'Levitate now, and I'll give you the money.' Dennis stood there and for a few seconds genuinely wondered if he'd be able to pull it off. Finally he turned to Fonda and said. 'Let's get the fuck out of here.'

Jack had a better idea: why not pitch their biker movie to his old *Head* collaborator Bob Rafelson and his producing partner Bert Schneider, who now ran their own production company with links to Columbia? The name of it was BBS. Dennis was already known to Rafelson, after the director had one night almost tripped over him at a party where he lay poleaxed on the floor. 'This guy is fucking crazy,' Rafelson announced to Schneider. 'But I totally believe in him, and I think he'd make a brilliant film for us.' When Jack chipped in that *Easy Rider* could be 'the *Stagecoach* of bike movies' Schneider seemed impressed and handed over a cheque there and then for $40,000, telling Fonda and Hopper to get down to New Orleans and shoot the Mardi Gras sequence as a test. If they didn't balls it up, he'd bankroll the whole movie.

Great news, but back at the Hopper homestead things weren't running so swimmingly. His marriage to Brooke was teetering on the edge, and her support for his latest venture non-existent; in fact she was downright hostile, adamant that he was going to fall flat on his arse. 'You've never wanted me to succeed,' Dennis fired back. 'You should be encouraging me, instead of telling me I'm going to fail.' He wanted a divorce, and Brooke was only too happy to oblige. Dennis left to make his bike picture.

Down at Mardi Gras, chaos was the order of the day thanks mainly to Dennis's self-confessed ego problems; as far as he was concerned he was 'the greatest fucking film director there's ever been in America' and he proceeded to tell his crew exactly who was in charge. 'This is MY fucking movie,' he yelled at them. Cruising down paranoid boulevard, Dennis saw conspirators on every corner. 'Nobody's going to take my fucking movie away from me!' This before a foot of celluloid had been exposed. Dennis was hell-bent on making his mark as a director. 'I mean, talk about obsession,' he later confessed. 'I didn't give a fuck if I ran over people in the street. If they got in the way, then they'd better get out of the way.' A few of the crew began seriously debating whether all of Hopper's marbles were present and correct. Fonda grew anxious as his ranting intensified. The shell shocked crew looked to their producer, but Fonda didn't know what to do. 'I'm fucked,' he thought.

As the scheduled five days went on people started quitting. There was confusion and bafflement amongst the three cameramen who'd been hired about what exactly they should be shooting. The tension escalated. 'Dennis was this semi-psychotic maniac,' said sound man Peter Pilafian. 'There would be a couple of handguns, loaded, on the table. He liked that kind of atmosphere.'

Tom Mankiewicz happened to be in New Orleans at the same time, working on a TV music special. 'I ran into Dennis and Peter by accident. Nobody had any idea that *Easy Rider* was going to become some sort of classic. But, my God, if I'd had the money I wouldn't have given it to these guys. They were loaded all day long.'

Come the final day the now infamous cemetery scene was shot, featuring Fonda with actresses Karen Black and Toni Basil. Baird Bryant was the sole cameraman on that and remembers Dennis bullying Toni to get undressed and 'crawl into one of those graves with the skeletons'. It was here that Dennis and Fonda clashed big time. Fuelled by a cocktail of speed, wine and lungfuls of grass, Dennis wanted Fonda to clamber atop a statue of the Madonna and open his heart on screen about his feelings for his mother. At the age of forty-two, after years suffering from mental illness, she'd committed suicide by cutting her throat with a razor in 1950, when Fonda had been ten years old. 'I want you to ask your mother why she copped out on you,' said Hopper.

This time Fonda thought Dennis had gone too far, this wasn't creating art, this was a family tragedy that he was being asked to expose to millions of cinemagoers munching on their popcorn. Reluctantly he did it, getting emotionally strung out. According to Bill Hayward, Hopper's brother-in-law installed as producer, Fonda never really got over that and a rift developed in their relationship, 'that never recovered'.

Still paranoid, Dennis demanded that his other cameraman, Barry Feinstein, hand over all the footage he'd shot; he wanted it locked in his room, safe. Pissed off, Feinstein lobbed the film cans at him and the pair ended up brawling and falling through a door into one of the motel rooms. They got up and stared at the sight in front of them, Fonda in bed with both Black and Basil (Black denies this). Feinstein wasn't stunned for long; he grabbed the TV set and hurled it in Hopper's general direction.

Karen Black later described the shoot in one word: 'Insane!' Not into drugs in a big way herself, she was in another universe from Dennis and co. Dennis would see some guy outside the motel window and say, 'Hey, man, you see that guy outside the window? I'm gonna get him!' And he'd go running out and lose all track of time. 'He was NUTS!'

So it had been an interesting few days in New Orleans. At the end of it Fonda called Brooke and suggested that maybe she and the children oughtn't to be in the house when Dennis returned. His reasoning – 'Dennis has gone berserk.' Terry Southern phoned Brooke with much the same advice: 'This guy's around the bend.' Brooke ignored them both; she'd handled Dennis before and she could handle him again.

But, waiting for him to come through the door, she must have felt like a beach-bar owner waiting for a hurricane to make landfall. Once home, Dennis locked himself away in his bedroom for three days, emerging only to view rushes of the Mardi Gras footage, which, in the opinion of Bill Hayward, was 'an endless parade of shit'. Not surprisingly, Dennis's mood blackened further, ably assisted by his increased drinking and drug taking. At this point Brooke categorised him as 'exceedingly dangerous'.

One night, according to Brooke, Hopper lost it when he found out the kids had eaten all the hot dogs being served for dinner. He began striding menacingly towards Brooke, but her young son blocked his path. 'Don't you get near my mother.' It was the final straw for Brooke. The kids were getting mixed up in all the shit with Dennis and she got out, sleeping with her young family for a week on the floor of a friend's house.

As Brooke set about getting a restraining order against Dennis, he was arrested for smoking dope while cruising down Sunset Strip and thrown in jail. He protested his innocence in court, saying the cops only pulled him over because his hair was too long and he was driving a battered old car. The cops said he threw a joint out of the window. No I didn't, pleaded Dennis, how could he when the only joint he had was still in his pocket?

The minute Brooke's father heard about the impending divorce he called up his daughter. 'Congratulations. That's the first smart move you've made in six years.'

Suing for divorce, Brooke claimed Dennis had a violent temper, used drugs and had struck her on several occasions. She also charged him with 'extreme cruelty'. Not surprisingly, she won custody of their daughter, and in the final settlement also received the house and the artwork Dennis had collected during their years together: Warhols, Lichtensteins and many others. Not long afterwards Brooke sold the paintings to private dealers. Today the collection would be worth in excess of $70m and is distributed amongst some of the world's finest art galleries.

Brooke also revealed that when the divorce finally went through she would have been within her rights to have claimed half of Dennis's profits from *Easy Rider*. She opted to not ask for a thing. 'I didn't want him coming after me with a shotgun.'

Dennis has blamed his behaviour towards Brooke on his drinking and the fact that she was a manic depressive. He claimed she'd be in bed for four or five days, in the dark, then give a party and be all jolly and hyper, then descend back into her moods again. 'I didn't know how to cope and I belted her.' It was a young and stupid mistake he's since admitted.

Dennis's behaviour baffled almost everyone who met him. When Schneider bamboozled Columbia into distributing *Easy Rider* Dennis stood up during one meeting and stuffed his finger up an executive's nose. If that's how he behaved in board meetings, what was he going to be like on location? Fonda had shown Schneider and Jack footage surreptitiously taken of Hopper ranting and raving out in New Orleans and told them his director had 'lost his mind'. Relations were bad. 'Everyone wanted to kill one another, put one another in institutions,' said Jack. To save the film Schneider decided that, because of his experience working on Roger Corman productions, Jack should be on the main shoot as a sort of sheriff. 'Just be there, Jack,' Schneider told him. 'And make sure that you and the rest of your dope-fiend friends don't go crazy. See if you can bring this picture in and keep 'em from killing one another.' And since Jack was going to be on set virtually every day, why not cast him as the third lead, an alcoholic lawyer called George Hanson who teams up with the motorbike drifters.

The role of Hanson was originally earmarked for Rip Torn, that was until Torn and Dennis almost knifed each other to death. Hopper burst into Fonda's New York town house one night, where the actor was entertaining Terry Southern and Torn, and barracked them all for getting pissed instead of working on the script. He was angry, having just come back from Texas scouting locations and hearing that kids with long hair were being sheared with razor blades like sheep. 'Take it easy,' said Torn, who hailed from that part of the country. 'Not everyone from Texas is an asshole.' Hopper pushed him away. 'Sit down, you motherfucker.' Things then got very serious when Dennis claimed that Torn pulled a knife on him. Torn would recall the event very differently, saying it was Dennis who grabbed a steak knife and waved it menacingly just inches from his head. Torn disarmed Dennis, knocking him back against Fonda, who fell on the floor. 'There goes the job,' thought Torn.

Subsequently Torn claimed that Hopper's version of the knife incident damaged his career, spreading an unjustified image of him as being something of a nutter. In 1994, just as Torn rejuvenated a stagnant career with success on the Larry Sanders sitcom, Dennis repeated his version of the legend during an appearance on a chat show. Fed up, Torn successfully sued for defamation. The judge ruled that Hopper was not a credible witness.

Filming began around California, then gradually hit the southern states and redneck territory, where the cast were subjected to bowel-loosening levels of intimidation. Every restaurant, every roadhouse they went in there was a Marine sergeant or a football coach who started with, 'Look at the Commies, the queers. Is it a boy or a girl?' Hopper went into one bar and immediately a guy swung at him, screaming, 'Get outta here, my son's in Vietnam.' Behind him was the local sheriff; his son was in Vietnam, too. As a joke Dennis said, 'Hi there, I'm hitch-hiking to the peace march,' whereupon eight guys jumped him.

This was really what *Easy Rider* was about. In the new, radically changing America, if youth were going to wear a badge, whether it be long hair or black skin, they'd better learn to protect themselves. This was the ultimate irony: in a country that talks about freedom and democracy it's people really can't bear anyone to be different from themselves. As it said on the poster: 'A man went looking for America. And couldn't find it anywhere', a tagline that, according to Richard Rush, Jack came up with.

When the crew hit Taos, New Mexico, Dennis and Jack dropped LSD and were driven over to the crypt of D. H. Lawrence, where they started hallucinating at the foot of the grave, imagining insects crawling over their faces. Later, as dusk began to fall, they hit the waffling inanely stage. 'We're geniuses,' said Jack. 'You know that? Isn't it great to be a genius?'

Brando: Half angel, half devil, and 'a walking hormone factory' according to one producer.

Two icons of the twentieth century: Marilyn and Marlon, their affair lasted several years. After one date back at Marlon's place he said, 'For God's sake Marilyn, get out of that dress. Those tits of yours look like they need to be liberated.'

A raging talent: Marlon habitually clashed with directors and indulged in fist fights with producers.

A lover on screen and off. Actress
Ewa Aulin got the shock of her life when
Marlon actually tried to penetrate her for
real, live on camera during their love scene.
Ewa, quite understandably, had a bad
reaction to it. Well, she freaked out.

Washed up and unemployable *The Godfather*
rescued Marlon's career. Still, he refused to
learn his lines and cue cards were pasted on
furniture, on fruit in a bowl, on the back of his
hand. 'But it didn't matter,' says producer Al
Ruddy. 'He was Don Corleone, he was the man.'

As Colonel Kurtz in *Apocalypse Now*. The filmmakers were thrown into a panic when it was discovered a grave robber was supplying the movie with dead bodies as set decoration for Kurtz's chaotic compound.

With his doomed son Christian, who in 1990 was involved in a fatal shooting and jailed for manslaughter.

Dennis Hopper: Before …

… and After. This is what drugs can do to you. It got so bad he once stripped naked and slept in a jungle, convinced World War Three had begun and aliens had landed. He pleaded with local police to shoot him.

Easy Rider. Filming the classic camp fire scene Dennis, Jack and Peter Fonda
smoked 155 joints of Mexican grass.

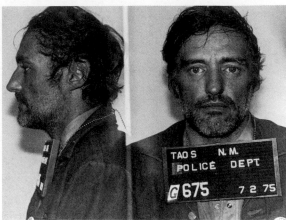

Would you give this man a job? Dennis arrested in 1975 in Taos, New Mexico after causing a traffic accident and fleeing the scene.

Working out the worst aspects of his alter ego: Dennis as deranged pervert Frank Booth in *Blue Velvet*; the start of his great comeback. No longer did he need to finish off a bottle of tequila or a pound of cocaine in order to play a scene.

Dennis and Jack, shooting the breeze at an LA Lakers' game. Other times they meet to play golf. 'Most of the guys who were heavy on drugs and stuff, we're all out playing golf and we're all sober,' says Dennis. 'It is weird.'

The great survivor. 'Dennis took a lot of drugs,' says screenwriter Tom Mankiewicz. 'He has absolutely no right to be still alive.'

Dennis agreed that it was. From somewhere a beautiful woman appeared – luckily for all concerned she was no hallucination – and took them to a nearby hot spring where they got naked. Dennis claimed the woman for his own, leaving poor Jack to return to his hotel alone. So, whacked out, he stood guard for several hours inside his room, convinced he was about to be raided by Red Indians. For a while he listened to the buzz coming off the television set, imagining himself a bunch of electrical circuits, all pumped up with energy. He went outside and started walking and saw that dawn was rising. Clambering to the top of a forty-foot tree, Jack looked down on a vast meadow, pulsating with patterned light. His eyes fixed on a large white rock in the centre. Suddenly the rock stood up and turned into a fabulous white stallion that went tearing around the meadow, throwing its neck up and bouncing and kicking. Then other smaller rocks began to mutate and transform into horses. 'The moment filled me with fantastic emotion.' Christ, he was out of it.

Hanson was a great role, perfect for Jack; certainly he made it his own. A man equally at odds with the heartland of America, he hitches a ride with Dennis and Fonda and around a campfire they philosophise and argue about what is wrong with the country they love. Mostly, though, they smoke dope. That one scene did more for Jack than all the Corman pictures put together; it made him a star.

It was difficult to shoot, not least because, for the sake of realism you understand, the actors smoked authentic dope. According to Jack's calculation, they dragged on 155 joints of pretty good Mexican grass. There was also the added difficulty of the men breaking into convulsions of laughter, verging on hysterics, with Dennis off camera rolling around in some bushes, 'totally freaked out of his bird', said Jack.

It remains an iconic screen moment. '*Easy Rider* was the first time people smoked marijuana in a movie and didn't go out and kill a bunch of nurses,' claimed Dennis. But to some extent the film normalised the use of drugs, and made cocaine fashionable. The plot had these two bikers smuggling a heavy load of drugs in order to fund early retirement. A motorcycle couldn't carry enough marijuana to score big bucks, and Dennis ruled out heroin, so came up with cocaine, a drug that at the time wasn't very well known or much used. After *Easy Rider* came out it became as common as heroin on the streets, while in Hollywood parties it was being handed round on trays along with hash. 'An unfortunate situation in my mind,' excused Dennis.

Post-production was conducted within a perpetual cloud of dope. Dennis edited like a maverick, tearing up the rule book, not giving a shit. One of his ideas was to run the credit sequence upside down. He was Orson Welles on acid. This was going to be his masterpiece and he wasn't going to compromise. His first cut ran something like four and a half hours. 'This isn't *Lawrence of Arabia*,' argued the producers.

Months went on and still Dennis was, in the words of one crew member, 'jerking off in the editing room'. Enter Henry Jaglom, now a respected independent director, then an actor who'd trained with Lee Strasberg at the Actors Studio. For some reason he and Jack were thrown into the editing suite to help out on *Easy Rider*. 'Each of us worked with an editor in white gloves who sat in front of us, trying to reshape the material in ways we thought would be helpful,' recalls Jaglom. 'Jack didn't want to touch the stuff he was in as an actor, all that campfire stuff, so I concentrated on that to begin with.'

About twice a week everyone would gather downstairs in Columbia's Projection Room 6 to look at where they were and discuss where they should go. 'These were exciting, often intense and frequently combative meetings,' recalls Jaglom. Jack, Dennis and Fonda attended, along with Bob Rafelson and Schneider. 'Everyone contributed what I think are important benefits to the film,' confirms Jaglom. 'But *Easy Rider* is at its heart fully Dennis Hopper's work and should be respected as such. It was Dennis alone who captured the zeitgeist that made the film resonate so powerfully with a generation.'

For years, though, Dennis and Fonda would feud over ownership of *Easy Rider*, both laying claim to the greater creative input. This infighting even extended to the music soundtrack. Fonda wanted Crosby, Stills and Nash; Dennis told the band that anyone who drove around in limos as they did could have no comprehension of his movie and wanted them out, warning, 'If you guys try to get in the studio again, I may have to cause you some bodily harm.'

After a preview screening Columbia's veteran chief executive Leo Jaffe stood up, hailing: 'I don't know what the fuck this picture means, but I know we're going to make a fuck of a lot of money!' At Cannes it was a sensation, and Fonda, Dennis and Jack wallowed in the attention. 'We were free to get loaded in those days,' says Jack fondly. 'The festival was a little more rocking than it can be in the streets today.'

On a modest outlay of something like half a million dollars *Easy Rider*, when it opened in July 1969, reaped in tens of millions at the box office, this at a time when bloated fare like *Hello Dolly* was almost bankrupting the studios. 'I was stunned by the response to the film,' says Jaglom. 'We all were. Except Dennis.'

Hopper and Fonda's little bike movie revolutionised Hollywood corporate thinking. The idea that young filmmakers could make a movie for their own people, about their own time, was something that just hadn't been allowed to happen before because formula films had frozen the industry. It was a unique period and heralded the new wave of American cinema that lasted well into the seventies, when studios threw money at any long-haired geek leaving film school to make more independent, risky movies – people like Scorsese, Bogdanovich, Spielberg and Lucas.

As for Dennis, he made the cover of *Life* magazine, which called him 'Hollywood's hottest director', and was hailed as a counterculture icon, a tag that has never truly gone away. Ironically, it was Jack who reaped the greater reward. After over a decade of hacking it in Corman movies and not making the slightest impact, critics were falling over themselves in praise and he ended up with an Oscar nomination at the very time he was contemplating giving up acting. As Richard Rush recalls, 'After *Easy Rider* Jack came up to me one day and said, "Shit, Dick, I think I'm going to have to become a movie star." Because he really wanted to be a director. And I thought he was a good director and a very capable writer, but I thought it was crazy for him to fight it; he had this clear path into stardom, might as well grab it and make all the world happy.'

There's nothing wrong with me. I mean, I don't like boys.

Warren Beatty had been spending a lot of time with Roman Polanski in London. The director was living it up while his wife Sharon was at home in Los Angeles preparing for the birth of their child. As the pregnancy drew to an end Sharon was constantly on the phone to Polanski, urging him to return. He promised he'd catch a flight in a few days' time.

Too late. While Polanski remained in London, Sharon was butchered by a group of maniacs. Warren rushed over to Polanski's house when he heard the news, but the director was inconsolable, distraught. How could this have happened? Why had they targeted Sharon? Who were they? Had there been danger signs? Polanski must have replayed in his mind all the events that led up to this terrible tragedy, a tragedy that for a brief time changed how Hollywood looked at itself.

Polanski and Sharon moved into Benedict Canyon, a popular residency in Los Angeles, in February 1969. Warren was amongst the guests at a housewarming party and frequently popped by, as did the likes of Dennis and Peter Fonda. Unfortunately the house was used for more nefarious purposes when the owners were away filming. Friends held wild parties there which often had to be broken up by the police. Drugs were also being used and supplied on the premises. To use the phraseology of the time, the house was getting a bad vibe. The couple decided to move.

Polanski asked Warren if he fancied taking on the lease. The actor viewed the house and seriously contemplated moving in until he met a couple of Polanski cronies who claimed they'd also been offered accommodation there. 'There's plenty of room for everyone, man.' The prospect didn't fill Warren with joy, since he knew these particular individuals were caught up in the local drug scene. He left. What Warren didn't know was that the house and the goings-on within it were under the watchful eye of a certain Charles Manson.

On 5 August the house was again the scene of a celebrity bash. Sharon had invited over Jane Fonda, Roger Vadim and a few others. Three days later she was busily organising another special evening in, this time a quiet dinner to which she'd asked, amongst others, Steve McQueen, a former lover. In the end McQueen got lucky with a girl and spent the night with her. His libido saved his life; Sharon wasn't so lucky.

Manson had ordered several of his 'family' to visit the house and murder everyone inside as nastily as possible. They arrived at midnight.

Sharon was tied up and had to endure the agony of watching three of her friends being butchered before begging her attackers to spare her life because of the child she was carrying. Her pleas were answered with a series of vicious stab wounds that penetrated her heart, lungs and liver. As she lay dying in a pool of blood, Sharon's last words were 'Mother . . . Mother.'

In London Warren could see Polanski was in deep shock so quickly took charge, arranging for first-class tickets home and an immigration official to escort Polanski personally off the plane and away from the expected press frenzy. In the horrible aftermath of the murders Polanski's closest friends did their best to keep up his spirits, lest he slide into total darkness. 'Warren kept up a stream of improbable stories,' Polanski later recalled. 'Mostly relating to his hyperactive sex life and containing details I'm sure were invented just to make me laugh.'

Sharon's memorial service was a moving tribute, but it was too much for some. People wept openly as her coffin, with her unborn baby wrapped in a shroud beside her, went into the ground. Warren attended, thoughts perhaps running through his mind that had he been in LA rather than London he might very well have been among the victims.

Hollywood, with its tales of murder, corruption and decadence had rarely experienced such a time. The Manson murders affected the place, no question. As Robert Towne said, 'That was the end of the sixties. The door was closed, the curtain dropped, and nothing and no one was ever the same.' Even Jack began sleeping with a hammer under his pillow.

Of course the cinema was blamed. The accusation that violent films somehow contributed to a cultural environment that could spawn a Manson massacre, and the general hedonistic lifestyle of the moviemakers themselves, stuck on Polanski and he was virtually blackballed in Hollywood at a time when the town should have been behind him. 'His situation was a very interesting case of what notoriety can do to you,' said Jack. 'He would be excommunicated by Hollywood because his wife had the very bad taste to be murdered in the newspapers.'

Strangely, when Charles Manson wanted his life story told as a movie he instructed his lawyers to get Dennis to play him. At first Hopper turned down an invitation to meet him in jail, but curiosity won out in the end and they talked for something like an hour and a half. 'It was interesting,' said Dennis. 'He told me his whole life was like a movie, and that he always thought there were cameras there.'

It took a while for Polanski to get his life back to some sort of normality. Going back to work, he wanted to make a film of *Papillon*, the bestselling book about Devil's Island, and for the lead it had to be Warren. Flying over to Paris to meet Polanski and read the script, Warren ended up spending the next forty-eight hours in clubs and with girls while the script sat unread back at the hotel. Warren was enjoying himself so much that the third day was a repeat of the first two, as was the fourth, and the fifth. 'I was so frazzled for lack of sleep I couldn't take any more,' Polanski recalled. 'We'd been in Paris almost a week and Warren still hadn't read a page of the book.' He liked it when he finally got round to looking at it, but there was a scene in which he had to appear naked and that was a no-no. 'I'm not going to appear bare-ass,' he told Polanski. 'It's a hang-up I have.' It didn't matter. Polanski, still persona non grata in Hollywood, couldn't raise any finance. *Papillon* was later made by Franklin J Schaffner as a star vehicle for Steve McQueen and Dustin Hoffman.

I move around a lot, not because I'm looking for anything really, but 'cause I'm getting away from things that get bad if I stay.

Jack Nicholson had always wanted fame, craved it, dreamed of it, but when it landed in his lap after *Easy Rider* it gave him pause, it was too all-encompassing and it affected him for a while. At times he could be incredibly arrogant with it, at other times show deep insecurity. Of course he missed basic freedoms, like being able to light up a joint in a public place or hang out at his old haunts. 'And I can't go around picking up stray pussy any more.' Maybe now they came to him. He was stuck with being a celebrity, for better or for worse.

He also felt uncomfortable as the poster boy of the counterculture and strongly denied that *Easy Rider* and some of his other films like *The Trip* could influence someone to try drugs, although he believed in the legalisation of grass and spoke out about America's 'insane' anti-marijuana laws that made criminals of normal decent people who merely smoked weed recreationally.

Jack had always been open and honest about his own private drug use, confessing that he smoked grass and used cocaine, now the 'in' drug, 'because chicks dig it sexually'. He referred unashamedly to certain practices of Errol Flynn, where the old-time movie star recommended placing some powder on the end of one's dick as an aphrodisiac.

Years later Jack tried to distance himself from such statements, claiming that at no time did he ever advocate the use of hard narcotics. Yes he admitted to having 'done all the drugs', and in the early nineties remained 'an old pot head', but never once was he enslaved to them. Back in the early seventies Jack's openness about drug taking shocked the establishment and really pissed off the anti-drug-abuse authorities, coming as it did in the aftermath of such drug-related celebrity deaths as Janis Joplin's and Jim Morrison's.

As the sixties died Jack was very hot indeed and top scripts were landing on his doormat. To the consternation of friends, and no doubt his bank manager, chances to appear in *The Godfather*, *The Great Gatsby* and *The Sting* were all spurned over the next few years, any one of which would have sent Jack's earnings through the roof. Instead he preferred to stay with BBS, who were flush and cool after *Easy Rider*. Their offices were really the place to be in Hollywood; these guys knew how to party, but they also, most importantly, knew how best to cultivate and exploit Jack's new screen image. It proved a masterstroke as Bob Rafelson, along with Carole Eastman, were composing a script especially tailored to his special gifts as an actor, one that would capitalise on both his *Easy Rider* success and his appeal as a counterculture figurehead. It was called *Five Easy Pieces* (1970) and would earn Jack his second Oscar nomination in a row. His performance is raw and startling, certainly amongst the best he's ever given.

The film's most famous scene is when Jack's drifter character loses it big time in a restaurant over an order of wheat toast, a case of art imitating life. Carole Eastman witnessed a Nicholson temper tantrum vented against a snooty waitress. 'You say one word,' Jack warned her, 'and I'll kick in your pastry cart.' In the early sixties Jack went into a restaurant with a girlfriend and Roger Corman and ordered steak. When it arrived it wasn't cooked to his satisfaction, but the waitress insisted it was what he'd ordered. Jack grabbed the offending meat off the plate and threw it up in the air – splat – hitting the ceiling.

Jack's anger is sudden and volcanic. It's rarely seen, but when it's unleashed – *wham!* One story comes from the early seventies when he was at an American football game and a group of rednecks sitting behind him were behaving insultingly to a group of women. Jack turned to his girlfriend and said, 'Would you like to get even?' Beaming, she agreed. Jack turned round to face them. Three had gone off to buy hot dogs so he focused on the one remaining guy, who nervously hid behind his wife. That didn't stop Jack. He grabbed the wife and dragged her over the seats in order to get hold of the redneck. Enraged, he unleashed a bad punch and cut his finger on the guy's glasses before making a hasty exit. 'I'm a coward, first of all, so when I get to that place, it's purely hysterical. When I'm angry and I can't control myself, I don't like it. I've never liked fighting. You know, I could get killed!'

During filming Jack's co-star Karen Black fell for him in a big way. 'I think working with someone like Jack, an actor of that quality, turns you on.' Nothing happened, though. Karen was in a relationship and Jack was still dating Mimi, although the lure of his other female co-star Susan Anspach ultimately proved too strong. Mimi was aware of Jack's dalliances and was getting pretty fed up. It was common knowledge around the offices of BBS that Jack hit on women at parties and entertained groupies at the office. 'When Mimi wasn't there,' said one BBS production member, 'it was any girl he could find.' There were drugs too. Susan Anspach claimed Jack took cocaine on the set. For one love scene Rafelson needed thirty-nine takes. 'Jack had one toot every six takes,' said Susan. 'He frequently left the set to snort cocaine.'

Jack's affair with Susan was very different from the rest; it produced a child, a boy christened Caleb. During the early years of his upbringing Susan never sought any assistance from Jack, later explaining that at the time she didn't want to complicate her life with, as she said, Jack's inadequacies and hang-ups. How could she trust him, she said, considering the way he handled relationships with women? It was a situation that years later would boil over into a particularly nasty public feud.

4

The Explosive Seventies

I'll tell you exactly what we have been doing. We have been doing sex!

I t was an odd time for Marlon Brando, the early seventies. If anyone was box-office poison, it was him. 'Everybody was a bigger star than Marlon then,' says Michael Winner. 'He'd had ten flops in a row, nobody wanted him. I thought, I've got Marlon Brando, now everyone will finance my film; quite the contrary, they ran away even faster.'

The film in question was *The Nightcomers* (1971), to be made in England, a sort of imaginary prequel to the Henry James novel *The Turn of the Screw*. Marlon liked the script and agreed to appear for just a percentage. 'He was incredibly professional,' Winner recalls. 'Very restrained, knew all the lines, didn't need an atmosphere of reverence on the set. He was giggling away, telling jokes, got up and did his scene, sat back down again telling jokes. It took a long time for him to get started in the scene, he fumbled and mumbled, rushed to the script to have a look and rushed back. Once he got going, outstandingly brilliant.'

During one take a prop guy dropped a piece of equipment which clanged nosily on the floor. Oh shit, thought Winner, but Marlon didn't seem to take any notice. 'I'm terribly sorry that someone dropped something,' said Winner afterwards. 'What?' said Brando. 'They dropped something; there was a big bang, and I thought you did very well, you didn't react.' Brando just stared back, 'What?' Winner said, 'MARLON, THEY DROPPED SOMETHING!' Brando gently hit his ear and out came an ear plug. 'He acted with ear plugs,' says Winner. 'So he could only hear the people next to him. Rather clever, I thought.'

Marlon particularly enjoyed his sex scene with co-star Stephanie

Beacham. Well, who wouldn't have? 'The trouble was,' says Winner, 'he insisted on wearing Wellington boots and underpants. I was on the floor crying with laughter. And he said, "What's so funny, Michael?" I said, "Marlon I don't know how it looks from where you are, but from here its absolutely fucking hysterical."'

During the shoot a large bearded man arrived on location. For days he hovered about in the distance, always on the periphery of the set. It was Francis Ford Coppola. Winner said one day, 'Marlon, isn't that Francis standing behind the barrier?' Marlon looked across and said, 'Yes.' 'Shall we let him through?' asked Winner. 'No,' Marlon replied firmly. Coppola had flown in from America to ask Marlon to appear in his next film, *The Godfather*.

After *The Nightcomers* Marlon became one of Winner's dearest friends, and they usually met up whenever he was in London. While filming *Superman* at Shepperton Studios Winner was invited to Marlon's rented home for dinner one evening. There were a few people there, including a Pakistani lady, a current flame of Brando's, who was spouting a lot of cobblers about the underclass in her country. Winner was wondering how the devoutly liberal Marlon could stomach such a woman when he whispered in the director's ear, 'She's a great blow job.'

When he wasn't in the country Marlon was prone to call Winner at all hours of the day and night, sometimes disguising his voice. 'I put the phone down on him six times once. I kept getting these calls. A man would say, "This is Baron Von Stumpel," and I'd put the phone down because I get nuisance calls. He called again and said, "This is Marlon Brando, Michael; you keep putting the phone down on me." I said, "Marlon, you use these fucking voices all the time – what do I know?" He was the most playful man in the world, Marlon, jokes all the time.'

I had fantasies like that, about being beat up. Did you ever have a fantasy about women beating you up? Or don't cowboys have fantasies?

Even after the success of *Easy Rider* Dennis Hopper had a tough job trying to set up his next movie. BBS had a gut instinct that his ego would now be about the size of Jupiter and he'd be completely uncontrollable. They passed. As did Warners and Columbia.

The picture Dennis wanted to make had been festering in his mind since the mid sixties, a parable about the impact of a visiting Hollywood film crew on a South American village. It was to be called *The Last Movie* (1971). For a time legendary record producer Phil Spector had agreed to come in as backer until his accountant said Dennis was too big a risk and he walked. Finally, Universal stumped up a million dollars, waving away concerns that Dennis was erratic and unreliable. The world was waiting for the next Dennis Hopper picture after *Easy Rider*, and by God Universal was going to give it to them.

As a token of faith Dennis took a modest fee as star and director in exchange for a large slice of the profits and full creative control. This was the new Hollywood Dennis wanted to be a part of, the old studio formula of making big soulless blockbusters was finished. 'We're gonna make groovy movies, man.' The problem was, although he was a film-maker of imagination and talent, the drink and drugs got in the way, fucked up his focus to tell a story coherently. *The Last Movie* became a mess and pretty much destroyed his career as a director.

Dennis intended shooting his movie in Chinchero, a village that nestled 14,000 feet up in the Peruvian Andes. Maybe it wasn't the best idea to make the film in Peru, one of the world's leading producers of cocaine, but there you go, hindsight's a wonderful thing. On the flight down, the plane was scarcely in the air before the film crew started passing round the drugs, much to the horror of staid South American businessmen who muttered, 'Damn gringos.'

Once in Peru Dennis managed to offend the government by spouting about the joys of marijuana and tolerance of homosexuality. The Catholic Church was spitting blood and the ruling junta started investigating Hopper's background, not liking one jot the information coming back about this hippie who spoke fluent revolution.

Drugs were everywhere. Brad Darrach, a reporter from *Life* magazine, could hardly believe his eyes when within hours of arriving a crew hand managed to score some cocaine, seven dollars for a packet that cost ten times that in the States. By the first evening some thirty members of the crew were sniffing the stuff, or smoking grass or dropping acid. By midnight the actors had trotted off to various beds. The reporter did the same, only to be awoken at 2 a.m. by screams he believed were from a young actress experiencing a bad trip.

There were wild parties aplenty. Darrach claimed one actor chained a young girl to a post because she looked like Joan of Arc and he wanted to re-enact the saint's immolation. There was also a rumour that another actor almost died when he took too many peyote buds at once. The reporter was at a loss to fathom why these young actors were taking so many drugs, other than the obvious reason, that it was the hip thing everyone did in the new Hollywood. 'It's also the hip thing not to get addicted,' Darrach wrote. 'But some of the people I saw in Peru were nibbling godawful close to the hook.'

Kit Carson was another reporter down there and one night in his hotel somebody knocked on his door. 'I opened it and there was this guy looking at me holding a bottle saying, "Hey, man, you want some ether? It's really good." I mean, everything you can imagine was being done in this hotel. That whole shoot, that was one of the most out-of-control situations I've ever seen.'

During one scene a horse bolted after hearing prop gunfire and fell off a high wall, breaking its back. A crew member pulled out a Colt .45 and put a bullet through its brain. Almost instantly a group of locals arrived armed with knives and began butchering the animal for its meat. Two of the cast fainted, the rest retired to the nearest bar. That night Dennis broke down and cried like a baby.

Kris Kristofferson was a young unknown singer when Dennis cast him in a small role as a wrangler. The sights he saw on that movie were enough to scare him off show business for life. 'I see the guy he's mellowed into now, and I love Dennis,' Kristofferson told the *Guardian* in 2008. 'But back then he was the most self-destructive guy I had ever seen! He got a priest defrocked because he got him involved in some kind of weird mass for James Dean. He antagonised the military and all the politicians. It was crazy.'

Besides drugs, the location was awash with groupies, or ding-a-lings as Dennis called them. He fell for Michelle Phillips, a member of the Mamas and the Papas, who had a small role in the film. When her work was finished and she left, Dennis moved in with a local lass who was often spotted shopping around for marijuana and cocaine. Dennis ultimately booted her out, convinced she was a spy for the government. This wasn't paranoia: the local government had posted spies amongst the crew, itching for any excuse to kick Dennis and his movie out of the country. 'This shit don't bother me, man,' Dennis told a friend. 'It's the old establishment disapproval, man. I got a picture to make. I got my art to express.'

As filming wound down cast and crew turned to booze rather than drugs as the temperature dropped markedly. At the end-of-shoot photo Dennis, bottle in hand, hollered, 'This picture was not made on marijuana. This picture was made on Scotch and soda.' Dennis's own personal supply of grass was actually stolen quite early on in production and for the rest of the shoot he had to bum from other people's private stashes.

Amazingly, in spite of all the drugs, boozing and whoring, *The Last Movie* was completed on schedule and within budget with Dennis, according to the *New York Times*, 'inspiring something akin to idolatry in his actors'. But he was physically drained and now faced the monumental task of editing his beast. Immediately he annoyed the studio by retreating to Taos in New Mexico, away from any Hollywood influence, a place so remote that one reporter found it hard to believe that there were actual roads that connected it to the rest of the world. Taos was where Dennis and Jack had spectacularly tripped on LSD together. He'd fallen in love with a house there, enchanted by its association with onetime occupant D. H. Lawrence, and when he learned it was up for sale, Dennis had to buy. It consisted of three buildings, a small living space where Dennis resided, a large residence left for visitors, family and staff, and a place Dennis filled with musical instruments for people to go inside and, like, jam, man. His dream was to create a commune, a hang-out for artists. Rooms were filled with the weird and wonderful, and Dennis's own art pieces. In the dining room stood a white plastic box, maybe eight feet long, that had an aluminium shaft sticking out of it and two very large balls. It was called *The Perpetual Erection Machine*. Before Tracy Emin, before Damien Hirst, there was Dennis Hopper!

Jack came down a few times and visiting reporter Kit Carson saw at first hand the interplay between these two emerging icons. 'They were competitive in a friendly way. I think they probably dared each other a lot, but that's how you act when you're two driven alpha male figures; you get off on that. Though Dennis went a whole lot further than Jack did in a way of bringing himself to the edge of the universe.'

It was at the house in Taos that Dennis sat down to edit *The Last Movie*. And, along with other dropouts and hangers-on, ingest an inordinate amount of drugs. 'I was only down there once in Taos,' says Tom Mankiewicz. 'Everybody was just blotto. You thought, everybody's going to die, everybody in this house is going to die.'

Not long after settling into Taos Dennis surprised friends when he turned his fling with Michelle Phillips into a more permanent arrangement. They married in the main living room, 150 candles burned and 200 guests gathered to hear them exchange vows. Michelle later confessed that she was drawn to Dennis in part by her 'Florence Nightingale instinct. I was so overloaded emotionally by this point in my life, I didn't know what I was doing.' She'd not long divorced from husband and former lead singer of the Mamas and the Papas John Phillips, by whom she had a daughter, Chynna, who would herself go on to become a pop star with the group Wilson Phillips.

According to Tom Mankiewicz, the wedding took place in something of a drug-induced haze. 'Apparently one night, and this is what I heard, everybody was getting wasted, dropping acid. Dennis married Michelle Phillips, and then the next morning literally woke up in bed and didn't recognise her; he had no memory of the ceremony whatsoever. It got annulled pretty much straight away, he didn't remember marrying her.'

In the days after the wedding Michelle alleged that the behaviour of her new husband was slightly disturbing. He let off guns in the house and handcuffed her to prevent her from fleeing, saying he thought she was a witch. In an interview with *The Times* in 2004 Dennis contested Michelle's assertion that he handcuffed her. 'Where did the handcuffs come from?' he asked. 'I didn't handcuff her. I just punched her out.'

By the end of the week Michelle knew she had to get out. She grabbed Chynna and together they made a dash for the airport. In the story she later told John Phillips, Dennis chased after them, driving his car onto the runway in an attempt to stop the plane taking off.

Back in LA Michelle's father dragged her to an attorney, saying, 'Men like that never change. File for divorce now.' It was going to be embarrassing in the short term. 'Everybody had the same question,' Michelle explained to *Vanity Fair* in 2007. 'A divorce after eight days? What kind of tart are you?'

Dennis, back in Taos, took a phone call from Michelle and begged her to come back to him. 'I love you, I need you. What am I going to do?' According to Dennis, Michelle replied, 'Have you ever thought about suicide?' Dennis paused for a moment. 'No. Not really.' And that was it. He was left devastated. The only sign that Michelle had ever been in Taos was a room Dennis had prepared for her daughter, a room the child would never see. It became a shrine almost, untouched, unlived in.

It wasn't long before Taos became a magnet for hip Hollywood, with actors, filmmakers, journalists, photographers all coming down, sometimes as many as twenty at a time. A frequent guest was a stuntman hired by Universal to be Dennis's bodyguard. In reality the executives had this guy spying on Dennis and reporting back about what progress was being made on the film. The ploy backfired: Dennis quickly corrupted him, even had him act as a courier for drugs on his frequent trips between Hollywood and Taos.

The editing continued. Dennis had to cut forty hours of material into a two-hour movie; it would take him over a year. Hardly a surprise when you think he compared editing a movie to 'having a child and cutting its arms off – putting its eyes out'. When the suits at Universal called asking when the damn thing would be finished Dennis went nuts and cursed them down the phone. Then when they came all the way from Hollywood to see a rough version Dennis ignored them and went into the local bar instead to get pissed. Friends thought he might be destroyed by his own movie. He was constantly changing the message he wanted to convey. As one friend revealed, 'None of us really thought he would finish the movie, we thought he would have a nervous breakdown long before that.'

Finally, it was ready, but things didn't look good. Certainly people expecting another *Easy Rider* were going to be disappointed. After a test screening at the University of Iowa Dennis was booed and jeered as he got on the stage. People were throwing stuff; they were really hostile. Dragged out into the lobby, Dennis spied a very attractive girl standing by a vending machine. 'Mr Hopper,' she said. Dennis smiled, 'Yes, my dear?' The girl walked over. 'Did you make this film?' Dennis said he had. Suddenly – thwack – the girl let him have it, straight on the nose. Blood spurted out. 'You sexist fucking pig!' she yelled. So, not the best preview in Hollywood history.

Universal certainly thought *The Last Movie* was a bucket of shit. One executive said to Dennis, 'Great, so you made an artistic film. What are we supposed to do, kill you? Only a dead artist makes money. We'll only make money on this picture if you die.' Dennis was livid. 'Don't talk to me like that. You're talking to a paranoiac.' And he wasn't joking.

Dennis refused to recut the movie into a more commercial form. Friends weren't surprised by his attitude. Jack sympathised, but again thought Dennis was going about things the wrong way. 'You don't take someone's bread and then walk across the street and say, fuck you.' It was Dennis playing the rebel again. 'I was young and thought I had power. I had no power at all. I had a big mouth.'

In the end audiences were puzzled and critics tore the film apart, calling it an ego trip, at best just plain bad. *Time*'s review summed it all up: 'That sound you hear is of checkbooks closing all over Hollywood. Dennis Hopper has blown it.' Universal played it just for a couple of weeks in LA before shelving the thing, despite the fact it had won the Critics' Prize at the Venice Film Festival, though this said more about how far the festival judges had their heads up their pretentious arses than the merits of Hopper's film.

Dennis was adamant that he never wanted to make another movie for Universal again. They felt much the same way. 'In fact,' said Dennis, 'they don't ever want to hear my name again.' And that pretty much went for the whole of Hollywood. Incredibly, Dennis had gone from unemployable rebel to industry saviour with *Easy Rider* and back to unemployable rebel again, all within about eighteen months. Asked years later if *The Last Movie* had damaged his career, Dennis replied, 'Did it damage my career? I'll tell you, man, it *ended* my career. But I've no regrets.'

However, this time the road back would prove much tougher as Dennis plunged into a self-created abyss of drink- and drug-induced psychosis.

Hey, pard, you know how to square a circle? Shove a four-by-four up a mule's ass.

After a mini sabbatical Warren Beatty returned to making movies, though with more muted raspberry than fanfare, replacing Frank Sinatra as a compulsive gambler who falls for chorus girl Liz Taylor in *The Only Game in Town* (1970). Astonishingly Beatty chose this bilge over *Butch Cassidy and the Sundance Kid* because 'I didn't feel much like getting on a horse and riding around.' Maybe the real reason was director George Roy Hill's contention that Beatty's demands frustrated him so much he told the star to take a hike and got Robert Redford instead.

Despite the fact that *The Only Game in Town* is set in that most American of locations, Las Vegas, Taylor insisted it be shot in Paris so she could be near hubby Richard Burton, then working in the French capital. So at huge expense Vegas streets, shops and casinos were recreated on a Parisian sound-stage. The film stiffed. Warren didn't mind working in Paris, far from it. While there he dated opera diva Maria Callas, still smarting after being dumped by shipping magnate Aristotle Onassis, and Princess Elizabeth of Yugoslavia. Indeed, Liz and Burton watched goggle-eyed as most of the female aristocracy of France arrived in Paris to sniff the stud over. Not for nothing did Liz Taylor rate Warren, physically, a 15 on a scale of 1 to 10.

Back in London, looking for fresh meat, Warren hooked up with Polanski again at a party, also attended by the stunning Britt Ekland. Warren saw his chance and together they hotfooted it round the capital's top night spots, ending the evening in one or the other's bed, having sex 'until sleep came from sheer exhaustion', as Britt later poetically put it. For a woman formerly married to Peter Sellers and romanced by the likes of Rod Stewart and Ryan O'Neal, it was quite a claim when she revealed that Warren was the most divine lover of all. 'I had never known such pleasure and passion in my life. Warren could handle women as smoothly as operating an elevator. He knew exactly where to locate the top button. One flick and we were on the way.'

The ride was brief, though, lasting barely two months. Britt must have known she didn't stand a chance when out in LA together Warren dodged photographers, fearful Julie back in England would see them together.

Julie was definitely still the one, and in a bid to cement their relationship further they decided to make a movie together. Or David Foster decided for them. A former publicist trying to produce his first movie, Foster had bought a book that would make a neat revisionist western, about a gambler who pitches up one day in a little mining town and goes into business by building a whorehouse. It was called *McCabe and Mrs Miller*. For director he hired Robert Altman, who'd just finished making *M*A*S*H*. Then, wearing his publicist hat, Foster thought what a coup it would be to get Warren and Julie, these two famous lovers, to work together for the first time. 'So I talked to Bob about it and he said, "How do we pull that off?" And let me tell you, my God, it was hot stuff, and I was right about getting them. I mean, we had to beat the press away with a friggin' baseball bat.'

Warren was in London when his agent told him about *McCabe* and that Altman was going to direct. There was a pause. 'Who's Bob Altman?' said Warren. (*M*A*S*H* had yet to open outside America.) 'And to Warren's credit,' says Foster, 'he got on a plane and flew to New York, saw *M*A*S*H*, loved it, got back on a plane and flew to LA to meet with us and made a commitment to do the movie.' But he wouldn't sign a contract. Verbal commitment is one thing, but in Hollywood studios wanted you to sign a contract before monies were paid and they officially green-lit the movie. 'Warren had a reputation for always being dragged kicking and screaming to commit to a movie,' says Foster. 'He kept saying, "I'll do the movie, I'll do the movie." But Warners were saying, "You've got to sign the contract." And he kept putting it off until finally we called his agent and said, "If he doesn't sign the contract by six o'clock Friday night we're going to get another actor." At quarter to six he signed the contract.'

According to Foster, almost from day one 'there was a strange relationship between Warren and Bob. I lived it and I'll never understand it.' Altman was so meticulous in his preparation, so knowledgeable about what he was going to do, it probably unnerved a guy like Warren. As a filmmaker himself coming off a huge success with *Bonnie and Clyde*, Warren obviously had his own ideas. 'Warren was very intense,' says Foster. 'And he'd constantly question Bob on set-ups and dialogue, and Bob was like, I'm the fucking director here!'

On location in Vancouver, British Columbia, clashes between the two men were frequent. Warren liked lots of takes, working his way into a performance, Altman preferred to shoot fast and loose. Take the scene in which Warren is alone drinking in his room: the bottle falls off the table, he catches it and pours out another shot. It was take twenty and still Warren asked for another one. Tired, and probably pissed off, Altman announced to the crew, 'Print seven and eleven – I'll see you guys tomorrow,' and walked out. The assistant director took charge of the scene and twenty more takes were completed before Warren was satisfied. 'Warren is basically a control freak,' Altman complained. 'He wants to run the show.' Altman got his revenge by ordering Beatty to do twenty-five takes of a scene in a biting cold snowdrift.

With such childish battles going on, little wonder that *McCabe and Mrs Miller*, when it opened in July 1971, was a stylised mess that didn't find an audience. Warren and Altman, predictably, blamed each other. 'Had I been the producer I would have killed Robert Altman,' said Warren. Altman's two cents' worth was that Beatty, in his view, was, 'really a bit of an asshole'.

Ironically, Warren's performance in *McCabe* is amongst his best, but he never gave due credit to Altman, says Foster. 'To the day I die I'll never understand it. Actors loved Bob, that's why he had this company of actors who always worked for him. Paul Newman loved him. Julie was the complete opposite to Warren, she put herself totally in Bob's hands and to the day he died she was close to him. The only guy he had a problem with was Warren.'

Who knows if bad feeling remained between the two men? 'But the last time that the three of us ever saw each other is burned indelibly in my brain,' says Foster. There's a chic little studio in LA called Lantana Studios. Inside is a wonderful restaurant and a lot of film folk go there because they don't get bothered by fans. Foster had a lunch date one afternoon with a director to discuss a film; around the early 2000s. 'I walk into the restaurant and there's Bob Altman. He jumps up: "Hey, Foster!" He was a big burly bear of a man. All of a sudden in walks Warren Beatty. And he sees me and Bob and walks over and we all throw our arms around each other in the middle of this restaurant, it was like a group hug. It was the last time we were all together and it was like a moment in history where all the bad vibes were gone.'

Warren and Julie's rented home on the *McCabe* location was the scene of numerous dinner parties and at one of them Jack turned up. He and Warren had never met before, but Jack certainly ingratiated himself by taking one look at Warren and declaring, 'Now, *that's* what a movie star looks like.' It was the beginning of one of Hollywood's most enduring and infamous friendships.

Warren and Julie's setting up home together, be it only on a temporary basis, suggested to some that marriage wasn't too far away. Although Julie confessed that the institution itself 'frightens me', she almost certainly would have taken the plunge if only she could have believed that Warren would be faithful. Of course he knew his failings, that monogamy would bore him, that marriage scared him to death. 'Why should I get married when I know I'll get divorced in two or three years?' said Warren, not unreasonably. Both he and Julie weren't living so differently from married people anyway, he thought; they'd just not signed a piece of paper.

After finishing promotional duties for *McCabe*, Julie went off to buy a cottage in Dorset. Very un-Hollywood. But then she did and always would shun the facile side of show business. She never craved adulation. And this made her so very different from Warren, who quite enjoyed playing the movie star. 'I always remember Julie sitting on the outer edges at parties,' said Altman, 'while Warren was at the centre of things.'

Is this an ultimatum? Answer me, you ball-busting, castrating, son of a cunt bitch! Is this an ultimatum or not?

With his *Easy Rider* earnings Jack bought a large property on Mulholland Drive, tucked away in a private canyon. Marlon was his neighbour. In the early seventies Jack's home became well known as 'the epicentre of the era's drug-soaked social scene', according to one report. A notorious late riser, for obvious reasons, a sign over the doorbell asked visitors: PLEASE, DON'T RING BEFORE 10 A.M.

Not just a home and retreat, Jack's place grew into one of the world's most prized private art collections, including paintings by Dalí, Picasso, Bacon and Magritte. It expanded to the point where there was little space left on the walls. One visiting reporter counted fifteen works of art stacked in the guest bathroom, including two Japanese prints and an Egyptian sculpture, waiting for free wall space.

Happy in the creative commune of BBS, Jack made his directorial debut for them. But, as usual with Jack, *Drive, He Said* (1970), a college drama, proved to be both unconventional and controversial. As indeed did his search for an actress to play a cheerleader, who had to briefly appear nude. Even though this was a minor role and had no direct relevance to the plot, Jack's resoluteness and unswerving dedication in interviewing a hundred girls, each of whom had to take their clothes off in front of him, was a testament to his professionalism.

Drive, He Said went further than any previous movie in its depiction of full frontal nudity and the sex act. After a screening at the Cannes Film Festival there were boos as well as cheers and some audience members got to their feet to wave indignant fists toward Nicholson. Then a fight broke out that had patrons running for the exit. Back home a scene where a couple fuck in a two-seater sports car was the subject of much discussion, with some critics finding it all a little degrading and unpleasant, having to watch a girl bent over the front seat taking it like a good 'un from behind. Jack hit back: thanks to personal knowledge, he could confirm that was the only position in which one can fuck in a sports car.

He came to terms with his directorial debut misfire, but relations with Mimi were near breaking point. An ambitious actress herself, Mimi was fed up being known only as Jack Nicholson's girlfriend, so had begun sleeping around within Jack's extended entourage. Not best pleased, Jack was in no position to complain as he was doing the same himself. But, hell, sex was an important part of Jack's life. He argued that if you're not releasing sexual energy, you're in deep shit. Away from home and, 'not relating to a chick', in Dr Jack's words, 'pretty soon that's all you're thinking about. Within three days in a new town you're thinking, Why can't I find a beaver in a bar?'

Eventually it was Mimi who walked out. 'We were two maniacs who couldn't live together or apart,' she bemoaned. As for Jack, he felt, 'dumped on' and for a time broke into a cold sweat at the very mention of Mimi's name. He sought solace with pal Harry Dean Stanton, who recalled Jack was, 'almost incoherent. I've never seen such despair.'

Jack always found it amusing that because of his reputation men would ask him for advice about women. Close friends never did. 'They think I'm too goofy about women. In love with love. Too easily injured. Idealistic.' In relationships Jack commits like a freight train, which means when it hits the buffers, the pain is that little bit stronger. When it comes to the opposite sex Jack has three guidelines: 'They're stronger, they're smarter, and most important they don't play fair.'

After years in the wilderness it must have felt strange for Jack to have directors like Mike Nichols, who refused to even let him audition for *The Graduate*, now falling over themselves to have him in their movies. Nichols described Jack as 'the most important actor since Brando' and personally cast him in *Carnal Knowledge* (1971) as Jonathan, an unrepentant philanderer, a role Jack was all too familiar with and gleefully took on, unaware of the backlash it would create. This was a character who didn't know how to communicate with women beyond fucking them, a situation Jack freely admitted he'd been in himself. 'When I began sexual activity in earnest, my point of view was simply to try to seduce everyone I could.'

The impact of *Carnal Knowledge* and Jack's performance caused the growing feminist movement, dubbed 'political lesbians' in Washington, to have a collective seizure. No matter how hard Jack tried to explain that he was merely replicating what the script required of him, which was, in his view, a legitimate portrait of male attitudes at the time, the women's libbers had their bras in their ears and weren't listening, ranking him public enemy number one along with other reprobates such as *Playboy* owner Hugh Hefner. Jack probably didn't do himself any favours with quotes such as: 'I've balled all the women, I've done all the drugs, and I've drunk every drink.' Such statements seemed deliberately antagonistic.

So, despite protesting that 'I am not trying to get into the pants of every woman I'm interested in,' Jack's role in *Carnal Knowledge* pretty much cemented in the minds of the public an image of Jack as an out-of-control shagging machine, male chauvinist and rabble-rousing establishment-baiter. He was never to live it down, if indeed he ever wanted to.

Still down in the dumps over Mimi, Jack hooked up with Michelle Phillips, taking care to first phone Dennis in Taos to say he was dating his ex. 'Best of luck, man,' said Dennis. 'It's over between her and me anyhow.'

Michelle was a stabilising influence, despite her being just as much of a free sprit as Jack and highly ambitious. Right from the start she'd been happy to accede to Jack's ground rules of not wishing to be tied down and refused to share a house. 'The idea of living with him was just horrible because he's set in his ways.' No problem, Michelle and her daughter rented a house nearby and Jack happily carried out stepfatherly duties such as taking the kid to school.

Soon he was coming out with stuff like, 'Expanding sexuality is not most satisfied through promiscuity but through continuously communicating with someone specifically.' Could Michelle be the one to stop his philandering ways? Jack admitted that in the past there had been weeks 'when I've been with more than four women'. He dismissed that now as being nothing more than an ego trip and also regretted having once told a reporter that he'd already bedded all the women he wanted to. 'Well, man, every chick I ever related to really resented that statement.'

I'm gonna make him an offer he can't refuse.

The film that threw a lifeline to Marlon Brando's floundering career was never seen as anything particularly special. 'Everyone forgets Paramount had no faith in *The Godfather*,' says its producer Albert Ruddy. The studio had bought an option on Mario Puzo's book prior to publication but done absolutely nothing with it. 'Because they'd made a gangster movie called *The Brotherhood* three years earlier that was a disaster,' Ruddy continues. 'And they said, who wants to do another fucking mob movie, we don't care how good Puzo's book is. But when it came out, the damn thing never dropped off the bestseller list, so they finally said, fuck it, let's do this, but do it as a cheapie.'

Every director Paramount approached turned them down. Finally, studio head Robert Evans insisted an authentic Italian get the job, if audiences were to 'smell the spaghetti'. Francis Ford Coppola's name cropped up. Evans wasn't sure: he'd only made three pictures and none of them had done any business, but at least he was an Italian. 'And he was born to do *The Godfather*,' says Ruddy.

So, I guess, was Brando born to play Don Vito Corleone, the mobster boss, arguably his most famous and certainly most lampooned characterisation. Coppola's determination to cast Brando put him on a collision course with Paramount. 'Marlon had a bad reputation and was death at the box office,' says associate producer Gray Frederickson. 'He was kind of washed up.' At a meeting with executives Paramount president Stanley Jaffe slammed his fist hard on the table and decreed that Brando would be cast in *The Godfather* over his dead body. It was a statement that saw Coppola succumbing to what seemed like an epileptic fit.

While Coppola put his career on the line for Brando, the actor repeatedly spurned his advances; he wanted no truck with a film that celebrated the Mafia. It was Marlon's assistant Alice Marchak that pestered him to read Puzo's bestseller. At one point he threw the book back at her howling, 'For the last time, I won't glorify the Mafia!' Marchak realised he'd warmed to the notion when she arrived at Mulholland Drive one afternoon to see Marlon sporting a drawn-on pencil moustache and asking, 'How do I look?' Every time she turned up at the house for weeks after he was wearing a different gangster-style moustache.

So keen was Brando now to play Don Corleone that he personally visited Bob Evans at his Paramount office. 'I know a lot of people in Hollywood say I'm washed up,' Evans would recall him saying. 'And I know you've heard a lot of stories about me, and some of them are true. But I can play that part, and I can do a good job.'

The studio power brokers were still to be convinced, so Coppola asked Brando if he might come over to Mulholland where they could do a little improv and put it on video to show his doubters. While Coppola set up his equipment Brando put shoe polish on his hair, stuffed a pillow up his jumper and pushed tissue paper in his cheeks. His idea was that Corleone had been shot in the throat years before, so muffling his voice. He also wanted the Don to speak quietly. Powerful people don't need to shout. As he looked at himself in the mirror, there was Don Corleone staring back at him. 'That's it,' Marlon muttered to himself. 'The face of a bulldog, mean-looking but warm underneath.'

Coppola took this footage over to New York to personally show Charles Bluhdorn, the Austrian CEO of Gulf+Western, who owned Paramount. Setting up the video monitor in a conference room, Bluhdorn poked his head round the door. 'Francis, vat are you dooink?' Suddenly Brando's face appeared on the screen. 'No! No! Absolutely not, I don't vant a crazy guy.' Bluhdorn changed his mind when he saw the transformation into Don Corleone. Coppola had got his man.

Francis faced another stiff battle over his casting choice for the key role of Michael Corleone, inheritor of the family business. Evans wanted Beatty, Jack, Redford . . . anyone except Coppola's favourite, Al Pacino, whom he felt didn't radiate star quality. 'We tested Al three times,' says Ruddy. 'The second time they said, forget it, why are you testing him, he's a fucking midget. Francis is pulling his hair out, we're gonna start shooting soon. I said, "Francis, let's do one more test, put the camera on the ground and shoot up so he looks like Clint Eastwood." I get a call from Bob Evans. "Ruddy, I run the fucking studio, right? I go to the dailies, what do I see? Fucking Al Pacino, the fucking midget again. Get him the fuck out."'

In the end Coppola won, as he did on practically everything else. He was a force of nature you couldn't compete with; battling to shoot on authentic New York locations, battling for more money, his energy and stubbornness turned *The Godfather* from a low-budget picture into a seminal event. But the first week of shooting was disastrous; they got behind schedule and the studio hated the footage they were seeing. Worse, Brando adopted a stray cat he saw wandering round the set and insisted on using the animal in a scene where he addresses a group of gangsters. 'The problem was, the fucking cat was purring so loud you couldn't understand Marlon,' says Ruddy. 'Evans went, "Is this movie going to have fucking subtitles or what! We can't understand what the hell he's talking about."' Rumours circulated that Coppola might get the boot, with Elia Kazan ready to step in. 'If you fire Francis,' Brando threatened, 'I'll walk off the picture.'

Could things get any worse? Well yes, a whole lot worse. Suddenly the real Mafia showed up, unleashing all sorts of threats against a production they didn't want to see happen. Evans was frantic after a series of bowel-loosening phone calls from hoodlums and told Ruddy to sort it out. Joe Colombo was the local mob boss and Ruddy got in touch to organise a meeting at his office so the mobster could look over the script. 'At three o'clock the next day Joe Colombo and two other guys arrived in my office. I gave him the script and he put his glasses on. It's a hundred and fifty-five fucking pages, right? He looks at page one for about five minutes and says, "What does this mean, fade in." With that he throws the script in the air. "You read it, Frankie," he says. "Why me, boss? Give it to Louie." And they start throwing the script around. Finally, it lands on my desk and Joe says, "Wait a sec, do we like this guy?" They say, "Yeah we trust him." Joe said, "Let's make the fucking deal." Just the threat of making them read a script, I made the deal. Fucking amazing. But believe me, I would rather deal with a mob guy than a Hollywood lawyer any day.'

The problems facing the film only brought the cast and crew closer together and Marlon was, for many, a role model, certainly for the younger actors like Pacino, James Caan, Bobby Duvall and Diane Keaton. 'It was like acting with God,' said Pacino. Although God was far from perfect, sometimes not reporting for work on Mondays and altering his own dialogue, but Marlon revelled in his newfound role of Svengali.

At first Pacino and the rest felt intimidated when Brando arrived on the set. 'It was like Christ coming off the cross,' says Ruddy. 'And then Marlon started being funny. He'd be mooning everybody, he'd start cracking jokes, got everyone to loosen up, it was a real love fest. He liked all the guys and they just adored Brando, he was very generous to them.'

The actors mooning at each other became a feature of the production.

'It started out with Jimmy Caan driving home one night and he had his butt hanging out the window, so they started mooning each other,' says Frederickson. 'And then Brando, during the big wedding scene, stood up on the stage and mooned the whole crowd.'

There was general ribbing amongst the cast, too. In one scene Lenny Montana, playing a hoodlum, stuck his tongue out at Marlon; the guys had written 'fuck off' across it. Brando loved that. According to Robert Duvall Brando talked about nothing else but, 'fucking Indians' for an entire week. As he left the studio to go home Duvall said goodnight to the crew and then to Brando. 'Have a good weekend, Philosopher King.' Marlon held up his middle finger and said, 'Sit on this and rotate.' Every once in a while it was good to stick it to each other. 'It was all ultimately in a good spirit,' says Duvall.

Marlon remained playful throughout the shoot. In the scene where he returns from the hospital on a stretcher, the extras playing the orderlies were struggling a little bit so Coppola asked the strongest crew hands to take over. While they left to get into costume Marlon ran over and grabbed weights off the camera crane and loaded the stretcher with them and then laid back down on top. On 'action' the crew were in hysterics as these hefty guys failed to lift the thing. 'That was Marlon,' says Frederickson. 'He wanted to have fun on set. But he was a serious professional. And he worked eleven hours, no more, no less. At the end of eleven hours he would finish the take but if you wanted another take, it was automatic, he would just say, "Goodnight, gentlemen," get up and walk off the set. There was nothing you could do.'

It was obvious to everyone that Marlon was creating a classic film character; his on-screen transformation was extraordinary. Out went the Kleenex tissues, replaced by a special mouthpiece, wrinkles were added by his make-up man and weights put in his shoes to make him walk slowly. 'It was ironic,' says Frederickson. 'On *The Godfather* Marlon had gone on a diet and showed up lean and mean and young-looking and we had to pad him up and make him look fat and older, and then later when we wanted him to look mean and lean on *Apocalypse Now*, he showed up weighing three hundred pounds and looking like Orson Welles.'

He was still trying to figure out a way to stop eating, though. He had this plan. He'd say to his assistant, 'Listen, after nine o'clock I want you to lock up all the cabinets and no matter what I say don't give me the key.' Then, come 9.20, he'd say, 'Alice, give me the key.' 'No.' His voice now trembling. 'I swear to God I'll fire you.' 'No.' So he went and got a crowbar and just busted all the locks.

True to the method, Marlon remained pretty much in character all the time, talking to the crew in that famous guttural voice. Refused to learn his lines, though. 'He came on the set and there would be a big card he would read off,' says Ruddy. 'But it didn't matter, he was Don Corleone, he was the man. It was just a fucking amazing experience to watch.' Actually Marlon had cue cards secreted everywhere, pasted on tables, on fruit in a bowl, written on the back of his hand or shirtsleeve, like a kid with exam answers.

He also invented a whole batch of quirks and mannerisms for Corleone, not least for his famous death scene where he collapses with a heart attack after playing in the garden with his grandson. The child actor wasn't reacting very well, so Brando stuck an orange peel in his mouth to look like monster teeth, something he'd done to amuse his own kids. Although the result makes him look like a Halloween version of Godfrey from *Dad's Army* there's something unsettling watching this evil bastard tearing around a garden chasing a giggling child

That scene was Marlon's last in the can. Like a lot of things on *The Godfather* it presented its own special set of problems. Coppola had been growing a nice little tomato patch to double for the garden, but on the eve of shooting a torrential downpour all but destroyed it. Because Marlon only had one day left, per his contract, and it looked unlikely they could shoot on the set, some quick thinking was called for. 'We had huge financial constraints on that movie,' says Ruddy. 'Marlon got a deal of fifty grand but if the film went over schedule we had to pay him another hundred. So I went to the hotel and said, "Marlon look, the set's wrecked, but if we have to shoot on it we will because we don't have the money to pay you the extra fifty. But if you care to give us a break and leave now, I'll pay your flight back here again when it's tarted up and looks good." He thought about it and said, "Well, you guys have been good to me, OK." His agent called me the next day and said, "You fuck, hustle my goddamn client." I said, "I didn't, I told him the truth, and it was his choice. He was kind enough to help out." The thing with Marlon and a lot of huge stars, they become highly distilled neurotics obviously, but they have built-in radars, they sense if you're trying to bullshit them, and if you try to bullshit them you are D-E-A-D, dead. If you're honest with them and tell them the truth, they'll go out of their way to help you. Marlon was great to everyone on this goddamn movie.'

The Godfather was an instant classic when it opened early in 1972 and a worldwide box-office smash. Ruddy remembers attending the first public screening with Al Pacino. 'We left halfway through to have a few drinks and returned for the final few minutes. When the movie was over there wasn't one clap, no applause. Al said, "It's a fucking disaster." He didn't realise they were stunned. The audience were wiped out.'

The Godfather turned Coppola from a flop director into Hollywood's hottest talent and created stars out of its young cast, but it was Brando's movie. His performance remains iconic, even carrying favour with real-life mafiosi, who told him they loved the picture because he'd played the Godfather with dignity. For years Marlon couldn't pay a bill in any restaurant in New York's Little Italy.

Perhaps the biggest irony of all was that here was a man who'd suffered perhaps the worst ever run of flops now starring in the biggest hit since *Gone with the Wind*. It was a remarkable resurrection, culminating in his Oscar for best actor. But when his name was read out as the winner there was genuine surprise when instead of Marlon a young woman in full Native American dress came onto the stage to tell the audience he couldn't accept the award owing to his concerns about the mistreatment of the American Indian. 'We really didn't know that Marlon planned not to show up,' recalls Gray Frederickson. 'Everyone was shocked when that woman appeared. But he really believed in those causes. When we were filming *Godfather* his big cause was the unfairness of the caste system in India, then he switched to American Indians by the time the Oscar came round.'

Marlon's stance didn't find much sympathy from his fellow performers. Michael Caine said that if Brando felt so strongly on this issue he should have had the guts to stand on the stage himself, not send a trembling squaw. Clint Eastwood joked, 'Maybe we should give an Oscar to all the cowboys shot in John Ford movies.'

But what happened to the Oscar itself? Actor Marty Ingles can throw some light on the mystery. 'For a time I was a celebrity broker and I came across a guy who had in his possession the Academy award that Brando turned down. This guy was there on Oscar night, he was in the wings and when the girl walked off with the award she didn't know what to do with it. My friend said, "I'll take it." Years later the press got to hear about it and I got some correspondence from Brando by fax which said: "I'm under the impression you have access to the award, I'd like to have it back." I'm a sweet guy but I'm not an idiot, and I replied, "Mr Brando, the law says it doesn't belong to you any more. You publicly gave it up. So it's not yours, let's make that clear, with all due respect to your genius. I think it would be nice if, maybe, we used it to bring something to humanity, like a giant fundraiser for the cancer foundation, perhaps even a fundraiser for the very Indians that you wanted to speak of." And he wrote back to say he wanted to give it to his daughter. I replied, 'Mr Brando, I love you dearly, but you did what you did and now I want to make it work for humanity, and I'd like to see if perhaps we can really do something good for some people that need it. And if you won't do that, then I keep the Oscar." And that's the way it was. My friend still has it.'

Good for nuthin's good enough fo' me.

After yet another two-finger salute to the ruling class in Hollywood, Dennis Hopper packed his bags and went into exile in Taos. He was bitter, he was paranoid, and he was deeply pissed off. What he viewed to be his masterpiece had been shat on from a quite considerable height. Would he ever direct again? Would anyone even want to hire him again?

He took solace, almost inevitably, in booze and drugs, while the artistic commune he'd hoped to establish at Taos began to crumble all around him. It was full of wasters, hangers-on and sycophants who did nothing much else but smoke dope with him. As Universal executive Ned Tanen said, 'It was hippie heaven. Dennis was the friend of every freak who was trying to get back and forth across America.'

One visitor was Kit Carson, former journalist turned filmmaker who'd decided to make a documentary on Dennis and his crazy world at Taos. Carson first met Dennis when he interviewed him at the time of *Easy Rider*. 'He loved the article and so did his friends. I sat with Dennis and Jack Nicholson going over the edit of the interview and Nicholson kept saying, "He makes you sound like you make sense, Dennis. It's really hard to do."'

While filming the documentary, Carson got to like Dennis enormously and enjoyed his playfulness. At one point Dennis said, 'Why don't you guys go get a whole bunch of girls and bring them up here for me.' Carson and his crew were up for that. 'OK,' they said. 'If you'll walk naked down the local high street then we'll go get your girls.' Dennis did just that. 'And in the documentary,' says Carson, 'there's this moment where Dennis gets out of a car, strips naked and hustles down a block, then we cut to three carloads of girls showing up and we had this sequence of Dennis playing with all those girls. Dennis was someone who rises to dares, that's who he is.'

Carson's documentary *The American Dreamer* is full of such eye-popping moments. Bearded and bleary-eyed (one reporter at the time thought he resembled, 'some kind of maniac bomb thrower'), Dennis babbles about his childhood, fires off semi-automatic weapons and shares a bathtub with three naked young ladies. There's also a nice caring, sharing moment where Dennis declares, 'I'd rather give head to a woman than fuck them. Basically, I think like a lesbian.'

These scenes played around with Dennis's own sexuality and reputation as a ladies' man. He'd always had a large sexual appetite and thought himself pretty irresistible to women. 'Dennis thinks he's very sexy,' says Carson. 'And so he will eyeball the women around him, and if they're in a room with him then they're sort of looking for the exit door because they know they're gonna have to get out of there sooner or later. But he's not pushy about his randiness. But it's there. It's one of the amusing things about being around him, just watching him thinking, he's the hottest dick in the room.'

And of course there were the drugs, lots of drugs. Amazingly, though, Carson didn't think that the inordinate amount of drugs Dennis was consuming altered his personality at all. 'By that time in his life he'd done so many varieties of drugs they didn't have a noticeable effect on him. Drugs were all over the place, mescaline, marijuana, speed, there was a lot of alcohol, too. One time a reporter from *Rolling Stone* arrived and went off on a mescaline trip; she walked out of the house and no one could find her. I went out scouting and found this journalist staggering around in the nearby desert. Years later she credits me with saving her life. She was stoned out of her mind.'

It was a weird existence at Taos, then probably the last vestige of the sixties left on the planet. 'Actually Dennis was the perfect host for you to experience the sixties with,' says Carson. 'It was like the final scenes of *Withnail and I* where they're trying to count down the end of the sixties but they really can't.'

Taos had been a strange place anyway to build a fortress of hippie power. The local populace largely resented them moving in, these strange people dressed in flower beads talking bollocks. It was rather a rough town, too, the last place you'd want to huddle round a campfire with guitars singing 'Mr Tambourine Man'. It was so enclosed an environment that when someone was shot, which happened rather too frequently for comfort's sake, you knew the person who'd been shot, and you knew the guy who'd done it and why he'd done it.

When Dennis first came out to Taos to set up his commune, 'it was bad, man. Suddenly there was me, this movie freak and all these hippies around, and the locals didn't dig it.' Many times when Dennis and others walked the streets cars would pull up with guys yelling from the windows, 'Hey, we're gonna rape your wife and your sister!' Dennis claimed that groups would go hitch-hiking in the mountains and get the crap beaten out of them by high-school kids while the cops watched. Rape was going on, too. Finally, one night Dennis said, fuck it, and got a gun. Walking in the street, he and his younger brother David were stopped and hassled by some local kids. 'OK, everybody up against the wall,' yelled Dennis, brandishing his gun. 'I'd seen too many John Wayne movies.' There and then he made a citizen's arrest and held them all at gunpoint until the cops arrived. When they did they were accompanied by a large mob, 'something like 150 people wanting to hang our asses. It looked like a scene out of *Viva Zapata* – pitchforks, machetes, the works.'

Naturally the police arrested Dennis and his brother rather than the baying crowd. They posted bail and were let out through a side door of the local jail, where sixty locals still held vigil. Some guys told Dennis to his face, 'We're going to kill you.' When Dennis pointed out this threat to the police they told him to shut up.

OK, thought Dennis, this is war. He made calls to some stunt buddies of his back in Hollywood. 'Look, I need your help because the police sure aren't gonna help me.' Then he and David visited a local sporting-goods store and bought every fucking gun in the place. 'Back at the house we set up machine-gun nests,' said Dennis. 'And rifles on the rooftops – good fields of fire.' It was like the Alamo. Kit Carson recalls, 'It got to the point where Dennis was carrying a loaded gun all the time. That was kind of interesting. In the house he'd be looking out the windows with a gun like it was a fort. The town was a little bit afraid of Dennis, actually; that was good, he liked that.'

Next Dennis and David, with guns hidden under their ponchos à la Sergio Leone, visited the high school and gatecrashed their assembly. Dennis bounded up onto the stage. 'Look,' he told the kids, 'I'm here and here I'm going to stay. What's more, there are more freaks coming in over the next few months, and though they may have long hair, they are not the love generation. They're back from Vietnam, and they're hard dudes. They will have weapons – like these.' With that Dennis and David whipped open their ponchos to reveal a mini arsenal. 'Macho is macho,' Dennis continued, 'and if this keeps up, somebody is going to get hurt around here. Just because these hippies are dropping acid, that doesn't give you the right to rape their women and cut their balls off.' According to Dennis, 'They listened, and they finally got the message.'

The locals pretty much left Dennis and co. alone after that. The authorities, however, still viewed him with suspicion. One time he was arrested by police in the main plaza of Taos for possession of a loaded .357 Magnum revolver.

Hey, stealing's a business, not a crusade.

After *McCabe*, Warren Beatty swapped Julie for the endearingly kooky Goldie Hawn. They made for a fun team in crime drama *Dollars* (aka *The Heist*, 1971), but the movie itself was poor, certainly not worth dying for, as Warren so very nearly did. Filming on some train tracks, Warren stumbled into the path of an onrushing locomotive. The crew were set up some distance away and could only look on in horror as an injured and groggy Warren staggered up, saw the train approaching at some speed and somehow summoned up the strength to hurl himself out of the way.

Missing Julie, Warren flew from the location in Germany to London every weekend to see her. Such strong attachment, however, didn't deter him from seducing Goldie, who at the time was in an 'open' marriage to director Gus Trikonis, the 'open' part of it being entirely Gus's idea. Gus was around the *Dollars* set quite a bit, but the moment he turned his back Warren and Goldie slipped into his trailer to make out.

With *Dollars*, Warren's choice of material was once again seriously affecting his career. He continued to play a blinder, however, when it came to turning down hit movies. Now it was the turn of *The Sting* to pass like sand through his fingers. He said he didn't want to do it because he kept dozing off while reading the script. *The Godfather*, too, was declined. To be fair to Warren, he'd no clue that these movies were destined for greatness, and during this period he was turning down something like seventy-five scripts a year.

Barbra Streisand was after him to co-star with her in *The Way We Were*. He didn't fancy it, though he definitely fancied her and happily succumbed when Babs, refusing to take no for an answer, indulged in a brief fling, perhaps hoping that as his lover she could change his mind. Warren did what he did best: fucked, wavered and waffled. Finally fed up, Barbra turned to Redford, who, according to director Sydney Pollock, found making the movie 'Like doing overtime at Dachau.'

Warren continued, in the words of Natalie Wood, 'to go through women on an industrial scale. Although he does it with great charm.' At one Hollywood party an actress sat in a deserted screening room watching a movie. Suddenly Warren walked in with a giggling girl and despite the acres of empty seats sat down right in front of her and proceeded to noisily make out, all the while winking at the actress over his date's shoulder, as if to say, 'How am I doing?'

But even Warren had the odd failure. At another party he met Kim Novak and, mistaking her natural exuberance for sexual interest, asked if he could go home with her. He ended up pounding on her bedroom door even after she bolted it against him.

Actress Lee Grant, who'd appear with Warren in *Shampoo*, assessed that his conquest success rate was about fifty–fifty. Those he couldn't conquer didn't want to be part of a crowd – one of Warren's girls. 'But the Peter Pan quality in Warren is very attractive to some,' she told *Time* in 1978. 'He teaches them to fly, and they have extraordinary experiences with him. Then they grow up and go on, and he keeps flying. Like Peter Pan, he always comes back to another little girl who's ready to fly off with him to Never Never Land.'

Politics was back in his life, too. In spite of the debacle over Hubert Humphrey, Warren joined another political bandwagon, this time for George McGovern, who was seeking the 1972 Democratic presidential nomination. As proof that this was a man he believed in, Warren took a whole year out of his movie schedule to travel across the country drumming up support, personally raising $2m. Warren's fundraising prowess was extraordinary. Democratic pollster and future producer of TV's *The West Wing* Patrick Caddell relates the occasion he witnessed Warren forcefully persuade a rich businessman to contribute to the McGovern fund. The man happily wrote a cheque for $50,000. According to Caddell, Warren berated the guy. 'I don't want your fifty thousand. People in your position give a hundred thousand.' Embarrassed, the businessman swiftly wrote another cheque for $50,000.

At the 1972 Democratic convention in Miami there was a young campaign worker for Senator McGovern whose job it was to garner dissenting voters. He zeroed in on this 19-year-old woman from his own home state of Arkansas and was determined to get her vote. She refused. 'Well is there any way in the world I can convince you to vote with us?' She said, 'Yeah, if you get Warren Beatty to walk on the beach with me.'

By pure chance thirty minutes later he got into an elevator and there was Warren. He explained the deal and Warren said, 'Sure I'll do it.' Later that afternoon Warren walked a hundred yards on the beach – that woman voted for the Democrats on every single amendment. Subsequently she became a school teacher and was always a keen supporter of the young campaigner. In 2008 he was in southern Missouri and there she was. 'I can't believe you're still here after all these years,' he said. Smiling she replied, 'I'm still paying off the beach walk.' The young impressionable campaign worker was Bill Clinton.

Taking a much more hands-on role in this campaign, becoming a strategist in such fields as public relations and the media, McGovern found Warren's ideas and advice both shrewd and valuable. 'He has a political maturity astounding in someone so inexperienced.' When he spoke at a rally and was roundly booed, Warren realised the public weren't interested in listening to film stars pontificate so wielded his power and influence behind the scenes, practically inventing the political fundraising concert. Pulling in favours, he managed to get Barbra Streisand and Simon and Garfunkel on stage, with the likes of Paul Newman, Raquel Welch, Dustin Hoffman, Goldie Hawn and Jack acting as ushers.

Inevitably, Warren's choice for president ended up losing to Nixon, who was returned to office with a landslide victory for a second term, where the Watergate scandal was waiting for him. Some colleagues even urged Warren to run for the US Senate, but that kind of public service required supreme selflessness, time and energy, none of which Warren could afford. He didn't like the mud-slinging that went on in politics either. Sure, that happened in his own profession, too, but 'I'm used to those showbiz interviewers who not only ask me who I slept with last night but in what position. In politics it's much tougher than that.' No, the more he thought of a political career, the harder the task seemed. He already knew friends were getting more than a bit tired of his politicking. Even Jack, who'd placed a halo above Warren's head, said that on certain subjects he could 'bore the shit out of me'. Jack's never been much of a political animal, preferring to stay at home and drag on a spliff rather than join an anti-war demo, shag a woman rather than campaign for some senator. For him celebrities and politics don't mix.

And what of Julie? Maybe as a way of compensating for the time he'd spent away, the subject of marriage was raised again, but the same old problems were still there.

Such statements as 'monogamy requires genius' and 'I'm not going to make the same mistake once' only reinforced what Julie had known all along: Warren was best not as a husband, but as a lover, and a short-term one at that. He was seeing other women, of course, like the future Mrs Richard Pryor, Jennifer Lee, who at the time was quite content to be part of the Beatty harem. 'The last stop before the ball and chain main squeeze, which is what Julie is.' Jennifer was also enjoying affairs with Ryan O'Neal and Art Garfunkel. One time Warren and Garfunkel were both staying at the same hotel in New York. Jennifer spent part of the evening with Garfunkel, then after a modest interval popped upstairs for part two with Warren, knocking on his door saying, 'Just happened to be in the neighbourhood.'

There was also a brief fling with Carly Simon, which, according to the singer, was not especially profound. 'I never took him seriously. He was great fun and very bright. But noooo . . . as a boyfriend.' It did, however, result in one of the great musical mysteries when Carly recorded the hit single 'You're So Vain' and refused to divulge exactly who it was about. Most people assumed it was Warren, as indeed did he, calling her up and saying thanks. 'You'd gone with him?' enquired one reporter. 'Hasn't everybody?' Carly replied.

While all this was carrying on Julie continued to love Warren deeply, and to be fair it was genuinely reciprocated. Warren reportedly proposed to her on more than one occasion but she always sensibly backed off, still suspecting that he could never be faithful. 'You can't just go swanning off with everyone who attracts you,' she said. 'It's greedy and selfish. It sounds great to do whatever you want. But it never works out in real life – only in the movies.'

It was a phone call that ended it, from Julie. Warren was alone at his suite in the Beverly Wilshire, a place that had come to almost symbolise his rootlessness. Although they remained friends, the emotional loss was crippling. Simon Relph, a producer on *Reds*, said the break-up with Julie was 'the only one that Warren still speaks of with regret'. His parents were upset too when Julie left; of all their son's girlfriends she'd been their favourite. 'I can't think of anyone I'd rather he married,' Ira Beatty said at the time. 'But I wonder if Warren will ever settle down. He's a nomad, like Shirley.'

In a bid to stave off the chill of loneliness Warren partied and cruised around with Polanski, but more specifically now with Jack. They had become the new deadly duo. In her autobiography Faye Dunaway wrote that she was wary of hanging out with either star. 'Jack was bemused that he and Warren, at different points in their lives, often ended up with the same woman. It didn't make him happy.'

It was ironic that here was Warren, one of the biggest sex symbols in the world, loved by millions of strangers, but by no one individual, in the truest sense. Julie, like Leslie Caron, had so far been his only hope for a meaningful and continuing relationship. With Julie now out of his life he'd come to realise, perhaps for the first time, that his hedonistic lifestyle had left him in an emotional vacuum. 'I have led a very indulgent life,' he admitted. 'Almost indescribably indulgent.'

He was about to bring a little bit of that hedonism to life on the screen in one of his most famous films.

I am the motherfucking shore patrol, motherfucker.

Jack Nicholson's friendship with Henry Jaglom went back further than their editing duties on *Easy Rider*. They used to hang out together in all-night restaurants on Sunset Strip, spending hours 'dreaming our movie dreams. Jack was an extraordinarily bright, funny and charismatic guy from the moment I met him. He and I were the two in the crowd who were most focused on becoming directors.'

Both had long since agreed that they'd act in each other's first film as a director. Jack beat Jaglom to the gun with *Drive, He Said*, in which Jaglom appeared. 'Now, a year later, when I directed my first film, *A Safe Place*, in 1971, Jack returned the favour – in spades. I no longer could afford to use him in my film as he had become a gigantic star, much to everyone's amazement. And yet, fulfilling our agreement, he made it possible for me to have him act in my first effort as a director by waiving the million-dollar fee he was entitled to and doing the part for a new colour TV set of his choice.'

Jaglom's directorial debut, a non-narrative story of the emotional vulnerabilities of a young girl, received a heated reception at the New York Film Festival. People screamed at it, praised it, condemned it and several stormed out. All of which surprised Jaglom as several European filmmakers had been working along the same lines and greeted warmly for their films. 'Jack suggested immediately one of the canniest ideas I have ever heard,' recalls Jaglom. 'He said we should pull the film, dub it in French, put English subtitles on it and change my then unknown name to Henri Jaglom. He insisted that it would be a huge hit if we did that. It was a commercial disaster of unbelievable proportions at the time.'

Jack was still hitched up with Michelle Phillips when he agreed to make Bob Rafelson's *The King of Marvin Gardens* (1972), playing a late-night radio DJ. Michelle visited the Atlantic City locations and her strong personality was sometimes overpowering. If she didn't get her way she tended to explode, calling Jack a stupid Irish Mick in front of everybody. It was an odd relationship: half the time she had him wrapped round her finger, the rest of the time it was a standoff. She wanted to rent a beachfront house; Jack preferred dossing in hotels. She left in a strop and Jack went back to the guys and hanging out with groupies. 'The minute she was gone,' said one crew member, 'he had his little entourage.' He and co-star Bruce Dern also hung out a lot. When actress Ellen Burstyn celebrated her birthday both of them and Rafelson surprised her with a serenade in the nude.

Marriage may never have been on the cards for Jack and Michelle, which is not surprising since they never actually lived together. At the time married life didn't appeal to either of them. 'I don't have a marriage policy,' was Jack's flippant response to matrimonial press enquires, 'thinking that was the more intelligent approach to life'. The inevitable did eventually transpire, and after two years the couple drifted apart. Michelle later revealed that it was Jack's jealousy and possessiveness that drove her away. 'He was always peering in the windows to see what I was up to.' She also objected to his continuing habit of sleeping around and hanging out in nightclubs until all hours, coming home stoned and drunk. Jack's house was party central and not for nothing did *Rolling Stone* magazine nickname him the 'Great Seducer'.

One guest at a party in New York during this period recalled seeing Jack reclining fully clothed on a bed practically smothered in women, all horny as hell. Jack just lay there with a big grin on his face. 'I think he likes women more than any man I've ever known,' Cher said once. 'I mean he *really* likes them.'

Career-wise, Jack was finding the kind of roles that perfectly suited his personality and screen image, that of a wisecracking anti-establishment figure, tough on the outside but soft and vulnerable beneath, a key to many future Jack characters. At a party Billy Wilder stood talking with Jack and said to him, 'You know, what the public likes about your characters is that you're always playing the guy who has this tremendous ability at any given moment to say, "Why don't you go fuck yourself?" And that's what people love because they can't do that.' One of the astonishing things about Jack's career is how long he's managed to be both a subversive and an institution.

The Last Detail (1973) had Jack as a naval officer escorting a young offender to prison who gives him one final wild night of freedom. It almost never got made because of the avalanche of swearing in Robert Towne's screenplay. At one studio meeting Towne recalled how an executive asked, 'Bob, wouldn't twenty motherfuckers be more effective than forty motherfuckers?' Towne thought it over then said, 'No they wouldn't.' This was how sailors talked, that was the whole goddamn point, and since movies were now supposedly more frank and adult in their outlook at portraying 'real' life, he wasn't prepared to back down. Jack stood firm behind him. In the end the studio caved in.

Other problems quickly surfaced, like when their director Hal Ashby, after scouting locations in Canada, was busted in the airport for possession of marijuana. Looking as he did – rose-tinted glasses, full beard, sandals and love beads – he might as well have walked around with a neon sign saying 'dope-head here'. Studio lawyers got him out of jail and flew him back to LA, with Ashby cursing the whole flight, 'Motherfucking customs inspectors.'

We are all alone until we look in the asshole of death.

Many of the great French actors had turned it down, Delon, Jean-Louis Trintignant; Belmondo called it a porno script. Nobody wanted to star in *Last Tango in Paris* (1972). Out of desperation, Bernardo Bertolucci contacted Marlon Brando and they arranged a meeting. 'For the first fifteen minutes he didn't say a word,' the director recalled. 'He only looked at me.' Bertolucci began explaining the story and the character he wanted Brando to play, that of Paul, an American expat living in Paris whose wife has committed suicide. By chance he meets a young woman in an empty apartment up for rent and they begin a short and ultimately doomed sadomasochistic affair. Marlon listened carefully and then said yes right away, without asking to read the script. Marlon later confessed to never really understanding either what the film was about or its message. 'Bertolucci went around telling everybody the movie was about the reincarnation of my prick,' said Marlon. 'Now what the fuck does that mean?'

It's the sex scenes that everybody remembers about *Last Tango in Paris*. Maria Schneider was nineteen years old when she was chosen over 200 actresses to play opposite Brando. She got the part of Jeanne because when she was asked to remove her clothes at the audition she did so with no fuss whatsoever. 'She was a little Lolita,' said Bertolucci. 'Only more perverse.' She later claimed that the infamous 'butter scene', where Paul uses the dairy product as an aid to anal intercourse, was not in the script and improvised at the last minute by Brando. Just before Bertolucci called action, Marlon told Maria not to worry, that it was only a movie, but during the scene she admitted to crying real tears. 'I felt humiliated and, to be honest, I felt a little raped, both by Marlon and by Bertolucci.' Luckily there was just the one take.

Actually, if Bertolucci had got his way the sex scenes would have been even more outrageous; he wanted his two actors to fuck for real. Marlon quite rightly refused. 'I told him, if that happens, our sex organs become the centrepiece of the film.' Bertolucci didn't agree but lost the argument. Marlon was against performing full frontal nude scenes anyway because 'My penis shrank to the size of a peanut on set.'

For *Tango* Bertolucci wanted Marlon to explore and experiment on celluloid as never before, to improvise heavily and act purely by instinct. It was a challenge Marlon relished, to play a role so completely derived from within himself, and as a result he gives his most personal and devastating screen performance. But ultimately he viewed it as a violation of his privacy, pulling out painful memories from his past, particularly his on-screen monologues about an unhappy childhood and remote parents. 'My father was a drunk, tough, whore-fucker,' he says at one point. During another scene Marlon had to explode emotionally. Suddenly he hit the wall so hard with his fist Bertolucci was convinced he'd broken his hand.

Very quickly the film earned a reputation as the most controversial movie ever made, receiving an instant ban in Italy. Obscenity charges were filed in the Italian courts against Bertolucci, Brando and Schneider, and although they were all ultimately acquitted Bertolucci lost his civil rights (including his right to vote) for five years and was given a four-month suspended prison sentence: a bit extreme for the nation that gave the world fascism.

A cause célèbre, *Tango* created a sensation wherever it was shown, in spite of one critic calling it a piece of 'talented debauchery that often makes you want to vomit'. In America it was slapped with an adults-only rating, usually the kiss of death for a film. For *Tango*, however, it merely guaranteed a media frenzy and queues round the block. In Britain the sodomy sequence was cut, presumably so as not to encourage public schoolboys.

The success of *Tango*, coming as it did right after *The Godfather*, put Marlon back in the top ten of box office stars and he was once again heralded as the greatest actor of his generation, a Lazarus-like comeback that put him on the cover of *Time* magazine. It seemed almost churlish of him, then, to take a three-year sabbatical from movies. Or was it something deeper? Marlon confessed to Bertolucci that he'd never suffered so much during the making of a picture and had decided never again to destroy himself emotionally on camera. In subsequent roles Brando gave up trying to experience the emotions of his characters, as he'd always done before, and simply played the part in a technical way. As he said, 'I decided to make my living in a way that was less devastating emotionally.'

In a distressed state, Marlon sought refuge on his Tahitian island with his kids. He also spent a lot of time campaigning for the American Indian

Movement, an organisation he'd helped found and to which he was the largest financial donor, taking a more radical stance than he had with any other political group. He appeared on TV declaring that he would give his house on Mulholland Drive to the Indians. Neighbour Jack was at home watching and almost collapsed. 'Jeez, what's the sonovabitch doing now? He's crazy.'

Marlon also posted bail for some of the Indian leaders held for violent crimes, and helped others avoid arrest. He took part in ancient tribal ceremonies, occasions that could move him to tears, and was one of the few white men to be so honoured. His involvement in the Indian cause wasn't universally welcomed by those he was trying to help; some dismissed him as a publicity seeker, which couldn't have been further from the truth. There were rumours that at one demonstration some tribe members had put a horse's head in his sleeping bag.

Brando's semi-reclusive semi-retirement was shattered when his family life once again erupted into the tabloids. He'd just finished *Tango* when news reached him that his ex-wife had spirited their son away to Mexico, an action that he interpreted as kidnapping. Immediately Marlon hired a detective to carry out a search for Christian, finding him in a hippie commune in California, the leader of which admitted that Anna Kashfi had promised them money if they'd hide the boy.

Over the years, Kashfi had become a shadow of her former self. Drink and drugs had taken their toll and she was now clinically paranoid, suffering from epileptic fits and terrible mood swings. Fearful for his son's welfare, Marlon fought for years to claim sole custody of Christian, telling friends he believed he might be 'destroyed by his mother's weird-ness'. Like most family squabbles there were two sides to the story, Kashfi often claimed that Marlon was hardly the perfect parent, that when staying with him Christian was exposed to his numerous lovers and rapidly expanding family. Christian himself called the Brando clan 'weird and spaced out. I'd sit down at the table some nights and there would always be some new addition, and I'd say, "Who are you?"' Christian also liked to tell the story of the time when, as a kid swimming in a lagoon in Tahiti, a shark swam by and Marlon just shouted 'motherfucker' and socked the beast on the nose.

Marlon was the best father he knew how to be, though admittedly this involved alternating between spoiling, ignoring and bullying his kids. 'The older he gets,' said his make-up man Phil Rhodes, 'the more Marlon resembles his father in terms of trying to control and dominate.' Shuttled between warring parents, sometimes offloaded on friends and relatives or dumped in boarding school, Christian had everything he needed except love and a sense of where he truly belonged. Little wonder he became disorientated, confused, and impossible to handle as a teenager, drinking and taking drugs. The consequences would be dire.

I ate cow shit one time, not too bad if you're hungry. Not hungry? Don't eat cow shit.

The communal idealism of Taos was heading for freefall. Dennis Hopper would struggle downstairs in the morning to get something out of the icebox and there'd be thirty people there he'd never seen before. He'd say, 'Where's the orange juice?' and they'd say, 'Who are you?'

Dennis made the odd debilitating foray to Hollywood to look for work. He'd try to be on his best behaviour, play their game, suck up to the bigwigs, but, sure enough, he'd soon explode. At parties he'd nail producers to the wall and demand to know, 'Why am I not directing? Why am I not acting?' The answer was pretty obvious. Nobody wanted to deal with a maniac. 'I got nothing, man,' he'd tell reporters. 'I'm a failure. I'm out on the street again.'

Dennis admits that his biggest mistake after *The Last Movie* was saying 'fuck you' to Hollywood and exiling himself in Taos, waiting and hoping for someone to come along with an amazing job offer. James Frawley, a young filmmaker, was one of the few people willing to take a chance on Dennis, casting him as the lead in *Kid Blue* (1973), a wry and interesting western that was shot in New Mexico. 'Dennis came down to the location not in the best of moods,' Frawley recalls. 'He was still depressed about the fate of *The Last Movie* but totally dedicated about doing the best job he could. I think he used the work to get rid of a lot of those negative feelings.'

Frawley was more than aware of Dennis's reputation for being difficult, but saw this as being primarily because he was such a political outlaw, an outsider that resented authority. 'When Dennis made *Easy Rider* he immediately became an iconic political figure for the radical left. He had real political power.' This was clearly demonstrated when Frawley and Hopper took off for a few days' holiday in Mexico City after wrapping *Kid Blue*. They were sitting at a table in one of the finest restaurants in the city when a guy came over and said, 'Mr Hopper, Mr Frawley, we know you've just finished your picture and we wanted to know how long you intend to stay in Mexico.' Dennis and Frawley looked blankly at each other. 'Why? Who are you?' The man presented his badge to them; he was the head of the secret service and the Mexican president's brother. 'They were keeping an eye on Dennis,' says Frawley. The man continued. 'You see those two guys over in the corner? They will be following you wherever you go in Mexico. And if you set foot on a campus or speak at a rally you'll be immediately arrested.' It was a stark warning. 'There was a lot of unrest at that time in Mexico, especially with the students,' says Frawley. 'But I was kind of amazed that this myth I was sitting with was not so mythological but actually somebody that the authorities were after or watching.'

Famously, Dennis was one of the most paranoid individuals on earth at the time, seeing conspiracies round every corner. 'It's true, he would tend to be paranoid,' says Frawley. 'There was a rumour that he thought John Wayne was out to get him. But then suddenly something like this happened, which was real, and you go, wait a minute this paranoia has a basis in reality. Dennis was a real political figure.' And an actor that Frawley believes was unjustly neglected. 'You were communicating with somebody who had a fertile mind and great passion, someone full of surprises. That was part of the joy of working with Dennis, he never did two takes exactly the same. It was lightning in a bottle; it was a pleasure to have been the bottle for a while.'

Back in Taos, Dennis's excessive consumption of alcohol and drugs, now in deadly combination with an interest in mysticism and local Indian spiritualism, was leading to hallucinations, and not always pleasant ones. He swore he saw the spirit of D. H. Lawrence wandering around the courtyard. One regular visitor recalled seeing Dennis in a paranoid state, utterly confused. Friends were worried he might lose his mind completely.

More than most, Dennis was suffering from the dying embers of the sixties and its repercussions. When his generation started using drugs it was all going to be wonderful, everyone was going to hold hands, stop the Vietnam War and find God. It wasn't the sixties that fucked Dennis up, it was the hangover into the seventies. The drugs that were free suddenly weren't free any more. 'We ended up at the drug dealer's door, man, carrying guns and in total madness.' Grass and LSD had given way to heroin and cocaine. Everybody was addicted and the party was over when people like Hendrix, Joplin and Morrison started dying. They weren't on a suicide trip; they just took too much shit. Looking back from the safety of today, Dennis knows he was lucky to get out alive. 'I should be dead or a serial killer.'

Then salvation arrived in the shapely figure of actress Daria Halprin, who'd been Antonioni's leading lady in *Zabriskie Point*. There was instant attraction and she and Dennis married in 1972. Soon Daria gave birth to a daughter and came to accept that motherhood and marriage had more or less put an end to her acting career; her place was by his side at all times. If she was to act again it would be in one of Dennis's movies, whatever and whenever that might be. But decent work – any work, really – was not forthcoming, even though Dennis had filled his Taos home with state-of-the-art editing facilities. 'They should be bringing me movies,' he ranted to one reporter. 'I mean, I'm, you know, a genius.'

Wild, too, and reports of Dennis's eccentric behaviour filtered back to Hollywood. Even Daria didn't quite know what to make of him sometimes, particularly his mood swings and his fascination with guns. He'd go out and shoot a pig with his pistol, just for the hell of it.

Face it, they know we're always trying to nail 'em and they don't like it.

Shampoo (1975) started life back in 1968, the height of the sexual revolution, as a cautionary tale for people like Warren Beatty who slept around too much. 'I wanted to explore contemporary sexuality through the medium of a Don Juan,' he said. According to Warren, a Don Juan doesn't get that way because he's a misogynist, impotent, or has a desire to degrade women; neither is he a latent homosexual who seduces so many women to conceal the fact that he really wants to seduce men. No, said Warren, 'He just wants to fuck because he likes to fuck.'

Screenwriter Robert Towne was hired to work on a story about a randy hairdresser who discovers porking everyone under the hairdryer is actually rather an unsatisfying way to approach middle age – a sort of *Alfie* with curlers, then. Warren revealed that *Shampoo* was his attempt to 'close out the promiscuous phase' in his life. It didn't work. He was shamelessly on his way to becoming the world's oldest adolescent, the only man alive Hugh Hefner envied.

Beatty liked Towne's finished script but suggested the female characters needed bolstering. Towne didn't agree and it got nasty. 'Although I don't know anybody who's a bigger prick,' said Towne about Warren, 'there's no one I love and admire more.' The relationship between Warren and Towne was one of the closest and most interesting in Hollywood. When producer Gerald Ayres decided to live an openly gay lifestyle it was Towne who warned him that his reputation might suffer. Ayres was furious, knowing how intimate he and Warren were, 'twisted together like a knot'. He told Towne, 'Listen, you and Warren squabble on the phone every day like a couple of lovers, go all over the world fucking the same women in the same room. If you two guys aren't lovers, you're the next thing to it.' Towne refused to speak to Ayres for years.

They ran hot and cold, Warren's feelings for Towne, and vice versa. After the impasse over the *Shampoo* script the atmosphere was definitely chilly and resulted in the project's cancellation and both men not speaking for a few years. But a thaw eventually set in and Towne returned to have another bash at it. *Shampoo* gradually came back to life. Warren, who'd installed himself as producer, pumped a million dollars of his own money into pre-production, assembling a top-notch cast including a couple of ex-girlfriends in Julie Christie and Goldie Hawn. The autobiographical nature of the project was now unavoidable. Warren said he 'didn't mind the suggestion of parallels too much'. He also hired the then unknown seventeen-year-old Carrie Fisher to play a wild Beverly Hills brat, not a huge stretch at the time, providing her with some of the film's choicest lines, such as 'Wanna fuck?' Years later Carrie admitted to *Rolling Stone* that Beatty unsuccessfully propositioned her.

Because of the personal nature of the story, Warren thought *Shampoo* was the perfect vehicle to launch his directorial career, but in the end lacked the confidence so hired Hal Ashby instead. For a week Warren, Ashby and Towne shut themselves away to get the script finished, working from nine in the morning till eleven at night. Creative differences still remained, however, between Warren and Towne. The writer always envisaged *Shampoo* as a Bergman-type film about relationships while Warren was keen to weave a political subtext into the narrative, a statement about the times. Towne was vehemently opposed to Warren's vision. 'He told me to do this and that,' said the writer, 'and we usually fought about it, and sometimes he really fucked things up.' Their 'discussions' became more and more fierce. 'You cunt!' Towne was sometimes obliged to say to Warren. 'You're just being a cunt. That's more cunt stuff.'

When filming began, hostilities broke out between Warren and Ashby. There was only ever going to be one winner: as producer Warren had hired his cronies in key positions and they'd tell Ashby what to do. According to cinematographer Haskell Wexler, a visitor to the set, 'Warren chewed Hal up and spit him out. He was like an office boy on that set.' Warren was able to seize creative control because Ashby hated confrontation of any kind, preferring to brood in a corner, anger and frustration squirming inside him. 'I can't take it any more,' he told production designer Richard Sylbert. Well, he obviously could, because he finished the film, but it was a steep learning curve, and Ashby never lost control on one of his sets again, telling colleagues who stepped out of line, 'Fuck you, this is what I'm gonna do; if you don't like it, stick it in your ear.'

Warren also put Julie through the mincer on at least one occasion, keeping her waiting until the middle of the night to shoot and then making her endure thirty-eight takes. They do share one memorable scene. At a fundraising event she is seated between Warren and a fat-cat Republican. 'I can get you anything you'd like,' says the oily politico. Julie ponders the offer. 'Well, first of all,' she says, looking at Warren. 'I'd like to suck his cock.' It was the most brazenly sexual line ever heard in mainstream American cinema and caused quite a stir. When the studio saw it they were so shocked they demanded it be removed. Warren refused.

According to friends, Julie was weighing up the pros and cons of maybe getting back with Warren. During filming they stayed at the Beverly Wilshire, but on different floors. Warren seemed more interested in getting into the sack with current Miss World, twenty-year-old American Marjorie Wallace. One colleague said this of Warren: 'He was afraid of commitment. This is a man who can only have an intimate relationship in a horizontal position. He thinks a hard-on makes for personal growth. He just wasn't ready for Julie.'

On *Shampoo* Warren was working himself into the ground, as producer taking all the decisions, working round the clock, sleeping sometimes in his dressing room. But far from the pressure eating away at him, he thrived on it. Friend Buck Henry thought him, 'psychotic' about the possibility of overlooking anything, adding, 'His attention to detail is maniacal. Easygoing is not a quality he has.'

Tony Bill, a former actor, now producer (with *The Sting* to his credit), was on the film for some five weeks and found Warren to be an extremely collaborative filmmaker. 'He was a total professional, always talking with the director or the cameraman or the writer; Robert Towne was on the set a lot. So it was very collaborative. And despite being the star, Warren was very much one of the guys, not at all unapproachable or overly serious.'

Shampoo turned out to be a huge hit but critics complained that the performance was easy for Warren; after all, he was playing himself, wasn't he? One magazine writer accused the star of exploiting his super-stud reputation. 'I sent his wife a letter offering to do her hair,' said Warren.

At the film's premiere at the USA Film Festival celebrity journalist Don Aly, who has no hesitation in naming Warren Beatty the 'stud-horse' to beat them all, observed the great man in 'action' at first hand. Warren was attending a press conference. 'I watched him sitting on stage, supposedly intently listening to questions. His eyes moved from row to row, but he was not looking at the folks asking questions. He was checking out the broads sitting there in their tempting low-cut frocks and new short skirts.'

The answers he gave were pap, almost rehearsed, then his attention was gripped by a pretty buxom blonde who looked like a young Jayne Mansfield and they got talking. 'You didn't have to hear what he said to understand what was happening,' says Aly. 'If you spotted Warren tossing his hotel keys in the lap of the girl with the big gorbanzas, then you pretty much understood what was coming down.'

When the press conference closed Aly followed the blonde out into the street, where she hailed a cab for Beatty's hotel. He asked if he might share the ride and split the fare. 'She seemed happy to do that, probably a little embarrassed that she was on her way to a little sex session with the great cinema lover!' Aly knew that Warren was now dating Michelle Phillips and that she'd accompanied him to the festival, but when he hadn't seen her at the press conference he'd assumed that Warren had left her behind in the hotel, as was his custom. 'That, of course, left him free to womanise with whomever he wanted and make arrangements for secret meetings later. Frankly, I knew what Beatty had on his mind. And since I wasn't privy to the exact relationship he had with Michelle, I didn't know if they played these little ménage-à-trois games frequently or not.'

After the blonde made her way up to Warren's room Aly decided to wait in the lobby to see what would happen, thinking it might make an amusing aside in his showbiz column. 'And as it turned out, it did. Just a few minutes later the busty blonde stepped off the elevator and deftly deposited Warren's key down a mail chute.' Aly got talking to her again and she explained what had happened in Warren's room. 'I don't know who that girl was up there,' she said, rather frustrated. 'I started to leave; I thought I had the wrong room.' Aly nodded sympathetically, and grinned.

Back home, preparing for the premiere that night of *Shampoo*, Aly called a friend, actress Morgan Fairchild, 'whom I know Warren put the hustle on on three different occasions. She turned him down each time, making her one of probably few women in Hollywood who had the gumption to say no.' They'd first met when Morgan, a sixteen-year-old high-school student from Dallas, worked as an extra on *Bonnie and Clyde*. Arriving for her first day on location in Texas, Morgan was looking for the film crew when she noticed this guy shuffling toward her. 'Is this the way to the set?' she asked. The guy looked up, 'Well, uh, yeah, yeah, the uh, it's down that way,' he said. 'And I thought, my God, that's the most beautiful man I've ever seen in my life,' Morgan recalled. 'And of course it was Warren. He just glowed.'

Aly told Morgan what happened with the blonde and that he'd also tried to get an interview with Warren but had been brushed off. 'Why, that skunk!' she exclaimed. 'Tell you what we'll do. I'll call my sister and invite her to the premiere. When you walk into the theatre lobby with the two of us on your arms, Warren will be all over you in a New York minute. Don't worry about a thing. We're gonna have a ball.'

That's exactly what Aly did, and when Warren saw them he made a beeline across the lobby and sequestered them in a corner. 'Hey, baby cakes,' he commented. 'What's shaking, baby cakes?' The three of them just looked at one another and laughed and completely ignored Warren, walking right past him to their reserved seats.

Once the movie was over, Aly spotted Warren heading for the men's room and followed him in. Standing side by side at the urinals Aly said, 'Hey, guy, enjoyed the movie. Oh, by the way, I'll give you Morgan's phone number if you'll give me a good quote.' Warren shot Aly the old evil eye, zipped up his pants and prepared to leave. Then he suddenly stopped and turned round. 'What's the number?' he asked. Aly wrote down the number of an escort service and gave it to him. 'Warren gave me a quote, but I don't usually repeat it in print or in mixed company. I never saw Beatty again and I'm glad. I think maybe he got the message. What a jerk.'

Ever since the LA Playboy Club opened on Sunset Strip in the mid-sixties Warren had taken good care to ingratiate himself with Hugh Hefner and his bunnies. More so at Hefner's LA mansion, which during the seventies became one of *the* celebrity hang-outs. Jack was a regular visitor too, especially on Friday nights, when Hefner threw lavish dinner parties. One day Warren was ambling along with a bunny girl on each arm when he met Hef, who enquired, 'Have you been robbing the hutch again, Warren?'

He also continued to cruise Sunset Boulevard with Jack, picking up girls. *Time* magazine reported that 'an occasional recreation of [Jack Nicholson] and Warren Beatty's is riding around town, skunk spotting on the street.' The *New York Times* added that Jack 'still sophomorically goes on random girl-hunts in a car with his friend Warren Beatty'.

Early on in the relationship between these two movie titans there developed an unofficial competition about who could score with the most voluptuous beauties; it was an ongoing challenge. Some wondered how much of their reputation as cocks men was pure hype. Bruce Dern said, 'Jack brags about a lot more pussy than he's ever gotten. I'd say if you cut half of his pussy in half, you'd have it about right, and still he probably gets more than anybody around. He and Beatty have contests about it.'

Warren and Jack were now so inseparable that it seemed only a matter of time before someone put them in a movie together. They were the dream team, but the film they chose turned out to be a complete nightmare. It was called *The Fortune* (1975), a period screwball comedy, and Warren breezed into the boardroom at Columbia and got Jack his first mega-buck deal, $1.5m, the same amount he demanded and received for himself. Shell-shocked, one executive commented, 'I don't wish on my worst enemy negotiations with that man.'

In business Warren had proved himself a tough operator, someone who refused to make commitments and negotiated tirelessly to get his fees up. Warren wasn't just smart and ruthless but also devastatingly charming: a dangerous combination. He got people to do what he wanted. He was also the most tuned-in celebrity in Hollywood. 'Warren talked to everybody in town all the time, and always knew what was happening,' recalled super agent Freddie Fields, whose clients included Newman, McQueen and Hoffman. 'He knew about weddings before people got married, and about divorces before couples broke up. He knew who'd get a picture before they knew. He knew release dates and grosses. He'd talk to Jack Warner, Harry Cohn, to studio heads, and the guys running distribution. He was on the phone all day. Part of what drove him is paranoia. He needed information like he needed sex.'

Apart from a script that was never really ready, a further strain on filming was that Jack's old girlfriend Michelle Phillips was now with Warren, as earlier she'd left Dennis to shack up with Jack. Feeling guilty, Michelle called Nicholson to make sure he wasn't too hurt about her getting it on with his best friend. 'I thought it was fabulous,' said Jack. 'Because I am fond of them both.' According to Michelle, however, director Mike Nichols eventually had to bar her from the set because she'd show up and disappear into Warren's bungalow, 'And it was terribly painful for Jack.'

There's a scene in *The Fortune* where Warren and Jack pass Stockard Channing back and forth between them like a football; some friends speculated that this reflected their attitude towards Michelle. This was unfair; Warren was genuinely serious about her. Jennifer Lee met Warren again around this time and recalls how deeply in love he obviously was with Michelle, though the old reprobate was never too far from the surface, suggesting they all have a nice friendly threesome. Jennifer was past all that; after numerous affairs she'd met the love of her life, comedian Richard Pryor.

Warren was determined that this relationship was going to work, though it didn't bode well that, although Michelle and her young daughter Chynna moved into his home up on Mulholland Drive, he still spent most of his time at the Beverly Wilshire. At least he played at happy families, driving Chynna to school, helping her with homework, but blotting his copybook somewhat by the odd bit of blatant womanising. Michelle quickly concluded that to keep the errant Warren away from temptation she shouldn't let him out of her sight.

When news broke that Warren and Michelle were preparing to marry it was a case of 'we'll believe it when it happens'. Both appeared to be serious, though, with Bali chosen as the perfect romantic rendezvous to tie the knot. On the flight over Warren started applying the brakes, talking about marriage as 'a dead institution', hardly a good sign for any potential bride. They returned to LA still single, and the press sensed storm clouds hovering. Warren waved them away, complaining that the media were behaving like 'anxious mothers' trying to push him up the aisle. Michelle felt different. 'He prefers shallow, meaningless relationships,' she said. 'He thinks they're healthier, or at least the only kind he can have. I don't respect his lifestyle, but I don't try to judge him.' No one ever did.

In one week, I can put a bug so far up her ass, she don't know whether to shit or wind her wristwatch.

Robert Towne was touting a new screenplay around town, a Chandleresque story about how fat-cat developers made LA into the city it had become, with a subplot about a father who's screwing his daughter thrown in for good measure. His detective hero was very much written with Jack Nicholson in mind, to suit his 'blue-collar arrogance'. Bob Evans over at Paramount couldn't make much sense of the labyrinthine story, but he liked the title, thought it was catchy – *Chinatown*.

It was Jack who suggested Roman Polanski direct the film. At first he was hesitant about returning to Los Angeles, the scene of his wife's terrible murder only a few years before. He was still damaged by it, carrying in his bag a memento of Sharon wherever he went, her knickers. Evans finally persuaded Polanski to fly over to discuss the movie. It was a depressing experience for him. 'Every street corner reminded me of tragedy,' the director said.

Jack got on well with Polanski, or 'the Little Bastard', as some called him, and adapted well to his martinet approach to directing. The feeling was mutual. 'Jack's on the wild side. He loves going out nights, never gets to bed before the small hours, and smokes grass.' Jack did arrive late a few times when the call was indecently early, his eyes bloodshot, but he not only knew his own lines but everyone else's. His lack of vanity also endeared him to Polanski, who insisted he spend half the movie with a large bandage on his nose, the result of a knife wound. He simply doesn't care about the way he looks. With Jack it's only the result that counts.

The real on-set fireworks were between Polanski and Faye Dunaway. Almost from the start of shooting she puzzled over her character's motivation. 'Say the fucking words,' an unsympathetic Polanski shouted. 'Your salary is your motivation.' She also fussed excessively over her appearance. In one scene the actress couldn't flatten a miscreant strand of hair that kept catching the light, so Polanski took matters into his own hands and ripped it out of her scalp. Faye couldn't believe it, screamed obscenities at him and stormed off the set.

Relations were even worse after that. Faye and Jack were in a car waiting for cameras to roll. She needed to pee rather badly, but Polanski wouldn't have it; he wanted the shot done. Faye wound the window down and threw a cupful of liquid in his face. 'That's piss,' he said. Faye smiled. 'Yes, you little putz.' And rolled the window back up.

The explosion between Jack and Polanski that people were waiting for didn't happen until near the end of the shoot. Jack's beloved Lakers were playing a vital basketball game on TV and during filming he'd rush back to his dressing room to catch the latest score while Polanski fiddled about with the lighting. At one point he failed to return on time and Polanski stormed in and smashed the television to pieces. 'You are an asshole,' he fumed at Jack, hurling the smoking hulk out of the door. (The TV, that is.) Jack's reaction was, in Polanski's words, 'dramatic in its irrational fury'. He tore off his clothes in the full glare of everyone on the crew and walked off the set. Too mad to continue, Polanski quit too.

On the way home, Jack pulled up at some lights. Looking over, he saw Polanski in his car. The two of them stared at each other in silence. Finally, Jack mouthed the words 'fucking Polack'. Polanski grinned and the two men burst into laughter as they drove off in opposite directions.

Still at his philandering best, boasting to one friend that a top fashion model had flown 10,000 miles just to spend the weekend with him – 'What can I do, I'm hot!' – Jack started to look for something a little more permanent. He found that special someone in Anjelica Huston, the daughter of veteran director John, who was a successful model at the time. They met at a party during the *Chinatown* shoot. It was instant attraction, he seduced by her feline sophistication, she by his hypnotic eyes and the famous Jack grin. 'His whole face lit up when he smiled. I wanted him!'

Friends agreed that Anjelica was perfect for Jack, and it was her love and understanding that brought him out of the self-imposed shell into which he'd retreated after his break-up with Michelle Phillips, nervous about plunging into another long-term relationship. Theirs would be a tumultuous love affair that lasted, on and off, for the next seventeen years.

It was a playful one, too. At home with a *Rolling Stone* reporter Jack, dressed in a bathrobe, was showing off stills from his latest movie, including love scenes with the sultry Valerie Perrine. 'Let me see that,' Anjelica said. 'No,' said Jack, defending himself as Anjelica jumped at him on the sofa and they began to wrestle, she making a grab for the hem of his robe. 'Help!' Jack cried. 'She's trying to expose my wanker to *Rolling Stone*.'

Chinatown was one of the summer hits of 1974 and received near-universal acclaim. Today it is justly regarded as an American master-piece, and one of the best films of the seventies. The icing on the cake for Jack was another Oscar nomination for best actor. Jack could now name his price. He'd truly arrived, his name mentioned in the same breath as Hoffman, Redford, Newman, McQueen and Beatty.

Jack has attributed his longevity in Hollywood to his determination to mix up his roles, playing in mainstream Hollywood movies followed by more art-house choices. 'I don't believe in pigeonholing, it's the death of any actor.' It was a policy that began when he agreed to make *The Passenger* (1975), mainly because the man doing the asking was Michelangelo Antonioni. He plays a burned-out TV journalist who assumes the identity of a mysterious stranger he finds dead in a hotel room. In Antonioni's hands, it is less a thriller than an existential-style meditation on identity and alienation. 'Antonioni is the absolute opposite of melodrama,' Jack said. 'A chase scene in his movies might be a camel walking for a very long time.'

Antonioni quickly got to work on Jack, stripping away all his trademark mannerisms, leaving him naked as an actor. It was a huge leap of faith to surrender himself totally; there was no communication, no give and take. According to co-star Maria Schneider Jack suffered during that movie. 'He was lost in Spain. He loathed the food, he had hamburgers sent from America, and he panicked because he wasn't being directed.'

Fresh from her controversial role in *Last Tango in Paris*, Maria accepted Antonioni's film in a bid to play something different. 'She didn't want to be typed as the sexy broad with butter up her ass,' said Jack helpfully. Unable to handle the instant fame and notoriety of *Tango*, Maria had descended into a drug-induced oblivion that lasted years. Jack recalled how in one scene he had to hold Maria upright because she was so zonked on painkillers. Another time she was holding a conversation with Antonioni and she was loaded and half nude, with her bathrobe open. 'I thought Michelangelo was going to die,' said Jack.

Hot on the heels of *The Passenger* came the film that for many remains the quintessential Nicholson movie – *One Flew Over the Cuckoo's Nest* (1975). It began life in the early sixties when superstar Kirk Douglas bought the rights to Ken Kesey's novel about a nonconformist in a mental hospital. Hoping to play the title role himself, Douglas spent thirteen years trying to launch a movie version, finally giving up and passing the rights over to his son Michael. But the son wasn't any more successful than Dad at hustling the property around Hollywood. 'How many films about mental illness made money?' studio executives would say. Enter Saul Zaentz, owner of Fantasy Records, keen to branch out into movies and together he and Michael were able to raise the budget independently.

For their director both men wanted Milos Forman, who'd fled his Czech homeland in 1968 when Soviet tanks rolled into Prague and had been looking for a Hollywood hit ever since. Forman grabbed the opportunity; after all, Kesey's book was about what he'd left behind – a totalitarian system. He also saw only Jack in the lead role of Randle P. McMurphy. Obviously Kirk was too old now to star and the likes of Marlon had turned it down. Burt Reynolds was also considered. (Did they envisage Reynolds escaping the nuthouse at the end by launching a souped-up red Ford Mustang over the fence?) Finally, logic prevailed and Jack signed on. It was a book he had always loved.

Given the filmmakers' intention to offer audiences their most realistic view yet of life inside a mental ward, highlighting vile practices like lobotomies and shock treatment, most institutions were understandably reluctant to accommodate them. Luckily the director of Oregon State Hospital in Salem was a fan of Kesey's novel and welcomed the producers, providing they employ as many patients as possible both as extras and to work alongside the crew. It would be good therapy for them. What no one on the film realised was that this meant employing some pretty wacko people. So you had an arsonist who'd tried to burn the hospital down a year before working with highly flammable turpentine as a painter, and a murderer working with the electricians, along with a couple of child molesters and rapists.

During filming, a crew member left a second-floor window open and a patient climbed through the bars and fell to the ground, injuring himself. The next day the local paper's headline read: 'One Flew OUT of the Cuckoo's Nest.'

Jack undertook painstaking research, talking to staff and even persuading them to allow him to watch inmates undergo electro-shock treatment. It was a chilling experience, watching the grotesque facial convulsions of the poor wretches when the technician unleashed the juice. He then took a stroll inside the maximum-security wing that housed the most dangerous mental patients in the whole of Oregon. He sat there quietly and alone as they were brought out of their cells; some even engaged in conversation with the actor, believing him to be a patient like themselves. Only a month earlier one of them had stabbed a guard to death. For Jack it was both fascinating and rewarding to sit, watch and learn from them, although a guard was never very far away. When he saw the finished film the hospital's superintendent, Dean Brook, said of Jack's performance: 'He was an absolute genius in getting across the character of McMurphy, a sociopath of whom there are plenty around. Jack's performance typified them.'

It was a long shoot, lasting some eleven weeks, and Anjelica came to stay with Jack. She was soon wishing she hadn't. Usually Jack had no problem slipping out of the skin of a character once the cameras stopped whirring, 'But here I don't go home from a movie studio, I go home from a mental institution.' Poor Anjelica didn't feel that she was living with Jack at all; the character of McMurphy was taking over. 'Can't you snap out of this?' she challenged him one day. 'You're acting crazy.' Jack couldn't, he was in too deep and Anjelica packed her bags and left. 'I'm no longer certain whether you are sane or not,' she told him. 'I'll see you when you come back into the real world.'

Cuckoo's Nest was a monster hit, beaten in 1975 box-office terms only by *Jaws*. It worked primarily because of Jack's performance, subtle and unashamedly crowd-pleasing at the same time. The culmination of critical acceptance was at the Oscars ceremony, when *Cuckoo's Nest* became the first film since *It Happened One Night* way back in 1934 to sweep the top five categories. Jack was there, sporting his by now standard dark glasses, and had brought Anjelica along for support. When his name was announced as the winner the audience yelled as he hopped onto the stage. 'I guess this proves there are as many nuts in the Academy as anywhere else,' he said. Walking off, clutching his award, Jack was heard to say, 'Jesus, I'm shaken up.' In the press room afterwards one hack asked, 'When you were doing *Little Shop of Horrors*, did you ever think it would lead to this?' Jack smiled, 'Yes, I did.'

You know what woke you up? You just had your throat cut.

After three years watching waves crash against the shore of his paradise island and agonising about how badly the American Indian was being shafted, Marlon Brando returned to the movies. His comeback couldn't have been more high profile, teaming up with Jack, two heavyweight acting champs in one movie. The result was a rather messy western called *The Missouri Breaks* (1976), with Brando as a psychotic bounty hunter and Jack as his prey, leader of a band of cattle thieves.

Although they'd been neighbours for a couple of years, the two actors were hardly what you'd call pally. 'We weren't up each other's ass all the time,' said Jack. Getting them together and fixing it so their schedules matched was quite a feat for producer Elliott Kastner. 'But he pulled it off,' says the film's associate producer Marion Rosenberg, 'by employing that old trick of telling Marlon that he had Jack, and telling Jack he had Marlon. That picture had to be made within a certain time period, so to get it done Elliott pulled out all the stops.'

There was one casualty, however: the script. It was never finished. Marlon, Jack and director Arthur Penn all agreed it needed heavy revision but no one sat down and properly worked on it. By the time cameras rolled, as Penn put it, 'We were out there tap dancing for our lives, making up the movie as we went along.'

Jack was giddy about working with his idol. 'I remember waking up one morning halfway through the shoot, and I couldn't move because I thought, wait a minute! I'm in a movie with Marlon Brando, the patron saint. I was practically immobilised by it.' Jack's deference to the great man was plain to see. He shot for two weeks prior to Marlon's arrival on location. 'And while Jack was working that first fortnight he was the star of the picture,' says Marion Rosenberg. 'For the crew, the minute Marlon arrived it was like, Jack who? But to his enormous credit, Jack just took a back seat and let Marlon get on with it. There was never a moment when Jack said, "Hey, what about me?" He's a total professional.'

Marlon's arrival was suitably dramatic. Trying desperately at the time to lose weight, Marlon didn't want to be around the cast and crew in a hotel, where people were socialising, anywhere where he could maybe be tempted to scoff himself stupid. 'So the production bought him this giant Winnebago,' recalls Marion, 'which he insisted on driving personally from Los Angeles to the location in Montana, almost a thousand miles, and no one could stop him. And the very fact he arrived was a miracle, because we were in the middle of nowhere, miles away from any town. How he found us I do not know, but this gigantic Winnebago came lumbering over the hill.'

Pretty quickly Marlon took control, his copy of the script simply awash with scribbles, crossed-out lines and his own personal additions. Jack and Penn were invited into his trailer for long discussions as the crew suffered outside in the searing heat. After an hour and still no show someone was heard to mutter, 'Has God's gift to the world appeared yet?'

Depending on your viewpoint, Marlon's performance as a schizophrenic lawman who grows into more of a fruitcake with each passing scene is either a darkly comedic tour de force or operatically self-indulgent. 'I know Marlon and Arthur had long talks abut his performance and his depiction of the character,' says Marion. 'And it's clear that Marlon got his way, because that performance is exactly what he wanted. And to this day I don't know if he was thumbing his nose at us or if he really felt that was the way the character should be.'

For his troubles Marlon received $1.25 million, plus a percentage, and worked five weeks, beginning a policy that continued until the end of his life to earn big bucks on a movie and work on it for the shortest time possible.

Jack wanted maximum authenticity for his character so stained his teeth a yellow-brown to get that frontier look. Penn admitted there were times when he couldn't tell Jack from the old cowboy wranglers around the set. It was an approach diametrically opposite to Brando's flamboyancy. For example, in one scene Marlon wears a dress and bonnet. It was here that Harry Dean Stanton lost patience with him. As the camera was about to roll on his death scene at Marlon's hands, Stanton jumped on the star, wrestled him to the ground and tore off the dress. 'I just couldn't stand the idea of getting killed by a man in a dress.' The two actors would clash again in 2001, when Marlon threatened to hurl

Stanton out of the window of a posh Los Angeles eatery for daring to light a cigarette. His action elicited a standing ovation from fellow diners.

Jack and Marlon's working methods were different, too. Jack was keen to get on the set and do the scene while Marlon was forever coming up with wacky and frankly bonkers experimental ideas for his character. Jack never got his head round Brando's use of cue cards, either. 'Who are they for,' he asked Penn one day when he first saw them.

'Himself.'

'Marlon?'

'Yes.'

'Why does the greatest actor in the world need cue cards?'

'Because he hasn't learned his lines.'

For one scene Marlon had the audacity to paste his dialogue onto the forehead of one of the cast members. When the actor complained that he'd at least like to look into Marlon's eyes, two holes were punched into the paper. When that didn't work out new cue cards were drawn up with large letters and stuck on a wall behind this poor actor. Cameras rolled and Brando began, only to stop suddenly. 'Shit,' he said, 'there's a plane coming into shot over your left ear.'

The legend of Marlon relying on cue cards grew over the years. Was he merely bone idle and never learned his lines or was it a practical aid to his acting, the belief that in life you don't know what words you're about to say, so why learn them? It looked more realistic on screen to be seen struggling with the dialogue, to have a real thinking process going on. Later on Marlon dispensed with cue cards to take advantage of technology. 'He'd use an ear piece,' says cameraman William Fraker, 'into which an assistant would read him his next line, he'd listen to it and then speak the line. And you'll notice on the screen that there's a little hesitation before he speaks each time.'

Jack had his own problems too. His screen lover on film was newcomer Kathleen Lloyd, but their personalities just didn't gel, she being something of a militant feminist, and when it came to their love scene Jack baulked. 'I wouldn't even fuck her myself,' he complained to a friend. 'How can I make love to her in this movie?'

For much of the filming Jack didn't see much of Brando. 'I think

Marlon and Jack had tremendous mutual respect for one another,' says Marion. 'But I wouldn't say they were good buddies, their lifestyles were completely different.' Marlon spent his free time playing bongo drums, roaring around on a motorbike or searching the prairies for grasshoppers. He was fascinated by the insects and Penn never forgot the time co-star Randy Quaid was feigning sleep and Marlon dropped a grasshopper in his mouth. Randy didn't mind, but it sure took him by surprise.

Another surprise was when the FBI showed up to interview Brando about a pair of Indians on the run from the police. Marlon took much pride in being as uncooperative as possible and later admitted that he had indirectly assisted the two men to escape.

As for Jack, he tended to hang around with his own bunch of friends like Harry Dean Stanton and much drinking went on at a motel a few miles out of town. One party Jack hosted must have been particularly good as the management asked the entire crew to vacate the next morning, while someone had added UN- to the sign outside which read WELCOME MISSOURI BREAKS.

Curiously, when Marlon's five-week stint on the movie ended he remained on location, living in his Winnebago. 'I remember a couple of his sons came to visit him,' says Marion. 'But Marlon would not let them come on set. He said, "I don't want my children to see me walking around in silly clothes." So he took them fishing. Marlon was wonderful, but he really despised acting, he didn't think it was the way for a grown man to make his living.'

It's your money or your life and it's in that order.

Isolated in Taos, Dennis Hopper's marriage to Daria naturally suffered. His drug-induced personality changes were the final nail in the coffin of his third marriage. Daria upped and left with their daughter and went back to her parents in San Francisco. Dennis was crushed. 'If I hadn't gotten on drugs,' he said years later, 'I'd be married to her today.'

Dennis was in despair about what was happening to his career, or what was left of it, trying all the time to get jobs in Hollywood, getting more and more depressed because it was the same guys he'd made rich on *Easy Rider* who now wouldn't give him a job. So with no offers from Hollywood he took whatever work was going, parts in low-budget independent movies, foreign films no one was ever likely to see. Some of these roles he was advised to turn down, the characters he was being asked to play lacking any redeeming qualities. But when his bank manager came calling, saying his account was empty, 'The role sounded redeeming to me,' said Dennis.

In Australia he appeared in *Mad Dog Morgan* (1976), at least that's what his filmography says, and there is actually a film to prove it, too. Just as well; Dennis can't remember a damn thing about it. 'I was out of my mind back then. I was on 150-proof rum and had no idea what the hell was going on.' The character he played was an outlaw, a sort of Ned Kelly type 'and very much attuned with the way Dennis was at the time,' says assistant director Michael Lake. 'He was still enjoying the good life and was persona non grata in Hollywood. He was still drinking and taking drugs, but hey it was the seventies, so some days he'd come to the set a little worse for wear, as many of us did. But Dennis was a true professional and that's the thing that really impressed me about him, that he could take all this stuff but once he got in front of the camera he could perform. And he really had a presence on screen.'

He turned up on his next picture equally spaced out to play a soldier returning home from Vietnam in Henry Jaglom's controversial *Tracks* (1976). It was a perfect piece of casting, says Jaglom: 'My anger and hurt about what the Vietnam War was doing to America – and to the Vietnamese – were best expressed, I felt, by the madness and lostness that Dennis, more than any other American actor, can reveal just in his face alone.'

At first Jaglom found the actor difficult to deal with, even though they'd been friends since the days of *Easy Rider*. But that quickly vanished as filming progressed and Dennis came up with the most extraordinarily creative ideas and acting choices, notably his last speech at the funeral of a fallen comrade. Jaglom had written what he thought was a rather brilliant six-page oration, about America's loss of its own innocence, that kind of stuff. Dennis ripped it up the moment Jaglom called action, threw it into the grave and started screaming, 'You motherfucker. You motherfucker. You motherfucker. You motherfucker. You wanna go to Nam? You wanna go to Nam? You motherfucker.' It was a barrage of fury and inarticulate rage, 'A thousand times better than all that smart stuff I had written,' said Jaglom. 'Dennis understood the anger and the hurt better than I did.'

Before the likes of *Coming Home* and *The Deer Hunter* made films about Vietnam fashionable, that particular conflict was seen as pretty much a taboo subject, so audiences stayed away from *Tracks*. 'The only thing Hollywood wanted less than a Vietnam War movie,' said Jaglom, 'was a Vietnam War movie with Dennis Hopper in it. But even though he fought me during filming he helped me enormously to get at the inarticulate rage of those men coming home from that misbegotten conflict. I realised much of Dennis's true genius on that film when we showed it to audiences made up of Vietnam veterans and I watched their faces looking at his face and understanding. In fact, understanding things that I would never, thankfully, have to understand.'

You ever listen to women talk, man? They only talk about one thing, how some guy fucked 'em over, that's all I ever hear about!

Early in 1977 it was reported that Warren Beatty's affair with Michelle Phillips was now 'friendly rather than romantic'. Soon stories were running about Warren and Kate Jackson, star of *Charlie's Angels*. Joan Collins once said that 'Warren always had to be with the girl of the moment.' Well, *Charlie's Angels* was the smash TV show of the moment, and Warren had three to choose from. He hit on Jaclyn Smith first, but she didn't return his call. Kate Jackson was more receptive and so began a brief affair. He never got round to Farrah Fawcett-Majors.

Not surprisingly, Warren and Michelle eventually split after three years. The fact it had lasted that long, she said, 'was a miracle'. Ultimately she'd been driven to despair by his lack of commitment, his belief that marriage or a one-woman relationship wasn't a happy, productive way to live. 'He feels that it's shallow and meaningless and boring,' said Michelle. So he went around having shallow, meaningless affairs. 'He also makes a point of not getting too close to you.' The closer he got, she felt, the more afraid he got, so off he went again on another affair. After a while, 'I couldn't live under the same roof with him; we were fighting all the time.' It was obvious Warren was never going to finish the relationship, so Michelle did it for him and walked, realising he didn't want to take the responsibility for their relationship breaking down.

A pattern was emerging here with Warren. Yet when his affairs ended it hurt, 'Even the promiscuous can feel pain,' but the truth was that whenever a relationship finished the decision was never his; 'It's always been the other person's.' A few of his girlfriends raised their eyebrows at that statement. Michelle Phillips claimed that she 'fell off the couch laughing' when Warren trotted out something similar on a TV show. Warren was rarely ungentlemanly enough to walk out on women; he conquered them, they fell in love with him, and he'd either overpower them or grow restless, bored even, and not be very good at concealing it. So in effect, Warren was right: the women did break up with him. 'That,' said Michelle, 'is what Warren *makes* his women do.' In a rare moment of honesty Warren once said, 'I'm really a bum of sorts.'

So, with Michelle gone it was open season as Warren's name was linked with almost every Hollywood beauty and beyond. They didn't have to be famous actresses, supermodels did just as well. And one of the biggest supermodels of the time was Texas-born Jerry Hall. Her encounter with Warren took place at a private party in a Manhattan restaurant. Engaged at the time to Roxy Music frontman Bryan Ferry, Jerry's not inconsiderable assets quickly brought her to the attention of another rocker, Mick Jagger, who promptly began chatting her up. Warren walked past Mick and Jerry, probably did a double take, gave Jerry the once-over and ingratiated himself into the conversation. Lord knows what Jerry was thinking with these two ageing studs drooling over her. Mick, totally ignoring his rival, whispered into Jerry's ear. When Warren attempted to butt in Mick snarled, 'She's with me.' Undeterred, Warren looked at Jerry, hoping for a sign that Mick wouldn't be getting any oats this time. In fact, neither would. 'I'm not with anyone,' she announced. 'And I'm engaged.' This didn't deter Mick, of course, who was full of English spunk. Still thinking he had a shot with Jerry, he pulled Warren over to a telephone booth. 'Now, Warren, listen, man . . .' he said, calling a friend of his to fix up the actor with another model for the evening.

Warren also had a soft spot for middle-aged divorcees and, shall we say, 'more mature' celebrities; deluxe milf, we could call them now. HRH Princess Margaret certainly qualified on that score. The Queen's sister was in LA on royal business and attending a special private dinner. The organisers had seated Frank Sinatra next to Mags at the top table, but she went out of her way to rearrange the seating plan so she ended up next to Warren. According to British royal journalist Richard Mineards Margaret was, 'A very unhappy woman. She was looking for some sort of solace, be it sexual or otherwise, and I remember there were two names that came up a lot: Warren Beatty and Mick Jagger.' According to Mineards, Warren visited the Caribbean island of Mustique, one of the world's most glamorous playgrounds for the rich and famous, where Margaret had a home.

Even Warren drew the line somewhere. That line was Julia Phillips, who is a member of the very small band of women who Warren preferred not to fuck. She was certainly successful enough, an Oscar-winning producer. At a party she spied Warren and started flirting with him. She got off to a bad start by dissing Julie Christie, whom she found nice enough but not very communicative. 'Let me put it this way,' said Julia. 'I did all the giving and she did all the taking – does that turn you on?' It didn't. And they didn't have sex, which must have been a major disappointment for Julia as she later wrote that 'Warren tries to fuck everybody.'

Maybe he did, maybe he didn't. As Warren once said, 'If I tried to keep up with what was said about me sexually I would be speaking to you from a jar in the University of Chicago Medical Center.' Warren did boast, however, of a photographic memory and could recite the phone numbers of most of the beautiful women in Beverly Hills. *Variety* editor Peter Bart tested him once and recalled, 'Of perhaps two hundred names, Beatty faltered only five or six times while smiling smugly.'

One young lady told *Playgirl* in 1976 of the time Warren called her up at a rather inopportune moment. After a few seconds or so Warren said, 'You're making love? Don't let me disturb you,' and hung up. 'That was Warren,' the girl said to her lover, who was doing very well indeed before the call and then lost all momentum. 'There went the evening,' the woman sighed. 'I guess men have a problem competing with Warren's image.'

What are you doin' here? You oughta be out in a convertible bird-doggin'
chicks and bangin' beaver.

In the midst of his Oscar success there was talk of Jack and Anjelica
marrying; his friends said they'd only believe it when they saw him
actually walking down the aisle. As Jack himself once joked, 'Marriage
in Hollywood is like a nice hot bath, it cools off after a short while.'
Harry Dean Stanton was convinced Jack had already decided never to
marry again. His long romances with Mimi and Michelle might very
well have resulted in marriage, followed by, let's face it, divorce. So by
his late thirties Jack could conceivably have had three ex-wives. It was
this fear of failure that put him off, and what he saw as the inequality
of the divorce laws, that an ex-wife had the legal right to financially
screw him to the wall.

Anjelica felt much the same way about marriage. She knew all about
the pain of divorce, her father having been through numerous wives.
She also knew what it was like to be referred to only as the offspring of
a famous father, and the pattern was repeating itself, except that now
she was Jack Nicholson's girlfriend rather than John Huston's daughter.
It also irked her that Jack sometimes took her for granted, and for a
period their relationship was on a decidedly unpredictable course. It
didn't help that Jack was up to his old tricks. In New York promoting
Cuckoo's Nest he went 'wild', a friend told *Cosmopolitan* magazine, with
a couple of models. Back home in LA, when Anjelica wasn't around,
there were frequent female visitors in the evenings or he'd be out hitting
the nightclubs with a string of dates on his arm. 'I'm such a wag!' he
claimed, winking. 'I'm a scamp. I don't deny it. I like myself.'

Anjelica soon got fed up and moved into her own apartment, then
jetted over to London, telling friends, 'What's good for the gander . . .'
Jack wasn't far behind, incensed at reports that Ryan O'Neal was sniffing
round his old lady. Jack was hurting. Anjelica's desertion, as he saw it,
hit him harder than even Mimi's or Michelle's. He flew off to San Tropez,
hiding out on Sam Spiegel's yacht. When he heard that a gang of press
photographers were on the nearby quay he dropped his trousers and
mooned them.

The couple's public spat lasted a whole summer, with Jack even seeking Papa Huston's advice. 'Be firm with her,' he ordered. So Jack demanded Anjelica's swift return to America. She knew by the tone of his voice on the telephone just how much he was missing her. 'I felt so crummy abandoning him – men like Jack you just don't find any more.' It wasn't long, though, before there was yet another bump. Jack left to go skiing in Aspen, holidaying with a group of friends that included ex-Bond girl Jill St John. Anjelica meanwhile was preparing to move her things out of Mulholland Drive. Jack expected an empty house to greet him when he got back, not for it to become the scene of one of the greatest scandals ever to rock Hollywood.

Since *Chinatown*, Jack and Polanski had remained friends. In March 1977 Polanski was bumming around Hollywood trying to set up movie deals, and shooting a photographic feature on adolescent girls for French *Vogue*, a nice excuse you might think to meet nubile Lolitas. He took one young wannabe model, just thirteen years old, to Jack's pad, gave her champagne and half a Quaalude, took risqué shots of her in various poses around the house, and then had sex with her. He was arrested the next day.

While this was all going on Jack remained in Aspen, heeding advice that he stay as far away from Mulholland Drive as possible to avoid even remote association with the scandal. But the police wanted his fingerprints to see if they matched those found on a box containing hashish that detectives had found in his house during a search. When after a couple of weeks Jack had still not returned, the police obtained a warrant authorising detectives to obtain his fingerprints. Jack complied willingly, asking the Aspen police to take his dabs, which in the end didn't match those found on the hashish container. He was soon cleared of any suspicion in the case and eventually flew back to LA, keeping a very low profile.

Polanski, though, was in deep shit, despite loyal friends talking up the theory that he'd been set up by the girl and her mother. He pleaded guilty to unlawful sex with a minor and the trial judge, Laurence J. Rittenband, wanted Polanski locked up for ninety days to evaluate whether or not he was 'a mentally disordered sex offender'. Polanski had no choice but to agree and on his last night of freedom Jack and an intimate group of friends threw a small dinner party for him. The rest of Hollywood, though, turned on him. The joke going around town was that his next film would be *Close Encounters of the Third Grade*.

After forty-two days in prison Polanski was released temporarily as his lawyers set about organising a plea bargain that in the end both sides were happy with, especially the prosecution, who had no desire to see the young girl face the horror of going to court and being publicly examined over the case's lurid details. Then, incredibly, the night before the hearing the judge changed his mind and decided he wasn't going to play ball; now he was gunning for the maximum sentence of fifty years. Polanski felt he'd no choice but to bolt and flew immediately to Paris, where, as a French passport holder, he was safe from extradition. He's been there ever since, in exile, aware that if he ever sets foot on American soil he'll be arrested.

Jack remained on friendly terms with the director, occasionally visiting him and reportedly using his influence with the LA judiciary to end his exile, without success. But the whole sordid episode, played out as it was in the public arena, affected him greatly, though he never admitted as much. As for Anjelica, she went back to Ryan O'Neal. Years later O'Neal's film-star daughter Tatum revealed that Anjelica 'became the official joint roller in our household because she was the best at it'. By early 1978 she'd returned to Jack's home; though tension remained. Attending a party given by Andy Warhol at which O'Neal was a fellow guest, the pop artist wrote in his diary that 'everyone was trying to keep Jack and Ryan apart so they wouldn't see each other'.

The horror . . . the horror.

If things had worked out differently *Apocalypse Now* (1979) would have been directed by George Lucas guerrilla-style, in Vietnam itself while the conflict was still raging. Rightly, no studio would finance such an exploit, for fear that Charlie might dislodge the filmmaker's lower intestines with a well-aimed bazooka blast. Imagine that: no *Phantom Menace*! Coppola's vision was far greater, far more artistic, far more bonkers. As he later raved during a Cannes press conference, his film wasn't about Vietnam, 'It *is* Vietnam!'

Based loosely on Joseph Conrad's novel *Heart of Darkness, Apocalypse Now* was about an officer called Willard sent upriver to find and kill Green Beret Colonel Kurtz, who had gone AWOL and nuts. Coppola had tried to lure big stars like Steve McQueen and Jack to the project. Pacino turned him down, saying, 'I know what this is going to be like. You're going to be up there in a helicopter telling me what to do, and I'm gonna be down there in a swamp for five months.'

Eventually he settled on Harvey Keitel as Willard and managed to lure Marlon on board as Kurtz with a mammoth deal. Dennis Hopper was also amongst the cast. Before going to the Philippines to start shooting Coppola called Roger Corman, who'd shot several films in the country, for advice. Corman's advice was simple – 'Don't go.' Too late, Coppola was already committed. Corman said he was going during the monsoon season, the worst time. 'It'll be a rainy picture,' said Coppola.

It was expected to be a fourteen-week shoot beginning in the spring of 1976, but logistics, weather and general disasters conspired against the film and turned it into an utter mess. Worse, Coppola fired Keitel after just two weeks, replacing him with Martin Sheen, who was at the time fighting his own alcoholic demons. When Sheen arrived he found chaos: Coppola was writing the movie as he went along and constantly firing personnel; people were coming down left, right and centre with innumerable tropical diseases and the helicopters used in the combat sequences were constantly being recalled by President Marcos to fight his own war against anti-government rebels.

As for the crew, they worked hard and boy did they party hard. Doug Claybourne, a Vietnam vet, was brought in as production assistant and was one of maybe two or three people working on the movie who'd actually been involved in the war. 'At the hotel where the crew were based, it was party heaven,' he recalls. 'We'd have a hundred beers lined up around the swimming pool, there were people diving off the roofs, it was crazy.' Then a typhoon hit, battering one of the locations, and the whole production was temporarily shut down.

After a month regrouping at his base in San Francisco to rethink his battle plan, Coppola returned to the jungle. Some of the crew mutinied and didn't go with him. Sheen went somewhat reluctantly. 'I don't know if I'm going to live through this,' he told friends. 'Those fuckers are crazy.'

Work now began on the sequences set around Colonel Kurtz's compound, where a shocking discovery was made. One morning, Sheen's wife woke up co-producer Gray Frederickson. 'You've got to come with me.' She took him down to the temple set, which was strewn with rubbish and smelled terrible. 'You've got to clean this up,' she said. 'It's a health risk, I won't allow Marty to work here.' So Frederickson went to the production designer Dean Tavoularis. 'They're complaining about you; there are dead rats in there.' Looking not bothered, Tavoularis said, 'That's intentional, it gives it real atmosphere.' 'Well you're gonna lose the actors,' said Frederickson. 'They're not happy working in those conditions.' There was a prop guy standing close by who muttered, 'Wait till he hears about the dead bodies.' Frederickson cried, 'What!'

He'd heard the rumours about dead bodies being on the set but discounted them as plain ludicrous. 'And they took me there,' Frederickson recalls. 'There was a marquee where we all ate dinner and then behind it was a tent where they stored props and we went in there and I saw this row of cadavers all laid out, all grey-looking. I said, "You guys are nuts. Where did these come from? We've got to get rid of this immediately." They said, "No, no, they'll be very authentic, we'll have them upside down in the trees." I said, "You can't do that." It turned out they'd got them from a guy who supposedly supplied bodies to medical schools for autopsies, but the police showed up on our set and said that this guy was robbing graves. Then the police said to us, "How do we know you guys haven't had these people killed because they're unidentified?" And they took all of our passports; I was worried for a few days. But they got to the truth of it all and put the guy in jail. And they showed up with a big truck and these soldiers were loading the bodies inside and they came over to me and said, "Where do we take these." I said, "I don't know, the cemetery." Turned out they couldn't take them to the cemetery because it costs money to bury them. "Oh, don't worry," they said, "we'll dump them somewhere," and they drove away. I don't know what they did with them. So for the scenes in the movie we had extras hanging from the trees, not dead bodies.'

When Marlon arrived he shocked everybody – he was like a blimp, maybe three hundred pounds; that's an awful lot of peanut butter. 'He was huge,' says Frederickson. 'You couldn't see around him.' This gave Coppola palpitations, for he'd envisioned Kurtz as a lean and hungry warrior. Also, what the hell was he going to wear? There was no Green Beret uniform on earth big enough!

Worse, Brando had neither read Conrad's book, learned his lines nor done any preparation whatsoever for the role. 'Francis had to literally start from scratch with him,' says Doug Claybourne. 'He had to bring him up to speed on what the thing was about and who the character was.' According to Dennis Hopper the whole production was shut down for a week while Coppola read Brando the novel out loud. 'Nine hundred people, the cast and crew, just sat and waited!' he said. 'We called it "the million dollar week", because Marlon was getting paid a million dollars a week.'

When Marlon finally got round to reading the script he didn't like it at all, and refused to play the role as written. Each morning Coppola would trudge over to Brando's dwelling and for hours they'd debate and pore over the dialogue. Coppola sensed Marlon was stalling because he'd yet to get a handle on how to play Kurtz. The director was also getting nervous. 'I only had him for fifteen days and I used up five of them just listening to him talk about termites.'

Finally, on the fifth day, Marlon shaved off all his hair and arrived at the idea of improvising his scenes and letting Coppola's camera capture whatever came out of his mouth. Self-conscious of his killer-whale appearance, Marlon also stipulated that he dress in black and for the most part be filmed in shadow. Coppola agreed to steer his camera away from his enormous belly.

Marlon also wanted nothing to do with Dennis Hopper. Coppola had cast Dennis as a character who doesn't appear in the book, a photo-journalist who's part of Kurtz's inner entourage. Dennis agreed to play the role on the understanding that he would be given at least one line of dialogue with Brando. 'That was my contract.' Dennis had idolised Brando since his teenage years. Early screen acting gods had been the likes of Orson Welles and John Barrymore, but they soon became old hat when the thirteen-year-old Dennis saw films starring Brando and Montgomery Clift in the same week. 'It changed my life.'

Marlon simply refused to work with Dennis, or even appear on the set at the same time. Instead he'd shoot one night, Dennis the next; that's how they worked to get their scene done. Dennis came in once and Coppola said, 'Last night Marlon called you a snivelling dog and threw bananas at you.' So the actor had to endure this prop man throwing fruit at him all night long. Crushed that his hero wanted nothing to do with him, Dennis wondered if he was 'giving off something that freaks him out'. Or maybe because of Marlon's experience of alcoholic parents he had a major problem with Dennis's drink-and-drugs lifestyle.

Dennis was certainly in a bad way on the film according to George Hickenlooper, who directed the seminal documentary *Hearts of Darkness* about the making of *Apocalypse Now*. 'Dennis recounted the story to me that he was asked, "What can we do to help you play this role?" And Dennis said, "About an ounce of cocaine." So he was being supplied by the film production drugs that he could use while he was shooting.'

Hopper's performance as the crazed photojournalist is, well, crazed. 'That's the way he was, on and off camera,' says Frederickson. 'He was pretty crazy on that film, but he was fun and everybody loved him, a great guy. There wasn't an edge to his craziness at all. Actually he's a lot more serious and less friendly now that he's not so crazy.' For some of the crew he was also taking his method acting a little bit too far. 'Dennis was notorious on set for never taking a shower,' says Doug Claybourne. 'You didn't want to stand too close to him.'

Dennis even managed to set his hotel room on fire, according to Frederickson. 'He had his girlfriend there and they were having a romantic night and he had all these candles and put them too close to the curtains and it caught on fire.' Claybourne also recalls the incident. 'Suddenly this flaming mattress came hurtling out of Dennis's hotel room window and landed in the river outside.'

Like Marlon, Dennis improvised many of his scenes. Hours and hours of footage was shot, but Coppola chose to use only a few choice moments. His death scene was also removed. When Dennis takes a photograph of

Kurtz he more or less signs his own death warrant and is hoisted up on a rope and shot to ribbons. A life-size dummy of Dennis was constructed and filled with ninety-eight squibs. 'Now that dummy cost more than I got paid for the entire fucking movie,' argued Dennis. 'So, y'know, who's the biggest dummy?'

Catastrophes continued to plague the production. Martin Sheen suffered a heart attack and Coppola, convinced he was to blame, one evening had an epileptic seizure, banged his head against the wall, rolled round on the floor and foamed at the mouth like a rabid dog. These were Coppola's darkest hours from a stressful shoot that would have felled most other directors. 'We had access to too much money,' he later confessed, 'too much equipment, and little by little we went insane.' Dennis said, 'Ask anybody who was out there. We all felt like we fought the war.'

Coppola, though, had more to lose than most. Some of the money being squandered was his own, several millions, in fact, and the director faced financial ruin if the film couldn't be completed. No surprise that Coppola's marriage almost collapsed as the pressure increased and the director suffered a nervous breakdown, declaring on three separate occasions during filming that he intended to commit suicide. He was ready to die out in the Philippines, do whatever it took to finish the film. Dennis could relate to that.

Sheen eventually recovered and work began again. When Marlon finished and it was time for him to leave, Coppola needed a big favour from his star. He approached Frederickson, 'because he knew I got along with Marlon. Francis didn't get along with him that well.' Coppola needed Marlon to come out just for a quick close-up of his lips saying, 'The horror, the horror.' Frederickson went to Marlon's hotel; he was getting ready to catch his flight to Hong Kong. 'My contract's up; I finished yesterday,' said Marlon. 'It's just a little favour,' Frederickson replied. 'We'll fly you out there, shoot it in an hour and then you can be on your way.' Marlon smiled, 'It's never an hour, you know that.' He then calculated how much he'd been paid for his stint on the picture. 'It comes to about $75,000 a day,' he said. 'I'm in the Marlon Brando business, I don't do anything else. I'm not in real estate or oil, I sell Marlon Brando. So you're asking me to do a $75,000 favour. Would you ask that of the president of General Motors?' Frederickson went back to Coppola. 'When I told him he was furious and raved, 'OK, tell Brando I'll pay him the $75,000, but I'm gonna keep him here all day long.'

After 238 days Coppola finally wrapped. The budget had ballooned from $13m to nearer $30m. United Artists wanted *Apocalypse Now* to be their big Christmas 1977 release, but the opening was pushed back and pushed back as Coppola worked frenziedly in his editing suite for months on end arranging some 200 hours of footage. Critics started referring to the film as 'Apocalypse When?'

Doug Claybourne stayed with the picture when it moved into post-production, working with the actors as they dubbed their lines, many of which were inaudible owing to background noise on location. Marlon came in for two weeks. 'I remember one time Francis came in late to the studio and Marlon said to me, "You've got to get me a water gun, Doug." So I ran out and bought a dollar water gun and gave it to Marlon. He filled it up and put it in his pocket and when Francis came into the recording suite he let him have it, wet him down good, saying, "You can't be late, Francis, you've got to be here on time." He loved to pull that kind of stuff. He was a real jokester, and a gentle guy and very sweet. Just a gentleman.' Martin Sheen also found Marlon extremely friendly. 'He went to great lengths to crack a good joke. The only thing he would not talk about was himself, or movies, or acting.'

Apocalypse Now finally opened in 1979 and is today rightly regarded as a masterpiece and a life-changing experience for most of the people who worked on it. Doug Claybourne recalls helping to organise the press screenings in New York. 'I had all the actors together at the theatre but I couldn't find Dennis. I had to go back to the hotel and I found him in his room, stark naked with his cowboy hat and his cowboy boots on.'

Years later, when George Hickenlooper made his documentary, most of the stars and crew were happy to talk about the movie. Except Marlon. Hickenlooper tracked him down to the set of a movie. As he walked to his trailer Hickenlooper made his move. 'Mr Brando, we're making a documentary on *Apocalypse Now*. Would you be prepared to do an on-camera interview?' Marlon turned round and stared like death into

Hickenlooper's face, his eyes boring into his psyche. 'Why are you making a film about that fat fuck? He owes me two million dollars.' Obviously Marlon was having issues with his royalty payments from Francis. 'You tell that fat fuck,' Marlon continued, 'that if he pays me the two million, you can film me taking a shit.' With that the trailer door slammed shut. Hickenlooper never got his interview.

Look at this fucking shit we're in, man. Not with a bang, but with a whimper. And with a whimper, I'm fucking splitting, Jack.

Dennis Hopper had been in the Philippines shooting *Apocalypse Now* for just over a month. On his last night he and Coppola got roaring drunk together. An assistant was looking on nervously; his task was to get Dennis to Manila to catch a flight to Germany, where he was due to start filming the Wim Wenders thriller *The American Friend* (1977). Dennis refused to leave until there was no more beer left in the house.

At Hamburg airport Dennis was dazed and confused, knowing neither where he was nor why he was there. Still wearing his character's costume from *Apocalypse Now*, at first sight Dennis gave Wim Wenders the impression that 'he was drugged out of his mind'. Maybe the Coppola shoot had taken more out of Dennis than he realised because the actor was 'totally impossible to work with for the first couple of weeks', according to Wenders. 'I told him that either we'd get someone else or he'd have to prove to me that he was the great actor that I knew he was. He was totally suicidal. He took every drug in the book.' In the end Wenders confronted Dennis, telling him straight, 'Are you gonna die tomorrow or are you gonna become an actor?'

Relations between Dennis and his co-star Bruno Ganz were even worse. The two of them had diametrically opposed approaches to acting. Dennis arrived on set entirely unprepared, not even knowing his dialogue, but once the camera turned he attacked the material with enthusiasm. 'He had an incredible presence,' said Wenders. Ganz, who came from a theatrical background, had been fretting for days about the scene, going over every gesture, every word, and so was completely thrown and disturbed by Dennis, who basically didn't give a toss. 'They actually had a fist fight in the middle of one scene because they hated each other so much,' says Wenders. 'There was no way I was going to work with these two maniacs.'

That night both actors decided to settle their differences and talked things through until the early hours of the morning. As dawn rose they'd reached an understanding and actually went on to become good friends. Overall, Dennis enjoyed the experience, later calling *The American Friend* 'probably my best film'. He and Wenders discussed making another movie together, and flew to Mexico to scout locations, but the trip ended in chaos when Dennis started shooting guns in a Mexican town and was summarily deported from the nearest airport. It wasn't until 2008 that the two of them reunited on a picture, *Palermo Shooting*, with Dennis playing, of all things, Death.

For Dennis, taking drugs or drinking like a maniac while working was always about the job at hand, not the drugs or the booze; they just kept him going. When work started to dry up, then the drug taking was about wallowing in self-pity and anger. For a while therapy looked like being a solution, but not for long: Dennis wasn't the type to sit in a circle for everyone to gawp at his insecurities and problems. 'Numbers of times through my life I have been asked to be in therapy. Or *demanded* to be in therapy. Or *forced* into therapy, but I just wore them out, I guess.'

Do I . . . play polo?

Somewhere amongst his bedroom-hopping activities Warren Beatty found time to make a movie, a romantic comedy called *Heaven Can Wait* (1978). Originally conceived as a vehicle for Muhammad Ali, a friend whom Warren regarded as a potential movie star, the great sportsman didn't want to quit fighting so the character was changed from a boxer to a footballer and Warren played it himself. He also tried to cast Hollywood legend Cary Grant as God, dropping by his house to try the personal touch. Grant said no and asked his girlfriend Maureen Donaldson, an entertainment journalist, to see Warren to his car. En route Warren asked Maureen for a date. One thing led to another and poor old Cary was ditched and Maureen moved in with Warren.

On *Heaven Can Wait* Warren again pushed himself to the limit, putting in eighteen-hour days working as star, co-producer, co-writer and director, having finally taken the plunge, calling the difference between directing himself and being directed the difference between making love and masturbation. To be on the safe side, though, he roped in friend Buck Henry to act as co-director and sought advice from the highly seasoned crew he'd assembled. Many in the industry wondered, though, if he'd listen to them. Buck Henry admitted there were plenty of disagreements on set. 'When Warren wants to do something his way, he has it all figured out, so you goddamn well better be prepared to argue your case if you differ with him.' David Foster, who produced *McCabe and Mrs Miller*, is the first to acknowledge Warren's pedigree: 'Of course he's a multi-talented guy, it's just hard for him to listen to other people, I guess. He's such an intense guy. To get an answer he'll check six different people. If a car drives by and he thinks it's silver, but he's not quite sure, he'll ask six people, "Is that silver or grey?" He'll question you to death. Intuitive, he's not. Everything has to be thought out and thought out, it's overkill. But he's been very successful, so what the hell.'

A big talking point on the movie was the return of Julie Christie, who was making her third and final film with Warren. Afterwards he graciously declared that he could not have functioned without Julie on *Heaven Can Wait*. What he failed to mention was she at first turned him down flat and he had to fly to London to persuade her to be in it. William Fraker was the cameraman and remembers Beatty arriving back in LA. 'He said to me, "We've got Julie, she's coming back to Hollywood and, Billy, I want her to be beautiful in this picture. Absolutely beautiful." I said, "OK, she's a well-trained actress, disciplined, she'll hit her marks, but Warren, you'd better hit your marks, too, if you want to look as pretty as Julie." And he was magnificent. They were both beautiful in that picture. And it was a lot of fun to make; Warren's a phenomenal guy, very generous.'

Observers couldn't fail to notice that Warren still carried a torch for Julie, she less so for him ('cool' might be the operative word). During one candid moment Julie made her views perfectly clear about the formulaic material Warren was wasting his talents on. 'I can't believe you're still making these fucking dumb movies when there are people all over

Europe making fabulous films, about real things, like Fassbinder, and you're still doing this shit.'

That was unfair; *Heaven Can Wait* is a supremely well-crafted movie. Audiences thought so, too, and made it a smash hit. The poster had Warren in tracksuit pants, trainers and angel's wings sprouting from his back. Bob Evans, a man whose marketing savvy Warren admired, was invited to comment on the artwork. Evans loved it, except 'No cojones,' he said. 'Your sweat pants, there ain't no crease. Looks like you're sporting a pussy.' Warren scrapped the campaign and ordered a reworking. Half a million dollars down the drain. Evans called it, 'By far the most expensive crotch retouch in cinema history.'

Warren was still very pally with Evans, but their friendship had an edge. When in a *Rolling Stone* article Warren claimed to be the fastest phone dialler in the world, Evans called him up to say his son Joshua was faster and could easily 'out-touch-tone' him. 'I'll wipe him off the street.' Warren said. They arranged to have a dial-off in Evans's screening room, which had two phones. When Warren arrived at the house he blasted, 'Where's the fuckin' runt?' Josh appeared and they began their dialling duel. Josh proved to be the fastest finger. Warren went into a huff and didn't speak to the boy for more than a year.

Most critics seemed to accept the fact that *Heaven Can Wait* was essentially lightweight, but the influential Pauline Kael, a supporter of Warren's since the beginning of his career, dismissed it out of hand. Warren felt betrayed, so issued a challenge that many a film director has wanted to offer a critic after a particularly foul review. OK, then, he said, see if you can do better, come out to Hollywood and make movies. It was the ultimate dare and Kael foolishly accepted a development deal Warren wrangled out of Paramount. In her rush to rise to Warren's bait Kael forgot one thing: she was a writer, not a movie maker. She was treated as a joke in Hollywood and soon fled back to New York, her reputation severely damaged. It was an incredible piece of calculated revenge. 'We're talking about manipulation on a level unknown to man,' Buck Henry called it. 'This is so Machiavellian; even I can't quite believe it, except that it was Warren.'

I ain't no slab of meat to be auctioned off, but, what the hell. Fine by me.

Following the aftershocks of the Polanski rape trial, Jack Nicholson set off for Mexico, hoping a change of scenery might do him good. The film was *Goin' South* (1978), very much a personal project which he intended to both star in and direct. It was a comedy western that couldn't possibly create any major problems, could it? Enter John Belushi.

A household name in America thanks to his inspired appearances on TV's *Saturday Night Live*, Belushi had yet to make a movie but was already hooked on the drugs that would eventually kill him. Jack hired Belushi because he'd heard he did a brilliant comedy impression of a Mexican, perfect for the small role of a sleazy local sheriff. People knew the cocktail of drugs Belushi was consuming altered his personality dramatically, but no one was expecting the sight that greeted them when he arrived late for the shoot, looking as if he hadn't slept for days. Shunning his hotel room, Belushi insisted on staying with Jack in the more luxurious bungalows up in the hills. 'I've gotta get outta here,' he grumbled. 'The hotel is suck-o, man,'

Back in the production office producer Harold Schneider had the un-enviable job of calming Belushi down. It didn't work and he continued to talk in an incoherent fashion before picking up a large kitchen knife which Schneider feared he intended to use on himself. Then the other producer arrived. Harry Gittes had hired Belushi on Jack's instruction and was taking no crap from a TV comic. 'You are a real asshole,' he blasted. 'You're acting like a complete asshole. You're going to put us all in deep shit.' Belushi seemed not to be hearing this. Instead he collapsed in a convenient chair and fell asleep. 'What's this?' snapped Jack, arriving back from the set. 'A crash pad?' He didn't want to hear explanations, he wanted Schneider to get Belushi back to his hotel room. Easier said than done. Stirred from his audible slumber, Belushi became wild and abusive and a pissed-off Schneider would surely have belted him one if he hadn't been restrained.

It was a coy and still rather hungover Belushi who emerged on the set the next day full of apologies. Jack was having none of it. 'You asshole,' he bellowed. 'Any other producers would write you out. You only stay in because they're my friends. If Paramount people were here, you'd be kissed off and your career in movies would be totally fucked.'

With Natalie Wood, among the first of Warren's cavalcade of celebrity conquests. Her jilted husband, Robert Wagner, contemplated killing Warren.

As a young actor Warren was tough. After working with him director Robert Rossen said: 'If I die, it'll be Warren Beatty who killed me.' He died.

Legend has it Warren offered to kiss Jack Warner's shoes if he financed *Bonnie and Clyde*. 'Get off the fucking floor you crazy bastard,' shrieked the mogul. But Warren got his way.

With Julie Christie. Director John Schlesinger, who'd launched Julie's film career, warned his protégé off the Hollywood lothario, describing him as a serial womaniser who, 'gets through women like a businessman through a dozen oysters.' She ignored him.

Warren the stud. Returning from work there might be a phalanx of girls,
larger than a Broadway chorus line, outside his door at the Beverly Wilshire Hotel.
Guests directly below often had difficulty getting to sleep.

Vampire love: Madonna
needed his credibility,
Warren needed her youth.

Warren and Jack, from skunk
spotting on the Sunset Strip
to Hollywood royalty.

A Roger Corman discovery, Jack toiled away in B-movie hell, acting alongside Boris Karloff and man-eating vegetables, for over a decade.

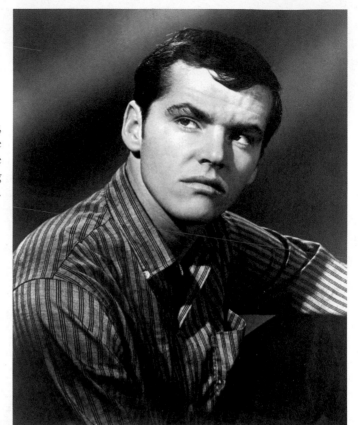

The killer look: Jack's way with women earned him the nickname 'The Great Seducer.' One top fashion model flew 10,000 miles just to spend the weekend with him. 'What can I do, I'm hot!'

'Here's Johnny!'

Next door neighbours, Marlon would raid Jack's fridge and leave behind his underpants.

With Anjelica Huston. Theirs was a tumultuous romance that lasted, on and off, for 17 years. It ended with a right hook delivered by Miss Huston.

Wild Jack. He once attacked a motorist with a golf club for cutting him up on a highway. He told police he selected a number two iron, while adding, 'You can bet I felt justified.'

His roistering days over, Jack's philosophy hasn't changed: 'More good times.'

As filming went on Jack wanted desperately to like the comedian, who was fundamentally a nice guy, someone he could take under his wing, but Belushi remained belligerent on set and had a problem controlling his anger. He also continued to make petty demands and fought with the producers. Partly in response to his behaviour, Belushi's role seemed to shrink. By the end of production he'd harsh words to say about the experience: 'Jack treated me like shit on *Goin' South*. I hate him. If I see him, I'll punch him.'

Besides the difficult Belushi, Jack found it awkward to balance his twin roles of star and director, setting up shots through the viewfinder one minute, then leaping into the scene and acting the next. 'I will never direct myself again!' he was heard to yell at the top of his voice after one particularly difficult shot. Most of the crew, though, seemed to enjoy the experience. Cinematographer Nestor Almendros likened Jack to 'a force of nature; exuberant, tireless, able to film ceaselessly from dawn to dusk, then go to a party and enjoy himself till daybreak'.

As the seventies drew to a close Jack's huge personality was threatening to swallow the parts he played. Bizarrely, the more famous Jack got, the more difficult his job as an actor became. Often he found himself having to un-Jack his characters in order to get audiences to separate the public persona from his work; un-Jacking meant toning down the mad eyebrows and cheesy grin and all the other Jackisms. It was a challenge because some directors hired Jack to be, well, Jack. As Bob Rafelson says, 'Jack is much bigger in all respects than the characters he plays. He would never throw a dog down a disposal chute, as he does in *As Good As It Gets*; he would choke it to death right on the spot.' Over the next few years Jack faced accusations that he was merely trading on his celebrated wild image, criticism that he couldn't care less about. 'I love to put myself somewhere where they can say, "Jeez, he's overacting again." Which I am, but damn, that's why I'm good!'

Your name is Kal-El. You are the only survivor of the planet Krypton.

It was one of the most anticipated movies of the decade: *Superman* (1978). Once the exhaustive search for an actor to play the superhero concluded,

195

with the unknown Christopher Reeve donning the cape, thoughts turned to who would play the pivotal role of Superman's father Jor-El. Director Richard Donner wanted Marlon Brando, and together with screenwriter and creative consultant on the film Tom Mankiewicz visited the great man at his house on Mulholland Drive.

Once inside they began discussing the script and Brando's role. What happened next, as Mankiewicz recalls, was bizarre to say the least. 'Brando looked at me and said, "You know that long speech I have, well maybe on Krypton we don't speak English, maybe we make electronic sounds you know, beep, beep, and we have subtitles." I went, "Yeah." He then turned to Dick and said, "And maybe we don't even look like people, maybe I look like a green suitcase." We said, "A green suitcase!" By this point Dick and I are sitting there and our spirits are just dropping so fast, here's our big legendary star and he's going to appear on screen as a green suitcase making electronic sounds.'

Donner couldn't take this nonsense any longer and said in a booming voice, 'You can't look like a green suitcase and make electronic sounds because every kid in the world knows that Superman's dad is a handsome guy.' Before he could finish Marlon roared with laughter. 'What was so obvious in that instant,' says Mankiewicz, 'he was putting us on. He wanted to know what kind of people he was working with.'

When Marlon signed on his fee of $3.7 million for twelve days' filming made headlines around the world. 'But he was a dream to work with,' recalls Mankiewicz. 'He gave us eleven free days on that picture that he didn't have to give us; we just had a ball with him. And he literally saved my life on *Superman*.' The film was produced by Alexander Salkind, whose wife Berta fancied herself a writer and repeatedly sent Mankiewicz script rewrites, which he ignored. After Brando's final day on the movie Mankiewicz and Donner took the actor to dinner on the King's Road. The Salkinds got wind of it and joined them unannounced, Berta squeezing herself into the booth between Mankiewicz and Marlon. 'She was drunk,' recalls Mankiewicz. 'And she turned to me and said, "I keep sending you these rewrites and you never reply to me." I said, "Mrs Salkind, I apologise, I'm just so busy." To the whole table she said, "You know how much my husband is paying him." And then she announced my salary to everyone; it was just awful. "You should get on your hands and knees," she said to me, "and thank my husband for hiring you." Well, Alexander Salkind was about four foot eleven, and I said, "Mrs Salkind, I'm always on my hands and knees when I'm talking to your husband so I can look him straight in the eye." Suddenly she grabbed a steak knife and went right for me – the knife was four inches away from my chest, I swear to God – and Marlon grabbed her hand and shoved her down in the booth saying, "Will you behave?" She nodded, and then came right at me again. You always wonder when something like that happens to you what you're going to do, and I'm afraid in my case I flunked, because I was so aghast I didn't try and stop her. So I do owe Marlon one. I tell you what, even at Marlon's age then, boy his reflexes were awful fast. Got her just in time.'

Marlon's scenes take place in the opening ten minutes of the film, in the lead-up to the destruction of the planet Krypton, and were played for the most part with Susannah York. 'He was absolutely enchanting,' she recalls. 'So nice to me, filled my dressing room with flowers and fruit. I liked him very much. I was certainly very astonished by cards being put up for his lines, that took me a bit of getting used to. And I remember asking somebody why he didn't learn the lines, because he obviously could, and this guy said, "I don't think Marlon has very much respect for the profession he's in." And that made me feel rather sad for Marlon because he was such a great man, and somebody so wonderful at what he did, and not to feel much respect for it was just enormously sad.'

Stunt man Vic Armstrong, doubling Christopher Reeve in the flying sequences, was also mystified by Marlon's use of cue cards. 'It was actually true what they said about him, that when he scratched his head it was to look over at the idiot boards. Guys were walking around with great big cards with lines of dialogue on in different parts of the set and he'd look at them and that's how he got those long thoughtful looks on screen. It was amazing. But Brando was a very generous, nice person. Of course I was in awe of him, he was an icon.'

I told her you had a small dick!

After his appearance in the belated release of *Apocalypse Now* Dennis Hopper was sure movie offers would come rolling in. At last he had exposure in a major movie that would be seen by millions. Nothing of any merit turned up. His agent suggested he move back to LA in case he be obliterated completely from Tinsel Town's subconscious. For a while he took the advice, but the sheer phoniness of the place had him yearning for his sanctuary back in Taos.

Waiting for him there was a predictable slide into excess. Things were starting to get a little crazy, even by his standards. He bought a two-ton Cadillac while high on drugs because he thought it was a tank. He gave interviews depressed about his career, the fact he'd had to look for film work in Europe instead of his native land. 'I can't say I wasn't angry and upset during that time,' he said later, 'because I was.' He was particularly desperate to return to directing, to prove himself once again behind the camera. He just had to make films, he said, 'because that's what I feel justifies my existence'. He was literally going nuts, and in need of some creative release picked up a brush and started painting again. 'I was stopped so many times from acting and directing that if I had not had art as an outlet, I don't know what I would have done.'

Still, there was an air of desperation about Dennis: his expression emoted pain, befuddlement and disillusionment; his angry eyes were soul-piercing. As one journalist put it, 'He has the face of a human train wreck.' At least he was still alive to feel miserable; three-quarters of his friends died before he was thirty. Talking to Bob Dylan once, Dennis said, 'When we hit forty, man, we can look at each other and really talk to each other, like hey, how did we do that?'

With no one prepared to gamble on Dennis he bummed around with some old friends including Dean Stockwell, Russ Tamblyn and rocker Neil Young, and together they churned out a movie that was something like five years in the making, with Young acting as co-director putting something like $3m of his own money into the project. It was called *Human Highway* and filmed partly on location around Dennis's home. The film didn't see daylight until the mid-80s, whereupon it was not well received. *Entertainment Weekly* said, 'The nicest thing you can say about *Human Highway* is that as a filmmaker Neil Young is a great guitarist.'

As might be expected of a Dennis Hopper movie, all did not run smoothly and he ended up in court on an assault charge. Actress Sally Kirkland alleged that one day a doped-up Dennis, who played a cook in the film, was performing knife tricks on the set with real knives. Fearful of an accident, Sally attempted to grab the knife off him and in the struggle received an injury to her hand serious enough to require surgery and two days in hospital. She sued Dennis for $2m, along with the producers, blaming them for not keeping the actor under control. Her lawyers alleged that Dennis and the crew were 'smoking and in other ways ingesting dangerous and illegal drugs and drugs known to cause violence and dangerous behaviour'. In the end no criminal charges were ever filed against Dennis.

Don't touch me unless you love me.

When *Heaven Can Wait* was showered with several Oscar nominations Warren Beatty turned up at the ceremony arm in arm with new girl-friend Diane Keaton. God knows what she must have thought when Shirley MacLaine bounded up onto the stage and joked, 'I want to take this opportunity to say how proud I am of my little brother, my dear, sweet, talented brother. Just imagine what you could accomplish if you tried celibacy!'

Warren met Diane Keaton at a party thrown by her former lover Woody Allen, and for days afterwards besieged her with flowers and calls. Would she go to dinner with him? Would she fly to Acapulco for the weekend? It had never failed before. Playing it cool, Diane turned him down several times before finally agreeing. Diane fitted the template of many previous Warren girlfriends: highly successful, a star in her own right. 'Warren likes ladies whose names appear above the title,' joked *Bonnie and Clyde* actor Michael J. Pollard. 'But he makes exceptions – lots and lots of exceptions.' Those exceptions might be waitresses, secretaries and Hollywood groupies. A few years back, at a party Roman Polanski hosted at the Chateau Marmont on Sunset

Boulevard, Warren parked his car and immediately started to flirt with one of the girl valets. A Hollywood executive was witness to this and it struck him as more than odd that here was Warren, a top movie star, trying to pick up a parking attendant in the middle of the night. 'His conquests were a matter of chemistry,' Robert Altman once said. 'And a hell of a lot of stamina.'

Diane Keaton had fancied Warren for years, of course, first laying eyes on him as a young actress browsing through the Beverly Wilshire bookstore. She looked up and there he was in the lobby. 'I thought, my God, he's so beautiful. He looked at me for a second, and then passed me by. I thought, I'll never know him. He'll never be somebody in my life.'

Theirs was a contentious, complicated relationship; 'volatile' was a word Diane once used to describe it. 'Warren,' she said, 'really likes women who kick his ass.' According to reports Beatty bought Diane a pair of handcuffs, an ironic comment on their relationship perhaps, or were they just kinky bastards? 'God help me, no,' Warren said when confronted with the suggestion. 'I've never been into that.'

Besides Diane, Warren was seeing other women. When Ali McGraw left husband Steve McQueen the news spread along the bachelor grapevine faster than meths goes down a tramp's throat. Warren immediately called her former husband Robert Evans. 'Your old lady, she's free. Do you mind if I call her?' Evans couldn't believe the nerve of the guy; everyone knew he was involved with Diane. 'If you weren't living with Keaton,' Evans replied, 'Ali would be the best thing that could ever happen to you, but she's too good a dame to hurt for the sake of a notch. You've asked me, so I'm telling you – pass.'

Amazingly, just two minutes after Warren's call, Jack rang Evans with the same question. 'Whaddaya think, kid? Now that your old lady's free, is it worth a dial?' Evans's advice to Jack was much the same as he'd just given Warren. 'Call her if you want, but you're with Anjelica and Ali's too vulnerable for you to play it shady. Got it?' There was a slight pause. 'Got it,' said Jack. Years later Evans recalled what happened next. 'One called and called, and the other passed. Who do you think called?' Doesn't take a genius, does it?

Did Warren make a habit of this, one wonders. Friend Richard Sylbert once said. 'I remember years ago Warren used to scan the trade papers, looking to see who was getting a divorce. He was great with wounded birds.'

Warren had no qualms about stealing the vulnerable Ali from McQueen, since the two megastars had been rivals for years. McQueen saw Beatty as white collar and limos, he was blue collar and motorbikes. Later, when Warren was dating supermodel Barbara Minty, McQueen exacted his revenge. After seeing Barbara's picture in a magazine, McQueen called her up for a date. Barbara was intelligent enough to know that her relationship with Warren was never going to lead anywhere, so agreed. They rode round for a while on McQueen's bike, and afterwards he confessed to a friend that the moment he felt her cruise missile breasts against the back of his leather jacket, 'I knew this was the woman for me.' As Bill Maher, McQueen's business manager, put it. 'She was Warren Beatty's girlfriend. Steve stole her away from him.'

Around this time Warren was dating Jackie Kennedy Onassis, whose second husband Aristotle Onassis had recently died. Once more a grieving widow, Jackie had moved into a flash apartment on Fifth Avenue in New York. How serious their relationship was is open to speculation. In 1997, when quizzed about it on television, Warren denied they ever had sex. Ever on the lookout, though, Warren was flirting like mad with Cher at one party and when the singer refused to leave with him his radar instead switched to a beautiful pair of girls. He knew they were lesbians but that didn't stop him having a go. In the end one of them said, 'What the fuck do we need you for?'

Wendy? Darling? Light, of my life. I'm not gonna hurt ya. I'm just going to bash your brains in.

Jack Nicholson had wanted to work with Stanley Kubrick for years and made no secret of the fact that he'd told Stanley if there was anything that he thought he was right for he'd drop everything and be on the first flight over to England, the American's home since the sixties.

As soon as he read Stephen King's chilling novel *The Shining* Kubrick recognised its cinematic potential and saw Jack as the only actor with the intensity to play the central role of a family man driven to mental collapse who tries to kill his family with an axe. 'The character is a desperate, driven man,' said co-screenwriter Diane Johnson. 'And Jack can play insanity better than anyone.'

Jack arrived in London in the winter of 1978, where he'd remain for the next year as the film progressed at a fairly methodical rate, befitting Kubrick's reputation for perfectionism. To an actor who learned his craft in the Roger Corman wham, bang, thank you, ma'am school of film-making, Kubrick's habitual fifty or sometimes sixty takes for the more difficult scenes was a real challenge for Jack and something quite new. 'He's demanding,' said Jack, with just a hint of understatement. Kubrick's approach was: how can we do it better than it's ever been done before? 'A lot of actors give him what he wants,' Jack went on. 'If you don't, he'll beat it out of you – with a velvet glove, of course.'

Jack's method of dealing with such eccentricity was to bitch and moan behind Kubrick's back, 'I'm a great off-stage grumbler.' Poor old Shelley Duvall had nowhere to vent her frustrations, storing it all inside to such a degree that she almost suffered a nervous breakdown. Apparently Kubrick demanded 127 takes from Shelley in one scene.

Seeing all this unfold at first hand was Leon Vitali, a former actor who'd become personal assistant to Kubrick. 'Stanley loved working with Jack,' he recalls, 'because as an actor he placed himself completely in Stanley's hands and just went with him. I think the secret of their relationship was that Jack never felt hindered from trying anything, and Stanley never felt hindered about saying, "Well, do a little more of that, push it further." It was a wonderful collaboration.'

According to Vitali, the way Kubrick liked to work was with a script that was never really finished, it would adapt and change all the way through shooting. 'Jack always used to laugh because every day there'd be so many changes and they were all colour coded, but by the end of it no one could remember which colour came last.' Rehearsal time was also very important for Kubrick. 'He'd kick everybody off the set,' says Vitali, 'so he could work quietly with the actors. It might take an hour or two hours, or even longer sometimes, with everyone else just waiting outside to come back on.'

Holed up in a palatial apartment on the Chelsea embankment while *The Shining* took shape, Jack was able to savour the London scene in much the same way pal Warren had done in the mid-sixties. At one of the numerous parties he attended given by London's social elite, Jack met Margaret Trudeau, wife of Canada's former prime minister Pierre Trudeau. Margaret had left her husband and was enjoying numerous flings around the world. She later confessed to being instantly attracted to Jack and they left the party together in his chauffeur-driven Daimler, she crouching on the floor to avoid the lenses of waiting paparazzi. It was on the journey home, Margaret later revealed, that she discovered 'just how much room there was in the back of a Daimler'. According to Margaret, she and Jack became brief lovers, and she never let go of the fanciful notion that there might be a chance of a longer relationship. But Jack never hid his love for Anjelica from her and gave the former First Lady of Canada the ultimate brush-off when he told her over dinner one evening, 'Guess who's coming tomorrow?' The fling was over, and Trudeau felt 'crushed . . . a fool'. But a fool who wanted more. Years later they bumped into each other again at a Hollywood party. According to Trudeau, Jack took her into the men's toilet for a quick fumble and throb.

Actor Burt Young, who'd appeared in *Chinatown* but is best known as Stallone's brother-in-law in the *Rocky* movies, was called over to Jack's table at a New York nightclub to meet some of his pals. 'This is a great actor,' said Jack of Burt. Deeply moved, Burt replied, 'Jack, y'know when I knew you were great?' Jack looked up and said, 'No, when?' Burt carried on, 'When I read in the paper you screwed Margaret Trudeau in the back of a limousine.' Jack smiled, 'Yeah, yeah – that was great!'

Jack was not altogether unfamiliar with car sex. Sixties party animal Bebe Buell, one-time lover of Mick Jagger, Iggy Pop and Jimmy Page, confessed to having sex up against a car with Jack around about this time. She hung out with him for about a year during the early eighties. 'He's a great guy,' she recalled. 'It was very cool. My first sex-against-the-car lesson with Jack.'

When Anjelica arrived in London she couldn't take much solace in Jack's company. As he had been during *Cuckoo's Nest*, he was toting some pretty heavy on-screen psychological baggage that couldn't be so easily packed away at the end of the day. She'd arrived during the shooting of those scenes where Jack was required to be unshaven, unkempt and very, very bonkers. Working hard and often late into the night he'd often return home, walk straight to the bed, collapse onto it and immediately fall asleep.

The famous moment where Jack is required to break down a bathroom door with an axe to get at his wife and child was worked on for several days. Originally the props department built a door that could be easily broken, but having been a volunteer fire marshal in his youth Jack tore it apart so easily they were forced to build a much stronger replacement. Poking his head through a gap, Jack announces, 'Here's Johnny.' That line, one of the most famous in screen history, was an ad-lib by Jack, an imitation of announcer Ed McMahon's famous introduction of Johnny Carson on his late-night TV chat show. Amusingly, Kubrick didn't get the connection; having lived so long in England he wasn't at all familiar with American television.

When it opened in the spring of 1980 *The Shining* was a huge commercial success, but critics were divided over Jack's performance, some deriding it as completely over the top. During filming Jack had been similarly concerned, querying, 'Jesus, Stanley, aren't I playing this too broad?' No, Kubrick insisted, the character should be an almost pantomimic villain. The result is highly memorable. 'I can't talk too highly about how good Jack was in *The Shining*,' says Vitali. 'It was a long schedule for him, and he was always up and ready for it. There's the scene where he's pushing Shelley Duvall up the stairs and she's swinging a baseball bat at him. We had two cameras set up, and there was this one take; it was just so amazing that there was a spontaneous outbreak of applause and cheering from the crew. As Stanley said, it was one of those things where the hands and the brain are all wired together, you don't know what you're doing, but everything you're doing is right.'

5

The Excessive Eighties

Let me tell you something. If I didn't have a son that still loved me, I'd blow your fuckin' brains out.

When Marlon Brando agreed to play a small role in the political thriller *The Formula* (1980) alongside George C. Scott, nobody knew that it would be the last time he'd stand in front of a movie camera for nine years. Again he was up to his old tricks, insisting his character wear a hearing aid that was in fact a radio receiver through which an assistant fed him his lines. There was also the customary taunting of his director, this time John Avildsen. On his first morning on the set Marlon summoned Avildsen to his trailer. The script was on Marlon's lap and he was eyeing it contemptuously. 'I can't say this shit,' he said. 'OK,' replied Avildsen, 'let's find some shit you can say.' The two men spent a most entertaining morning swapping stories and jokes and then finally arriving at some dialogue Marlon was happy with. 'It was delightful working with him,' Avildsen later recalled. 'He was worth the quarter-million dollars he insisted on getting each day. In cash.'

For years now Marlon had been dividing his time between his home in Mulholland Drive and his paradise island, where life seemed much simpler – but was it? In the mid-seventies he'd sunk a small fortune into a hotel complex that was doomed from the beginning. Storms and high tides meant flooding was a perpetual problem and Marlon was driven nuts by middle-aged ladies crying, 'Mr Brando, we loved you as Napoleon,' and asking for his autograph. It was a bad idea that was eventually scrapped. What possessed him to do it in the first place? 'I love having projects, even bad ones,' he told the press. 'I don't want to sit on an island like a meditative Buddha.'

His other projects included the establishment of a research station to find ways to tap solar and wind energy and to extract protein from seawater. He believed the planet was in peril due to overpopulation and pollution and these problems had to be solved quickly. When one reporter congratulated Marlon on persuading a tycoon to invest in one of these schemes he replied, 'Wasn't hard. All I had to do was rub his hump with yak butter and suck on his earlobe a little.'

His island served another purpose, too, as a sanctuary for his children away from the decadence and corruption of Hollywood. Producer Albert Ruddy recalls Marlon telling him, 'I'm keeping that island, I like that island, I don't want my kids to grow up in LA, I want them to grow up in Tahiti.' Nice idea. 'But the tragedy of his life,' says Ruddy, 'is that his kids still grew up troubled.'

Jesus Christ, she's a dyke.

Dennis Hopper was off to Canada after agreeing to play the role of an alcoholic father just out of prison for ramming his truck into a school bus full of kids in *Out of the Blue* (1980). But he got fed up after two weeks of just bumming around in his trailer and not working. The film was in a mess, it was going to be shut down, the director Leonard Yakir hadn't any usable footage. It was Dennis who came to the rescue, agreeing to take over. It was an amazing chance to direct again, the first time in ten years, and it had fallen straight into his lap.

Dennis didn't muck around. Once in charge he made swift and drastic changes, such as throwing away the script and starting all over again. If I take the movie over on the Saturday, Dennis was thinking, I have Sunday to write it, and we start shooting on Monday. From a routine film about a teenager from a broken home Dennis turned *Out of the Blue* into a thoroughly depressing picture of angst-ridden family life. The mother became a drug addict and the daughter a punk rocker who stabs her father with scissors and then blows up herself and her mother in a truck. In the original script only Dennis's character died. 'Now the whole family goes.' Hopper went on a blitzkrieg and had the movie wrapped in four weeks. When it opened, opinion was polarised: people either hated it or loved it. Dennis didn't care. He saw himself as a protest artist, making statements about what he saw happening in his country. 'And what I see is a corrupt place, which I kind of enjoy.' Leaning forward for effect, Dennis whispered to his interviewer, 'I'm kind of corrupt myself.'

He flew to London with his daughter Marin for a film-festival showing of *Out of the Blue*. In the arrivals lounge he ran over to her, ecstatic. 'Oh my God, I've just been through customs and I've gotta let you know something. I have drugs all over my body. *I have drugs all over my body!* And I got through customs.' Marin sunk her head in her hands, as if to say, 'OK, thanks for that, Dad.'

Though he had proved he remained capable behind the camera, Hollywood still refused to take notice. Executive Ned Tanen of Universal, for example, knew that 'Dennis has more talent in one hand than most of the people making a fortune in the film industry.' But, 'Sadly, it can't be pointed in the right way.' His drinking and wild behaviour were still barring him from mainstream cinema. As director James Frawley says, 'Dennis's reputation in the media, and what he represented, over-shadowed his ability as an actor and director, no question. Because he's a wonderful performer.'

Perversely, Dennis's drinking was never particularly detrimental to his work. As he liked to say, he drank all day and still managed to write and direct *Easy Rider*. He was able to function normally when he had to, without appearing disorientated. (No more than usual, anyway: he thought he was doing fine so long as he wasn't rolling around on the floor insensible.) And it was all done in plain sight, no rushing to the bathroom between set-ups for Dennis. 'In those days I was doing it right out in front of everyone.' If he wanted to get totally blotto and black out the world he'd start lining up shots of tequila and hit them, bang bang, one after the other.

Years later Dennis confessed that in spite of all the drugs, psychedelics and narcotics he did, he was at heart an alcoholic. 'Honestly, I only used to do cocaine so I could sober up and drink more.' At the time he didn't think he'd ever be able to live without booze. His idea of a perfect retirement at the time was to buy the biggest bottle of alcohol he could, sit in an armchair somewhere and live perpetually pissed. Is it any wonder that *Empire* magazine once said, 'If Dennis Hopper didn't exist, Hollywood would be required to invent him?'

You dream that if you discuss the revolution with a man before you go to bed with him, it'll be missionary work rather than sex.

Warren Beatty had long held an ambition to make a film about American writer and activist John Reed, who charted the bloody birth of the Soviet Union in his classic book *Ten Days that Shook the World*. Reed had been dubbed 'the playboy of the revolution'. Warren could relate to that.

He knew *Reds* (1981) was going to be a tough pitch. 'It's not the most attractive thing in the world to a studio, a three-and-a-half-hour movie about a communist who dies.' He tried Paramount first and met with its chief Charles Bluhdorn. 'What's it going to cost?' Warren said twenty-five million. Bluhdorn couldn't believe it. 'Why are you doing this? Do me a favour, Warren. Take twenty-five million, go to Mexico, spend a million on another movie, and keep twenty-four for yourself. Just don't make this movie!' It was tempting, but Warren said, 'I'm sorry, Charlie. I really am gonna have to do this.' Against his better judgement Bluhdorn agreed to back the project; after all, Beatty was still hot after the success of his last movie. 'Warren could dictate what he wanted to make,' said Robert Evans. '*Reds* was his come shot after *Heaven Can Wait*.'

To bring his vision to the screen Warren hired acclaimed British playwright Trevor Griffiths, considered by many to be an odd choice. 'Maybe it was,' says. Griffiths. 'I don't know. Warren wasn't a theatre man, in fact he didn't like the theatre, he didn't like actors or acting, or at least this is my understanding of it. He said to me, "Actors are people who jump through hoops," that was the definition he gave me. But I thought he was incredibly smart and very connected.'

They first met at Mike Nichols's wedding in America. Esteemed playwright Lillian Hellman, an old friend of Warren, was also there. She was then in her seventies and a frail creature. Griffiths recalls her spotting Warren and hobbling over towards him saying, 'Warren, my dear Warren,' and him picking her up above his head. 'Oh God, the millionaire,' she said. Warren smiled. 'Billionaire.'

An early meeting between director and screenwriter was at London's Claridge's Hotel, from which Griffiths was kindly asked to remove himself because he wasn't wearing a tie. Warren wasn't standing for such stuffy tradition and offered to buy the hotel. Griffiths was allowed to stay. As he began working on the screenplay Griffiths quickly saw that Warren's obsession about the subject matter was what his obsession always was: 'With himself. I don't say that viciously, he just happened to be part of a very winning narcissism that pervades American life, particularly American Hollywood life.'

Ultimately the partnership ran aground when Griffiths submitted his screenplay, which Warren liked but only with, inevitably, a whole bunch of changes. Together they sat in a hotel room for months on end pounding away on a new version. Fed up, Griffiths left for London – he wanted his life back, to put it bluntly – but Warren followed him and they resumed the work until, after one row too many, Griffiths walked out and that was it. Perhaps the problem was that Griffiths's angle focused too heavily on the politics to the detriment of the romantic elements that Warren saw as equally important to the story. Reed had a tumultuous relationship with fellow scribe Louise Bryant, a role he'd already cast Diane Keaton in. Warren took over the script himself, with assistance from Elaine May and Robert Towne.

As for Griffiths, he looks back now with a combination of, 'pain, bitterness and joy'. His Hollywood sojourn was not completely devoid of merit or pleasure. He recalls bumping into Jack on numerous occasions, even attending his first A-list party as the guest of Jack and Warren. 'I had no tie on and hair down my back. Nobody knew who I was so they asked Jack and he told them I was his Native American gardener, so for the next hour people kept coming up to ask me if I'd do their garden for them. They were all women, so Jack had obviously told them a lot more than that. That really amused me.'

When *Reds* went before the cameras not only was Warren the star but he'd installed himself as director. He'd had no choice: 'I felt that no one had the power to make it but me, that I had earned the right to make that movie.' It took a whole year out of his life, shooting on several continents, often without a full script. 'Warren Beatty is *mysterium tremendum*,' said co-star Edward Herrmann. 'We never saw a script. We could have been shooting *Casablanca* for all we knew.'

Warren didn't want to overlook anything, even taking time out to explain to his extras what the film was about. After a lecture on the rights of the working man during filming in Spain, the extras took his message to heart and refused to return to work, having suddenly decided they were being exploited. Warren rolled his eyes, smiled at the irony and increased their wages.

Warren was having trouble casting Eugene O'Neill, the American play-wright who stole Reed's lover Louise Bryant. He went over to Jack's place for advice. 'What do you think the part needs?' asked Jack. Warren thought a bit and said, 'Above all else, you need to believe unquestion-ably that the character can take the leading lady away from me.' Jack smiled. 'Well, there's only one actor who could do that – me.'

During filming, rumours circulated that Jack had fallen in a big way for Diane Keaton; they had been seen out together, so naturally to a hack journalist's mind they were shagging. When asked if the story was true, Jack confessed it did feel a little bit like that. 'I thought, my God, I've got a real crush and, holy fuck, this is my best friend and his girl-friend!' Nothing happened, of course, Jack would never two-time his buddy. 'I'm not an asshole.'

Again during filming, the perfectionist in Warren's soul came to the fore and he demanded multiple takes from his actors. In one scene played between Jack and Diane, Nicholson raged at Warren, 'Just tell me what the fuck you want and I'll do it.' Jack was visibly shaking.

Esteemed Broadway star Maureen Stapleton, who attended the Actors Studio in the fifties with Brando, was giving a speech to a large crowd of workers in a rainstorm. After each take Warren said, 'That's great. Terrific,' but asked her to do it again, and again and again. After one very good delivery Warren went, 'Great.' Everyone on the crew relaxed, not least Maureen. Then. 'One more time, please.' Maureen exploded. 'Are you out of your fucking mind?' The whole crowd of extras broke into cheers.

Warren had a habit of pushing and pushing his actors. 'What do people say: he's not a perfectionist, he just does it until he gets it right,' says *Dick Tracy* producer Jon Landau. 'Warren knows what he wants, and as a director knows that you can't tell an actor what to do, you have to lead them to that place. The actor has to discover it themselves but the director has to be the one influencing them.' As Robert Towne puts it, 'Warren works everybody to a frazzle, but always wins them back.'

Well, not quite everyone. Gene Hackman agreed to play a cameo role in *Reds* as a favour to Warren, who'd launched his career with *Bonnie and Clyde*. Despite appearing in only two scenes, Warren made Hackman complete fifty takes for one of them. When he called a few years later to ask Hackman to appear in *Dick Tracy* the answer was, 'I love you, Warren, but I just can't do it.'

Some scenes in *Reds* took so long to film they actually impinged upon the domestic lives of those involved. Cameraman Vittorio Storaro's family were based in London and during the filming of Warren's death scene, which was dragging on interminably, as he'd return home his kids would yell at him from the window, 'Pa! Pa! Is he dead yet?' Storaro called back, 'No, not yet, but he's very sick.'

Warren was just as tough on Diane, and their relationship took a mighty battering. Warren likened making a movie with your partner to 'running down a street with a plate of consommé and trying not to spill any'. Diane was at a loss sometimes as to what Warren was after in a scene, as he demanded yet another take. 'Warren was very fastidious,' observed George Plimpton, a magazine editor who was offered a small role in the film when he nearly tripped over Beatty as the actor lay sleeping on the floor of the Playboy mansion. 'He did thirty or forty takes, all the time. Diane almost got broken.' Plimpton thought perhaps Warren was deliberately causing friction so that their relationship would mirror that of their on-screen counterparts. Well, it worked; they broke up. Before *Reds* was in the can Diane had gone, straight into *Shoot the Moon* with Albert Finney, a film that centred, ironically, on a relationship breaking down. Its director Alan Parker recalled, 'If anyone mentioned Big W, she'd just walk away. There was no way she was going to share all that.'

To be fair, although *Reds* placed a huge strain on their relationship – Warren was so completely obsessed by it there was very little room for anything else, Diane included – a number of other factors contributed to its breakdown. 'I adored him. I was mad for him,' she later confessed. 'But we were never, ever to be taken seriously as one of the great romances.' It drove her crazy that he wanted a child with her but continued to indulge in quick flings, including an attempted one with another actress working on the film. In London he invited himself into her trailer and the first thing he asked was, 'Do you fuck?' The woman was quite startled by this but managed to reply, 'Yes, but not you.' Poor Warren was somewhat puzzled. 'Why not me?' 'Because I'm a lesbian.' Warren paused, and then said, 'Can I watch?'

Around the same time Jurate Kazickas, a writer and filmmaker, was invited by Warren to LA after a mutual friend said they'd be perfect for each other. She was collected by limo from the airport and was taken to Mulholland Drive, where the dinner table was laid romantically for two. Warren came in, took one look at Jurate and his face fell. 'It was the most painful moment,' she later lamented. They ate and made interesting conversation but she could tell he didn't fancy her. Every twenty minutes Keaton called. Before his driver whisked her away Warren kissed her on the cheek and said, 'Jack Nicholson would just adore you.'

As *Reds* continued, costs started to spiral out of control. Paramount production chief Barry Diller stopped talking to Beatty in an effort to make the star feel guilty about using so much of his money. When the budget rose to a reported $40m a state of cold war existed between star and studio. Rumours of another *Heaven's Gate* began to spread and Michael Eisner, then president of Paramount, lamented in a memo the studio's decision to green-light *Reds*. It really was the ultimate irony that it was costing so much American capital to make a film about a communist.

By the time *Reds* was finished Warren had exhausted himself; he was spent both physically and mentally and had lost something like thirty pounds. During location shooting in Finland co-star Jerzy Kosinski said Warren was 'coughing all the time. Sick. Emaciated.' Maybe he'd taken too much on. Certainly there was an element of megalomania in wanting to star, write, produce and direct so epic a picture. Strange, then, that after such a Herculean effort Warren should choose to give no interviews or other publicity when his film opened in December 1981. His love life would get in the way, he said; he wanted his work to speak for itself. Years later he admitted this was a calamitous mistake. *Reds* did only average business at the box office.

The critics on the whole liked it, though, and when the Oscar nominations were announced *Reds* was up for twelve, the biggest haul since *A Man For All Seasons* in 1966. Warren was now the only person, other than Orson Welles, to receive Oscar nominations in the same year for acting, directing, writing and producing – something he achieved twice (for *Reds* and *Heaven Can Wait*), Welles just the once for *Citizen Kane*. It didn't win the big gong, however. *Chariots of Fire* carried off the best film award, Warren making do with an Oscar not for his acting but, curiously, as best director. Still, a fine achievement. 'In the past the Academy has always been a little reticent to give Warren his due,' said Jack. 'They hold back because he's too pretty and cute.'

They hang people for that, Cora!

For years Jack Nicholson had wanted to remake the classic film noir *The Postman Always Rings Twice* (1981), this time ratcheting up the sex, making it far more explicit than the censor had allowed the 1946 Lana Turner/John Garfield version to be. Jack would play the grungy Depression-era drifter who begins a sadomasochistic affair with the bored, lustful wife of a roadside café owner, and together they plot his murder.

For the randy wife a number of star names were spurned in favour of Jessica Lange, then still known only for her role in the heavily panned seventies *King Kong* remake. Having been in his fair share of Corman schlock, Jack leapt to her defence – 'If anyone ought to know what it's like working with giant apes and moaning carrots, it's me' – while tipping her to be 'the sex star of the eighties'.

With Lange as his co-star no wonder Jack was eager to make the sex scenes as real as possible, as close to porn as modern sensibilities would allow. One really has to raise one's hat to his professionalism here and meticulous eye for detail, insisting for the famous fuck-on-the-kitchen-table scene on a genuine stiffy to show through his pleated pants – 'This bulging railer.' That had certainly never been seen before in a movie, said Jack. 'It would be a stunner.' First he thrust a dildo down his trousers, but that didn't work. 'Jeez, Jack,' said director Bob Rafelson. 'If you're so red hot about this, go upstairs and get a boner.' So off Jack went and began 'whipping my pudding' for a few minutes, trying to flush out of his head the image of an entire movie company listening in. Ultimately his anatomy did not wish to cooperate. 'Somebody might have said I was a pervert,' he said later about his failed effort. 'But in my terms, this would've been extremely artful.'

Our Jack was not to be defeated, however; the great erection shot would one day be his. Ten years later and working with Rafelson again on *Man Trouble*, a disappointing comedy, Jack wanted to try it again, turning up on the set with dildos of various sizes. 'Now we're gonna do this,' he challenged. 'All right, goddamnit,' said Rafelson. 'You've been driving me nuts, we'll do this shot.' This time the dildo worked. 'Now don't you fucking cut this thing out,' ordered Jack, 'or I'll kill everybody involved.' The shot stayed in the movie. Jack invited some of his friends to a screening and as they filed out he asked, 'What do you think of the codpiece shot?' Not one person saw it – not one. 'I was stunned,' Jack admitted. 'I was surprised that nobody noticed the fucking thing. Another lesson in filmmaking.' Nor would this be the last time Jack showed up on a movie set with a giant dildo.

But back to 1981. Though rather dull, *Postman* is charged with a primitive erotic and sexual tension, but the rancid sex went down badly with American critics. As Rafelson said, 'They didn't like the idea that a guy who looked like a sloth could touch the pussy of Jessica Lange. And touch it he did, by God!'

Postman also saw a small appearance by Anjelica Huston, who in personal terms had arrived at a crossroads in her life, not sure where to turn. Acting and the film world had been an inescapable part of her life since childhood. For years she'd spurned offers of work from her father because of 'nepotistic embarrassment' and later rejected Jack's help for the same reason. As a result she hadn't done much of anything in the last few years, save being around Jack's orbit, which was all very nice and great fun, but hardly personally fulfilling. She was rapidly becoming disappointed in herself for having no focus in life.

Things changed early in 1980 after she was involved in a car accident. In hospital Anjelica had plenty of time not just to convalesce, but to sort her life out. She made a decision to embrace acting wholeheartedly. It was the beginning of what would become a distinguished film career, but it drew her away from Jack. In an interview he admitted there had been a standing invitation for marriage for years, but Anjelica had yet to pick it up. 'Or sometimes there might be days when she said, "Today is the day," and I might run off to Alaska or something.' It seemed that both had settled down into a kind of open relationship, allowing each of them to conduct their own independent adventures. Both insisted their love life was better for it.

Jack had now been a star for ten years and worked almost like a man possessed. He needed a break and took one in Europe, though with the paparazzi, not Anjelica, for company. Naturally stories surfaced of him romancing the likes of Princess Caroline of Monaco and actress Rachel Ward.

There was also Janice Dickinson, then at the height of her modelling career and partying hard. She was also getting through her fair share of famous studs, so inevitably got round to Jack. They met at a star-studded party in New York and Janice was debating which celebrity she might sleep with that night. Warren Beatty was too good-looking; Dustin Hoffman too short; Robin Williams too frenetic; and Jack too much of a wolf. 'But Jack did have a great smile, he was irresistibly funny – and he really, really wanted me.' Even though he was surrounded by a bevy of lovelies, Jack behaved as if Janice were the only woman in the room. 'So I left with Jack – much to Warren's chagrin.'

They went back to Jack's suite in the Carlyle Hotel, where he ordered champagne and lobster; he was the perfect host and they made love. It was ruined the next morning when, according to Janice, he asked if she didn't spread it around that they'd had sex. Enraged, Janice turned up for a modelling assignment. 'So, how was Jack?' Asked her make-up man. 'Yes, it's true,' Janice yelled at the top of her voice. 'I've been up all night fucking Jack Nicholson. And I don't think he will be getting an Oscar this time out. Now, can we get to work?'

' Film projects came and went, including *Road Show*, where Jack would have played a cowboy wrangler. With director Richard Brooks he went off scouting locations in Kansas City, but almost got the pair of them arrested when he mooned some tourists. Instead Jack made a film for Tony Richardson, *The Border* (1982), about the problem of illegals entering the US from Mexico. 'He's what the thirties and forties stars were like,' Richardson said after the experience. 'He can come on the set and deliver, without any fuss. "What do you want? OK." And he just does it straight off.'

Shooting in El Paso, Jack was in shocking back pain one day when an emissary of the local mayor arrived with a letter. The president of Mexico was arriving in town for some festivities and because Jack was his favourite movie star desperately wanted to meet him. 'I needn't tell you how much these informal meetings contribute to positive relations between our two countries,' the mayor's letter pointed out.

Geez, international politics, thought Jack as he began formulating what he might say to El Presidente in his bad Spanish. Just then two huge guys, Mexican secret service, Jack assumed, ushered him outside, where a motorcycle escort awaited. Still in pain, Jack lay flat out in his limo as it zipped in and out of traffic, the bikes in front all sirens blaring.

By this point Jack was starting to get edgy; something didn't seem right. 'I start to wonder if I'm being kidnapped.' Just then his driver said, 'Uh-oh, Jack, you better sit up and look at this.' Jack peered out, there were 200 bikes all in formation along the road. As they passed, the bikers pulled out and followed. Now I know there's something weird going on, thought Jack.

The limo and bikers pulled into a big football stadium that was packed with people, complete with a full marching band. 'I'm wondering, what the hell!' recalled Jack. 'I'm now half-convinced that I'm being kidnapped while still mentally rehearsing my wimpy speech about friendship between our two great countries and trying to remember my Spanish so I won't insult the president.'

As Jack stepped from the car a bank of fireworks ignited, spelling

JACK IS NUMBER ONE. Holy God, thought Jack. The president of Mexico must be my biggest fan. As the crowd cheered and the band played 'The Yellow Rose of Texas', forty women in bikinis and high heels sauntered over towards Jack. 'When they got close enough I said, "Ladies, what is going on here?" One of them said, "Anything you want, Jack?" I thought, Jesus Christ, what a night for my back to be out.'

Just then Jack started paying attention to some of the faces of the bikers and picked out Dennis, plus a couple of guys he worked with on *Hells Angels on Wheels*. The whole thing was one big ruse, the letter from the mayor, the limo; it was all a joke by this one grand nut whose idea it was to make the ultimate bike movie with Jack as the star.

We train young men to drop fire on people. But their commanders won't allow them to write 'fuck' on their airplanes because it's obscene!

In 1982 a series of personal tragedies befell Marlon Brando. Jill Banner, an actress he had an on/off relationship with over many years, was killed in a car crash. Marlon attended the funeral but kept away from the main mourners, watching proceedings perched in a tree. Then his trusted business manager Norman Garey inexplicably shot himself.

As the eighties drew on Marlon became even more of a recluse and fortified his Mulholland Drive home with security systems. 'Privacy is not something that I'm merely entitled to,' he said. 'It's an absolute pre-requisite.' As for his career, it might as well have been over. When producers had the temerity to send him scripts he placed them in his freezer until they hardened and then tossed them high up into the canyon below his home and blasted them into smithereens with a shotgun.

Clearly, Marlon was happy doing nothing in particular, save adding a few more kids to his family, usually by different women. 'I had a real Ford assembly line going throughout much of my life,' he once confessed. 'If you're rich and famous, getting laid a lot isn't that difficult.' His attitude to women, though, hadn't altered much from his early days. He liked to joke that he had a long bamboo pole with a leather loop on the end. 'I slip the loop around their necks so they can't get away or come too close. Like catching snakes.'

He also caught up with his reading and gave some thought to life and what it all meant, trying to figure out what it is he wanted to do with his. 'I never really knew.' He also travelled back and forth to his island, his one true sanctuary. 'He worshipped his island in Tahiti,' says producer Albert Ruddy. 'Spent most of his time there. He didn't like hanging around LA, didn't like Hollywood people.'

To fill in the blank moments of his life Marlon would call his friends around the world at all hours of the day and night or fire up his amateur radio. Marlon was a keen radio ham. It was one of the few ways that he could be anonymous. He could shoot the breeze, his voice disguised, and not be fearful that people were saying and behaving in a certain way because he was Marlon Brando. 'He talked on that radio all the time, to people all over the world,' says Gray Frederickson. 'I guess he started it because that was his main way of communicating from his island in Tahiti. When we were doing *Apocalypse Now* he was running over to Hong Kong all the time buying electronic gadgets and had it all set up in his little bungalow on location. So he talked to the world on that little ham radio.'

And he ate; boy did he eat. Friends would often find him curled up in bed with a huge tub of ice cream. The last time Gray Frederickson saw Brando was outside a Baskin Robbins shop and he was tucking with relish into a huge ice-cream sundae. His weight fluctuated wildly. Robert Duvall ran into Marlon when they were looping *Apocalypse Now* and remembered him saying, 'I'll be fat for ever.' Comfort eating is often a problem for children of alcoholics. Terrified that they themselves might turn to booze, they turn to food instead. 'Food has always been my friend,' Marlon declared. 'When I wanted to feel better or had a crisis in my life, I'd open the icebox.'

As his career faded, his obesity, along with an increasingly troubled family life, attracted more attention than his acting. His friends were saddened: 'It disturbs me that toward the end, all some people could speak about was his weight,' said Jack. 'What Mr Brando does for a living ain't done by the pound.'

Every now and then, a person comes along, has a different view of the world than does the usual person. It doesn't make them crazy.

Dennis Hopper had been existing on a steady diet of largely crap roles. There were even plans to reunite him with Peter Fonda for an *Easy Rider* sequel that was to take place a hundred years in the future after a nuclear holocaust, a world of mutant motorcycle gangs. Dennis and Fonda's characters are resurrected to restore the American way of life. 'It's a satire,' said Dennis. Jack would have played God. It didn't happen.

Coppola once again came to Dennis's rescue, casting him in *Rumble Fish* (1983) as an alcoholic father; Dennis was good at playing those, no research required. 'I hire Hopper for the two per cent of ultimate brilliance, not the ninety-eight per cent horse shit,' Coppola said. *Rumble Fish* was an interesting film that brought Dennis back into some kind of relevance, appearing as he did with up-and-coming stars Matt Dillon and Mickey Rourke.

Another rising star, Sean Penn, turned up one day to watch filming. He'd never met Dennis before and was fascinated to see the old pro in action. The scene they were working on had Dillon's character talking about his mother. 'Was our mother crazy?' Dennis is supposed to reply, 'No, your mother wasn't crazy. She just saw things differently than other people.' Coppola demanded quiet, then, 'Action.' Dillon asked the question. 'Dad, was our mother crazy?' Dennis looked him in the face. 'No, your mother wasn't crazy! She just saw things – she saw – she saw a buffalo's feet on an elephant! Have you ever seen rainbows going up a duck's ass? No, your mother wasn't crazy.' The crew fell about. As for Penn, 'Now I knew that everything I had learned about acting I could just throw out.'

When Dennis arrived on the set of Coppola's movie he'd been off the booze for months. The reason? His father lay dying, 'and I wanted him to see me sober for the last year of his life'. There had been very little contact between father and son up until that point, or with his mother, even after the success of *Easy Rider* and the birth of grandchildren. At least there was some form of reconciliation prior to his death. 'He was really a decent guy,' Dennis would say of his dad. 'I just didn't know him.'

Although he was temporarily off the sauce, Dennis's belief back then was that for some scenes you had to be authentically rat-arsed on camera, not act drunk. There was one such moment in *Rumble Fish*, a scene in a bar. 'If we don't get it after the third take,' Dennis told Coppola. 'I'm going to start taking shots of cognac.' Coppola was horrified. He didn't want Dennis back on the bottle, at least not on his film. After Coppola had calmed down they shot for eighteen hours. 'I consumed a bottle of cognac,' said Dennis. 'And I stopped drinking again the next day.'

But on the set of his next film, the Sam Peckinpah thriller *The Osterman Weekend* (1983), one journalist recalled interviewing Hopper in his dressing room and he was drinking beer and pulling on a joint at the same time. Dennis was facing his demons again. Amazingly it still didn't affect his work. He was on time and did the job at hand, the perfect professional, although sometimes when he hit the stuff hard no one knew who was going to come out of the dressing room, Dr Jekyll or Mr Hyde.

But his personal life was a real mess, 'a nightmare'. Back in Taos, Dennis's girlfriend was becoming ever more perturbed by his habit of firing guns into the wallpaper. He imagined intruders or phantoms hovering about the rooms. It was said that he slept with a gun under his pillow. It was the same old paranoia. Dennis was himself hovering pretty close to insanity and planned to demonstrate it to a disbelieving world by literally blowing himself up with dynamite as the culmination of an exhibition of his art work, aptly called 'Art on the Edge'. As a boy Dennis had watched in awe as a stuntman performed this daredevil feat at a rodeo in Kansas, surrounding himself with sticks of dynamite and emerging from the smoke unscathed after they had detonated. It was an illusion, of a kind, but a dangerous and seriously misguided one. The basic theory is that the blast from twenty sticks of dynamite placed in a circle will shoot outwards, creating a central vacuum like the eye of a storm, leaving anything there intact. That is, if everything goes as it should. Some small oversight or miscalculation, or a few sticks failing to detonate simultaneously, and you could be blown to bits.

It wasn't just the public who crowded into a speedway track in Houston, Texas to see Dennis kill himself; friends had flown in for the party, too.

Was this all a giant charade, the artist's ultimate statement? Or was he literally on the edge, now, as never before? 'People,' he reasoned later, 'were worried about my sanity.' George Hickenlooper, who made a documentary on Dennis, believes he was 'at the nadir of his existence then. He was on drugs, his career was in the toilet, he was living on the edge, and it was a way for him to garner some attention, I guess, or at the same time end his life. He would have appreciated either at the time, considering the state he was in.' So if he lived it was a piece of art; if he died it would be a glorious exit.

The crowd watched with bated breath as Dennis strapped himself into a chair, the explosives arranged around him and then – *ka-boom!* When the smoke cleared, Dennis was unharmed, although his tongue was left so numb that he lost the power of speech for several days. When asked years later if he would ever repeat it he deadpanned, 'No. I don't think I'll try that again, thank you.'

Dennis's life at this point was about as unbalanced as it had ever been, his consumption of booze and drugs frankly frightening. He really was on course for hell and damnation. The statistics were awesome. At his peak Dennis was consuming daily – wait for this – a half-gallon of rum with a fifth of rum on the side, in case he ran out, twenty-eight beers and three grams of cocaine, 'lines the length of a fountain pen every ten minutes'. These are amounts that would kill most people.

His paranoia was working overtime, too. For some reason he believed there was a contract out on his life. Even the sanctuary of Taos felt unsafe. He had to get out, so called on a bunch of friends to form an armed escort to the local airport. He fled to LA, where he booked into a hotel and called over some female company for a welcome-home orgy. Between bouts of wild sex Dennis was snorting his way Scarface-like through vast quantities of cocaine. He was even shooting the stuff, taking coke directly into his bloodstream. (The effect was instantaneous and dramatic, but it left his body just as quickly.) At times he was shooting it every ten minutes, plus speedballs, coke and heroin mixed, the lethal combination that had killed John Belushi only a few months earlier.

Still convinced there was a contract out on him, Dennis moved from town to town. At one point he confronted a local mobster he believed was out to get him. The meet was in a deserted parking lot and Dennis wanted answers to questions. When he wasn't satisfied with the answers he pulled a knife. Luckily the crook felt pity for the miserable Dennis and didn't have him killed on the spot.

Let's face it, I fucked them all.

Following her romp with Jack, supermodel Janice Dickinson managed to snare Warren Beatty next. They kept bumping into each other in New York and Janice invited him to the notorious nightclub Studio 54. Warren declined, that just wasn't his scene. She'd got his attention, though, and Warren invited her to his suite at the Carlyle, where she'd romanced Jack. Warren's suite was considerably bigger, she noticed.

Warren got chatting to Diane Keaton on the phone as Janice made herself comfortable. Just then the second line rang; it was new conquest Mary Tyler Moore. Deftly Warren put Diane on hold and proceeded to make Mary 'feel deeply loved, too', recalled Janice, who watched, marvelling, as he telephonically juggled both women for a few minutes.

Eventually royally seduced, Janice recalled that Warren hung on her every word, making her feel like the centre of the universe, and when they made love she wasn't disappointed. 'He knew where everything was and what to do with it. Of course he'd had lots of practice. I tried not to think about just how much.' Janice woke up at around 3 a.m. to find Warren wasn't in bed; instead he was standing admiring himself in the mirror. When she asked what he was doing he said, 'I'm trying to get that just been fucked look.' Janice dated Warren for the next few months before their passion petered out naturally. 'I never let myself fall in love with him,' she said. 'As I knew he was making half a dozen women feel the same way at the same time.'

Including Sylvia Kristel. Warren bumped into the *Emmanuelle* star at an LA party and called her a few days later. Sylvia felt seduced almost by his voice alone, writing in her autobiography: 'When you hear him murmur "It's Warren Beatty" you immediately realise he's actually saying: might the prospect of sleeping with me be agreeable to you?'

Sylvia agreed to meet Warren at a luxury hotel, despite a friend's warning that he always carried the key to a suite, just in case he got lucky. They had lunch, though Sylvia was curious that he'd brought along another woman, 'That week's conquest.' Sylvia later found out that Warren thought she was bisexual and was hoping . . . well, Warren lived in eternal hope. She arranged another meeting with him, but this time with the caveat that 'Sylvia is not Emmanuelle.' So began an affair that lasted a few brief though memorable months. Sylvia saw that for Warren the pursuit of women was 'an irrepressible urge, an endless hunting ground'. She found it amusing to watch Warren constantly on the lookout for new prey like an animal, knowing that few women could resist but that all would suffer the 'frustration of becoming no more than a memory a few hours later'.

By the eighties, of course, Warren's reputation as a ladies' man was already legendary. 'But it was a puny thing compared with the reality. It really was,' says screenwriter Trevor Griffiths. 'He used his sexuality the whole twenty-four hours of his day. It really was like *Shampoo*; there was no way of getting away from the next erection. We'd be driving down Sunset Boulevard or wherever, and he'd stop next to some woman in her Mercedes. He'd just look at her, she'd look at him, and something would happen behind their eyes. He'd mouth "hello" and they'd pull over and there would be an exchange of telephone numbers. Now, you imagine that and put yourself in his position and that is a very strange life to lead.'

Rolling Stone magazine had fun revealing some of Warren's chat-up lines – 'You're the most beautiful woman I've met who's not an actress or model,' or, 'Your grandmother, she was one of the sexiest women I ever knew.' Amazingly, he still succeeded in avoiding marriage while remaining friends with many of the women in his life. 'No matter what has happened,' he once revealed, 'I've never felt very apart from any of the women with whom I have been involved. Some feeling always remained.'

If you wanted to get me on my back, all you had to do was ask me.

It wasn't often that Jack Nicholson scooped up a Burt Reynolds cast off, but that's exactly what happened with *Terms of Endearment* (1983), and he ended up with a second Oscar. It was a gem of a role, Garrett Breedlove, a pot-bellied, balding, hard-drinking ex-astronaut who chases young women around. Perfect casting for Jack, you might think, but director/writer Jim Brooks, who'd come from a highly successful career in TV with *Rhoda* and *Taxi*, initially offered it to Reynolds. After the mustachioed one turned it down Jack was happy to come on board, not giving a rat's arse about what the role might do to his image. Indeed, critics praised him for taking a part that called for an overweight, middle-aged man, just the sort of casting many Hollywood leading men actively avoided. And Jack went all out with the role, asking Brooks on set, 'How much gut do you want?' It also represented a nice change of pace after playing an assortment of sex maniacs and nut jobs. 'I was looking for a slightly more socially redeeming character,' Jack said.

As filming began tension emerged between Jack's co-stars Shirley MacLaine and Debra Winger, playing mother and daughter. The two women did not get along and Jack often had to act as mediator. While watching rushes one day, Shirley reached over to touch Debra's arm. She missed. 'You grabbed my tit!' Debra shrieked, and to the amazement of everyone punched MacLaine and had to be pulled off her by crew members. If anything Debra's behaviour became more deranged. During Jack and Shirley's love scene the actress crept under the bed sheets with them and licked Shirley's leg. Fuming, Shirley got in her car and made to drive off. Brooks couldn't have his star go AWOL so one of the producers threw themselves onto the hood of the car to stop her leaving.

Shirley's relationship with Jack was far more positive. Although she was Warren's sister, Shirley didn't know Jack at all well before starting work on *Terms of Endearment* but it ended up being a dream partnership. 'To have Jack in bed was such middle-age joy.'

Regardless of the frictions, *Terms* was a huge box-office success and won a clutch of Oscars. Strolling over to the podium to pick up his best supporting actor award Jack punched the air and roared, 'All you rock people down at the Roxy and up in the Rockies, rock on.' Not your typical acceptance speech.

While publicising the film in Britain, Jack discovered that his reputation was beginning to get in the way of his work. A British tabloid claimed he'd had a 'string of drug busts in America'. Jack sued, and the paper was forced to pay him substantial damages. Maybe someone forget to tell Jack that if you dance with the devil, expect to get pricked by his horns. Maybe someone forgot to tell the paper, too.

It wasn't only on the cinema screen where you'd catch Jack; he often took a starring role courtside at home games for his beloved Lakers. A basketball fanatic, Jack sees his local team as often as work permits, sometimes chartering his own plane to away games for himself and select buddies. He's gone down in Lakers history as their number one fan, entering the arena sporting sunglasses to huge cheers. *Sports Illustrated* feels that Jack's affection for basketball is just part of his 'successful project to have more fun than anybody on the planet'.

A highly vocal fan, ranting and raving at the referee or opposing players, stories of Jack the fan are legion. Back in 1980 when the Washington Bullets were playing the Lakers a lively exchange broke out between Jack and the visitors' coach, Dick Motta, who claimed Jack made a grab for his leg. 'You touch me again and you won't need a frontal lobotomy,' Motta yelled, alluding to Jack's *Cuckoo's Nest* role. Jack hit back, saying it was Motta who was breaking the rules (he had strayed out of his coaching area). 'Say, pal,' Motta responded, 'if you wanna be a coach, buy me a team and I'll make you my assistant. Now sit down.' 'Sit down yourself,' said Jack. 'I pay money for these seats and, by the way, pal, it'll take somebody bigger than you to make me sit.'

The crowd loved it, of course. Jack's antics are usually deliberately orchestrated to raise the temperature of a game, firing up both the team and the fans. Once his courtside tantrum was so heated, screaming at a ref who had penalised a Lakers player, that the official warned security that if Jack threw another fit he should be escorted out. It did the trick, though; the Lakers stormed to victory. His gamesmanship is equally outrageous at away games, most notably against arch rivals the Boston Celtics, where he reportedly mooned at thousands of their fans at the Boston Garden Stadium. Red Auerbach, the Celtics general manager, told *Sports Illustrated*, 'I've seen a lot of fans in my day, and to me there's a difference between being an ass and being a fan.'

After that incident Jack was public enemy number one with the Celtic fans, but still enjoyed the away games in Boston. 'Until you've had 15,000 people in Boston Garden screaming, "Fuck you, Jack!" you haven't lived.' It's all good-natured banter, and as he takes his seat he gestures obscenely to the baying crowd and laughs at their hostile banners – CHOKE ON YOUR COKE, JACK. But even in this maelstrom of hate he had his supporters, two teenagers standing in the corner, wearing dark clothes and sunglasses. As Jack saw them they flipped over a small cardboard sign that read NICHOLSON YOUTH.

You know in 15 years, you're going to be playing soccer with your tits. What do you think of that?

Besides not making films, Marlon Brando was still trying, unsuccessfully, not to gain the proportions of a humped-back whale. One of his girl-friends apparently dumped him when he failed to keep his promise to lose weight. He said he was dieting, but never seemed to get any thinner. She later found out that deliverymen were throwing bags of Burger King Whoppers and McDonald's Big Macs over the gates of his Mulholland Drive estate at night to relieve his hunger pangs.

Tales emerged that Marlon's idea of a snack was a pound of cooked bacon shoved into an entire loaf of bread. Hardly surprising, then, that he was hit by a series of grave illnesses, though somehow he always managed to survive. 'He has the constitution of a horse,' said friend Phil Rhodes.

At Mulholland Drive there were rumours that he'd stay in his bedroom for days on end, a loaded pistol and 12-gauge shotgun tucked under his bed. When he went out it was usually in disguise, once with his whole face wrapped in white gauze, like the invisible man. He really would have been better off making movies, but his hatred of the profession, or those in charge of it, never left him. 'I notice,' he once said, 'that the width of a Hollywood smile in my direction is commensurate with how my last picture grossed.'

As a novice actor Marlon became a great observer of people, watching and mimicking their quirks and gestures. When fame came along that particular weapon was ripped from his actor's armoury and instead he became the observed. Or maybe he never forgave acting for stripping him of what he held most precious – his privacy. 'Acting is a bum's life in that it leads to perfect self-indulgence.'

Producer Albert Ruddy recalls one day sitting with Marlon when they were shooting scenes at a New York hospital for *The Godfather*. He'd taken a shine to a little Puerto Rican boy who ran the elevator and they were all chewing the fat when this kid confided in Marlon that he wanted to be an actor. 'And Marlon berated him,' says Ruddy. 'He said, "You want to live your life as an actor, having other people put lines in your mouth?" I was stunned, it was like Frank Lloyd Wright asking, "Why do you want to be an architect?" I was shocked. But that's how he felt. That's why he was frustrated and got involved with the Indians and all that. He felt he was pigeonholed and just didn't want to repeat this success over and over as the greatest actor in the world. The guy had accomplished everything that any actor ever did in their life.'

How would you like to have more fun than you've ever had in your life?

As the eighties continued it was a miracle Dennis Hopper's liver and kidneys hadn't divorced themselves from the rest of his body, which was in remarkably fine fettle, considering. But it was his mind that went AWOL first. He'd gone to Cuernavaca in Mexico to make a film called *Jungle Warriors* (1984), playing of all things head of the US drug enforcement agency. He arrived smashed out of his skull on booze and drugs. Checking into his hotel he convinced himself that people were being tortured and burned alive in the basement. Sensing he was next in line for similar treatment, he made a bolt for it, out into the warm Mexican night, stripped himself naked and wandered into a forest. He spent the whole night there, totally out of his mind. He sensed bugs and snakes crawling over and inside his skin, he had visions of an alien spacecraft landing and followed the glowing lights. 'I thought the Third World War had started. I masturbated in front of a tree and thought I'd become a galaxy – that was a good mood!'

By dawn, his revelries in the wood over, Dennis wandered back into town, still naked. Some police tried to dress him but Dennis screamed at them, 'No, shoot me like this! I want to die naked.' Wrestled into the local jail, the hallucinations continued. Telephone wires started talking to him and he heard friends of his being lined up outside and machine-gunned. Fearing that they might soon have a dead film star in their cells, the police dumped him into hospital. There Dennis watched terror stricken as doctors approached him with needles. In his paranoid state he thought they were part of the great conspiracy to kill him.

It didn't take the film's producer long to conclude that Dennis was in no fit state to take part in his movie and organise two hulking stuntmen to accompany him back to the States. On the plane Dennis was convinced he was being filmed by Francis Ford Coppola and Wim Wenders, because he'd seen them with cameras as he was boarding. He hadn't, of course, but Dennis's life had become its own mad movie. Waiting for take-off, Dennis peered outside and in his raddled mind saw the wing catch fire. He broke free from his bodyguards and tried to open the escape hatch. 'I was just totally gone,' he later related. 'But it's always very impressive when you do things like that.' The airline company said it would ground the flight unless Dennis was securely restrained for the whole journey.

Back in LA friends checked Dennis into rehab. 'Really a drag,' Dennis called it. 'Not cool.' He was still in a bad way, hearing voices and secret messages being passed down to him via telephone wires. Friend Paul Lewis visited him. 'He reached the point where he was insane. I'd say hello to him and between hello, how are you, was maybe ten minutes; for three words.' Dennis's daughter Marin later remembered doctors telling her that her father was practically brain dead and they were moving him to an insane asylum. While there he somehow got hold of a pair of hedge clippers and went wild with them until a pair of orderlies put him in a straitjacket. Staff placed Dennis on a regimen of anti-psychotic drugs but for months he had the shakes and found it difficult to string a simple sentence together, nor could he eat properly, unable to manoeuvre a fork into his mouth. His friend Bud Shrake, who wrote *Kid Blue*, visited Dennis at the hospital and saw a pathetic figure. He guessed they must have given him the wrong kind of medication because his arms were drawn up like a praying mantis's and he was trembling as if suffering from Parkinson's disease. At one point they gave him another drug and he froze completely. Doctors would also march him round to different groups of patients, his tongue hanging out, and say, 'Now how many of you have ever seen *Easy Rider*?' They'd all hold up their hands. The doctor would say, 'Well, this is one of the guys who starred in it. You see what drugs will do to you.'

Still suffering the symptoms, Dennis checked himself out of the clinic and was driven back to Taos by his girlfriend. He could barely speak, nor even steady a cigarette in his mouth long enough to light it. How the hell was he ever going to act again? He felt depressed and suicidal. 'I can't go through life like this,' he said. The girlfriend was suitably alarmed to take Dennis to a doctor, who put him on a new course of drugs which seemed to calm him down; at least he could light a cigarette now. 'That was the start of my coming back.'

It had been a horrific experience and one Dennis had come to realise had been induced more by alcohol than by drugs. 'Alcohol drove me insane.' To eradicate booze from his life Dennis went into an Alcoholics Anonymous programme and came out determined to quit. His warped strategy to stay off booze was to keep doing drugs. 'So rather than having a beer in the morning, I would have cocaine.' Sounds logical, if you happened to be Dennis Hopper circa 1983. (The logic being he could stop cocaine anytime.) The flaw in his plan was that he was getting through half an ounce of cocaine every two or three days. He'd turn up at AA meetings piously admitting 'I'm an alcoholic' with half an ounce of cocaine in his pocket. He was heading for oblivion.

Dennis remained at Taos into 1984. He played a small role in a Robert Altman movie, *O.C. and Stiggs* that tanked big time. He hit the bottle again and the hallucinations returned. So too the voices, voices of people suffering torture and murder. 'And the radio was talking to me and the electric wires – boy, I was out of it.'

In April 1984 Dennis checked himself into rehab again in LA. The hallucinations by this time were so powerful that the staff feared he would commit violence upon either himself or a fellow patient. He was put on anti-psychotics again and transferred to a psychiatric ward at a state hospital, where he wandered about the place like an extra in *Dawn of the Dead*, zonked out on a cocktail of prescription drugs for a change.

He was essentially trapped there. There was no family to take responsibility for him: his daughters were too young, his father dead, his mother remarried and no longer part of his life. And certainly Dennis was in no fit state to check himself out.

Bob Rafelson went to see him one day and was appalled that the hospital was pumping more drugs into him. He got him out of there and took him to the home of Bert Schneider, Dennis's old *Easy Rider* producer, who gave him sanctuary and the right environment to begin the long road to recovery. Friends like Dean Stockwell were there for him, too, lending moral support. And slowly but surely Hopper's mind balanced itself out again, found its natural plateau of normality. But it was that old cliché of one day at a time. He went back to AA, this time with the guts to admit he was a drug addict as well as a boozer. He faced the truth about himself and it wasn't pretty, but it was enlightening. He went back over his life, every fucked-up relationship, every violent outburst, each clash with authority, and realised that not once had he been sober, that every bad situation, every mad Dennis moment, had been fuelled by his addictions. In the end it was a simple rationalisation: all he had to do was stop drinking and the paranoia, the schizophrenia, would melt away.

There was no turning back now; his addictive personality meant that he could never do drinks or drugs again. One glass of wine with a meal and he'd want to know where the case was, or the vineyard, and then why the liquor store was closed. As for cocaine, he couldn't sit down and do a line. Bullshit. He'd want to do an ounce.

Dennis's rehabilitation led to welcome reconciliations with his children and his mother. At last he saw the damage he'd done, not just to himself but to those closest to him. There was also a willingness to help other people who, like him, had reached the absolute nadir and were grasping for a new start, a new life free of drugs. 'I don't think people can stop taking drugs until they've bottomed out, spiritually and morally, or they die. That's how they get off drugs.' Customarily with Dennis, his rock bottom was more rock bottom than anyone else's.

Dennis was never to touch booze or hard narcotics again. 'I'd only go back on drugs if sixty per cent of Americans voted that I should,' he once joked. Did he miss them? No, not really. Sure he puffed on the odd joint now and then, but that was purely for relaxation. Question was, had he subconsciously been trying to kill himself with all that stuff? 'No,' he once said, 'I was having a good time.'

Look at the upside: we're not livin' lives of quiet desperation.

In 1984 Warren Beatty returned to heavyweight politics when he supported the presidential aspirations of Colorado senator Gary Hart, marking a new era in the relationship between Hollywood and politics. The pair had met while collaborating on the 1972 presidential campaign for George McGovern and bonded quickly after realising they shared a passion for, well, women. Jennifer Lee remembers Warren introducing her to Hart at the Beverly Wilshire. 'Warren says he's a political hopeful,' she wrote in her diary. 'But he seems more like a poor man's version of Warren.' That would be his downfall.

Hart was intoxicated by Warren and listened to his opinion on key policy matters, but there really was only ever going to be one winner in that year's presidential race, ex-actor Ronald Reagan. Years later Hart would launch another bid for the White House and once again Warren came on board as kingmaker. The political ramifications this time, however, were to be of an altogether more momentous kind.

With no film in the pipeline Warren happily pottered around Hollywood. Nearing the big five-o, he still looked in pretty sound nick. This was due not to hanging out at fancy LA gyms but healthy living habits. For one, he didn't smoke, take drugs or drink excessively. 'It doesn't take much to get me loaded.' Ex-girlfriend Janice Dickinson claimed that because both Warren's parents had been drinkers he'd decided early in life that he'd never go mad with booze or drugs.

Warren was also fastidious about what he put in his mouth. He chewed vitamin pills and steered clear of rich fatty foods. His idea of sin was eating ice cream. Michelle Phillips said he once went on a courgette and string-bean diet for months. He refused to eat anything else. 'He's a complete freak about his health and his food,' she said.

Mike Nichols called him 'a postgraduate hypochondriac'. One time

Warren crossed wires making a call and overheard two strangers discussing the symptoms of a friend about to have her gall bladder removed. He listened and then broke in. 'Hey, she doesn't have gall bladder problems, she should be tested for hypoglycaemia.' Sure enough, he was proved right.

Asked once why he never married any of his many girlfriends, Warren replied, 'Just because you need a quart of milk doesn't mean you have to go out and buy a whole cow.' Well, Warren was certainly making more than the average number of visits to the dairy.

Model and socialite Carole Mallory remembers calling him up to suggest a rendezvous: 'He said he'd be right over. We continued our date on the kitchen table.' It was a one-night stand that didn't stretch to two; she refused to see him again after he passed her name on to Jack.

Warren continued to have his fair share of rebuffs. One of the classics was perpetrated by Sandra Grant, former wife of crooner Tony Bennett. She recalled Warren asking her to invite a girlfriend to her home to make up a threesome. She did just that and when Warren arrived both girls told the by now probably drooling Lothario to undress and get into bed. Teasingly, the girls told Warren to wait while they went into the bathroom to disrobe. Warren waited and waited . . . and waited. But the women never came back. Deciding it was time to puncture his ego, they'd crept out of the front door and gone to the cinema. 'He was adorable,' said Sandra. 'But he had to be taught a lesson.'

Do I ice her? Do I marry her?

In 1984 Hollywood was alive with rumours that Jack Nicholson had agreed to make a sequel to one of his most famous films, *Chinatown*. Once again he would play embittered detective Jake Gittes, Robert Towne would both write and direct, while ex Paramount supremo Robert Evans, who'd started his career as an actor, would appear in front of the camera for the first time in over twenty-five years. Contracts were signed, a production company was formed and the trio went out seeking financial backers.

One such was Texan tycoon Charles Langston, who was invited to

Evans's palatial mansion in LA to talk about the movie. 'Bob was very gracious,' Langston recalls. 'But he was what I would consider a little bit odd. He sat there for four hours out by his swimming pool totally naked as he told me the story of the movie. He'd just gotten out of the swimming pool. Occasionally the phone would ring and he'd pick it up, chat, and then he'd hang up and say, "That was Jack." And then it would ring again, he'd pick it up, "That's Warren, we're all gonna meet tonight at a restaurant on Sunset Strip."' Sure enough, Langston found himself at a table with Jack, Warren and Evans. 'And it was wall-to-wall women. The conversation was nothing about movie making, it was about all the women they had bedded. That evening was wild; you could tell that the bad-boy fraternity had arrived. And you can imagine there were tons of women at that bar, it was about four-deep all the time trying to get in to talk with Warren and Jack.'

Over the course of the evening Langston witnessed and came to appreciate the camaraderie that existed particularly between Jack and Warren. 'They had real respect for each other. And they were helping their buddy out, Robert Evans, because Evans had a money guy in town and they were gonna show the money guy a good time. They had a charisma about them that was magnetic. Back then, this was one of the deals where I wouldn't want to take my girlfriend, not around these guys because, who knows she'd wanna stay. But in their own way, if she did stay they'd make you feel good about it, heh, we're gonna take care of her, don't worry about it, you come back tomorrow and pick her up.'

In the end, though, Langston never got his cheque book out and the *Chinatown* sequel, provisionally entitled *The Two Jakes*, collapsed before it even started. A great supporting cast had been assembled that included Dennis, Harvey Keitel and Joe Pesci, but as the schedule loomed Towne voiced reservations about Evans, that he simply wasn't up to the task of playing the second lead role and should be replaced. Jack remained faithful to Evans and fought his corner. 'Bob used to run Paramount and you can't treat him like a piece of shit,' barked Jack. 'Friendship is more important than money. And if my friend Bobby Evans doesn't do this part, then I don't do this movie.'

It's all about loyalty with Jack; loyalty to his friends is the glue that binds his life together. It's something he grew up with on the streets of New Jersey, a certain belief in honour. 'Jack is tremendously loyal,' says *Witches of Eastwick* director George Miller. 'He had this personal driver who'd been with him for years, drove his Winnebago around while Jack often slept in the back. One day he turned up late on the location and the whole roof of this trailer had been ripped off. He'd been driving along and there was this low bridge and despite all the warning signs he'd ploughed on and shaved off the top. Jack was lying in bed when he saw the roof literally disappear. Of course most people would have sacked the guy. Not Jack, he kept him on.'

Jack certainly stayed loyal to Evans throughout the producer's many turbulent episodes, not least the time he was financially wiped out and lost his beloved mansion. When he heard, Jack got on a plane and flew to Monte Carlo to meet the new owner, went into the guy's bathroom while he was shaving and got down on his knees and begged him to return Evans's house. The guy thought he was crazy and went all over the south of France that summer telling friends, 'Can you believe Jack Nicholson flew over and bent in the bathtub asking for this guy Evans his house back?' In the end he sold the property back to Evans. 'And when I got back into it, I found a drawing Jack did and it said, "Back Home". Beautiful.'

There wasn't a happy ending for *The Two Jakes*, though. Hearing of the acrimony between the partners, Paramount pulled out and the project folded before a foot of celluloid was exposed. A million dollars' worth of sets already built had to be destroyed. Worse, the partners were sued by creditors to the tune of $3m. It left a nasty taste in the mouth and some very bad publicity. Jack was left reeling, while Towne retreated and licked his wounds, not making another movie for three years. *The Two Jakes* finally appeared in 1990 under Jack's direction and was met with a muted public response.

Jack had great affinity for Anjelica's movie-director father John, then in his eighties, the days of directing cinema classics like *Moby Dick* and *The Maltese Falcon* long behind him. Producer John Foreman had come across a property called *Prizzi's Honor*, a nice little black comedy about gangsters. He arranged lunch with Anjelica and told her about it. She loved the idea, there was even a nice little part in it for her, but then came the catch. 'What about your father to direct and Jack to star?' Anjelica was thinking: Don't do that to me. Please!

Jack plays Charley Partanna, a dour mafioso hit man who marries fellow assassin Kathleen Turner only to discover they each have a contract out on the other. He's a bit of a dumb-bell, and so put Jack through the wringer, forcing him to give up everything the public loved about his screen persona – his smile, his charm, his wit. During filming, Huston's continual advice to Jack before takes was, 'Remember, he's stupid.'

Invariably happy to concede near total control to the director, Jack likes to think of himself as the solution rather than the problem. 'I pride myself on being low maintenance.' George Miller recalls a conversation he had with Jack about his relationship with directors. 'Jack said to me, "If Stanley Kubrick wanted me to walk through a door for the hundredth take for some reason only known to him, that was my job, to walk through that door a hundred times." And then when he made *Prizzi's Honor*, John Huston was very ill and directing out of a wheelchair with an oxygen bottle, and Jack said, "I knew that I needed to give John my performance in take one or take two." And that's Jack's brilliance, it's whatever gets the movie made. If that's what Stanley wanted, that's what Stanley got, if that's what John Huston needed, that's what he got.'

Jack loved to refer to himself jokingly as Huston's son-in-law. Maybe the director was a surrogate father in a way, for, as Jack admitted, 'He's one of those people in life whose approval I seek.' Anjelica, though, had to separate her private from her professional relationship with these two powerful males who had shaped her life. During filming in New York she took a separate hotel room from Jack, who again brought his role back home with him. 'There were elements of the hit man in Jack at the time and I didn't want to be around him too much.' Jack had soaked up the gangster milieu by frequenting Brooklyn bars and gambling joints where these sorts of characters hung out, mastering their dialect and gestures. He also ate a lot of pasta to gain a more squat physique than usual. For his squinty-eyed expression he borrowed the look from his dog, 'When he had just killed another dog.'

Prizzi's Honor was only a mild hit when it opened in the summer of

1985 but critics loved the film and it was duly recognised with a host of Oscar nominations, Jack got his eighth best actor nod. But it was Anjelica who walked off with best supporting actress. A delighted Jack was at the ceremony, of course, although his left elbow was in a cast following a skiing accident, and he thanked God Anjelica's prize came early in the evening. 'I was legitimately stoned on pain pills.'

Marlon Brando – In Tahiti, probably.

Baby wants to fuck! Baby wants to fuck Blue Velvet!

It had become the biggest story around Hollywood. 'Hey, did you hear about Dennis Hopper? They say he's gone straight, no booze, no drugs.' People couldn't quite believe it, but there was a new Dennis in town, lean, mean and fit, not the bedraggled devil creature of a few years before.

He'd beaten his obsession, the hardest part of his rehabilitation. 'I don't give a fuck if you put a pound of cocaine on the table, I don't want it.' Sitting in the company of other drinkers no longer sent him off the deep end. He'd no desire any more to join them and get hammered. 'I have a great time not disorientating my mind.' His only vice now was a good cigar.

And he was eager to work, ready to prove to the world that he could be relied upon. No longer would he finish off a bottle of tequila or snort cocaine to help him play a scene. He discovered it was a lot easier now without the mood swings, the anxieties; he fell back instead on his drama training. Bizarrely, it was the sober and clean Dennis that would provide cinema with some of its most perverse and psychotic screen madmen.

Kit Carson, who so memorably caught Dennis's mad era in his documentary *The American Dreamer*, had written the sequel to Tobe Hooper's seminal horror movie *The Texas Chainsaw Massacre* and wanted Dennis to play an avenging sheriff in pursuit of the cannibal killers. It was shot in Austin, Texas, and the cast and crew all stayed in the same hotel. 'Every morning,' recalls Carson, 'Dennis would be in the commissary, going, "OK, I've got to do something today and it's not going to be drugs. So it's gonna be golf."' Dennis had befriended singer Willie Nelson, so every day when he wasn't shooting he'd go off and play golf with Willie. The sport became a passion; he'd play with Neil Young and Bob Dylan, sometimes Jack. It seemed to Dennis that most of America's golf courses were full of former wild men. 'Most of the guys who were heavy on drugs and stuff, we're all out playing golf and we're all sober. It is weird.'

Still, the madman was never too far from the surface. On the set of *Chainsaw Massacre 2* (1986) Dennis celebrated his fiftieth birthday. 'And he insisted on cutting his cake with a chainsaw,' says Carson. So there wasn't a huge change in him then. 'It was clear, however, that he had got more focused on having a relationship with parts of his family that he had neglected in his own egotistical trip,' says Carson. 'I saw a gentleness in him.'

One man who still hadn't heard about the new and improved Dennis, who still thought he got flaked out on drugs and slept with his gun, was director David Lynch. Hopper's name was one of several that came up in meetings about playing a sadomasochistic gangster called Frank Booth in Lynch's new movie *Blue Velvet* (1986), but it was always shot down. Then word reached Lynch that the guy was on the wagon for real. One afternoon Lynch took a phone call he's never forgotten. 'I have to play Frank.' It was Dennis, breathing heavily down the phone. 'I have to play this part because I *am* Frank.' This hardly inspired confidence, in fact it scared the living shit out of Lynch. 'Yeah, David was apparently pretty shaken up by my call,' laughed Dennis. Immediately he put the phone down Lynch called Dean Stockwell, whom he'd already cast in the movie and knew to be a long-time buddy of Hopper. 'My God, Dean, I've just spoken to Dennis Hopper and he said he had to play the part because he *was* Frank. And the scariest thing is, I believe him!'

Agents and industry people warned Dennis to stay clear of Frank Booth. 'This part has no redeemable character. It's beyond redemption.' Bring it on, said Dennis. 'The part is a fucking dream, man.' He knew exactly the kind of guy Frank was. He'd lived in a very dark area of alcoholism, addiction, drug running, outlaw glory. He'd seen

Franks. He'd known them, they'd been friends. 'It was something I really understood.'

Lynch had to concede that Dennis was the only person who could play Frank – 'He's one suave fucker' – and that as an actor he had the same quality as Jack, 'You can't stop watching the guy. He's got a presence.' His savage rape of Isabella Rossellini, inhaling amyl nitrate through an oxygen mask to heighten the sexually violent act, was amongst the most obscene ever shown in a mainstream movie. In the original script Frank inhales helium, which merely has the effect of altering his voice; it was Dennis who suggested amyl nitrate, so altering Frank's mind. It leaves one wondering how the scene would have played with Frank on helium sounding like Donald Duck. 'Now that would have been really creepy,' said Dennis.

It remains an astonishing performance, one that Lynch remembers coming to life with unbelievable power. There was an odd feeling on the set, a disturbing quiet when they finished a take. 'It just astounded me,' said Hopper's brother David. 'Definitely Dennis, in Frank Booth, worked out the worst aspects of his alter ego.'

On release *Blue Velvet* turned Dennis once again into a cult figure, this time for a new generation of moviegoers. Even though he called Frank the most perverse, decadent and degenerate man he'd ever played, Dennis also, rather bizarrely, saw him as one of cinema's great romantic leads! He was deadly serious. Yes Frank was a bit of a sicko, but his desire for Isabella's character was real and he went to any lengths. 'He kidnaps her, cuts her fucking husband's ear off with a pair of scissors, which isn't an easy thing to do, even shoots the cop he's in cahoots with. Now if that isn't true love, what the fuck is?'

Next for Dennis was a role opposite Gene Hackman in the basketball drama *Hoosiers* (1986), playing a drunk who ends up in rehab, a case of art imitating life. The film proved somewhat of a crowd pleaser and earned Dennis a well-deserved Oscar nomination for best supporting actor. It was an acknowledgement of a kind, an acceptance back into the mainstream, and it didn't faze him at all when he lost out.

Dennis was now on a roll, jumping from film to film. *River's Edge* (1986), featuring an early lead role for Keanu Reeves, was a dark fable about America's current crop of disturbed youth. Dennis played a burned-out hippie who sells dope to kids and lives on his own with an inflatable doll. Then Warren asked him to play yet another alcoholic father in a film he was producing, *The Pick Up Artist* (1987), starring the then very hot brat-pack actress Molly Ringwald. There was even a short stint in Spain on cult director Alex Cox's wacky hommage to the spaghetti westerns, *Straight to Hell* (1987). Dennis numbered amongst a truly eclectic cast including Clash front man Joe Strummer and singers Courtney Love and Elvis Costello. Cox had wanted to use Dennis years before on his debut movie *Repo Man*. 'We met for lunch and he was very nice and reasonable and not at all intimidating. In the end I didn't cast Dennis because of money. His agent wanted more than we had, so we went instead with Harry Dean Stanton.'

On *Straight to Hell* Dennis was on set just for one day. He worked fast, luckily, and came well prepared. 'Dennis was just wonderful to work with,' says Cox. 'He didn't act like a big star in any way. Dennis is a real person. Very relaxed and easy to get along with, and a magnet for the other actors. Five were called that day; twenty-five showed up to watch him work.'

I think that something went wrong and now I own a blind camel.

Warren Beatty was having a lot of fun, but he wasn't making movies. With no strong family ties, plenty of money and no compulsion to work, he'd take off for months on end to hop around the world, read, dabble in politics and bed beautiful women, of course. This is the strange contradiction within him: Warren is a workaholic given to gaping periods of hedonistic idleness.

There were always projects on the go, fingers in numerous pies, which made a nice change. Michelle Phillips recalled how Warren could spend five hours a day on the telephone. Practically all his business was conducted on the damn thing. Playwright Trevor Griffiths was amazed to see Warren deftly managing between four and ten projects simultaneously. 'I've been at his suite where he's had six or eight different phone calls all on at the same time, and moving between them. In fact

I was going to write a play for the Royal Court in the eighties called *Warren*, which was just about that. And he said, "I hope you don't, it'll cost you a lot of money."'

The problem with Warren was he's always been a bugger to commit to anything, and that goes for women as well as movies. 'I've made a whole career out of not working,' he liked to joke. For him, making a movie was like vomiting. He really didn't look forward to it, but after he did it he felt a lot better. But the gaps between his films were getting longer, to the extent that each time he made a movie it felt like a comeback. After six years away from screens the project Warren chose to make his return in couldn't have been more of a pilchard, a movie that has become synonymous with box-office disasters – *Ishtar* (1987). Hard to believe, but at the time it looked like a pretty good idea to team Warren and Dustin Hoffman as a couple of luckless cabaret singers lost in Arabia, then throw in Euro totty Isabelle Adjani and a funny camel. But it fell foul of almost everyone who saw it. Roger Ebert in the *New York Post* said, 'It's not funny, it's not smart, it's interesting only in the way a traffic accident is interesting.'

Warren was annoyed that most reviewers dealt with how much the film cost (something in the region of $40m) rather than its merits. Personally he thought it was funny, but the rest of the planet didn't. When asked about the disaster Isabelle Adjani replied, 'Oh, I took it the way Dustin Hoffman did, as a nice holiday in Morocco.'

Promoting *Ishtar* in New York, Warren stayed at the Ritz Carlton. At lunch one day he spied the familiar face of Julia Phillips. He knew the producer was staying in the suite across the hall to his and motioned for her to join him. 'So tell me, Julia,' he said. 'Don't you ever have an inclination to knock on my door late at night?' Phillips, you might recall, had been keen to jump into Warren's pants a few years before but had been rejected. 'Not in the least,' she replied. Far from dissuaded, Warren asked. 'What would you do if I knocked on your door?' She answered, 'I'd tell you to go away.'

Warren was romancing Isabelle at this point, but his roving eye was ever alert. One evening he went out to dinner with a friend and his date, an attractive model. At the end of the meal the waitress took their order for dessert, chocolate or vanilla ice cream were the choices. The model decided on both. For the rest of the evening she could sense Warren staring at her from behind his sunglasses. Next day, sure enough, he called, discussing of all things the fact she'd wanted both ice-cream flavours. 'You like to try everything,' Warren concluded. 'Have you ever made love to a woman? Do you want to? It will be my present to you.' All the time the poor girl was thinking, Just because I ordered both kinds of ice cream!

Anyway, they eventually had a little fling and the model came away duly impressed by his lovemaking and stamina, he could literally go at it all night. Returning home she wrote in her diary, 'I've been Warren-ized.'

There was another affair, with tomboy beauty Joyce Hyser, formerly Bruce Springsteen's squeeze. Reports emerged that Warren was going to settle down with her after Hoffman had convinced him of the joys of married life during the shooting of *Ishtar*. 'Do you want to go on like you have until you're ninety and wind up with the girls laughing at you?' Hoffman had remonstrated. But Warren was still drawn to women almost half his age, and had established not a single emotional root during his roving years, so the fate of Joyce was to be no different. Despite telling friends that she was both a friend and a lover, 'not just a wiggle and a jiggle', Warren was soon alone again. Over the years he'd found stability and a sense of belonging with the temporary family of successive movie crews, or he might attach himself to the families of friends like Hoffman, who genuinely felt for his buddy, seeing in him an essential loneliness. 'I can see him dying alone,' Hoffman told a journalist. 'With nobody there to love him and hold his hand. It hurts to think about that.'

I always like a little pussy after lunch.

The press by now had gotten used to Jack and Anjelica's peculiar relationship in which each seemed to flit in and out of the other's life. But hearing tales of Jack's infidelity must have caused her grief nevertheless. In February 1986 Jack held a party at his holiday home in Aspen, where he met British model and aspiring actress Karen Mayo-Chandler. It was a memorable evening. Jack played the perfect host, Karen recalled, drinking champagne but not excessively. She was, however, surprised by his casual lifestyle, epitomised by his clothes, which she thought looked dishevelled for a rich film star.

Obviously Karen made quite an impression on Jack, for he invited her and a friend round the next evening for more champagne. It was here, Karen claimed, that she refused Jack's suggestion that the three of them finish off the evening in his bedroom. But they remained in touch, meeting occasionally, going out to restaurants, parties, even catching a private movie at Warren's house. Their relationship would deepen later, with scandalous results.

It was back to movies and one of Jack's wildest roles in *The Witches of Eastwick* (1987), based on John Updike's novel about three women in a sleepy town seduced by the devil himself. Really there was only one candidate for the role, since he'd been practising for it his whole life. But it was too obvious a casting choice for director George Miller, who looked at other actors until realising he was crazy not to go with Jack. When they finally met, Jack's first words to Miller were, 'What kept you?'

Jack approached the role with deadly seriousness, reading numerous heavy tomes on medieval witchcraft. He told Anjelica that he wanted audiences to believe that he was indeed the devil incarnate. The quietly suffering Anjelica couldn't miss this open goal, assuring him that such a feat wouldn't be too difficult, research or not.

At first Miller approached Jack with trepidation. 'I thought he was a crazy man, that public persona, and that I was walking into the most difficult situation, and it was like falling down an elevator shaft into a pool of mermaids, he was completely the opposite of my expectation.' At an early meeting Jack said to Miller, 'You're paying me a lot of money, and what you're getting is not an actor but a filmmaker.' Time and time again Jack proved to be absolutely right. 'And he did everything he possibly could to make the best possible film,' said Miller.

And *Witches* needed a solid rock at its centre as too often it threatened to veer completely out of control. 'We had somewhat dysfunctional producers in Peter Guber and Jon Peters,' says Miller. 'And I still don't know why, but it was all pretty crazy. I remember one weekend *Aliens* had just come out and was a huge hit and suddenly Peters was saying, "Let's have a horror movie scene like the alien." And then the next weekend, whatever was number one at the box office, he'd want some of that. There was no logic to it, it was like a kid in a candy shop not knowing which candy to take.'

The film had all the pathologies of Hollywood and Miller actually quit twice. 'The only reason I stayed was because of Jack, and he coached me through the film because I'd never really worked in Hollywood before.' Miller had come to prominence in his native Australia with the *Mad Max* movies but *Witches* was his first American movie, and he admits now to not really knowing the score. In early budget meetings he tried to be helpful, save the producers a little money by saying he didn't really need a trailer. A nice gesture, you'd think, but in the Hollywood-speak of that time it signalled, 'This dumbass is negotiable on everything.' So when Miller wanted three camera crews on a particular day, he only got the one. If he needed 200 extras, half that many would turn up. It was Jack who said, 'George, your politeness is your weakness, you've got to make them think you're a little crazy.' Miller suddenly realised that not only were you punished for good behaviour but you got rewarded for bad behaviour. 'So if I didn't get my third camera I just walked off the set and suddenly, with Jack's coaching, I found myself enjoying the bad behaviour. Jack had seen all this stuff before and was endorsing it. He told me, "Just walk off the set when the producers arrive." And I did, and they never came on the set again. Jack knew all the tricks.'

The friction on the set deeply affected Jack's co-stars, a trio of remarkable women, Michelle Pfeiffer, Cher and Susan Sarandon. They were brought close to tears sometimes, and there were reports of them trying some amateur witchcraft of their own to inflict a nasty dose of herpes on the producers. Again it was Jack who provided the comfort zone, a shoulder to cry on. And a professional aide, able to adapt his performance to the requirements of each actress. Sarandon, for example, was best on the third or fourth take, Pfeiffer on the first. He'd even turn up on his days off to read lines to the girls behind the camera.

Things were a little different with Cher. 'She was very nervous,' recalls

Miller. 'She hadn't done much [acting] and was used to being a diva but here she was in an ensemble piece. Jack had this one long speech with her and every time the take was blown by Cher. We got to about take nine and everyone on the crew was grinding their teeth saying, look, Jack's doing all the running and then you blow it. But Jack didn't get angry at all, he was very kind and encouraging towards her. On the take we ended up using, there is one moment where she had to move into her light, and not only is Jack saying the dialogue and carrying the weight of the whole scene, he puts his hand on Cher's shoulders and turns her body into the light. As part of the character he found a way to get her through it, and I thought, fuck, this guy's a total master. He's a master technician.'

On another occasion, early in the shoot, the crew were rigging lights on one of the big sets, banging and clattering, shouting instructions and making a terrible racket. 'Suddenly Jack walks to the very centre of the room with his script and throws it down on the floor,' Miller recalls. 'And this slam echoes all over the place and everyone just froze and went silent. And then he stormed out again. As he passed me he winked. I thought, what the fuck's going on? I went into his trailer and he said, "George, don't ask me to do your work for you." And I realised he needed the quiet to concentrate, and that was his way of telling me.' After that the crew conducted their work in, shall we say, a more serene manner.

Witches was a big hit for Jack but his performance, grandiose and operatic, was criticised in some quarters. There were accusations of over-acting. Not so, says Miller. 'Working with Jack was like dialling the volume on an amplifier, you started on one and then you could go up to two and three and four. So we'd start on take one and he'd do a performance which was nothing too flamboyant, pretty naturalistic, and then we'd just ramp it up, and it often got to about take eight or nine and then he hit the sweet spot. And then the next take it just went too far. It was like calibrated. It was an amazing thing to watch. It takes a lot of creative courage to get big.'

Justice and law are distant cousins, and here in South Africa they're simply not on speaking terms at all.

As rumours circulated that Marlon Brando planned a screen comeback after almost a decade away, people were asking just where the hell had he been and what had he been doing with his time off, apart from eating lard sandwiches. Such questions always irked the Great One, as if the rest of his life was spent taking time out. The simple fact was making movies was time out for him, it was the rest of his life that was real. 'I'm not an actor and haven't been for years,' he said. 'I'm a human being who occasionally acts.'

The film that tempted Marlon out of his creative idleness was an anti-apartheid drama called *A Dry White Season* (1989). And to prove wrong those critics who claimed he was only returning for the money, Brando donated his hefty salary to an anti-apartheid charity, a gesture that also served to show the world his commitment to toppling South Africa's evil regime.

Inevitably Brando's return to movies made headlines. What wasn't known was that on his first day on the set he was too nervous to leave his dressing room. Despite all that bravado, the image, Marlon was essentially a deeply vulnerable individual. As he once admitted: 'I put on an act sometimes, and people think I'm insensitive. Really, it's like a kind of armour because I'm too sensitive.'

On set co-stars Susan Sarandon and Donald Sutherland and the crew all waited for Marlon to appear. The director Euzhan Palcy – the first black woman to direct a major Hollywood film – went to see him. 'OK, darling,' assured Marlon. 'I'm coming.' Another twenty minutes went by, no show. An assistant went to see him this time. 'Yeah, yeah, yeah, I'm coming.' Still no Marlon. Euzhan went back, sat down next to Marlon and they just talked. She couldn't believe Marlon could be so apprehensive; after all he was a genius, wasn't he? 'But he was first of all a human being. And this guy hadn't worked for years, and he knew that all these actors were there waiting to see the master, the myth. And he needed to wait a little bit to overcome his apprehensions.'

It was a nice little performance, an extended cameo really, but the

Academy felt it warranted an Oscar nomination. Despite the plaudits, his considerable girth still bothered him more than he let on. Karl Malden went to see the picture and felt compelled to write to his old friend telling him: 'I don't care if you are 500 pounds or 50 pounds. You are a fucking genius.'

You don't wanna get laid, man. It leads to kissing and pretty soon you gotta talk to 'em.

With films like *Blue Velvet* and *Hoosiers* in the can, Dennis Hopper's remarkable transition from train-wreck personality to respected actor was complete. He decided to leave Taos and move back to Hollywood after his doctor suggested it might be best if he left his Mexican hideaway and came back to reality. 'Reality? In LA?' scoffed Dennis. He didn't quite walk back into the lion's den. He hated Los Angeles so, recalling fond memories of listening to beat poets and cool jazz in the late fifties at Venice Beach, bought a property there instead. Situated to the west of LA, Venice is home to a thriving artistic community, so suited Dennis perfectly. The fact it was also a war zone didn't seem to faze him. The place boasted something of a schizophrenic personality: funky boutiques and smart restaurants jostled for space with burned-out cars and drive-by shootings. 'It's a low-income place you can actually walk round,' said Dennis. 'If you don't mind being mugged.'

Paranoia has always been one of the great themes of Dennis's life and it was no surprise to anyone that his house was Paranoia Central, a modernistic fortress, a bunker rather than a home with its corrugated steel façade, no windows, heavy-duty entrance door studded with bolts and surrounding 15-foot fencing topped with razor wire. Even the patio sported a steel mesh roof in case a wandering gang member attempted to lob a grenade in from the street. Don't expect either anything as straightforward as a doorbell; instead visitors had to punch in a special code and wait to be escorted within.

Gray Frederickson, who'd worked with Dennis on *Apocalypse Now*, recalls visiting the Venice house. 'Dennis lives in a gated, guarded, almost prison-like compound right in the gang area of Venice, and I remember he walked me out to the car and I started up a conversation and he said, "You better get in the car and go, this is not a good place for us to be standing." I said, "Why do you live in a place like this, Dennis?"' Because he revelled in it, he loved to reel off the latest crime statistics to visiting journalists. 'On my corner there's seven people killed on average every two weeks,' he told a reporter in the early nineties.

By the 2000s the area had calmed down a bit, only to be blighted by yet another gang war. Again, Dennis was on hand with the statistics, this time to the *Sunday Telegraph*: 'On my corner seventeen people were killed and seventy wounded during a three-month period in a Mexican–black drug war,' adding for good measure, 'And they shot the neighbourhood watch person a couple of blocks away, shot him sixteen times.'

Remarkably, not only did Dennis feel safe in the area, he'd never experienced any trouble. Maybe the muggers and gang bangers were too afraid of him. Walking home one day, he overheard a couple of locals say, 'Don't go in there, man. It's that crazy person lives in there. Any person that chooses to live in a prison is a crazy person.' But he was always on guard, ever aware of what suddenly might happen, like stumbling innocently upon a drug deal going down on some otherwise deserted stretch of pavement. 'That would definitely constitute adios, Dennis, and that would be a fucking shame.'

A prison it may look like externally, but inside the place resembled more a piece of industrial art. Incredibly, in the living room, like in a Bond villain's lair, there is a steel wall that rises up to allow Dennis to drive in and park his car – inside the house! There's also a studio for his own painting and photography, which he'd recently taken up again. Then, on the walls, a stunning collection of contemporary American art – Warhol, Basquiat, Julian Schnabel, several million dollars' worth of prime museum fodder housed in one of the highest-crime areas in the USA. Only Dennis. 'That house is very much a reflection of who he is,' says filmmaker George Hickenlooper. 'It stands for the post-*Apocalypse Now* Dennis, the Dennis who became much more serious about being sober, became more serious about finance and more conservative. There's an iconoclastic aesthetic to the house too; it looks different than any other house in the neighbourhood.'

Rehabilitated, Dennis ironically was emerging as a hero to a whole new generation of disaffected actors such as Sean Penn and Mickey Rourke. They sought his advice and knowledge, held him up as this iconic figurehead of chaos and rebellion, someone who'd strayed pretty substantially from the path most of us trod, done his own thing, survived and returned to tell the tale.

Sean Penn, Hollywood's current badass, had a script about cops fighting gangs in Chicago and wanted Dennis to direct. 'I read it and told him it was the worst piece of shit I'd ever laid eyes on.' There was no bite, said Dennis, no relevance to what was happening on the streets today. Dennis wanted to relocate the story to LA, where he knew the gang situation was out of control. 'Are there gangs in LA?' one studio executive asked Dennis at a script meeting. Looking incredulous, Hopper replied, 'Jesus, there are gangs in my alley!'

It was an amazing turnaround, Dennis directing a mainstream Hollywood movie after years of Hollywood refusing to even give him a shot at directing traffic. 'As everyone knows Dennis was slightly an erratic character,' says producer Robert H. Solo. 'It was like pulling teeth really dealing with him, though he kept making a big deal about the fact that he was now clean, that he wasn't drinking or smoking or taking drugs, because the studio was afraid to hire him. They only agreed because they loved Sean Penn and wanted Sean to do the movie. And because he wanted Dennis Hopper, he got Dennis Hopper.' Now he had a chance to prove himself a better director clean than he was off his face. 'And to be honest once we got going, Dennis was ok, he did a good job,' admits Solo. 'And was on his very, very best behaviour.' No, Dennis wasn't the problem on *Colors* (1988), his star was: Sean Penn. Dennis genuinely feared that Penn might end up in prison before the film was finished, such was his reputation and tendency to violence. During a break in filming an extra took a photograph of Penn, who ran towards him and knocked the camera out of his hand yelling, 'You bastard. Don't take any pictures of me between takes!' and then punched him in the face. Somehow Dennis guided Penn through the film and they ended up close friends. Penn would name one of his sons after him, Hopper Jack, a tribute to both Dennis and Jack.

Much of the film was shot on Dennis's home turf of Venice, due to the inordinate amount of gang activity in the area. He also took the gamble of employing real LA gang members to act as extras and technical advisers. The day 140 gang bangers arrived at the studio to audition scared the shit out of the movie executives. The cops said they'd never seen so many gang kids in one location in their lives. 'We also shot the film right in the real gang territory,' says Robert H. Solo. 'We used to get threats and often I needed a bodyguard to see me safe out of the location site and back home. We were in the black gang territory, the Latino, the Hispanic, and they would all come around. So it was a bit frightening at times. But Dennis thrived on it. He absolutely loved it. The more outrageous it was, the more he liked it. But that's Dennis, that's his nature, that's his personality.'

When *Colors* opened it courted huge controversy, particularly in LA, due to its depiction of Latino and black gangs. Protesters marched outside cinemas accusing the film of glorifying violence. Dennis watched on closed-circuit TV as members of the Guardian Angels, the famous community-protection group formed in New York, paraded outside his home calling for his film to be banned. Nervous theatre owners beefed up their security, fearful of gang shoot-'em-ups in the aisles. In the end there was little bloodshed in the stalls, save for a few arrests of wanted gang members attending screenings.

In 1989 Kit Carson invited Dennis to be guest of honour at a film festival he'd organised. After a screening of *The Last Movie* Carson hosted a discussion on stage. 'Dennis, tell me what method acting is like?' Dennis looked at Carson, 'Sure,' he said and then stared down at the table between the two of them and began moving his fingers around the glass surface. 'I'm thinking about my father's death,' he said. 'After a while he looked back up at me,' Carson recalls, 'and there were tears coming down his face and his voice broke. And the whole audience, about four hundred people, just gasped. That's how real Dennis is, he can put himself into another reality and be absolutely real there. That's what making movies is about. It was a stunning moment, that he put himself back in the moment when he learned that his father had died.'

They say a Martini is like a woman's breast: one ain't enough and three is too many.

In 1987 Gary Hart looked a shoo-in to claim the Democratic presidential nomination, but his opponents took comfort from the fact that he still consorted with Warren Beatty and sometimes stayed at Mulholland Drive. There were even occasions when Hart used the house when Warren was away, leading to speculation that he was being unfaithful to his wife. Hart and Warren did seem to be spending a lot of time sitting round swimming pools with young ladies. His advisers warned him of getting too entangled with the Hollywood set, but he ignored them and stayed loyal to his backer.

Such criticism obviously hit home, forcing Warren to refute suggestions that his 'supposed' lifestyle would hurt his candidate. 'Maybe twenty years ago, but not today. I don't believe the majority of people in this country are interested in what your sexual preferences are.' Warren was soon to be proven very wrong. The public, and most importantly the press, were very interested indeed in Hart's sex life. And Warren's naivety on this point made him something of a liability in Hart's bid for political glory.

Sick and tired of the rumours that he was playing around, Hart challenged the media to follow him 24/7 to check that he was indeed keeping his pants on. It was a stupid tactic, a self-inflicted wound that would prove fatal. Reporters gleefully took up the challenge and three weeks into Hart's campaign the *Miami Herald*, after camping for days outside his Washington residence, revealed that a woman had stayed overnight while his wife was in Denver. Hart did what all politicians do when faced with such accusations: he denied everything.

What happened next couldn't be so easily waved away. A photograph appeared showing a very sexy twenty-nine-year-old swimsuit model called Donna Rice sitting on Hart's lap. Oh dear. That didn't faze people like Jack, who chipped in helpfully: 'I'm a Hart supporter because he fucks. Do you know what I mean?' Clearly, Jack was voicing the minority view. The bulk of the country saw only a liar and a hypocrite and many of Hart's supporters defected. Warren told him to stand firm but it all went pear-shaped when the *Washington Post* threatened to publish more lurid details. That was it: Hart threw in the towel, his political aspirations apparently over. Charles Manson had more chance of becoming president than he did.

Incredibly, Hart re-entered the presidential race in 1988, his wife loyally by his side. It was a decision, according to the *New York Post*, that Warren had a major hand in, telling Hart that he had every right to keep his private life completely separate from his political career. But no one took Hart's candidacy seriously and after a few weeks he pulled out yet again.

Looking back, it does seem as if Warren wasted a lot of his time on someone who turned out to be a political also-ran, but screenwriter and friend Tom Mankiewicz isn't surprised Warren gravitated towards him. 'I think it was no coincidence that Gary Hart was very good-looking and was the guy that got caught with the girl on the boat. It was just so fitting that that would be the politician that Warren would have a proclivity for; it was perfect. People said at the time, when Gary Hart was running for president, the problem is Gary Hart wants to be Warren Beatty and Warren Beatty wants to be Gary Hart.'

Tell me something, my friend. You ever dance with the devil in the pale moonlight?

Ever since a Batman movie was first mooted in the early eighties Jack Nicholson was favourite to play The Joker. Batman's own creator Bob Kane envisaged the actor in the role above anyone else, using a doctored photograph of him from *The Shining* to show studio executives, replete with green hair and kabuki-like white face. 'Get Jack Nicholson,' he'd roar. 'He is The Joker. Get the man!'

The project was in limbo for years until producers Jon Peters and Peter Guber picked it up and offered the directorial reins to Tim Burton, who'd recently scored a hit with the wacky comedy *Beetlejuice*. Burton was someone determined to turn the direction of Batman away from the campy TV show of the sixties back to the dark, noirish original DC comics of the forties. It was during the making of *The Witches of Eastwick* that Guber and Peters first asked Jack to play The Joker. It was four o'clock in the morning when they rang and Jack, yawning, heard them make the offer. 'The Joker!' he replied. 'In *Batman*! Babe, you've got to be joking. I wouldn't do that even if the studio paid me fifty mil.'

Warner Brothers, who were already throwing millions at the project and desperate to land Jack – he was their insurance – told Guber and Peters to make the actor an offer he couldn't refuse. And indeed they did. Jack duly signed on, giving huge momentum to the whole enterprise. 'It was mainly because of Jack that the adrenaline ran so high on that movie,' said production designer Anton Furst. 'His casting was so fucking obvious. I don't think there was ever a part more tailor-made for him.' It also turned out to be the shrewdest financial deal Jack ever made. On top of his $6m fee he also negotiated a percentage of the box office and, crucially, a piece of the merchandising action. When *Batman* became the biggest grossing film of 1989, with toys and other spin-offs selling by the bucket load, Jack reportedly benefited to the tune of a whopping $60m. Such colossal remunerations caused commentators to suggest that stars' salaries were driving up the cost of movies to breaking point. But as Jack helpfully pointed out, 'They won't pay it to us if you ain't worth it. Period.'

Batman was filmed at Pinewood Studios under a cloak of secrecy with a cast that included Michael Keaton as the dark knight and Kim Basinger, who famously referred to Nicholson as 'the most highly sexed individual I have ever met'. He had amazing stamina, too. According to his driver, during the making of *Batman* Jack was out gallivanting most nights until four in the morning. Then he'd be up at seven to be picked up for work.

As for Burton and Jack, it was a real melding of minds. When they first met, Jack offered some advice: 'Don't do this thing too bright. I'm a fan of Batman – it takes place at night.' Burton agreed completely. 'I liked the darkness as a kid,' said Jack. 'The wild, deranged complexity of The Joker.' Burton called Jack one of the most intuitive actors he'd ever worked with, someone who got to know his character inside out and then had fun with it. 'He's absolutely brilliant at going as far as you can go, always pushing to the edge, but still making it seem real.' Jack himself was particularly proud of his performance as The Joker. 'I considered it a piece of pop art.'

After *Batman* Jack's marquee value had never been higher, but his personal life was about to take a tumble. His relationship with Karen Mayo-Chandler was becoming increasingly high profile. For years Anjelica had put up with his wanderings just so long as they didn't make her look foolish in the eyes of the public. Maybe he'd gone too far this time. She walked away, saying that she'd had a wonderful time with Jack but now she needed to find a relationship that gave her what she most wanted in life: to be a wife and, hopefully, a mother, too. Friends said Jack was dreadfully hurt, having lost not only a woman he loved and cared for deeply but also a close friend. He made numerous calls in an effort to patch things up but Anjelica wasn't budging. More bad news arrived a couple of days later when Karen revealed to the press that she'd broken off her relationship with Jack, too.

The old rascal wasn't alone for long. During a visit to a nightclub he met Rebecca Broussard, an aspiring actress with just the right qualifications: blonde hair, blue eyes and about half Jack's years. The only downside was the fact she was married, although in the throes of separating from her record-producer husband. It wasn't long before a gossip columnist spotted Rebecca driving Jack's black Range Rover in Aspen. She also jumped at the chance to play a small role in *The Two Jakes*.

The rumour mill began to grind again when Anjelica showed up on the *Two Jakes* set, Rebecca sensibly making herself scarce for the day. Was this a reconciliation? Were all the years of being together, however distant 'together' had sometimes been, worth throwing away over the silly romp with Karen Mayo-Chandler? And how much did she know about Rebecca?

But all that became irrelevant after Karen did a kiss-and-tell for the December 1989 issue of *Playboy*. A salacious exposé of his sex life was the last thing Jack needed. 'He would hold me down,' Karen gushed, 'rip off my clothes and make incredible, mad, wild, wonderful love to me.' At times Karen came over like a lovestuck teenager. 'We did not sleep a wink that first night. He's a guaranteed non-stop sex machine,' who, she said ate peanut butter in bed, 'to keep his strength up'. She added, 'He really ought to write a book and call it *How to Make Love to Women*. It would be a best seller.'

Most middle-aged men might feel well chuffed about a very sexy young woman making such complimentary if terribly personal revelations, and, had Karen stopped there, so might Jack. Instead she went on to reveal a kinkier side to their bedroom antics, fun and games including spankings and bondage, whips and Polaroids. She alleged that he also enjoyed 'chasing me round the room with a ping-pong paddle'. 'Spanking Jack' became Karen's favourite nickname for him. (Jack has confessed that he doesn't see much wrong with a woman wanting a good spanking, and, gathering up Warren and a bunch of friends one time, Jack announced, with a mischievous grin on his face, 'How about a night out with Spanking Jack?')

Angry enough to live up to the nickname, Jack phoned Hugh Hefner to complain. The *Playboy* boss said Jack ought to get over it, that the piece was only a bit of fun. Jack wasn't laughing and called Hefner a shit. Trying to dismiss the article as a 'non-event', Jack did admit that 'it caused me some problems with Miss Huston'. Indeed, as Anjelica said to friends, 'An article on Jack's sexual prowess at Christmas is hardly my idea of a nice present.'

It couldn't get any worse, could it? Well, yes, when a gossip column printed rumours that Rebecca was pregnant with Jack's child. On hearing the news Anjelica was incandescent with rage and drove over to Paramount Studios, where she knew Jack was working. As he confessed to *Parade* magazine in 2007, 'Her first response was, "You have to support this woman." Her second response was to beat the hell out of me. She really beat me up. I tell you, Anjelica can punch!'

An unwanted child himself, Jack had always been against abortion, and besides, he wanted another kid, middle age and all. Jack and Rebecca's daughter was born in April 1990, six days before his fifty-third birthday, and christened Lorraine. He was present at the birth and took to the job of being a father again with enthusiasm. Speculation began that maybe Jack's wild times were over, a debatable point as he was quick to dismiss talk of marriage, his intentions all too obvious when he installed Rebecca and the baby in a separate house not far from Mulholland Drive. It was an unusual arrangement, even by Hollywood standards, one Jack said gave them both their independence. Several times in the past he'd been through periods when he needed to spend time alone, 'So I can think devilish thoughts.' And because he has a loner streak in him. And that takes some understanding on the part of any woman. Certainly the last twenty-five years or so had shown Jack that he was no good at cohabitation.

And what of poor Anjelica? She walked out of Jack's life, this time for good, her dream of him fathering her children obliterated, leaving only painful thoughts of what might have been. The double blow of Karen's kiss-and-tell revelations and the media scrum surrounding Rebecca's pregnancy was the kind of public humiliation undeserved by a woman who had loyally spent the last seventeen years of her life devoted to the Jack project. Her fury must have been incalculable, as must her feelings of loss and abandonment.

6

The Redemptive Nineties

I'm getting too old for this nonsense.

It was one of cinema's greatest gags, Marlon Brando sending up his Godfather image as an ageing mobster in *The Freshman* (1990). It also marked the first time he'd shot on location in New York for something like fifteen years. On that first day of shooting in Manhattan, around Little Italy, word soon got out and the streets quickly filled with paparazzi and fans. Director Andrew Bergman was at a loss as to how he was going to get Marlon out without him being photographed or mobbed. A solution was found: Marlon was put into the trunk of his car, which was no easy task, and driven out.

For everyone concerned the film was a memorable experience. Producer Mike Lobell remembers receiving an alarming call from Marlon midway through filming, saying he was in a friend's Lear Jet, flying out to Tahiti for the weekend. 'Don't worry, I'll be back by Monday.' It turned out that Marlon was phoning from his hotel and had rigged his room with sound effects to make it appear he was aboard a plane.

William Fraker was the cameraman on *The Freshman*, his first film with Marlon since *Morituri* back in 1965, and recalls the big man's final day on the shoot. 'We finished in the afternoon and Marlon brought a whole stack of photographs of himself and he sat on the tailgate of the grip truck for two hours and signed those pictures for every member of the crew.'

Still despising Hollywood, Marlon was adamant that none of his children would become actors. One of them, Miko, did gravitate toward the glamour of showbiz, for a time becoming Michael Jackson's bodyguard, famously saving the singer's scalp when his hair caught on fire during the filming of a TV commercial.

Quite naturally, Marlon felt closest to his first-born, Christian. Ironically it was Christian who was the most troubled Brando sibling, at various points in his life addicted to alcohol and drugs. After an abortive attempt to become an actor he'd worked at a host of menial jobs, including tree surgeon and welder. Christian didn't get on that well with his brothers and sisters. His closest relationship was with his half-sister Cheyenne, a beautiful but troubled young girl who also dabbled in drugs. On the night of 16 May 1990, Christian, Cheyenne and her boyfriend Dag Drollet were over at Mulholland Drive. By the end of the evening Drollet was dead, a bullet in his brain.

There were stories and claims that Drollet beat Cheyenne, even though she was pregnant with his baby, and Christian wanted to teach him a lesson that night, scare the shit out of him. He got a gun and pointed it at Drollet; the two struggled and it went off. 'And I saw the life go out of him,' said Christian. Brando was at home that night, so too was Cheyenne's mother Tarita. Both ran to the scene when they heard the shot. Brando took the gun from Christian's hand, then he phoned the police.

Christian was charged with first-degree murder and the subsequent trial was a press sensation. It fitted horribly into the stereotype of the dysfunctional Hollywood family, something Brando had so desperately tried to avoid. 'I think I perhaps failed as a father,' he confessed on the witness stand. It was an attempt, genuinely felt or otherwise, to shoulder some responsibility for the crime, recognising that his tumultuous relationship with Christian's mother Anna Kashfi had caused his son irreparable damage.

The full truth of what happened that night will never be known. Cheyenne fled to her father's paradise island, safe from any attempt to extradite her back to the States. There she attempted suicide several times, distraught at being denied legal custody of Tuki, her young son by Drollet. Though she was placed in hospital and well cared for, nothing could be done for her state of mind and eventually in 1995 she hanged herself in her bedroom at the Brando estate. She was twenty-five.

Because the absent Cheyenne had been the only witness to the crime, the first-degree murder charge was reduced to voluntary manslaughter, to which Christian entered a guilty plea and served five years in prison. In 2005 Christian was in court yet again, this time pleading guilty to two counts of domestic violence after his ex-wife claimed he frequently beat her and threatened to kill her. This troubled man's life ended in 2008 when he died in a Los Angeles hospital after suffering from pneumonia.

There's something going on here that I really don't understand, but I like it.

Although his entry in the international film encyclopedia described him as 'the most freaked-out personality in films', Dennis Hopper had calmed down greatly by the time the nineties began, though he still revelled in his image and was more than happy to let the old Dennis out of the cage for show. During one interview he was perfectly responsive and polite answering questions. Asked to, 'get into character' for a photograph, Dennis slowly removed his glasses, looked for a suitable place to put them, then walked over to the camera, stared straight into the lens and screamed 'FFFUCK YOU!'

The success of *Colors* had also resurrected Dennis's career as a filmmaker and he won two directorial assignments back to back, each presenting him with a unique set of problems. First off was *Catchfire* (1990), which Dennis also starred in as a hit man who first rapes and then falls in love with his target, played by Jodie Foster. Dan Paulson was the producer and still remembers his first meeting with Dennis. 'This was one of my idols from the sixties, the counterculture, *Easy Rider*, he walks in with a white shirt, tie and a grey suit. He was driving a Cadillac Seville, not the chopper from *Easy Rider*, and it was a bit of a shock. He'd really changed his image; he was now more establishment, more of a serious artist.'

Working with a low budget, Dennis pulled in favours from acting buddies to swell the cast. 'They all loved him,' says Paulson. 'And we got them for practically nothing: Dean Stockwell, Vincent Price, what a classy gentleman he was. I remember Joe Pesci on the set of the movie telling me he was going to leave the business, this was before *Goodfellas*, John Turturro, Charlie Sheen, it's a great cast.'

Dennis's relationship with Jodie Foster started badly though. On the first day of filming there was this long dolly shot of her in a hotel room and Jodie, who'd ambitions to direct herself, yelled: 'Cut.' Dennis wasn't amused, as Paulson recalls. 'He very discreetly took her off to the side to tell her, "Don't ever do that again." Ultimately he got on very well with her, but he's in charge when he's on the set, no doubt about that.'

Dennis's next battle, however, he was never going to win. The backers were Vestron Pictures, who, when they saw the movie, didn't like it at all, took it off Dennis and recut it themselves. He was furious – 'I went nuts when I saw it' – and ordered his name be removed from the credits and replaced by Alan Smithee, which is the standard Hollywood pseudonym used by any director who is too unhappy with the finished film to put his real name on it. It was like the good old days again, Dennis railing against the system. 'He's a guy that's not afraid to speak his mind,' says Paulson. 'He has an opinion and he stands behind it. He just doesn't cave in like a lot of filmmakers do who are thinking of their next job and play nice.'

Ironically, Vestron then went bankrupt so *Catchfire* didn't receive a proper theatrical release. Years later Dennis returned to the movie and brought out a director's cut on video, renaming it *Backtrack*. It's a version Paulson prefers and he looks back fondly on working with Dennis. 'As a director he knew exactly what he wanted, very decisive in making decisions. I knew the legend Dennis Hopper, and I saw beneath that and the legend was a very professional, buttoned-down guy.'

Dennis next took the directorial reins of a rather tired thriller called *The Hot Spot* (1990), casting Don Johnson despite never having watched a single episode of his TV hit *Miami Vice*, thinking him just right to play 'An amoral car salesman/bank robber/fuck-the-women kind of guy.' Asked if he had much in common with Johnson, Dennis gave a lengthy pause before answering. 'We had some of the same girlfriends, which he pointed out to me.'

There was an air of tension on the set with Johnson scarcely endearing himself to either the crew or Dennis, who raised an eyebrow at the ancillary personnel that hovered around the star's orbit: a cook, a helicopter pilot, a personal hairdresser and make-up man, a driver, a secretary. He also had a heavily muscled bodyguard on hand at all times. When the bodyguard sprained his foot and was immobilised, Hopper burst into laughter. 'We had about ten people thinking, oh, good, now we can kick the shit out of Don Johnson.'

Wearing that dress is a step in the right direction.

In the new decade commentators wondered if a certain amount of lustre hadn't worn off Warren Beatty, if his boyish looks had surrendered to the ravages of middle age and his box-office prowess faded. Out of all our bad boys the eighties truly belonged to Jack, who churned out eleven movies, critical and box-office smashes amongst them. Marlon was about as visible as Big Foot in a tutu, Dennis's career resembled an out-of-control rollercoaster while Warren had managed a measly two features, both dubious in terms of bankability – *Reds* and *Ishtar*. Warren was now no longer considered a 'star' by the current cinema-going public, lapping up the likes of Cruise, Ford and Arnie. Luckily, Warren had maintained good relationships with high flyers within the Hollywood establishment such as Jeffrey Katzenberg at Disney, who'd bankroll his next film, *Dick Tracy* (1990).

Even Warren's Casanova image was dented, looking positively prehistoric in this age of women's lib and a youth-obsessed society. But he was still out there, chasing like a good 'un, maybe in an attempt to latch on to the kind of girlfriend that would make the world sit up and say, wow, he can still do it. If that was indeed his intention he certainly hit the bull's eye with Madonna.

The affair essentially sprang from a business deal. Warren was setting up *Dick Tracy* and Madonna was aching to play snazzy seductress Breathless Mahoney, seeing the role as vital in salvaging her dire movie career. After exploding onto screens in 1984 with *Desperately Seeking Susan*, Madonna hadn't found another vehicle to match it. Her personal life was in turmoil, too, with her marriage to Sean Penn about as stable as Paris Hilton's knicker elastic.

Warren didn't want Madonna, he was thinking of more experienced actresses like Michelle Pfeiffer or Kim Basinger. But her persistence was such that Warren caved in and agreed to a lunch meeting. 'I know you've heard a lot of terrible things about me,' Madonna said as they sat down to eat. 'And I'm here to tell you that they're all true. How about you? I've heard a lot about you.' When Warren remained silent, she said, 'Just as I thought. All true.' After their meal Warren, as always the perfect gentleman, took the pop star home and they kissed hungrily, we might imagine, outside the door, after which Warren is alleged to have said, 'We have lift-off.'

Whatever the misgivings about Madonna's acting ability she was signed on, Warren eager to exploit the singer's huge popularity with the MTV generation, who now made up the bulk of the movie going public. Let's face it, most teens hadn't heard of Dick Tracy, or Warren for that matter. Everyone was happy then. Well, except Sean Penn. He was livid, since Madonna had promised she'd undertake no major work in the next year so they could try and rescue their marriage by having a baby. When he heard she'd signed for *Dick Tracy* he became so violent that studio security guards had to drag him out of Madonna's bungalow. Penn was now a very angry man, and at this stage in his life it was not advisable to be in the same continent as he was, let alone shagging his missus in the same town. He started following Madonna and Warren around as they began to date more frequently. He once parked his car outside Warren's house as the couple arrived and was still sitting there come dawn.

Then, in a blind fury, he broke into Madonna's Malibu home and, she says, assaulted, bound and gagged the singer, leaving her bruised and bleeding for nine hours. Madonna finally broke free and went to the nearest police station. Fearing reprisals, she was forced to hide in the house of her manager. Penn was arrested, but Madonna ultimately dropped all charges. Penn would later deny Madonna's version of events. For Madonna, being around Penn must have felt like living in Peyton Place on acid. She wanted out and Warren, two decades her senior, was perhaps the sort of fatherly influence she needed. There was a benign element about Warren that appealed to Madonna, in other words he could be pushed around, unlike Penn. She felt she could be the aggressor in this relationship, a role that she had always preferred. No matter how much she taunted Warren she knew he'd never physically hit out at her. At worst, he might leave the room until he controlled his anger. 'I understand rebellion,' said Warren, 'so I understand Madonna.'

Of course another attraction for Madonna was the Warren image, the womanising legend. 'Sometimes I think he's been with the world's most glamorous women I go, oh my God? Then there is the side of me that says I'm better than all of them.' They certainly made an odd couple in Hollywood. *Rolling Stone* called the affair vampire love. 'She needs his credibility, he needs her youth. They are evenly matched legends, hers is louder, his is longer.'

They matched sexually, too. 'He's into all aspects of sexuality,' Madonna revealed. 'He says to me, "If you misbehave, I'll just have to spank you." I love that. Everything to him is living out his sexual fantasies.' According to a Hollywood insider, Warren once telephoned Madonna from his car as he drove to her home, demanding she remove item by item all of her clothing, one at each intersection or set of traffic lights. Pulling into the driveway, Warren instructed her to 'get in bed and wait'. Madonna must have been quivering as Warren entered the bedroom, anticipating the greatest bang since the one God let off.

Over dinner one night at a smart restaurant Madonna leaned across the table to ask Warren if he'd ever done it with a man. He didn't answer, except to say that he was willing to set her up with a lesbian. 'It will be my present to you,' he said. Warren was only too aware of Madonna's close friendship with Sandra Bernhard and asked the comedienne to join them the following night. 'Warren,' Sandra said, 'you know Madonna and I share *everything*.' Later Sandra recalled that Warren's 'eyes lit up like a kid in a candy store. A wild ride, I thought to myself. A very wild ride.'

Although *Dick Tracy* was seen by many in the industry as something of a make-or-break movie for Warren, it was a measure of the respect he had in Hollywood that the likes of Al Pacino, Dustin Hoffman and James Caan were happy to appear with their famous features obscured by grotesque make-up, befitting the story's comic-book origins. 'We're all wearing prosthetics except the women and Warren,' said actor Paul

Sorvino. 'So we're all ugly as hell and Warren looks beautiful. It's a Warren Beatty dream.'

Hoffman came to work on the movie the day after he'd won the Oscar for *Rain Man*. 'And I remember Warren getting down on his knees and bowing to Dustin,' says producer Jon Landau. Pacino is the baddie of the piece, grandstanding as Big Boy Caprice, a role he was attracted to because Warren talked him into it. Discussions about the role on set went something like this: AP: 'What should I do, Warren?' WB: 'You'll think of something.' And it worked. 'This was the best direction I have ever had,' laughed Pacino.

Cast as Tess Trueheart, Tracy's virginal girlfriend, was Glenne Headly. On the set one day Warren was telling a journalist about press mis-interpretation of his image when he made a grab for Glenne as she walked by. 'Look at those legs,' he sighed. Frowning, Glenne turned and said, 'See, that's how you got your reputation, Warren.'

Behind the scenes Beatty the perfectionist was driving some of the crew nuts as he constantly pushed for levels of excellence that matched his own. 'I actually think Warren is a very collaborative filmmaker,' says producer Jon Landau. 'He doesn't care where the good ideas come from. He was that way as related to the script, the casting and on the set. He was always encouraging people to give him input and to give him feed-back.' Disney executive Jeffrey Katzenberg also revelled in the star's company, and indulged him, according to some. Warren's charm and magic also extended to some of Disney's high-level female executives, real ball-busters by day, but on the set they were putty in his hands, draped on his lap dressed in cowboy boots and tight jeans.

Tension between Warren and Madonna was always inevitable, she being just as much a perfectionist and workaholic as he was. Hanging about while Warren fastidiously set up his angles she'd nag, 'Hey, Beatty. Are you going to shoot this fucking scene or not, you asshole?' They did behave like a married couple on set, their romance not hidden from the crew. They were even caught in a highly compromising position in a dressing room. But what the hell, they were in love.

Their social life was even more interesting, Madonna dragging him round clubs night after night. 'He'd come in looking like hell,' said a crew member. Places he would ordinarily avoid like the clap, a gay night-club in south central LA, for example. Madonna was frenziedly gyrating on the dance floor. 'Hey, pussy man, come on out here,' she berated him. Completely out of his element, Warren declined. 'No, I'm just fine. I can't even breathe, let alone dance.' Madonna sauntered over to where two women were dancing and started thrusting and throbbing rhythmically with them. 'I should'a come here with Rob Lowe,' she bellowed above the music. 'Now, he's a guy who knows how to party.'

Madonna often flirted with other women. Warren didn't mind. (Of course he bloody didn't), unlike Sean Penn, who in similar situations exhibited all the restraint of a bulimic at an all-you-can-eat buffet. However, Warren drew a line when it came to his male friends, especially Jack. Living as close by as he did, Jack often popped round and was delighted to learn of Madonna's keen interest in art. They became very pally; he intrigued by this vampish pop princess, she flattered by the attention of so iconic a movie star. Warren, though, was less than happy with their friendship, knowing Jack the way he did.

Slowly and surely Warren began introducing Madonna into the high echelons of the film world. He turned out to be useful in other areas, too, such as teaching her some of his business acumen, suggesting, for example, that she start up her own record label. (Madonna did just that in 1992.) Rumours soon circulated that marriage was on the cards, with Warren supposedly telling friends that Jack would be his best man. But rifts began to open up, often spilling out into the public domain. At a restaurant one night Madonna told Warren to 'keep your stupid opinions to yourself'. Warren paid the bill and left Madonna alone to yell 'Stop staring at me' to the other patrons. Maybe Warren had had enough. He spent hours one night on the phone to Jack complaining that Madonna and Sandra Bernhard were planning a spectacular wedding ceremony and that Sean Penn was on his back for fucking his ex-wife. 'I'm too old for this,' he said. 'Old enough not to want to look foolish.' Friends and colleagues made their opinions known, too. Barbra Streisand phoned Warren to tell him he was 'crazy for falling for a young floozy'.

It seemed that the blush had well and truly worn off the rose. Warren had developed the habit of holding the telephone at least two feet from his ear whenever Madonna called, wincing at the screech of her voice. It was almost a relief when the singer went off on her Blonde Ambition tour, which included songs from *Dick Tracy* in the running order. At one point in the show she turned to the audience and said, 'Dick. That's an interesting name. My bottom hurts just thinking about it.' Subtlety is not a word in the Madonna lexicon.

Tensions remained, however. Because of post-production commitments to *Dick Tracy* Warren was unable to meet Madonna's demands for emotional support during her tour. At the very least she expected him to turn up for the opening night, sending a private plane for him to fly out to Houston. He didn't get on it. Madonna couldn't comprehend Warren defying her and when the show hit New York and he turned up with Jack they were refused entry to her dressing room.

The simple truth was that Warren did not fit into Madonna's rockstar world. He felt uncomfortable in it. The fact that practically everything they did was being recorded by a film crew didn't help. Madonna had commissioned a documentary on her life, *Truth or Dare*, and when it was finished proudly screened it at Warren's home in front of an invited audience of friends. Warren did not like what he saw. He particularly disliked how some scenes made it appear that he was under the thumb. The next day he got in touch with his attorney to demand that the offending segments be cut from the film. In other words, Warren was threatening to sue his partner, which never goes down well.

As the tour continued across America Madonna got increasingly steamed up, and by the time they hit LA she was ready to explode. Warren paid a visit backstage at the moment she was balling out her stage crew. He did his best 'I'm not here, just ignore me, folks' act, but some of the dancers spied him and cried out 'Uncle Warren' and 'Dad'. Madonna now piped in, 'Don't hide back there Warren, get over here. You pussy man, what's with you? Can you believe I have to do this every night? Are you going to be nicer to me now, Warren?' Er, no. When Madonna was invited onto Arsenio Hall's TV chat show and asked, 'What does Warren Beatty have that we don't have?' she replied, 'About a billion dollars.'

Disney had pined much of their hopes for the movie year on *Dick*

Tracy, hoping it would be another *Batman*. Katzenberg was indulging in a phoney war with fellow executive Don Simpson over at Paramount, overseeing their big summer release, the Tom Cruise car-race movie *Days of Thunder*. Simpson sent a fax over to Katzenberg saying, 'You can't escape the Thunder!' Katzenberg promptly faxed back: 'You won't believe how big my Dick is!'

Big it was. The final budget was a whopping $47m, with Disney spending an additional fortune on marketing. The merchandising alone was huge, ranging from toys and games to action figures of Warren. 'I think I've been made into dolls before,' he joked, 'but they had pins in them.' With this kind of financial outlay Katzenberg had gotten Warren to commit to promoting the movie, something he hadn't done even for his pet project *Reds*. Warren's dislike of interviews and promotion was well known, but it was an attitude hopelessly out of date in this era of media saturation. So he went all out for *Dick*, even submitting to an interview with *Rolling Stone*, but when the questions got personal, primarily revolving around Madonna, he clammed up. Reporter Bill Zehme wrote, 'To interview Warren Beatty is to want to kill him.' But Warren has never hidden the fact that in interviews he protects the privacy of his lovers. 'Fuck and suck' was his pet term for scurrilous articles about his sexual profile.

Vanity Fair asked Warren to pose for top celebrity photographer Herb Ritts. He did so, but couldn't hide his boredom and disapproval of the whole thing. Apparently one of Ritt's female assistants bared a breast in order to raise a smile out of him.

Ultimately *Dick Tracy* made money, but it wasn't the massive hit Disney had hoped for. And when an inter-office memo from Katzenberg was leaked to the press, in which he lamented, '*Dick Tracy* made demands on our time, talent and treasury that . . . may not have been worth it,' relations cooled, you could say, between him and Warren. Maybe Katzenberg's and Disney's problem, countered Warren, was they had to put up with someone who had complete artistic control, 'And they didn't ordinarily affiliate themselves with gorillas like me.' Katzenberg sent a peace offering to Beatty of a dartboard with his own face on it, two white doves in a gold cage and an olive tree. It didn't work; Beatty wouldn't speak to him for years.

In spite of the recriminations and sour ending, *Dick Tracy* is still a movie very near and dear to Warren, according to its producer Jon Landau. 'It's still the character that he gets and understands and believes people get and understand. When the Dick Tracy comic strip was introduced, I think there are a lot of analogies to where we are as a society today. People are looking for a heroic character that's also relatable. You can have great action heroes that are rippled with muscles and fire guns that nail bull's eyes hundreds of yards away, that's not relatable, but I think in Dick Tracy people can see themselves in some ways. Warren gets that.'

Warren's busted affair with Madonna also sank into recriminations. 'He tossed me aside like a piece of old meat,' she complained. Warren moved onto supermodel Stephanie Seymour, but not for long, she soon dumped him for Guns n' Roses frontman Axel Rose, and Warren was alone yet again. But as usual, it wasn't for long.

You can't handle the truth.

In the early nineties Jack Nicholson became part owner of a West Hollywood nightspot called the Monkey Bar, perhaps sometimes exploiting its facilities too willingly. Somebody driving past the place late one night spotted Jack outside the door howling like a wolf at the moon. The bar attracted all types of Hollywood revellers, notably Heidi Fleiss, who then ran America's most notorious prostitution ring selling sex to the stars in Beverly Hills. Jack said he didn't understand why men went to hookers. 'I'm too Calvinist. Besides, I'm big Jack. I don't have to pay for it,' although stories around town hinted that Jack wasn't averse to accepting the odd freebie from one of Heidi's girls. He bagged the main prize too, Heidi herself. 'He is very kinky,' Heidi later revealed, 'and loved spanking my bottom in bed. He gave me twenty orgasms that night.'

Jack was now such a legendary figure in Hollywood that his mere presence was enough to guarantee a film high-profile status. Producers had to pay through the nose for it, though. Even a supporting role, as in the military court drama *A Few Good Men* (1992), had a price tag of $5m for just ten days' work. But look what they got, a grandstand performance that contributed immeasurably to the film's massive global success.

On set Jack found himself acting with the cream of the new generation of stars, Tom Cruise, Demi Moore, Keifer Sutherland and Kevin Bacon, all of whom idolised him as Jack had idolised Brando. 'When I walked in for the first time,' he confessed, 'I felt like the fucking Lincoln Memorial.' As a young unknown actor Cruise and pals Sean Penn and Emilio Estevez used to drive past Jack's house late at night. If the lights were on they'd think, wow, he's home, let's knock on the door. But they always chickened out. Nah, nah, he'll never let us in, they thought. One day on the set Cruise confessed all to Jack, who roared with laughter. They'd got the wrong house.

In February 1992 Jack and Rebecca had a second child, a son this time, christened Raymond, a more suitable name than Jack's first choice – Landslide. Jack remained reticent about settling down with his growing family – they still maintained separate residences – and there were rumours he was up to his old tricks. Then he decided to do the decent thing and proposed, only to be rejected. Rebecca perhaps knew he'd never change his lifestyle, and besides, she'd begun a new relationship; Jack was history. It was a decision that hit him like a frying pan in the face.

In Rebecca, Jack sincerely thought he'd found a lady that he could spend the rest of his life with. 'It's tough accepting that it turned to dust.' None the less, he fully intended to live up to his duties as a father and developed a strong and close connection with the two children, who became the most important things in his life. He'd take them to nursery school and loved it, although they were in the morning class. (Unlucky for Jack. 'Morning ain't my deal.') He'd struggle later on to not sound like a hypocrite when lecturing them about avoiding alcohol, drugs and random sex. All he'd tell them was, 'Everything they say is bad for you is bad for you.' And Jack can speak from some experience.

After a year of personal problems Jack wisely disappeared from view for a while, but couldn't keep out of the headlines for very long. Despite the man's Olympic-standard shagging history, there had never yet been even a whisper of a paternity suit. This was even more remarkable, given his confessed hang-up about using condoms. 'It's always a problem,' he once said about them. 'You can't feel your wanker.' Such sentiments look Jurassic in the post-Aids era, but were less so before that epidemic 'brought the death fuck into the world'. For Jack, whose life revolved so much around women, the Aids scare seriously impinged upon his activities. It didn't stop him enjoying sex, but he ranked the hysteria surrounding those early Aids cases as 'right up there with the atomic bomb as events that impacted our culture for the worse'. In the fiftieth-anniversary edition of *Playboy* magazine he wrote: 'We were moving to a freer society before Aids. Most people who investigated this knew that if you were not shooting up or getting fucked in the heinie, you were as likely to get Aids as you were to have a safe fall on your head while walking down Wilshire Boulevard.'

Jack had always been a target for women who might have designs on trapping him with a paternity suit. He knew the risks well enough, and inevitably his luck ran out when in late 1993 an ex-waitress called Jenine Gourin claimed to have become pregnant by him when she was twenty. When she threatened to sue, Jack's lawyers took over with promises to pay for the child's upkeep and education, and the story quietly slipped out of the public's consciousness.

Then it emerged in 2005 that Jack had another secret love child, this one from Danish supermodel Winnie Hollmann. Born in 1981, Honey Hollman waited until she was twenty-four before finally speaking out about her dad, confessing they shared some of the same personality traits. 'I have the same temper as him . . . I scream and shout a lot.'

If we don't sight land in three days you can cut off my head.

Desperate for cash after his son's financially draining trial, Marlon Brando took any old tosh going. You'll pay $5m for twenty days' work on *Christopher Columbus – The Discovery* (1992)? That will do nicely, thank you. His benefactors once again were the Salkinds, who'd paid him an outrageous sum once before, for *Superman*. All this for a man who once said, 'Never confuse the size of your paycheck with the size of your talent.'

Director John Glen, who'd just come off directing five Bond movies in a row, was excited about the prospect of working with Marlon and they met for dinner before location filming in Madrid. 'He was extremely charming,' says Glen. 'One could understand why he was so powerful on the screen because he had a certain charisma about him.' Marlon also had his own ideas about how he wanted to portray the role of Torquemada, the Spanish Inquisition's prime torturer. 'One of the things he wanted to do,' recalls Glen, 'was to have these outrageous nails growing like talons on his hands. I sort of looked at him a bit sideways and thought, well I hope that idea goes away.' Another ludicrous suggestion was that Marlon should stalk his torture chamber while young naked women were boiled alive in oil; and this was supposed to be a family movie! Anyway the dinner went well. 'But then the second night I wanted to see him again,' says Glen. 'I went to his room and I couldn't get past the security guards, even though I was the director they wouldn't let me anywhere near him.'

When Glen began shooting Marlon's scenes there was an immediate problem. The great man didn't turn up. 'I was anticipating trouble. When you're a director you have to box a little clever sometimes and I'd cast a very good actor called Michael Gothard as Brando's assistant, the idea being that if Marlon didn't turn up any time I would put Gothard in. And sure enough, on the first day, Marlon was a no-show, so I put Michael in and he took Marlon's lines.'

Marlon's invisibility on the set that first day caused ructions amongst the cast, notably with Tom Selleck, who approached Glen that evening. 'John,' he said, 'I admire your work, but really the only reason I did this film was because Marlon Brando was going to be in it. Now he's not turned up and he's not gonna play the thing, I'm not going to do any more, I'm off.' A bit taken aback, Glen replied, 'I appreciate your honesty, Tom, and wish you all the best.' Obviously word filtered back to Marlon that Selleck had walked and that another actor was delivering his dialogue. 'Because Brando turned up the next day,' says Glen. 'Actors being actors, they hate to lose their lines, and I just reshot that section. Naturally Tom Selleck reappeared, too.'

Despite these early problems, Glen got on extremely well with Marlon. 'He was very compliant when it came to direction, not difficult at all. I'm always very honest with actors and upfront with them and I think he appreciated that. It wasn't until later in the shoot that I realised he'd got a little sound piece in his ear and he was having his lines relayed from an adjacent room by an assistant.'

What surprised Glen even more was the incredible press interest in Brando's involvement in the film. All the time they were in Madrid the paparazzi hounded them. Driving to locations they'd have about thirty cars full of reporters following behind, all trying to get pictures. 'It was rather like the Diana scenario where the fame is so great that it becomes completely restrictive. It was a real trial. I think Marlon saw more kitchens in hotels than anything else, because that was the way he used to get into the hotel, round the back, past the dustbins and into the kitchens, that was the story of his life. I think he accepted it, he was almost numb to it.'

The Columbus movie opened to an apathetic public and Brando's lazy performance was harshly derided. American critic Richard Scheikel wrote, 'We are watching a man, broken by unhappiness, going through the motions to pay his bills.' But Marlon was completely honest about the fact that he'd made the film purely for the filthy lucre. 'I went to see Marlon in his caravan one day,' says Glen, 'and he said to me, "The only reason I'm doing this film is to pay the lawyers." His son had been involved in a murder case and it had cost Marlon a bloody fortune.'

'Cause you, you're part eggplant.

Thanks largely to his darkly majestic turn in *Blue Velvet*, Dennis Hopper was garnering something of a reputation as a rent-a-loon, creating over the next few years a dangerously intense series of misfit characters, cornering the market in miscellaneous perverts, druggies and wackos. He was master of the unsavoury and the unbalanced. 'I wouldn't like to mess with Dennis myself,' said actor Ed Harris. 'Nobody plays a monster quite like him.'

Certainly Dennis had more fun playing social deviants and psychopaths. Not that he was in any way like that in real life, of course. 'But I guess I could have been a top-class serial killer if things had turned out differently. I was the weird kid. Hated my parents. I could have been a killer, but life turned out differently.' Strange that he was being asked to inhabit such roles now he himself was rehabilitated and 'normal'. His old friend and fellow art collector Vincent Price told him back in the early sixties, 'I think you'll end up playing villains.' Dennis was put out at the time, seeing himself as leading-man material. But Vincent was right. And when playing baddies Dennis has always tried to give them human qualities so when they carry out their atrocities it's all the more alarming and disturbing.

Dennis played a true sicko in *Paris Trout* (1991), a bigot and wife beater who uses a broken bottle as a sex aid. Director Stephen Gyllenhaal admitted feeling nervous working with him, 'He's something of a myth,' but later attested to his total professionalism, not at all methody, unlike co-stars Barbara Hershey, who stayed in character throughout the shoot, and Ed Harris, who'd call Gyllenhaal at 3 a.m. to discuss his role. No, at the end of a scene Dennis trotted back into his trailer to watch ice hockey on TV.

In quick succession Dennis appeared in Sean Penn's directorial debut *The Indian Runner* (1991), played a renegade cop in *Nails* (1992), taking karate lessons and weightlifting classes to get into shape for the physically challenging role, teamed up with Wesley Snipes for the action thriller *Boiling Point* (1992) and was a cartoonish villain in the risibly awful *Super Mario Brothers* (1993), a film so bad that John Leguizamo confessed he and co-star Bob Hoskins frequently got drunk just to make it through the experience. 'The worst thing I ever did,' Hoskins dubbed it. 'It had a husband-and-wife team directing, whose arrogance had been mistaken for talent. After so many weeks their own agent told them to get off the set! Fucking nightmare. Fucking idiots.'

Perhaps the best critic of the film, which was based on the world-famous computer game, was Dennis's four-year-old son Henry. After seeing *Super Mario Brothers* he asked his dad, 'Why did you do that?' Dennis replied, 'To buy you shoes.' Henry looked at Dennis solemnly. 'I don't need shoes that badly.'

Dennis played just a brief supporting role in his next film, a flop at the box office on first release but later surfacing as a cult favourite – *True Romance* (1993). With an early script by Quentin Tarantino and direction from Tony Scott, *True Romance* had an outstanding cast: Christian Slater, Patricia Arquette, Gary Oldman, Val Kilmer, Brad Pitt and Christopher Walken as a mafia boss whose interrogation of Dennis and humiliation at his hands, through Tarantino's plenty-controversial dialogue, is an all-time classic. For sheer acting class it's hard to beat. 'That should go into a time capsule for future generations to look at,' said Tarantino.

At the end of it Hopper gets three bullets in his skull. Scott had a special gun that shot out flames. Dennis was understandably concerned. 'Tony, you're not putting that gun right to my head.' Scott assured him the gun was one hundred per cent safe. 'It's fine,' Scott called over a crew guy. 'Do it to me.' The crew guy took the gun and fired it against the director's forehead. He fell on the floor, blood pouring from a nasty wound. 'OK,' said Scott. 'That won't work.'

Meyer, we have known each other since we were too young to fuck.

In 1976 Goldie Hawn said, 'Warren Beatty will marry. It will take a very special woman. She'll have to be non-smothering and non-clinging. And strong! The stronger the woman, the better her chances of holding Warren.'

He first met that special lady at a showbiz party just after *Dick Tracy*. 'Interesting girl,' a pal said. Warren followed his gaze and rested on the fragile figure and classic beauty of a young actress called Annette Bening. 'Ooooh, yeah,' said Warren.

Warren had decided to make a biopic of gangster Bugsy Siegel, the man who more or less founded Las Vegas. He knew it was vital to cast the right actress to play the love of his life, Virginia Hill. Besides putting bullets into people, Siegel was something of a randy bastard, but after meeting Virginia never chased women again. He found someone who accepted him for who he was. Director Barry Levinson was thinking box office and Michelle Pfeiffer; Warren recalled that actress at the party and set up a lunch date. When Annette's agent heard the news he was dead set against any meeting, convinced the old Romeo just wanted to hit on his client. 'And it turned out he was right,' said Warren.

It was love at first sight for Warren, who fell for Annette in about ten minutes flat. 'I felt very conflicted because I was so elated to meet her, and yet at the same time I began to mourn the passing of a way of life. I thought, oh, everything's going to be different.' Of course the selfish part of him wanted to hang on to his playboy bachelor existence, probably until his bits withered and died, but he knew he was in the last-chance saloon to bag himself a scorching young bride and save himself endless reams of tabloid tittle-tattle about being a sad old lecher. Let's face it, Warren's adolescence ran about three decades longer than everyone else's. 'Being adolescent never got boring to me,' he's confessed. Or as sister Shirley once helpfully said, 'He's fifty from the neck up and fourteen from the waist down.' Fortunately that was all over now, and not a moment too soon. 'I stood a good chance of reaching the end of my days as a solitary, eccentric . . . fool.'

Desperate to have her there and then, Warren behaved, as always, like the old smoothie he is. 'As much as I am inclined to make a vulgar move upon you,' he said to her, 'I will refrain from doing so because I think it is terrible when people have to work together, if they have that pressure.' And Christ, he should know. On *Bugsy* (1991) they worked like a dream, so much so that critic Rex Reed noted, 'The chemistry is apparent and juicy. Their love scenes don't look like acting.' On set, however, Warren's romancing of Annette was so discreet that not even director Levinson knew what was going on.

Once *Bugsy* was in the can, Warren took Annette out to dinner. Between courses he came right out and asked if she wanted him to make her pregnant; this from a man who'd been running scared from fatherhood for decades. It was so off the wall a proposition, how could the poor girl refuse? 'Well, I would like to do that right away,' said Warren, and, er . . . they did. It was also perfectly in keeping with Warren's character. The guy's a gent, and a puritan under all that Don Juan stuff. He didn't litter the world with little bastard Warrens, he wants to go to heaven, so only impregnated the woman he knew he was going to marry.

The baby arrived early in 1992, a daughter, named Kathlyn after Warren's delighted mother. The event sent shockwaves through the industry. 'Is this the end of civilisation as we know it?' asked the *Washington Post*. The greatest lothario in Hollywood history, the man who had bedded the most desirable beauties of the age, was now a father, changing dirty nappies and cooing like an idiot. There were reports he'd fainted while watching birthing videos with Jack, but he denied it.

In March Warren and Annette were married in a small ceremony attended only by close relatives and friends. It must have been an awe-inspiring moment for Warren to say, 'I do.' Former lover and very nearly Mrs Warren Beatty Michelle Phillips commented, 'I love Annette and I pray for her every day. She can manage the guy, and I never could. He drove me nuts.'

A family man, and now a married man! Friends and Warren watchers couldn't quite believe it. Others, though, always guessed that, unlike Jack, fear of being alone would eventually drive him into matrimony. 'I think people do things that at the time are right for them,' says Tom Mankiewicz. 'I think if the Warren Beatty I knew in the seventies had gotten married, he'd have gotten a divorce right away. Playing the field wasn't really a statement. Warren fucked everything that moved, he just did. If he was in a movie and there were three girls in the movie, it was – bang, bang, bang. Now he's a terrific father and Annette's a wonderful mother. They make a great family.'

Warren has categorised his life into two distinct phases, 'Before Annette' and 'With Annette'. He'd avoided responsibility for so long, his life had been one long free buffet, but now it was time to end the party. Incredibly, married life seemed to suit him. 'I think stability is part of what Warren saw in Annette,' said sister Shirley. As for Robert Evans, he saw a distinct change in his old friend, who until his marriage had stood alone as the single most competitive person he ever knew. A man whose obsession in life was to be first: 'First with the new hot girl in town, first to be shown the new hot screenplay, the new hot role, or for that matter the new hot anything – as long as it was new and hot.'

Commentators wondered whether a man whose life was dominated by chasing women could settle down and be content with just the one. 'Women are his profession,' said one colleague. 'Movies are his hobby.' But Warren was determined to stay the course and he'd a better chance than most, due mainly to his compulsive nature. Divorce would be seen as a failure and, according to Robert Towne, 'Warren is terrified of failure.'

He must succeed because he cannot bear to fail. Warren will do anything short of murder to win.'

On his fifty-fifth birthday Warren attended the Oscars, Annette glowing on his arm. She'd been just three years old when he'd made his first trip to the ceremony, escorting Natalie Wood. As he entered the building a woman on the other side of the door just stopped dead when she saw Warren. 'I love you,' was all she could utter. Warren gets this a lot and sees it as part of the job of being a movie star. 'I've never seen Warren not be receptive to a fan coming up to him in a public situation,' says producer Jon Landau. 'Even when somebody is staring at Warren, then Warren will actually go up and introduce himself.'

In spite of all the failures, politics still held great sway over Warren. He advised Bill Clinton, then running as a presidential candidate, to jazz up his speeches by yelling 'fuck' a few times. Clinton ignored him, unlike McGovern and Hart, and won the election. Warren and Annette, along with Jack, were amongst the guests at his inauguration in January 1993. Clinton proved to be a Teflon politician, particularly where sex scandals were concerned. The danger of revelations about his private life had always been a factor in Warren not running for office, but the Clinton experience once again opened up the possibility that one day he might set his sights on the White House.

In this town I'm the leper with the most fingers.

Jack Nicholson burst back into the headlines in February 1994 when he attacked a motorist with a golf club in a rare public display of rage. It happened in LA, when Jack claimed a driver in a Mercedes cut him up. Incensed, he grabbed a golf club and ran over to the offending vehicle and gave it a good whack, Basil Fawlty style. The owner, one Robert Blank, claimed the star shattered the windshield and dented the roof, all of which resulted in a slight personal injury to himself from flying glass. All very bizarre. And in spite of Jack's wild image, completely out of character.

Questioned by the police, Jack admitted selecting a number two iron to dent the man's car, adding, 'You can bet I felt justified.' Later, when he'd calmed down a bit, Jack excused his behaviour by saying he was deeply upset, having just heard that a close colleague had died. 'I was out of my mind. He had died that morning and I was playing a maniac all night. It was a shameful experience for me. I don't like to lose control or to be angry.'

Blank intended to pursue a civil suit against Jack and the star faced prosecution for assault and vandalism, each charge carrying a potential six-month jail sentence. For a while it was squeaky bum time, but in the end Blank settled out of court and the charges were dropped. To many it seemed that Jack's power and money had triumphed over justice. The *Los Angeles Times* wrote, 'With the flick of a pen on a personal check, [Nicholson] can make things go away. Sue him for breaking your wind-shield with a golf club? There, a little cash ought to cover it. Bye bye lawsuit. So long, criminal charges.' The piece concluded that Jack was 'someone who seems exempt from the rules that govern life for the rest of us'.

Neither the golf-club incident nor the paternity suit did anything to diminish Jack's popularity. His stature in the film community was also never higher. Just a month later the American Film Institute honoured Jack with their Lifetime Achievement Award, justly deserved, if a little premature. Past recipients had been such well-wrinkled veterans as Hitchcock, Bette Davis and Henry Fonda. Jack was the youngest ever to receive the honour and dubbed it the Prime of Life Award.

He arrived on stage to the tune of Steppenwolf's 'Born to Be Wild' and star guests such as Shirley MacLaine, Cher, Bob Dylan, Faye Dunaway and Robert Evans, along with Dennis and Warren, all wore shades in tribute. 'I'm touched,' Jack said. Then, alluding to the road-rage incident, 'And I'm lucky to be at large.' Jack had wanted to make the occasion even more special by inviting swathes of family members, many of whom he'd not seen for years. The audience also included his ex-wife Sandra Knight and their daughter Jennifer, along with Rebecca Broussard. There were, however, some notable absentees, namely Susan Anspach and their son together Caleb. Susan had to wait a couple of days to see the cere-mony on television and after watching it called Jack. It was past midnight. 'This has to stop,' she said. 'This is really rude. If you don't want to invite me or Caleb, fine, but at least make a nice comment about your son.' Jack's voice, Susan recalled, was just a little slurred; he sounded stoned. 'Don't you know it's really late? I don't know what all this hysteria is about. You call me at this hour with this shit.'

When a few weeks later in a *Vanity Fair* interview Jack waxed lyrical about his young family with Rebecca but again failed to mention Caleb, Susan was seized with a mother's anger and sent a letter to the magazine's editor, hoping to rectify the omission. Jack called Susan, 'as mad as hell', in her words, that *Vanity Fair* planned to publish her letter in full.

Since their break-up Jack and Susan's relationship had always been a little shaky – Jack described her as 'fucking unpredictable' – but now it hit the skids with a vengeance. Some years earlier Jack had been happy to help Susan out when her career had taken a nosedive and she'd found difficulty keeping up with the mortgage repayments on her house in Santa Monica. Through a company operated by his financial manager, Jack arranged a large loan. After Susan's letter was printed in *Vanity Fair* the company suddenly requested that the loan be repaid, along with a daunting amount of interest. Refusal on her part, said the notification, would result in foreclosure. 'He's trying to ruin me absolutely,' Susan complained.

The row was getting ugly and spilling out into the public arena, as Susan was hounded by Jack's legal beagles for several months. The *Los Angeles Times* called it 'the misplaced trust between a Hollywood God and the mother of his child'. Jack must have known this wasn't playing very well, after all it was a comparatively small sum of money compared to his overall fortune, and eventually the whole matter was settled out of court. With Susan bound by a confidentiality clause, all the frenzied media could get out of her was the happy comment, 'I'm still in my home.'

After all that Jack needed some fun and headed to London, one of his favourite cities, where he frequented nightclubs, got roaring drunk and was seen in the glittering company of various British totty including Naomi Campbell, Kate Moss and Amanda de Cadenet, with whom it was reported he was having a fling following her estrangement from husband John Taylor of Duran Duran.

Jack also made time in his busy schedule to catch a performance of *Revue Voyeurz*, a lesbian musical that had dancers exposing themselves on stage, simulating sex, performing fellatio on rubber penises and gang raping a protesting virgin. It was Jack's kind of musical and he happily posed for pictures with the girls all wearing chains and bondage gear backstage after the performance. They couldn't wipe the smile off his face for two months.

Inevitably, wherever Jack went, the press followed. They camped outside his hotel watching a parade of nubile maidens going in and out at all hours, then wrote snide reports about it the next day. He was dubbed 'Jack the Sad'. 'Even if endless nymphets are happy to feel old age creeping over them,' wrote one hack, 'you just might not be up to it any more.' Of course he was used to being hounded by now. Nine days in ten since the mid-seventies he hadn't walked through a door without there being photographers around to capture the moment. It's one of the reasons he took to wearing sunglasses; they're primarily a defence against fifty flashbulbs going off in his face, and part of his personal armoury. 'With my sunglasses on, I'm Jack Nicholson. Without them, I'm fat and sixty.'

I have seen the devil in my microscope, and I have chained him.

When director Richard Stanley was given the green light to shoot his modern remake of the horror classic *The Island of Dr Moreau* (1996), he wanted Marlon Brando to play H. G. Wells's mad scientist. The idea intrigued the actor. Maybe he saw some parallels between himself and Dr Moreau; like Wells's character he had tried to create his own Utopia on his private island. He'd also in recent years pumped millions into various scientific schemes including genetics, the idea being that it was too late to repair the post-industrial environment mankind had created for itself, so, like Moreau, shouldn't the human race think of genetically modifying itself to fit the new environment? He'd invested too in alternative energy and terraforming: adapting other planets to support colonisation from earth. 'I think at that point in his life he had a very low opinion of the craft of acting,' says Stanley. 'So he was constantly trying to find causes to put his money into, feeding the Third World or creating alternatives to gasoline, terraforming Mars, space travel, ideas that he felt were real jobs. A part of him was in danger of turning into the Moreau character. Another very Dr Moreau touch that Marlon had in real life was he had these guard dogs in the house which were trained to attack anything he pointed his laser pen at. He had this laser pen and he'd point the dot at the wall and the dogs would leap at it, their jaws biting at the laser beam. Very Dr Moreau.'

Stanley felt confident, he had Brando voicing interest and a great script, but then he heard rumblings that backers New Line Cinema didn't want him as director and were planning a coup, replacing him with Roman Polanski. Stanley wasn't going without a fight and demanded a showdown with Marlon; he wasn't even put off when he heard that Brando wanted to skin him alive. (Why? Who knows? He just did.) 'Actually New Line didn't think I'd last five minutes with Brando,' says Stanley. 'And it was intimidating, pulling up into Mulholland Drive, the gates opening, TV cameras everywhere, excessive security. I was surprised when I finally met him because I was expecting him to be more of a monster than he was, because the build-up was so huge. He seemed smaller than I expected, but old. Obviously he wasn't Brando as we'd seen him in the movies. But all the time I was sitting down I was thinking, James Dean played bongos with this guy, he went out with Marilyn Monroe and fixed Tennessee Williams's plumbing.'

New Line had insisted on having a representative at the meeting, a fly on the wall to see exactly what went down. It was a woman executive. 'And quite early on she complained that it was too hot in the room,' recalls Stanley. 'Marlon turned up the thermostat. "If you turn that up any more I'm going to go to sleep," she said. And he just continued to edge it up very slightly, during which time he scarcely made eye contact with me. I was totally nervous; I don't think we exchanged a single word. Instead he made light chat with this woman, all the time gradually edging up the heating, and within about twenty minutes she was completely unconscious. That was weird. He just put her to sleep. As he turned up that dial she just got drowsier and drowsier until she was gone and right out of the meeting. At which point he looked at me and we started talking.'

Successfully. Stanley was back on his own movie, Brando was happy and New Line had to lump it, for the time being, at least. He returned to Mulholland Drive several times. 'After one meeting I was given a ride back to my hotel by his daughter Cheyenne. I remember as I was getting out of the car she looked at me and said, "Are you afraid?" I said, "Of what?" But she didn't answer and I still don't know what she meant by that, and it was the last time I heard from her. She was dead not so long afterwards.'

Things looked good for Stanley, that is until he actually started making the movie. He lasted about four days before New Line finally got their way. Since subtlety hadn't worked, they simply fired him, bringing in veteran John Frankenheimer, who had the script completely rewritten. Incensed by the way he'd been mistreated, Stanley sneaked back onto the set. 'I was curious. I wanted to see what was going on. It was a good thing to see because it was such a shambles, just complete chaos.' There were days when the crew didn't know what scenes were scheduled to be shot, actors would be in make-up for five hours being transformed into Grizzly Man or Rhinoceros Man only to find out they weren't needed that day. It was just a complete mess. And Brando was also up to his old trick of baiting his director, according to cameraman William Fraker. 'Marlon was tough to work with, no doubt, if you were a director or producer. He'd want to hear the director's ideas for a particular scene and then he'd have an explanation as to why he thought that was all wrong. And they'd sit down for hours and talk. In fact on one day during *Moreau* we sat down for eight hours while Marlon and Frankenheimer worked it out. So directing Marlon was a chore, really tough.'

David Thewlis was hired for one of the leads and on the night he arrived on location Marlon told him, 'David, go home. This is not a good film to be on. It's cursed.' It ended up driving Thewlis pretty nuts, but he did later recall one amusing incident. Brando still used a radio earpiece that an assistant used to feed him his lines. Suddenly in the middle of one scene he started getting police messages. 'There's a robbery at Woolworth's,' he announced to everyone.

One night Stanley managed to get into Marlon's trailer and they talked for hours. 'He was in a bad way. Christian was in jail and then Cheyenne had killed herself; it all started to get on top of him and he was pretty much broken. What was happening to him was a million times worse than what was happening to me. I was losing my movie, he'd lost his daughter. It was very sad. He offered me a lot of money which I now really regret not taking.' And Stanley's pretty sure why Marlon was offering the cash: 'Guilt. He knew I'd been screwed, he'd seen it all happen and he knew he hadn't helped me and he knew he could have helped me. But he just didn't have the fight left in him to try and keep me on the project or to stop New Line from tearing the movie apart.'

If you'll notice the arterial nature of the blood coming from the hole in my head, you can assume that we're all having a real lousy day.

Making movies has always been Dennis Hopper's crusade, his true vocation. During interviews he's never shy in pointing out that he's a talented director (and he is), or that he should have been allowed to make more movies (and he should). Back in the days of *Easy Rider* he told everyone about his dreams of changing Hollywood, of changing the way movies were made. Dennis was at a dinner party one night with Peter Bogdanovich, the new vanguard, and George Cukor, who represented the old. Hopper couldn't resist sticking it to him. 'Old Hollywood,' he kept saying. 'We're going to bury you, man.' And what happened? Not a lot. All the things he was going to do. 'I was full of shit,' Dennis admits.

His final feature to date as a director came in 1994. *Chasers* was a pretty lowbrow comedy knock-off of Jack's *The Last Detail* about a pair of US Navy police escorting a beautiful female prisoner, played by Erika Eleniak, an American *Playboy* Playmate best known for her role in *Baywatch*. Her chest is the best thing about the film.

It was as an actor that Dennis still fared best, picking up supporting roles in blockbusters, still cast as the crazed loon. In *Speed* (1994) he played a nut who puts a bomb on a bus that will explode if the vehicle goes below 50mph. Dennis tells Keanu Reeves's gormless bomb-disposal cop: 'A bomb is made to explode. That's its meaning, its purpose. Your life is empty because you spend it trying to stop the bomb from becoming.'

As soon as he got on the set Dennis realised that first-time director

Jan De Bont was making a hell of a movie. 'It had so much energy. It was like a big rollercoaster ride.'

Audiences certainly reacted that way to it, turning *Speed* into a massive success. Executives knew they were onto a winner when at the test screenings audience members would walk backwards when they needed to go to the bathroom so as to miss as little as possible.

It wasn't much of a surprise, having played so many screen nutters, that Dennis might attract a real-life loon. Sure enough in 1994 he was the victim of a stalker who believed he was the reincarnation of James Dean. Dennis took out a court order to stop the guy coming anywhere near his home.

His next essay in nutballism was on the infamous Kevin Costner action epic *Waterworld* (1995). Prior to *Titanic* the most expensive movie ever made, everything that could go wrong on location in Hawaii did go wrong: crew injuries, tsunami warnings, the main set sinking, a budget that ballooned from $100m to God knows what and rumours that director Kevin Reynolds walked off the set with two weeks of filming left, leaving Costner to complete the film. Joss Whedon flew out to do last-minute rewrites on the script. He later described it as 'seven weeks of hell'.

Dennis had a ball, though; there are worse things than having to stay for months on end in Hawaii. It shows in his performance as a scuzzy pirate and leader of a gang of cut-throats who roam the sea on a flooded planet Earth in a polluted future. 'Dennis was great,' recalls Kevin Reynolds. 'I'll never forget when I met him, we talked for a moment and I guess knowing that his reputation precedes him, he said, I won't give you any trouble, and he didn't, he was a total pro. Needless to say *Waterworld* was an incredibly difficult shoot, but Dennis was a trooper. What I admired about him was, this kind of role, which was so over the top and could be really intimidating to a lot of actors, the kind of thing that you have to throw yourself into completely or it won't work, he wasn't the least bit intimidated and really went for it and that's what made it work.' Even more impressive as Dennis wasn't Reynolds' choice but the studios and was parachuted into the film after they'd already begun shooting. Immediately Dennis seized on the comic potential of the character and Reynolds allowed him free rein to run with it. 'As a director you're hoping that a guy like Dennis will show up who will bring a lot to the set and be inventive. The last thing you want to do, especially on a movie like *Waterworld* where you've got a million other things to deal with, is to have to stop and try to push buttons to get a performance out of someone. That was never the problem with Dennis, he showed up and got it, and when you have a guy like that you just turn him loose.' It's a cartoon villain and a suitably cartoonish performance, with one eye and scarred features. 'I'm ugly, man,' said Dennis. 'This guy is really bad news!'

Inevitably, considering the obscene amount of money spent on the film, it was seen as a financial failure, despite a solid box-office performance. Unfairly it was dubbed 'Fishtar', after Warren's box-office bomb *Ishtar*. 'At the time so many people were gunning for us,' says Reynolds. 'But particularly gunning for Kevin, who had reached that point in his career where the press decided it was time to knock him off his pedestal. So because of the cost *Waterworld* just became this huge thing that the press wanted to hate. I'll never forget the first screening in New York, they wanted it to be a bomb and afterwards one of the critics walked out and said, with disdain, well, it didn't suck. It was like damning with faint praise.'

You know that I've never been faithful to anyone in my whole life.

Warren Beatty had taken to fatherhood with a delight and joy that surprised many. Not least sister Shirley, who once couldn't imagine Warren with children. 'When he first met my daughter, he examined her quietly as though she were just a specimen of human life instead of his niece.' In the end he and Annette had four kids. 'Warren's a blithering nut,' said Jack. 'He just turns into a goo machine around his children. Nothing's come close to making Warren as happy in his life as these children. Nothing.'

Annette once laughingly revealed that when one of the kids asked her dad what an orgasm was his unusual terminology for it was, 'It's a sexual sneeze.' Some wag suggested that before marrying Annette Warren must have suffered from chronic hay fever.

Not unnaturally, tensions existed in the marriage, namely about how Annette could juggle motherhood with movies, for she undoubtedly still wanted a career and she is an exceptionally fine actress. There was also an attempt to establish them as a screen partnership, misguided at best both artistically and commercially. *Love Affair* (1994) groaned under its own autobiographical weight in its story about a one-time lothario who meets his match. Everyone said it was a mistake; *Variety* called it 'a textbook exercise in narcissism'. But after the darkly gothic *Bugsy*, Warren wanted to make an unashamedly light romantic movie.

Yet again, his vision caused friction with his artistic partners. Originally Robert Towne was set to both write and direct the film, marking the first time they'd worked together since *Shampoo*. Months into the process Towne complained that Warren was encroaching too much, trying to modernise what Towne felt was essentially a traditional period piece. They argued. Towne was also playing around with Beatty's suave screen persona, having his character endure an on-screen proctology exam, for example. After numerous drafts Towne either walked or was asked to leave. There were also reports that in postproduction Beatty took over the creative reins from director Glenn Gordon Caron, who was hardly seen.

According to some sources, *Love Affair* did not entirely live up to its title, in that it put undue strain upon the couple's marriage. There was a report about a shapely blonde Warren hadn't seen in a while visiting the set. Just to be polite he invited her inside his trailer for a chat, but Annette saw them leave and went off the deep end. 'You don't take bimbos to your dressing room,' she decreed. Annette had to admit she didn't think Warren had changed all that much since their marriage; he still eyed the pretty girls, quite naturally. 'What has changed, I hope, is that he doesn't seem to have that urge to bed these ladies. And Warren respects me.'

Maybe it was because age was finally catching up on him. More than one critic commented that perhaps Warren was getting a little too long in the tooth to be playing romantic leads. And he was obsessing more than ever over diets and health foods. In one hotel in New York, after ordering an oil-free egg-white omelette with vegetables, he went into the kitchens to supervise the cordon bleu chef himself. Annette some-times kidded Warren about his scrupulously healthy habits. Few colleagues have seen Warren put anything gastronomically indecent in his gob. At a restaurant he was eyeing a particularly tasty looking titbit on his wife's plate. 'What is it?' he enquired, finally. 'Goat cheese,' she replied. He reached over with his fork and said, 'I think I'll try some.' 'Good,' said Annette. 'Live it up, Warren.'

Sell crazy someplace else, we're all stocked up here.

Director Sean Penn pulled off one of the casting coups of the year when he got Jack Nicholson to star opposite, guess who, Anjelica, both playing divorcees who, well, hate each other. *The Crossing Guard* (1995) marked the first time the ex-couple had worked together since *Prizzi's Honor* and Jack confessed they hadn't been in touch since their split, so the set could have turned into the ultimate nightmare of recriminations and reprisals, but Penn claimed they were both professionals and there were no prob-lems. Jack said they just did their job and avoided the obvious; none of the trauma from their seventeen years together came up. 'It was a privil-ege to work with her again,' said Jack, genuinely glad that she was now a happily married woman. He also playfully speculated as to why Anjelica might have agreed to play the role. 'She's got a lot of hideous things to say to me in the movie. I'm sure that's why she wanted to do it. I'm only kidding, but our scenes are all vicious.'

Jack also found himself acting opposite Penn's own mother Eileen Ryan in a quirky scene that had him licking her fingers. 'Don't worry, I washed my hand,' she told him before filming. 'You're the one that best worry,' Jack replied. 'I didn't wash my mouth.'

Jack next teamed up with old pal Bob Rafelson for another low-budget movie made outside the mainstream, the tough crime thriller *Blood and Wine* (1996). Agreeing to cut his usual fee, although not by all that much, Jack demanded, due to his hatred of commercial airline flights, that he travel only in private jets for the duration of shooting, at $50,000 a trip, which hiked the budget considerably. He also clashed with Rafelson over the not inconsequential backside of Jennifer Lopez, appearing in an early film role. Jack's argument was simple, 'Jennifer Lopez was going to be famous for her ass,' and with his experience of female anatomy, he should know. When, according to Jack, Rafelson overslept the actor himself staged a short dance number, 'with my hands on Jennifer's ass'. But Rafelson wouldn't put it in the picture. 'Bob, you're insane!!' Jack was later told the studio had insisted on its removal.

Although their personalities couldn't have been more different, Jack got on well with co-star Michael Caine. After a day's shooting Jack would go out to party and play, Caine would return to his wife. Jack's idea of play, according to reports, was snorting cocaine. Indeed, a production source claimed Jack made no attempt to hide the habit. In recent years Jack rarely spoke about drugs publicly. Sometimes when the subject was raised he could be riled into making a heated response, spitting into the face of one reporter, 'Yes, I smoke marijuana! Do you want to see me do it?' As late as 1987 he publicly acknowledged that he still enjoyed getting high, but never admitted in print any cocaine excess, though articles on his life routinely referred to his drug use. In Hollywood rumours were rife that he had a capacity to snort vast quantities.

Things turned awkward for our Jack in October 1996, when self-confessed hooker Catherine Sheehan accused the star of duffing her up after a sex romp. She alleged that Jack called her up one morning at 3 a.m. and asked her to come round to Mulholland Drive, and to bring a friend. According to court documents the women arrived, were greeted cordially and taken upstairs. Catherine claimed the three of them engaged in various sexual activities which stopped at around 7 a.m., when she noticed Jack was 'fatigued'. I'm not surprised, poor guy.

It was when the issue of payment was raised that Catherine alleged Jack became, 'loud and abusive, stating that he had never paid anyone for sex as he could get anyone he wanted as a sexual partner'. She also claimed Jack pushed her, then grabbed hold of her hair and showed signs that he might become more violent. He then asked both women to open their purses to see if they had stolen anything before chucking them outside. Once in her car, Catherine called the police. A squad car arrived shortly afterwards and Jack was interviewed by two officers, though no arrest was made. Catherine meanwhile had admitted herself to hospital, later discovering that a silicone implant in her breast had ruptured. In November Catherine's lawyer advised her to file a civil action against Jack claiming unspecified damages for assault, battery and emotional distress. Once again Jack settled out of court.

It was probably a relief to get behind the camera again, a romantic comedy this time, *As Good As It Gets* (1997), playing one of his most disagreeable characters, a novelist with an almost paralysing obsessive-compulsive disorder. He has phobias about germs, a fixation on tidiness and a nice patter in rudeness, insulting blacks, homosexuals and Jews with equal veracity. He even throws his gay neighbour's little dog down a garbage chute. Jack was quick to assure people that he was much nicer in real life, but could be just as obnoxious. 'I rather jump from immaculately polite to violent! There's not much rudeness in between. Rude is for amateurs.'

Jack has always taken delight in the fact that the public have no real clue as to who the real Jack is behind the shades, behind the grin. He's cultivated this enigma, this mystery that there are two of him, the person people think he is and the person he actually is. From his interchanges with the public he knows half of them think he's a raving lunatic, and the other half that he's a pretty rational guy. 'You see, I'm real nice, ultra-polite, raised by women. But inside I'm a right cunt.'

With *As Good As It Gets* Jack was back with a tried and tested partner, *Terms of Endearment*'s James L Brooks, a man he loved working with because, 'I can call him a shit and know that it won't harm our relationship.' For his lead Brooks had to think of someone who could play this monster, but not completely turn the audience off, someone who could in the end be loved. 'Jack was just the only choice.' And yet he found the role one of his toughest and the early weeks of filming so problem-laden that he quietly took Brooks to one side and said, 'Look, Jim, if you feel like you've got to replace me, don't worry about it.' Brooks just laughed; he thought Jack was crazy. And he was right, it was another prize-laden performance. Picking up a Golden Globe Jack told the audience, with a hint of sarcasm, 'I warned Jim, if I got this, it would give me licence to misbehave for ten more years.'

Perhaps Jack's anxiety about the role was that at sixty he would be romancing on screen an actress (Helen Hunt) who was twenty-five years his junior. If so, such reticence didn't extend to his private life, where he was still naturally drawn to younger women, though, as he confessed, 'I'm pretty old, so almost everyone is a younger woman to me!' In the end the film won him more fans and plaudits, with the *New York Times* hailing him as the poster boy for older guys who end up in bed with younger women.

The final measure of bravery is to stand up to death.

There's only one recorded occasion when all four of our bad boys have been at the same place at the same time. This little moment in history took place at the wedding of Sean Penn to Robin Wright in 1996. The ceremony was scheduled to begin at 4 p.m., but one guest hadn't arrived yet. Marlon Brando. An hour later he turned up, fat, sweating and tipsy, and proceeded to fall asleep in a chair and snore loudly. 'Not even the loud buzzing of a news helicopter could rouse the dozing don,' one guest reported.

Marlon slept through the entire ceremony, finally waking up during the toasts. He got up, began to ramble incoherently, even attempt a bit of off-key singing. Jack, alert to the potential embarrassment, took Marlon by the arm and attempted to sit him back down. 'Thank you very much, Marlon, for those sentiments. I'm sure they were very touching.' But Marlon wasn't ready to go quietly. Grabbing Jack's trousers, he pulled them round his ankles, and in this state Jack finished his toast to the bride and groom. It was Warren and Tim Robbins who restrained Marlon long enough for Jack to pull up his pants. Dennis watched with a wry smile on his face. The whole thing was like something from an insane sitcom.

Jack and Marlon had lived almost next door to each other now for over twenty years. They weren't the kind of neighbours who popped round much for cups of sugar but were always friends and there for each other if one of them needed help. Jack treasured the conversations they shared, genuinely touched that he was one of the few people Marlon allowed to call him Bud. Jack loved his humour, too. Brando's favourite holiday was April Fool's Day, when he could really let rip with practical jokes and pranks. 'And, trust me, the guy pulled a couple of real cracker-jacks at my expense.'

Yeah, she's a regular Meryl Streep. Her idea of improvisation is putting a dick in her mouth sideways.

Dennis Hopper was now working like a man possessed, a man on a mission, pretty much taking any acting job on offer; his record was eight movies in one year alone (1999). It wasn't because he was a workaholic. No, he just remembered the years when he sat around and wondered if he'd ever work again.

His quality control was busted, though, that's for sure; most of the movies were of the straight-to-DVD variety. As he joked himself. 'I've done over a hundred and fifty films, but I think most of them are only shown in Eastern Europe or Fiji or somewhere and they go right to tape.' Some never even got released. Take 1997's *The Good Life*, co-starring Frank Stallone. When older brother Sly agreed to appear in a cameo role and the producers started promoting the movie as if he were the star, old Rambo sued and the movie never saw daylight.

You can't make that many films and not strike lucky a few times. In amongst the tripe, with asinine titles like *Lured Innocence* and *Bad City Blues*, was the odd nugget, such as a deliriously sleazy turn in *The Blackout* (1997), from *Driller Killer* director Abel Ferrara. Co-star Matthew Modine, of *Full Metal Jacket* and *Birdy* fame, recalls fondly working with Dennis. 'I was curious about Hopper because the film we made together was dealing with drugs and alcohol abuse, and I wondered how Dennis would feel about me playing a character that was out of his mind from drugs and booze. I was working with an actor who had, let's say, a strong understanding of the character I was playing. It was wonderful to be in the scenes with Dennis because there was always a sense of danger. If he said something like, "I'm going to punch you in the face," there was always the sense that he might actually do it. Fantastic!'

One important role that slipped away from Dennis was the TV reality boss in *The Truman Show*. There are conflicting reports as to exactly what happened, that Dennis walked off the set after just one day's filming alleging 'creative differences', or that he was fired by the producer, who never wanted him anyway. Whatever, Ed Harris came in as a last-minute replacement and went on to win a Golden Globe for best supporting actor and an Oscar nomination. Dennis managed to see the funny side of it.

Everybody just gotta keep fuckin' everybody 'til they're all the same colour.

After the lacklustre *Love Affair* Warren Beatty backed off from not only making movies with Annette, but making movies full stop. Annette continued working, establishing herself as an actress of distinction in films like *American Beauty*. The same year she turned forty, and boy must Warren have regretted once quipping: 'My notion of a wife at forty is that a man should be able to change her, like a bank note, for two twenties.'

After a break of four years Warren at last made another film, a pretty good one, too. *Bulworth* (1998) was a biting political satire and one of the most radical American comedies in years with Beatty playing a US senator who speaks politically incorrect truths on sensitive issues. Warren claimed that 'just about everything' in the movie was likely to offend audiences, which takes pot-shots at blacks, Jews, the rich and Hollywood. He even poked fun at power-mad media moguls, moguls presumably like top Republican contributor Rupert Murdoch, whose 20th Century Fox bankrolled the satire. When executives over at Fox first read the script 'they thought I was demented', said Warren. 'They hated it, though at least they were honest enough to say so.'

Once again Warren's perfectionism reared its head during filming. According to reports he'd spend hours in the production office hovering over people seated at their computers and micromanaged every aspect of the film. The crew made up a T-shirt that read: 'I survived Bulworth.' Another bore the legend – 'I worked on Bulworth and all I got was – (a) an ulcer; (b) psychosis; (c) a migraine; (d) facial tics; (e) all of the above.'

Karyn Rachtman, who produced the film's musical soundtrack, confessed that Warren is the only person in the business she's ever hung up the phone on. 'He really works you hard. He would say things like, "I'm trying to figure out what your ulterior motive is." It was like, "Warren, I don't have one." He just wears you out, but he really gets the best out of people. Everything's very important to him; there was nothing that was just a throwaway. He's tough and brutal, but there's an element of charm about it. He gets his way.'

Karyn had been specifically brought to the project to assemble a stellar talent pool of rappers and hip-hop artists. 'Warren made it clear to me that he wanted the most hardcore and controversial rappers, the biggest names, the smartest, just get them all. He wanted the film to have real street cred.' So Karyn got the likes of Dr Dre, Wyclef Jean, Ol' Dirty Bastard, Ice Cube and Chuck D. It was an odd sight to see Warren, then over fifty, hanging out with these musical bruisers. Far from seeing him as an old wrinkly has-been the rappers dug Warren: he was Dick Tracy, Clyde Barrow, Bugsy Siegel, shit he'd fucked Madonna! 'The fact Warren had been with all these women was a big thing to these guys,' says Karyn.

As for Warren, he enjoyed dipping his toe into that culture and sincerely respected the art form, seeing these rappers as street poets almost and their songs the music of social protest. 'It was very important to him that he got their respect,' says Karyn. 'And twice a week he'd have a dinner party at his house and invite some of the rappers over, and it would be just the funniest dinner. Annette would be there sometimes, she was cool and the kids were crazy and cute. And a lot of the time Warren and these rappers would talk politics. He was really in awe of a lot of them.' He even tried a rap himself in the film, an unlikely mix used for comic effect. 'The way to make the rapping mildly amusing is to not be good at it,' said Warren. 'I had no trouble not being good at it.'

By using these artists Warren's hope was that young black kids interested in the hip-hop scene would come and see the movie. Didn't quite work that way. The audiences were mainly white middle-class liberals, despite all the controversy surrounding its deliberately clichéd view of black ghetto society, seen as brave by many, condescending by some.

When black film-maker Spike Lee was asked to comment on *Bulworth* he said: 'It was just unbelievable to me. Someone who looked like Halle Berry would not be with Warren Beatty – I think that's his own fantasy.'

Going out on a publicity tour, Warren subjected himself to the Howard Stern radio show. Inevitably the shock jock asked him about his sexual conquests and Warren clammed up. 'God, you're a lousy interview,' Stern said. But *Bulworth* was a movie and a message Warren passionately believed in. 'Obscenity is not words like cocksucker or motherfucker, it's the disparity between rich and poor, and the fact that it's increasing.' Warren couldn't give two hoots if he offended people, he never ran for office so Senator Bulworth fulfilled his fantasy of the liberal politician who says exactly what's on his mind without regard to the consequences. And far from getting him booted out of the Democratic establishment, it ended up with Warren asked to consider running for the presidency. David Letterman thought it a great idea, joking on his TV show, 'Warren Beatty has vast experience in screwing people and leaving them happy.' Close friend Garry Shandling advised Warren, 'If you get elected, make sure you get your name above the title of the country.'

The worm has turned and it is now packing an Uzi.

In the late nineties Jack Nicholson entered the longest sabbatical of his career, four years without making a film, leading to speculation that he might retire. Asked by a female reporter whether he might contemplate retirement, his answer was vintage Jack: 'I feel you'd miss me, honey.'

His private life, however, was as busy as ever. There was a trip over to Cuba to attend a film festival, along with a three-hour chinwag with Castro. 'We smoked a few good cigars. He stays up late, like I do.' Some political commentators back home were severely miffed. For company he'd taken Rebecca, leading to press speculation that the pair were getting back together, only for it to emerge that Jack the Lad was seeing another actress, Lara Flynn Boyle, best known for her role in *Twin Peaks*. They met in 1999 at a film function and struck up an immediate rapport, despite the thirty-odd-year age gap. 'The whole country has a love affair with Jack. Why can't I?' she told reporters. Some say it was Warren's wife Annette who played matchmaker here, worried that a footloose and fancy-free Jack might encourage hubby to relapse into his old playboy ways.

Jack's relationship with Lara Flynn again raised the issue of his preference for, let's say, younger women. Jack made no bones about the fact that he had a 'sweet spot' for them, even suggesting that it wasn't psychological but partly glandular; 'It has to do with mindlessly continuing the species.' His remark annoyed more than a few people close to him. 'I've got every woman I know up my ass on this one,' he told Meryl Streep. 'Deservedly so, my love!' she replied.

But marriage seemed about as likely as Steve Guttenberg winning an Oscar. 'It is difficult to imagine a woman of Boyle's appetites sitting up there in the hills, sharing muffin recipes with Annette Bening,' wrote *Talk* magazine. Lara was something of a wild child; according to her ex-boyfriend, actor David Sherrill, having sex with her, 'was like trying to jack off a bobcat with a handful of barbed wire. She was too wild for me, bro.'

Jack and Lara would enjoy, if that's the right word, a typical on/off relationship. 'Sleeping with Jack is like sleeping with Einstein,' she reasoned. But returning from holiday in the south of France Lara was allegedly incensed at Jack after finding a bracelet in his luggage not intended for her. 'It is so over with Jack,' she told reporters. Hounded by the paparazzi, Lara was photographed in a New York club with Harrison Ford, then having his own marital troubles. Jack swiftly got in touch, keen for reconciliation. It worked, and they were all smiles again for the showbiz marriage of 2000, between Michael Douglas and Catherine Zeta Jones in New York. 'Lara has a sense of fun and daring to her,' said Jack. 'That's probably why we like being together.' But for how long?

In any case, Jack had other problems, such as the time a very large female fan stripped naked and ran round his house demanding sex. After driving her car through security gates at Mulholland Drive she started banging on doors demanding, 'Make love to me, Jack!' Staff alerted police and the thirty-five-year-old nymphomaniac was taken to a mental hospital for observation.

Over the years Jack had come to expect the unexpected – being one of the most recognisable people on earth had its drawbacks. For the most part, though, Jack has always been comfortable with fame; if you don't like the attention, go live in the desert and run a gas station. Pursued one night by paparazzi on his way to Kennedy International airport to pick up a girlfriend, Jack had his limo stop at a neighbourhood liquor store in Queens, where he graciously shared a pint of Jim Beam with the snappers and local strangers. One time in London he spotted a very shapely young lady looking at a shop window display. He sidled over to her, put his face into hers and grinned. The girl squealed with delight upon recognising him, Jack stepped back, tripped over an ice-cream stand and nearly fell on his arse.

Another public encounter had a couple stopping him in a store to ask, 'How long have you been a Jack Nicholson lookalike? How much do they pay you?' When he told them he really was Jack Nicholson they just laughed at him. 'There was no way I could convince them that it was really me!'

7

And Then There Were Three

My God! Let me get a look at you. You know, you look like shit. What's your secret?

When Marlon Brando agreed to make *The Score* (2001), playing another supporting role in what was a decent heist drama, no one knew it was going to be the last movie he'd ever make. It was a hotly anticipated picture. Marlon was to appear on screen for the first time with Robert De Niro, the meeting of two industry monoliths. It was to prove a rocky journey. Before Marlon showed up he called producer Gary Foster to introduce himself and ask a couple of practical questions. Foster finished by saying, 'I'm looking forward to meeting you, we're going to have a lot of fun.' There was a pause on the other end of the line. Then Marlon spoke. 'How do you know we're going to have fun?' Foster said, 'Well, I usually try to have a good time when we work.' Marlon laughed, as if to say, 'We'll see.'

It wasn't as though Foster hadn't been warned. While setting up the movie he'd run into *Dr Moreau*'s John Frankenheimer and told him he was about to work with Marlon. Did he have any advice? Frankenheimer just looked at Foster and said, 'Here's what I'll say to you. If I was penniless and desperate and the only job available was working with Brando, I'd rather lie down in the gutter and die.'

When he arrived on location Marlon charmed the socks off the crew; after all it was Marlon Brando, oh my God! Foster wanted to rehearse that evening the scene they intended shooting the following day, Brando in De Niro's jazz club. 'We don't need to rehearse,' said Marlon. 'We'll just go to work tomorrow.' That was cool, smiles all round. A little while later Foster was summoned to Marlon's trailer. 'We had a really nice chat, it wasn't even about the movie, he wanted to know more about me.' Then it happened, Marlon said he didn't want to shoot the jazz-club scene the following day but something completely different, the moment he hits a villain with a fire poker. Foster said that scene wasn't prepped yet, but Marlon was adamant. 'Why don't we get the director?' So in came Frank Oz, who backed up Foster's argument. 'Look, Marlon, we're not ready to shoot that scene, we haven't finished the work on the prosthetic arm.' Marlon asked, 'What prosthetic arm?' Oz said, 'The prosthetic arm for the guy you hit.' Marlon looked dumbfounded, 'How the hell do you know I'm going to hit him in the arm?' Frank said, 'Because that's what's in the script.' Marlon, with feigned shock said, 'Oh my God, you're pre-directing the movie.' He then turned at Foster and roared, 'Get out.' Foster did just that. 'And I don't know what tran-spired afterwards, but five minutes later Frank Oz stormed out of the trailer saying, "Nobody fucking talks to me that way." Frank was just beside himself. And he never told me what was said, and Marlon never told me what was said, but it was, oh my God, what's going to happen now?'

What ended up happening was a battle between Marlon and Oz for the rest of the three weeks that Marlon was on the film. 'There were periods of time when it was fabulous,' says Foster. 'Everyone got along, and then there were periods where Marlon couldn't stop himself poking at Frank.' It didn't help that Marlon insisted on calling Oz Miss Piggy, the Muppet character he'd voiced on the classic seventies show.

Things got so bad that the studio talked seriously about replacing Marlon. 'Because three weeks of this kind of crap,' says Foster, 'we wouldn't be able to stand it. So Marlon was put on notice that he had to cooperate. De Niro was unbelievable, playing at being diplomat. Clearly he didn't have to get in the middle of it, but he wanted this one experience of appearing with Marlon not to be chaos. There were moments when Marlon and Frank had a disagreement on set and Bob went over to Marlon and said something and Marlon calmed down. We got through it, but it was a trying process.'

Marlon continued to have issues, like pitching script changes that Foster didn't think were appropriate. 'Well, if I was to appeal above you, who is the power behind all this?' Marlon demanded. 'Who do I talk to?' Foster said, 'The head of the studio, Peter Guber.' Marlon asked. 'And where is he, in Hollywood, hiding behind his desk?' Suddenly Marlon got into this whole diatribe on power, as Foster recalls. 'He started saying, "You wanna see power? I'll fucking show you power," and he started doing Don Corleone right in front of me, and he was loving it. And I was smiling because there was the Godfather talking to me. But Marlon definitely had this issue with authority.'

In another scene Marlon begs De Niro's character to do one last bank job for him because his life is on the line. Finally, he breaks down and De Niro agrees. It was 5.30 in the morning when Foster's phone rang. It was Marlon. 'I'm calling to let you know I am not going to cry, it's not going to happen.' Foster didn't argue, instead he went to the set early and told Frank Oz and De Niro. Between them there was no real understanding of how it was going to get resolved. 'But what happened when we shot it,' says Foster, '– and this was brilliant Robert De Niro – Marlon said, "Can you do this?" and Bob took his eyes off Marlon and put his head down, just didn't respond. So Marlon started improvising. Bob still stared at the ground, he would not acknowledge Marlon until Marlon realised he had no choice but to make Bob look at him, which caused him to get to a place he didn't want to go to. When Bob finally felt that he had gotten the most honest performance he looked up at Marlon and said his line, "OK, I'll do it. I hope you're not fucking me up." And he got up and he left, he literally walked off the set and out the building. Marlon sat there for a few minutes, emotional, and then erupted. But we got the scene.'

Brando's last day on the film proved just as difficult. His last scene had him lying on a bed watching a news report on TV about the robbery and letting out a smile when he realises his friend's gotten away. 'We did about ten takes,' says Foster, 'and Marlon gave us this completely sour face. Frank asked, "Come on Marlon, just a little smile." He wouldn't do it. I cleared the set. Marlon was on the bed. "Come on up," he said. So I got on the bed. "Listen," I said. "You want to go home, let's get this over with, do one take where you smile, I'll put you on a plane tonight." Marlon looked at me. "I won't do it." I said, "Why are you doing this?" He glared at me and said, "Get off the bed." I went to the cameraman and told him, let's do one more take, see what happens, and then we'll wrap him. And that's what we did, he didn't smile, and we wrapped. He made a lovely speech to the crew thanking them for their time, and then wandered off, into the sunset. I never heard from him again. So it was a little bittersweet. None of us knew, and I don't even know if he knew, that would be the last movie scene he was ever going to do.'

Strange that even right at the end Marlon was defying direction, still rebellious, this is my performance, I'm going to do it my way. Although in post-production a computerised smile was added to Brando's face. 'I do think that Marlon had some pride in his craft,' Foster admits. 'But he told me, "Do you understand how hard it is to get to that place, how draining?" It was debilitating to him, or he couldn't get there or didn't want to get there. It was a shame, but I think he felt he'd got to a certain point in his career where it's pay your million dollars and you get Marlon Brando, you get that brand, it wasn't really about hiring an actor. You look at some of the choices he made in the later part of his life and you think, why the hell did he do it? Because they paid him! I would hope that he did *The Score* for more than that.'

To the three Bs – Bikes, Beer and Booty

While Dennis Hopper was busy every other Tuesday making movies, his personal life hadn't been entirely without incident, especially on the marital front. Back in 1989 he'd married his fourth wife Katherine LaNasa, a former ballet dancer turned actress and thirty years his junior. (Go, Dennis!) They had one child together, a son Henry. But the marriage didn't last and they divorced in 1992.

In court Katherine claimed Dennis used violence towards her during their marriage, something he strenuously denied. Though with his past reputation there would always be doubts. 'I know that I've belted a few women,' Dennis told the *Daily Mail* in 2006. 'But I had taken years of abuse before it got to that stage, and some of them had belted me first.

I'm not going to feel bad about doing what I did.' Indeed, he'd never felt any compunction about treating a woman the same as a man; if they went for him he'd retaliate as if it was Jake La Motta throwing the punches. But all that kind of shit, Dennis said, ended when he took his last sup of alcohol.

Dennis never understood why Katherine raised the issue of domestic violence in court, but maybe it had something to do with the fact they were battling each other for custody of their son. Dennis had missed much of his other kids' upbringing and wanted so much to be involved in this one. 'But karma has dealt me the same kind of hand again – it's been hard on me.'

Depressed about the divorce and custody battle, Dennis was eating alone in a restaurant one evening when a very attractive young lady approached him. She'd just seen an exhibition of his artwork and wanted to discuss its finer points. Dennis was delighted. Her name was Victoria Duffy. They've been together ever since. As with Katherine, Victoria was almost thirty years younger than Dennis and when they married in 1996 he did feel conscious of the fact that one of his own daughters was older than her new stepmother. But Victoria was no bimbo. Dennis was proud of the fact she was a three-day-event champion who trained her own horses. 'She has been a very subduing influence on me,' he revealed. In 2003 Victoria gave birth to their first child, a daughter. Dennis remains on good terms with his other children, and like Jack has been open about his problems with drugs and their dangers. 'When you get into the depths of drink and drug addiction, insanity and death are really the only outcomes.'

Career-wise, Dennis continued to appear with alarming regularity in all manner of piffle that brought shame and disgrace to bargain bins everywhere, like crime movie *Luck of the Draw* (2000), in which Mickey Rourke walked off the set when the producers refused to let him include his pet Chihuahua in the movie. And *Ticker* (2001), an action movie that Dennis worked on for one whole day and never even met its stars Tom Sizemore and Steven Seagal. There was the odd breathing space of a decent role in a decent product, a guest appearance in several early episodes of the groundbreaking TV drama series *24* as, yes, you guessed it, a baddie. 'I usually play some sort of nut. I'm very good at it.' And he played an evil tycoon in George A. Romero's first zombie flick for twenty years, *Land of the Dead* (2005).

While his talents as an actor were going largely to waste, Dennis's flair as a cutting-edge conceptual artist was being recognised around the world with exhibitions of his work in major capital cities. Especially pleasing was becoming the only living American artist ever to show at the Hermitage in St Petersburg.

Then came a flood of Dennis product in 2008, an incredible six films in total, the kind of output Michael Caine with a Spitfire engine up his arse would find hard to beat. He gave a chilling performance as an abusive father in *Sleepwalking*, starring and produced by Charlize Theron; there was the superior drama *Elegy* with Penelope Cruz and Ben Kingsley (oops, sorry, Sir Ben Kingsley, even Dennis confirmed in interviews that he likes to be called Sir Ben), which was followed by Kevin Costner's *Swing Vote*. There was no escape from Dennis in 2008, even at home, with a starring role in *Crash*, the spin-off TV series to the Oscar-winning film about racial tensions in LA. It was a return to the mad heights of Frank Booth, playing a demented music mogul into knives, drugs, orgies and talking to his penis; yes, that's right, he regularly holds conversations with his dick.

There was also *Hell Ride*, produced by Quentin Tarantino, a grind-house inspired motorcycle movie about revenge, drinking beer and getting laid, with the added inducement of seeing Dennis hop on a hog just like his old *Easy Rider* days. It's something he still does in real life: hits the open road when the mood takes him, with a gang of like-minded bikers that include stars Jeremy Irons, Laurence Fishburne and former model Lauren Hutton. They've been on various road trips, cycling from Munich to Salzburg or making a 1,500-mile trek around the United Arab Emirates. So the sprit of *Easy Rider* lives on, a spirit that was there from Dennis's early beginnings. As a young actor in New York he'd tear around the city on a Vespa scooter, one time with fellow struggler Steve McQueen sharing the saddle. Some idiot opened a car door once and – whack – Dennis and McQueen hit the road literally, ending up with a mouthful of tarmac. Late for rehearsals,

McQueen split, leaving Hopper to clean up the mess. Naturally, neither had a licence.

No more women, OK?

Back in the sixties, Leslie Caron remembered, 'If you woke Warren Beatty in the middle of the night, before his defences were up, if that is ever possible, and asked him what he wanted to be, I think he would say president. I don't think he'll stop until he's president.'

Talk of Warren's possible bid for the White House had been steadily growing for a number of years, and he spoke of campaign finance reform and Medicare for everyone, impressive and radical policies. But it was all for nought, he didn't run. Just as well, according to his friend Buck Henry. 'Easygoing isn't a quality Warren has. You know how presidents age in office? If Beatty were president, either he would be dead after the first year, or the country would be dead, because his attention to detail is maniacal.'

Tom Mankiewicz believes Warren never had any intention of running for high office. 'He's always been genuinely politically involved. At the same time he loved the fact that people thought from time to time that he was going to run for public office. And he would encourage people to think that. He would make campaign speeches on behalf of causes or other politicians and then he would sort of drop in a little something which suggests that maybe one day he might run. And then the crowd would go crazy. And I think he loved every minute of that, and never had any intention of running for anything. Can you imagine Warren in the Congress? He'd be just one of a hundred senators, and Warren Beatty's never been one of a hundred anything. And he wouldn't be able to lead the kind of life that Warren likes.'

After the radical *Bulworth* and the restoration of some critical reputation, Warren fell back into complacency on his next film, *Town and Country* (2001); it turned out to be his biggest disaster. He hasn't returned to the screen since. Many saw it as a mistake, especially at his age, to play yet again a man who seduces lots of women. The *Daily Express* reported from one test preview that audiences no longer accepted Warren as a serial philanderer. 'They couldn't stand Beatty because he was after only one thing from women – sex – and he didn't seem like the sort of guy who would be able to get much.' Interestingly the film featured previous flames Goldie Hawn and Diane Keaton.

Quickly the film started to court bad press, with some insiders once again blaming Warren's perfectionism for complicating matters. There were script rewrites, reshoots, God knows what else, all conspiring to push the budget towards $90m, that's *Ben Hur* proportions and this was a light, fluffy romantic comedy. What was going on? Stories came back that Warren was at loggerheads with the director Peter Chelsom, that Chelsom couldn't control the star and was being pushed around by him. Cameraman William Fraker was on set and saw the whole thing unfold. '*Town and Country* was a complete disaster. Peter Chelsom was a great guy, really understands cinema, but Warren was off on a track. I don't know what was going on with him on that picture, there were major discussions and problems. They just didn't get along at all.' The film stiffed big time at the box office.

Maybe to let off steam, Warren tore around Mulholland Drive daily on his Harley-Davidson motorcycle. Annette said that, since he'd passed the age of sixty-three, perhaps he should give up the Harley. 'No way,' came the reply.

As is the way in Hollywood, their senior citizens are suddenly deluged with awards, lest they peg it. Warren was no exception. In 2007 he got a Lifetime Achievement Award from the Golden Globes. 'What balls this man has,' said host Tom Hanks. 'And by balls, I mean artistic vision.' In 2008 it was the big one, recognition from the American Film Institute, with the whole of Hollywood turning up to salute him: Jane Fonda, Dustin Hoffman, Diane Keaton, Quentin Tarantino, Faye Dunaway and Halle Berry; political friends too like George McGovern, Bill Clinton and Gary Hart. Don Cheadle amusingly related the sometimes torturous direction he was subjected to by Warren on *Bulworth*, saying that, as directors, Clint Eastwood and Warren Beatty typically require 140 takes per scene – Eastwood does one and Warren does 139.

One notable absentee was Jack, over at an important Lakers champion-ship game a few miles away. 'Rumour has it that he might have been sitting courtside in a tuxedo,' joked Hoffman. Of course he showed up later, rather bedraggled, and pitched in with his tribute, saying Beatty had, 'Received eight times as many awards as he's made pictures. You get all these honours because of your passion and your dedication to excellence. This is why I'm crazy about your work.'

I have never lied to you, I have always told you some version of the truth.

After years away it was Sean Penn who finally lured Jack Nicholson back onto our screens. Since *The Crossing Guard* the two men had forged an affectionate and admiring friendship. Penn called Jack one of the greatest gifts to American culture. 'You can't imagine what it's like at 6 a.m. in some distant location and out of the car comes that face, and says, "Morning, boys, let's go to work."' Penn's latest project was *The Pledge* (2001), a dark and dour psychological thriller, a big risk at a time when commercial escapism dominated the multiplexes of the world. But then going against convention has always been a great attraction for Jack.

By the summer of 2001 Jack was keen to get some kind of semblance of normality back into his private life. Still seeing Lara Flynn Boyle, he invited Rebecca over to London for Wimbledon and took her along with him to the Moscow film festival. In Russia Jack took time out to meet President Vladimir Putin, who was quite lost for words before confessing that *One Flew Over the Cuckoo's Nest* was his favourite film. Back home Jack was one of the recipients of the Kennedy Center Honors, an annual prize for excellence in the arts. Old pal Warren was on hand to host a collection of clips from Jack's movies, telling the audience, 'He's everyman; he's us.' To which one media commentator added the post-script, 'Well, let's hope not.'

Jack deliberately looked like shit in his next film *About Schmidt* (2002), playing the ultimate grumpy old man, a completely depressive old git. Worried about his appearance, he never once looked in a mirror throughout the whole of filming, thinking, What if I get stuck in this character? What if I can't get back to me? It was genuinely shocking. But Jack isn't averse to looking kind of extreme up there on the screen. He's not the most vain person anyway, 'But getting older has certainly made me less vain.' Jack's never been particularly fond of birthdays, signifying as they do the marching of time. He ignores them. 'I started in 1972 to simply eliminate the calendar.' He may feel inside like the gallivanting Jack of old, but he knew that person was buried long ago. As he admitted to *Newsweek* in 2002. 'There are a lot of crazy nitwit things that I can't do any longer. I can't work on a movie for twelve hours a day, then go out and burn the streets down to the ground all night and get wild. I don't have the energy for it. I don't have the same libido.' It used to be that Jack couldn't go to sleep unless it involved some amorous contact. 'If I was alone two or three nights in a row, I'd start writing poems about suicide.' Now, shock horror, most nights he slept alone, and he'd found it rather liberating. 'My fear is that I'm beginning to prefer it.'

The success of *About Schmidt* showed that even in advanced middle age and in a youth-obsessed culture Jack continued to be one of the most bankable stars in the American film industry. 'Why has Jack lasted so long?' asked friend Danny DeVito. 'You know what I think it is? You always like him. What can you say? The guy played the devil! You gotta love him!' For many the movie's most memorable scene had the rather rotund actress Kathy Bates climbing starkers into a hot tub with our Jack, who was far too bashful at this time of life to remove for real all his clothes. 'Come on,' urged Kathy. 'You don't need to wear those boxer shorts. I won't look, I promise.' Away from the cameras Jack wasn't so bashful, stunning neighbours at the home he rented in Nebraska during the location shoot by strolling around the place nude, obviously not giving a shit whether the curtains were drawn or not. Locals were thrilled when the star moved in. 'I mean, we wanted to see Jack in person,' said a spokesman. 'But this was ridiculous.'

Away from Hollywood, Jack was coming to terms with being dumped once again by Lara Flynn Boyle, this time for good. It hurt him badly and friends were worried that he was losing weight and looking haggard. Some relationships certainly seemed to shatter him for longer than the average person. He once admitted that at some point he'd asked every woman he ever lived with to marry him. 'But they knew me too well.' As did Jack himself. He knew he'd always roam, so wisely never married again in order that he wouldn't have to cheat on his wife. And, like Warren, he holds affection for every woman he ever loved and regrets her departure, without entirely regretting whatever he might have done to hasten it. 'I know I've caused pain to some of the women I've loved, but I won't defend myself because I've never pretended to be something I'm not.' On bleak nights, though, alone up on Mulholland Drive, a little part of him envies the family men who have spent their lives with one woman. But not for long.

Now in his mid-sixties, Jack, it seemed, had at last come to terms with the fact it was probably unattractive for him to be seen fawning over young bits of crumpet, but joked he'd still like to whisk young women away for a night of passion if the prying paparazzi couldn't identify him. 'If I could slip them out the back entrance wrapped in a blanket, that's a different story.'

But his role in *Something's Gotta Give* (2003), a romantic comedy for the Viagra-popping generation, sounded all too familiar: an ageing playboy who enjoys chasing young girls and is scared of commitment. But there's a neat twist in that he ends up falling in love with the mother of his current girlfriend. As his female foil, director Nancy Meyers pulled off a perfect piece of casting with Diane Keaton. It was Annie Hall versus The Joker. Who would come out on top? The two were old colleagues, of course, having made *Reds*, but Meyers got the feeling they hadn't seen each other in many years and were catching up. 'This was a reintroduction into the world of Jack,' said Diane. 'This time, I really did get to know him.' So well, in fact, that rumours flew around of impending romance, something Jack did little to discourage. When one journalist asked, 'Are you seeing Diane?' Jack smiled and gave a leering look. 'She turns into a screaming banshee every night. I couldn't shut her up.' Of course, all this love-affair stuff was deliberately stoked up to sell the movie, but the Oscar-winning actress did admit to having the biggest crush on Jack for twenty years. 'How can you not, even now? He's irresistible. He's a once in a lifetime guy.'

Nancy Meyers enjoyed her Jack experience too, impressed particularly by the fact that he read the script every week from beginning to end, just to keep it fresh in his mind, something that she'd never seen any other actor do. It wasn't the first time they'd met either. Twenty years before Meyers and her sister were eating in a small restaurant when Jack came in and sat right next to them. 'My sister and I couldn't eat. She was rummaging through her purse looking for something to calm her down. It was so thrilling to be next to the Big Guy.'

Jack had been working non-stop for almost three years with scarcely a break when Martin Scorsese asked him to play mob boss Frank Costello in his brutal crime drama *The Departed* (2006). Nicholson couldn't say no and was out 'to kick this movie in the ass' by making Costello even more evil and seedy than he was in the script, keen to explore the sexuality of a powerful villain. 'He's a mad, bad nut job, so he's evil sexually too. Fuck 'em, kill 'em, you know.' In other words, he was out to spice things up a bit – Jack style. That meant in one scene dusting the arse of an actress with cocaine and waving a strap-on dildo poking out of his trousers towards a suitably bewildered Matt Damon. Jack was having a great time, but pity poor old producer Graham King, whose job it was to report back to the studio executives every day. 'Yeah, shooting is really going well. Oh, and Jack wants to wear a strap-on.'

Damon knew what Jack planned to do. Scorsese had called him the night before. 'Hello, Matt, it's Marty, your director. Listen, a little thing about tomorrow, Jack is going to show up with a giant dildo, OK?' Turning up for work, Damon saw Jack in this trench coat and hat, with the fabled giant dildo. Jack just looked at Damon and said, 'I just thought the whole thing would be better if I had the dildo on.'

Scorsese pushed Jack to go further, more extreme, and to improvise during shooting. Before one scene, in which Costello interrogates Leonardo DiCaprio's character, Jack told Scorsese, 'I don't think Leo's scared enough of me. I have to be scarier.' DiCaprio came in the next day and immediately got nervous. Jack's hair was all over the place and he was muttering to himself. One of the prop guys came over. 'Hey, Leo, Jack's got a fire extinguisher, a bottle of whiskey, matches and a handgun somewhere.' Such information didn't help with the nerves. 'So I sat down at the table not knowing what to expect, and he set the table on fire after pouring whiskey all over the place and stuck a gun in my face.' That was the take Scorsese kept in the film. 'This is what happens when you set me loose,' said Jack.

It was back to comedy next with *The Bucket List* (2007), teaming up with Morgan Freeman as a couple of terminal cancer patients who make a list of things to do before they literally kick the bucket. With the exception of *The Departed*, Jack had been making largely comedy movies, a deliberate strategy and his personal response to the 9/11 tragedy which knocked him out emotionally. Jack didn't want to make his living any more by depressing people with angst-ridden movies, he wanted to make them smile and in the process maybe found his true calling. 'I'm going over there to the clowns where I belong.'

What are they gonna say about him? What are they gonna say? That he was a kind man? That he was a wise man? That he had plans? That he had wisdom? Bullshit, man!

After *The Score*, Marlon Brando became increasingly reclusive, scarcely straying from the confines of his home and seeing only a select group of friends, including Johnny Depp, whom he rated as the finest actor of his generation. His primary contact with the outside world continued to be his beloved ham radio and the internet, often going into chat rooms to start arguments.

Another close friend in these last years was Michael Jackson. Marlon enjoyed staying at his Neverland ranch and even guested in the singer's pop video for 'You Rock My World'. But his appearance at Jackson's thirtieth anniversary concert in New York's Madison Square Garden left jaws on the floor. Brando came onto the stage and took a seat, introducing himself by saying, 'You may be thinking, who is that old fat fart sitting there?' Instead of a glowing tribute about Jackson, Marlon enlightened the packed crowd by removing his watch and informing them, 'In the last minute, 100,000 children have been hacked to death with a machete.'

Such wacko behaviour probably appealed to Jackson, and Marlon's son Miko revealed that the last time his father left Mulholland Drive to spend any significant time away was at Jackson's Neverland. 'He loved it. He had a twenty-four-hour chef, twenty-four-hour security, twenty-four-hour help, twenty-four-hour kitchen, twenty-four-hour maid service.'

As the end drew ever nearer Marlon's eccentricities took on sinister tones. According to his long-time make-up man Philip Rhodes, Marlon installed a monitoring system in his home enabling him to record all telephone calls and eavesdrop on conversations in every room. When someone called, Marlon might ask, 'How's your sex life? You getting any on the side?' So he had all these people talking about their sex life and every word was being recorded.

Marlon Brando once said, 'I'm going to live to be a hundred and then I plan to clone myself, with all of my talent and none of my neurosis.' It was a nice thought, but when death came it was inevitable and messy. In October 2003 it was reported that Marlon had told family and friends he was preparing for death after learning that he was suffering from congestive heart failure, along with advanced diabetes and pulmonary fibrosis, damage to the tissue inside the lungs resulting from a recent bout of pneumonia. Those closest to him feared Marlon had simply lost the will to live. When doctors suggested they insert tubes carrying oxygen into his lungs, thus prolonging his life, Marlon refused. He spent his last months in a reclusive state, reflecting on a lifetime that had brought him enormous acclaim and wealth but also failed marriages and troubled children.

He even made his housekeeper pregnant three times. Chatting with Michael Winner on the phone one evening he explained how it happened. 'You know my bedroom, I've got all that electrical equipment in it. I dropped a tiny screw on the floor and she bent down on all fours to look for it under the bed and that's when the relationship changed.' Like all his relationships, it ended in tears. 'You know I've given up sex, Michael,' Marlon told Winner years later. 'I just watch the porno channel and jerk off. It's much simpler.'

On 1 July 2004 Marlon Brando passed away, the cause of death revealed as lung failure. He was eighty. Contrary to press reports at the time suggesting he'd died penniless, Marlon left a fortune of $21m.

He'd wanted no public tributes, no funeral service, 'no weeping widow', no cluster of mourners all sobbing at his passing; the very thought was enough to make him vomit. Even worse was the notion of being buried in a Hollywood celebrity cemetery and becoming a tourist attraction. Instead his ashes were scattered partly on his beloved Tahitian island and partly in Death Valley, California, where those of Wally Cox had been; back together at last.

Marlon's home lay empty for several months. Jack admitted he couldn't go up to the old place. 'I just had this weird juju.' Fearing it might be bought by developers and thus impinge greatly upon his privacy, Jack bought it in May 2005 for $5.5 million. Advised that it would be too expensive to renovate the derelict building, plagued as it was by mould, Jack demolished it, planting a garden where it once stood.

It's been said by many that Marlon was an enigmatic misery, his whole life a sham because he was ashamed of what he did professionally. Michael Winner disagrees. 'He was the most playful man in the world. Jokes all the time. But complex. I think he was the greatest actor. A couple of years before his death I said to him, "Marlon, you should be playing King Lear at the Old Vic." He said, "I hate acting. I've always hated acting. I never wanted to be an actor." I asked, "Why did you go to drama school then, Marlon?" He replied, "To get laid." Well, it's a good answer, isn't it?'

Maybe he detested the profession so much because it was no effort for him; it came so damned easy. Paul Newman used to confess seething anger towards Marlon, 'Because he does everything so easily and I have to break my ass to do what he can do with his eyes closed.' Perhaps there was a certain amount of guilt about his talent because it was nothing he earned. Like a woman being complimented on her beauty, it wears thin after a while because it's not an accomplishment.

Yet his legacy is huge. Jack used to say that other actors never went round discussing who the best actor in the world was, because it was obvious, it was Marlon Brando. Warren used to say that when Marlon goes, everyone moves up a place. 'There was a young actress who came into my office once,' says *Godfather* producer Albert Ruddy. 'I said, "You look like Natalie Wood." She said, "Who?" I said, "Have you heard of Marlon Brando?" She said, "Actor, right?" If you want to be in this fucking business you better learn the legacy of the art form. The greatest gift in the world is to sit there and run *On the Waterfront*, *Streetcar*, any movie Marlon Brando ever did. I say you will learn more running one of his movies than you learn in an acting class.'

Put simply, Brando is now beyond legend. 'There's a temptation to compare Brando to King Lear or some hero of a Grecian tragedy,' says Richard Stanley. 'But it's futile, he's actually beyond that. He's Brando. He's not King Lear. He's too much of a myth himself for any analogy to make sense.'

Dennis Hopper is the first to admit that his story is one of enormous potential that was largely squandered, undermined by a rebellious nature and self-destructive hedonism which as good as derailed his career for well over a decade and nearly killed him. 'When I look at my career and I look at Jack's there is a vast difference, isn't there?' There have been high points, of course: *Easy Rider*, *Apocalypse Now*, *Blue Velvet*. Those are the ones he's most proud of and yet they're so minimal in a vast body of, well, crap, 'This river of shit that I've tried to make gold out of.' But when he enters a museum with an exhibition of his paintings, is he disappointed? No way. 'I think that is a fucking miracle.'

Life is pretty good now he's part of the establishment, even mocking his old image in a TV ad for a car that had him appearing snappily suited driving alongside a superimposed image of himself as the wild-haired biker of *Easy Rider*. He's almost Hollywood royalty, revered, iconic, not necessarily because he has at last been accepted by the system he once so detested, 'But because I survived it.' In the words of his old friend Tom Mankiewicz. 'Dennis took a lot of drugs. I'm so happy that he's alive because he has no right to be alive. He has absolutely no right to be still alive.'

Henry Jaglom voices similar sentiments. 'I am beyond amazed, relieved and gratified that he survived. And every time I see him I am impressed by the fight he made to overcome his difficulties and survive and continue to produce a stream of thoroughly creative and singular work.'

For George Hickenlooper Dennis sums up what Hollywood is all about, a place that epitomises the ultimate American dream. 'Unlike Europe, where you're born into status or not, in America you can create yourself from nothing and then if you rise to the top and then plummet in a fiery crash you can be reborn and rise again; you have unlimited chances and Dennis just epitomises that more than any other actor. That's what makes him iconic too, he's risen from the ashes so many times and just doesn't give a shit what people think and that's the sign of a true artist.'

It's an amazing life story that would make for a pretty good film. The only problem is no one would believe it! Someone really should make the Dennis Hopper story one day. 'But I'm not playing that,' he said. 'I already did it. It's a bitch.'

Warren Beatty is simply a unique figure in Hollywood, one of the smartest cookies ever to grace the place, someone who has managed to stay at the very top of his game for decades. He's been in a fair number of flops, but whenever his career seemed a tad shaky he'd just go off and star in and direct a wonderful movie and be safe for another half decade.

After *Town and Country* he didn't appear to have the appetite for another comeback. Maybe because Warren's greatest successes have come when he's running the whole show, acting, directing, writing and producing. Now in his seventies, one wonders if he's got the energy for all that. He was almost tempted out of retirement by Quentin Tarantino's offer to play the role of Bill in *Kill Bill: Vol. 2* (2004). He finally passed and, ever the acute filmmaker, told Tarantino to cast David Carradine.

I guess the longer he stays away from the cinema, the more his mythical status as a playboy will begin to eclipse his genuine cinematic achievements. As Robert Downey Jr once said, 'Warren Beatty is really knowledgeable in a lot of areas, especially fucking.' But his achievements as a filmmaker must not be overlooked: few were better in Hollywood at persuading, cajoling and charming the pants off studio bosses into financing movies nobody else wanted to make, radical films like *Reds* and *Bonnie and Clyde*. 'He's one of those people where when you run into them and you see them, you start grinning, because you just know you're going to have a good time,' says Tom Mankiewicz. 'I've always liked Warren; liked him enormously, there's a spirit in him.'

* * *

And as for Jack Nicholson, in spite of his colourful, sometimes freak show of a life, he just might possibly be the finest screen actor America has ever produced. 'You learn a tremendous amount from the people with whom you work,' says director George Miller. 'But I doubt whether I've learned as much from anybody, both professionally and personally, as I have from Jack.'

Even though his roistering days are over, Jack's basic philosophy hasn't changed – 'More good times' – though, how he might go about implementing it understandably has. He might say to a date, 'Look, I just can't do the dance any more. If I do, you've got to be a really good dancer.' Neither is he the social gadabout he once was, holding magnificent court in the nightspots and clubs of London, LA or Monte Carlo. Meryl Streep, much to Jack's amusement, has called him 'That lovable old wreck'. And far from being, as one scribe prophesied, on course to be a ninety-year-old who is a danger to the nursing profession, Jack has settled into a kind of humdrum domesticity. You could also say that he's the last bad boy standing. After Marlon passed on, Dennis sobered up and Warren swapped bed-hopping for family bliss, Nicholson is king of Mulholland Drive, the old devil still capable of raising hell. Backstage at the Oscars in 2006 Jack propositioned Nicole Kidman, not realising she was engaged or that she was standing with her fiancée. He teasingly refused to divulge the comment, though seemed to relish the gasp it drew from Kidman. That's maybe the secret as to why we love Jack, it's because he's lived his life so openly and unapologetically.

Maybe the best thing you can say about Jack is that despite all the fame, the adulation, the money, he's not changed all that much from the aspiring actor of the sixties, desperately searching for his big break. 'Jack is Jack,' says Henry Jaglom, 'was always Jack, will always be Jack. There is something unchangeably American and buoyant about his cynicism, a contradiction that he embodies as did some of the great movie stars of earlier eras – Bogart, Cagney, Tracy, Gable. He's one for the ages. I knew it from the moment I met him and told him then, as he likes to quote me, "Just smile, Jack. That's all you have to do. Just smile your biggest smile." And boy does he.'

Index